YELLOWSTONE TREASURES

The Traveler's Companion to the National Park

JANET CHAPPLE

with geological text and advice by
Bruno J. Giletti
Professor Emeritus of Geological Sciences
Brown University

~

To my sister, Joan Orvis,
whose love and encouragement
have always guided my life
(1931–2001)

~

© 2002 Janet Chapple
Second printing 2003
ISBN: 0-9706873-0-3
Library of Congress Card Number: 2001116138

Park Archivist Lee H. Whittlesey reviewed this book for historical accuracy.

Front cover photos: Old Faithful Geyser by Don Forsyth; fireweed, Yellowstone Lake sandbar, mule deer, Lower Falls of the Yellowstone, bison, and Minerva Terrace by Bruno Giletti. Back cover: Beauty Pool by Leslie Kilduff.

Editor: Beth Chapple
Cover designer: Elizabeth Watson
Book designer: Alice Merrill
Printed by C&C Offset Printing Co., Ltd.
Published by Granite Peak Publications, LLC
P.O. Box 603120, Providence, RI 02906

www.yellowstonetreasures.com

CONTENTS

NATURAL AND HUMAN HISTORY

Selected Topics

PREFACE

So she sat on, with closed eyes, and half believed herself in Wonderland,
though she knew she had but to open them again and
all would change to dull reality . . .
　　　　　　　　　—Alice's Adventures in Wonderland,
　　　　　　　　　　　　　Lewis Carroll, 1865

A late summer day begins at Yellowstone Lake.

Some people in our fast-paced age make Yellowstone just one stop on a whirlwind western tour. But if you can allow several days or a week or two to savor it, Yellowstone will reward you fully. This guide is intended for such relatively unhurried first-time visitors and for the many thousands of us who return to explore anew.

I am one of the fortunate few who have spent many summer months in the park, first as an impressionable small child, later as an adult who could never get enough of the Yellowstone country. My association with the park and its surrounding mountains goes back two generations to my maternal grandfather, Fred Inabnit, a Swiss native who organized hiking trips and popularized the idea of appreciating the mountains—particularly the Beartooth Range—by exploring them. He spent months constructing the table-sized relief map of Yellowstone now belonging to the Yellowstone County Museum. After his death in 1928, a mountain was named for him not far from Montana's highest mountain, Granite Peak, which he just missed conquering.

For four idyllic summers of my childhood I lived near Old Faithful Inn, where my father was transportation agent. My sister Joan and I played countless games of Parcheesi while waiting for Great Fountain Geyser to erupt. Once my parents got us out of bed late at night to see Giant Geyser play. I played hide and seek with Joan when most of Old Faithful Inn's guests had left for the day's excursions and Mother was rehearsing music in the lobby with the Ladies' Ensemble. On rainy days, we read Frances Farnsworth's *Cubby in Wonderland* and *Cubby Returns*. Sometimes we left Daddy at his favorite hole above Firehole Cascades to catch a mess of trout for supper.

Yellowstone means many things to many people: bears and bison, geysers and colorful pools, hikes and horseback rides, distant vistas and the stillness of the backcountry. It can also mean clear dry western air, spectacular sunsets, and night skies so full of stars you think you're seeing to the end of the universe. Author Owen Wister said it for me back in 1891: "I have tested the power of the moon by consulting the second hand of my watch and reading a letter with rapid ease. But that's a poor mathematical way to talk or think about such magic. And all through the still air, the clean sharp odor of the sage. Not dust, as it smells at noon, but cool, like something a fairy would give you to make you suddenly well. Nobody, nobody who lives on the Atlantic strip, has a notion of what sunrise and sunset and moonlight can be in their native land till they have come here to see."

Yellowstone Park was called Wonderland by many writers in the early days, traceable to the publication of *Alice's Adventures in Wonderland* shortly before the park was created. Since the first Hayden Survey in 1871, scientists and other curious people have learned much about the origin of the park's wonders and how they function, but there are still countless wonders to be explained.

The visitors to Yellowstone Park now span six generations, from the explorers who braved some danger and considerable discomfort, to today's backseat youngsters with their handheld electronic games. Like so many others, my parents and sister and I in the third and fourth of those generations came with a copy of the *Haynes Guide* in our hands. I have followed that guide's organizational plan, and I honor the memory of pioneers F. "Jay" and Jack E. Haynes, who, for more than 75 years, published their comprehensive guidebooks full of information about park features, animals, plants, and photography.

Acknowledgments

There are four people without whom this book could not have been written. Robert J. English conceived of the idea of creating a new guide based on the

Haynes Guide. My husband, Bruno J. Giletti, not only wrote about Yellowstone's geology, but served as adviser, photographer, reader, field assistant, and moral support. Historians Lee Whittlesey and the late Aubrey Haines researched and wrote their many books about Yellowstone as labors of love. This guide relies heavily upon them.

Almost as essential to the book as the four men above were my wonderful editor and daughter, Beth Chapple, and my friend Linton A. Brown, who, in addition to reading the entire manuscript very critically, spent hundreds of hours perfecting the maps.

The majority of the color photographs were taken by Bruno Giletti and many others by Leslie Kilduff. Additional photographs come from numerous sources and are credited at the back of the book. Bengt Dellby and Tom Monego scanned the transparencies and Kristy Welch the black and white photos for printing. Nathan Welch sketched four panoramas.

A few of the many intelligent and exceptionally dedicated Yellowstone Park ranger-interpreters who helped me in my research are: Bob Fuhrmann, Bob Greenberg, Harlan Kredit, Ted Parkinson, Sandy Snell-Dobert, and Mary Taber.

Special thanks go to Sarah Broadbent, Vanessa Christopher, Virgil Hall, Tim Hudson, Laura Joss, Susan Kraft, Catherine Lentz, Cheryl Matthews, Tom Olliff, Jim Peaco, John Sacklin, and Eleanor Williams of the National Park Service, and the Yellowstone Association's Pat Cole. Co-hikers: Thomas and Kathie Brock, Karen Chapple, Donald Forsyth, Alan and Nathan Fox, Margie and Bob McCoy, Bev Peterson, Roberta Ryan, Henry and Caryl Seidenberg, Mary VanBuskirk, Rachel Weinberger, and Marylor Wilson. Yellowstone Institute teachers: Duncan Foley, David Fountain, Aubrey Haines, John Martin, Wayne Phillips, Anna-Louise Reysenbach, and Jennifer Whipple. Libraries and librarians: Mammoth Hot Springs N.P.S. Library and Archives, especially Lee Whittlesey, Barbara Zafft, and Kathryn Kirby; Brown University's Science, Rockefeller, and John Hay Libraries; and Providence Public Library. Advisers: Vic Benson, Thomas Brock, Mike Condon, Niklas Dellby, Tamsen Hert, Marcia and Phil Lieberman, Lisa Morgan, Lisa Nelbach. Readers: Holly Bartlett, Nancy Chapple, Ann Deutch, Duncan Foley, Laura Giletti, David Goldberg, Karl Hoppe, Tom Hougham, Jeanne Johnson, Greg Kroll, Joan Orvis, Brian Suderman, and Lee Whittlesey. Bed-and-breakfast-providing friends: Carol Critelli, Kay and Durwood Johnson.

My loving gratitude goes to my three Chapple daughters, Nancy, Beth, and Karen, for the support they gave me toward publication of this book.

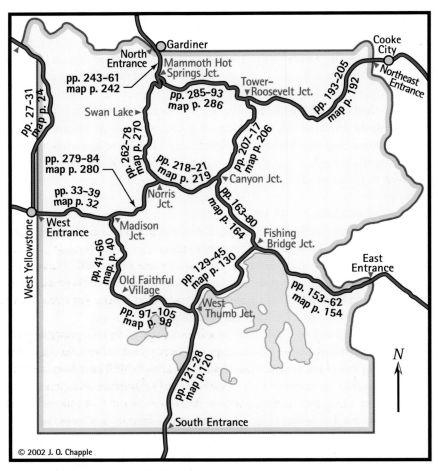

Gardiner

Cooke City

North Entrance

Mammoth Hot Springs Jct.

Northeast Entrance

pp. 243–61 map p. 242

pp. 285–93 map p. 286

Tower–Roosevelt Jct.

pp. 193–205 map p. 192

pp. 27–31 map p. 24

Swan Lake

pp. 262–78 map p. 270

pp. 207–17 map p. 206

pp. 279–84 map p. 280

pp. 218–21 map p. 219

pp. 33–39 map p. 32

Norris Jct.

Canyon Jct.

pp. 163–80 map p. 164

West Entrance

Madison Jct.

West Yellowstone

pp. 41–66 map p. 40

Fishing Bridge Jct.

East Entrance

pp. 129–45 map p. 130

Old Faithful Village

pp. 153–62 map p. 154

pp. 97–105 map p. 98

West Thumb Jct.

N

pp. 121–28 map p. 120

© 2002 J. O. Chapple

South Entrance

Key to the Park Roads

INTRODUCTION

Although the principal sights like Old Faithful Geyser and the Grand Canyon of the Yellowstone are notorious for crowds, you'll surely want to see them. But in addition, there are myriad other ways to enjoy Yellowstone. Imagine yourself walking a half mile (0.8 km) to a quiet lily-covered lake—like Harlequin Lake near Madison Junction. Maybe you'd enjoy hiking or biking on a level road through untouched meadows to see an eruption of Lone Star Geyser, or waiting with other wildlife watchers for wolves to appear in Lamar Valley. Here are a few hints for maximizing your enjoyment of Yellowstone.

When to go and what to see

In June or September, you'll find fewer people than in midsummer (see "When Is the Best Time to Visit?" for other seasonal information). If you can arrange your stroll around Upper Geyser Basin or the Mammoth Terraces for early morning or late evening, it may be yours to enjoy alone. Above all, what you need to truly enjoy the park is adequate time spent out of your vehicle, in order to observe and savor all the park's treasures.

Check the Best Sights of Yellowstone list on page 12 to help you plan your visit. Of the park's many geysers, I recommend only predictable ones. I also list less-known places I love, none more than one-half mile (0.8 km) from a road.

This road guide is designed for visitors traveling in their own or a rented vehicle or by bus, particularly during the warm months of the year, when all destinations are accessible. This is high mountain terrain, and most roads in Yellowstone are not plowed between early November and mid April. Winter travel by snowcoach or snowmobile is limited to only a few places in the park. Most accommodations are open from mid May or early June until mid September or early October.

You'll encounter the best weather in July and August, but also the most people. Weather in Yellowstone's summers is unpredictable, ranging from hot sun to rain and hail. Lightning storms are common, especially in late afternoons. It can snow or the temperature can drop to freezing any month of the year.

Safety and Hiking

Remember that you must not approach or feed any wildlife in the park. Park regulations tell you, "You must stay at least 100 yards (91 m) away from bears and at least 25 yards (23 m) away from bison, elk, bighorn sheep, deer, moose, and coyotes." For your safety and the animals' welfare, especially avoid all wildlife with young. Never hike alone. Make some noise, so that you will not surprise an animal.

When Is the Best Time to Visit?

Spring—May, June

When the snow has melted from the lowlands and the red bison calves are trailing after their mothers, you know springtime has come to Yellowstone.

TEMPERATURE RANGE (DAY–NIGHT): 50s–60s °F (Teens °C); 30s °F (0–4°C)

PROS: Baby animals numerous, wildflowers (at lower elevations), waterfalls at their peak.

CONS: Some mountain passes closed, biting insects common, meadows flooded, streams very high.

Summer—July, August

It's a time to enjoy hikes in the high country, long vigils in the geyser basins, and picnics along the riversides.

TEMPERATURE RANGE (DAY–NIGHT): 70s–low 80s °F (20s °C); 40s °F or below (below 9°C)

PROS: Wildflowers everywhere; drier trails in mid July and August; ripening berries in August; clear, starlit nights; fishing best in late July into September.

CONS: Visitor numbers at their peak, late afternoon thunderstorms, hordes of grasshoppers in dry years.

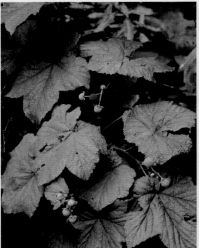

Thimbleberries may be found along some park trails in late summer.

Autumn—September, early October

Brisk nights, cool but pleasant days, and great light for photography are some of the joys of this season.

TEMPERATURE RANGE (DAY–NIGHT): 40s–60s °F (5–20°C); freezing and below

PROS: Fewer visitors, elk gather in herds and bugle, aspen turn golden.

CONS: Cold nights, greater chance of rain and snow.

Winter—mid October through April

A snowcoach can take you to Old Faithful or Canyon, where you'll marvel at the beauty of steamy pools and frozen waterfalls.

TEMPERATURE RANGE (DAY–NIGHT): Well below freezing to a few degrees above; usually freezing, often below 0°F (-18°C)
PROS: Cross-country skiing, ice-encrusted "ghost" trees, animals gather near roads.
CONS: Extreme cold, heavy snows and severe storms, most roads are closed to cars.

What Yellowstone is not

Although efforts are being made to make more sites and sights available to disabled persons, the accessible places are still limited to a relatively small percentage of the developed area. For more information, ask for the latest version of the "Visitor Guide to Accessible Features" by writing to Accessibility Coordinator, P.O. Box 168, Yellowstone National Park, WY 82190, or by calling (307) 344-2018.

Yellowstone is most suitable for able-bodied adults and children over about five years of age. Some places are dangerous for small children, and there are no playgrounds, no wading pools, no television, and very few radio stations that can be heard in the park.

What to expect

A woman touring Yellowstone in 1912 complained to visitor L. Louise Elliott: "There is such a sameness to it all. . . . Now, I supposed I should be seeing something different and interesting constantly without all the long, dusty rides between places. I thought the park fairly teemed with graceful fawn and antelope and other animals, and truly, I see more animals right at home in our city park, you know."

Reflecting on this complaint, Elliott wrote:

> I understand now as I never did before why so many people are disappointed when they come here. It is because of the fact that it is called a park and they come with the expectation of seeing a man-made park, similar to those of the cities, only on a much larger and vastly grander scale; with the curiosities all conveniently grouped, and the animals collected in large numbers in enclosed corrals. They forget that it is merely a district controlled by the Government and preserved as far as possible in its wild and natural state, and that the wild animals, native to this territory, are permitted to roam at will over miles and miles of country, and that the greater part of them come down to the mainly traveled districts only when forced to do so by hunger, when the snow gets deep and the grazing poor.
> —from *Six Weeks on Horseback through Yellowstone Park*, 1913.

How this guidebook is organized

The "Five Approaches to Yellowstone" chapter helps you decide which way to enter the park.

The Road Logs and Destinations sections start with the gateway communities and sights outside the park, and then follow the entrance roads onto the Grand Loop Road. Pairs of mileage indications show the distance from an entrance station or major junction as well as the distance from the other direction. Our mileage figures should serve as general guidelines; park road improvements will change a few distances. Metric equivalents for the distances are provided in the introduction to each road segment and on the maps.

Destinations you encounter along the way are described in detail as you come to them. In the hydrothermal areas, we describe only the most readily visible, historically interesting, and fascinating geysers and hot springs. Since geysers are notoriously changeable, eruption details are kept somewhat general.

We explain names of historical importance or general interest. If there's more than one spelling or version of the name currently in use, for example, Lake Hotel and Lake Yellowstone Hotel, the historical form of the name is used primarily. Keep in mind that you can't necessarily expect to find a certain animal or plant near a feature bearing its name.

After the Road Logs are chapters on Yellowstone's geologic past, its human history, and its flora and fauna. Practical help for planning your trip is found in the "Travel Tips" chapter. This includes a chart of the facilities available in Yellowstone and a list of recommended short walks.

Best Sights of Yellowstone

Ratings: ★★ Don't miss! / ★ Worth making time for or taking a detour

Artist Point★★, gorgeous view of the Grand Canyon of the Yellowstone and Lower Falls, page 174

Beauty Pool★★, outstandingly colorful hot spring in Upper Geyser Basin, page 85

Black Sand Basin★ & especially its Emerald Pool, page 64

Castle Geyser★ & Crested Pool★ in Upper Geyser Basin, page 93

Daisy Geyser★, Punch Bowl Spring★, & Black Sand Pool★, on a side trail in Upper Geyser Basin, pages 94 and 95

Dunraven Pass★ & its trails, outstanding mountain pass for wildflowers and panoramas, north of Canyon Junction, page 216

Firehole Canyon Drive★, scenic and geologically interesting side road, page 43

Firehole Lake Drive★, outstanding and accessible thermal features, page 53

Fountain Paint Pot★ north of Old Faithful Village, page 49

Grand Geyser★★ in Upper Geyser Basin, page 84

Grand View★, best view of Canyon colors on North Rim Drive, page 178

Great Fountain Geyser★★ on Firehole Lake Drive, page 54

Inspiration Point★★, outstanding view of Canyon colors, page 178

Lake Hotel★ & lakeshore view, pages 141–44

Mammoth Hot Springs & Terraces★, large travertine terraces, page 256

Midway Geyser Basin★★, especially Excelsior Geyser and Grand Prismatic Spring, pages 57 and 58

Mud Volcano★ & Dragon's Mouth★, best thermal features in Mud Volcano area, pages 166 and 167

Norris Geyser Basin★, especially Echinus Geyser★ and Porcelain Basin's★ outstanding vista, pages 222–34

Old Faithful Geyser★★, the world's most famous geyser, Old Faithful Village, page 72

Old Faithful Inn lobby★★, historic and awe-inspiring architecture, page 68

Riverside Geyser★★, graceful and rewarding geyser at Upper Geyser Basin, page 87

Tower Fall★, popular high waterfall, page 211

West Thumb Geyser Basin★, thermal features along a scenic walk, page 132

LESS WELL-KNOWN PLACES

Apollinaris Spring, a verdant spot graced with historic stonework north of Norris Junction, page 274

Brink of Lower Falls near Canyon Village, page 179

Firehole River behind Old Faithful Geyser, page 178

Floating Island Lake, a pleasant site for bird-watching west of Tower-Roosevelt Junction, page 291

Lake Butte view, east of Fishing Bridge Junction, page 158

Lamar Valley from the Buffalo Ranch area, viewed in evening light, page 199

Moose Falls, a small waterfall and tranquil site near the South Entrance, page 122

Nez Perce picnic area, by the Firehole River on Fountain Flat Drive, page 45

Yellowstone River from Chittenden Bridge, quietly flowing water above the tumult, south of Canyon Village, page 171

DRIVING DISTANCES

	Alpine, WY	Ashton	Big Sky	Billings	Bozeman	Canyon Junction	Cody	Dubois	East Entrance	Fishing Bridge
Ashton, ID	98									
Big Sky, MT	207	109								
Billings, MT	319	272	186							
Bozeman, MT	245	153	44	142						
Canyon Junction	152	95	92	177	119					
Cody, WY	216	189	186	103	211	94				
Dubois, WY	124	159	214	309	242	140	204			
East Entrance	163	136	133	156	160	41	53	151		
Fishing Bridge	137	110	107	182	134	15	79	125	26	
Gardiner /N. Entrance	189	109	106	169	80	38	132	178	79	53
Idaho Falls, ID	73	56	165	328	203	151	245	177	192	166
Jackson, WY	37	72	189	282	217	115	179	87	126	100
Livingston, MT	244	164	70	116	26	93	187	233	134	108
Madison Junction	149	70	67	202	105	25	119	137	66	40
Mammoth Junction	184	104	101	176	86	33	127	173	74	48
Moran Junction	68	103	158	255	186	84	148	56	95	69
Norris Junction	162	83	80	189	107	12	106	152	53	27
Northeast Entrance	199	142	139	130	133	47	81	187	88	62
Old Faithful Village	135	87	84	219	122	42	119	123	66	40
Red Lodge, MT	269	212	183	60	149	117	62	257	115	132
South Entrance	95	130	121	224	159	57	121	83	68	42
Tower Junction	171	113	110	159	104	18	113	158	60	34
West Entrance	154	56	53	216	92	39	133	151	80	54
West Thumb Jct.	116	103	100	203	138	36	100	104	47	21

Chart shows shortest distances in miles on fully paved roads.

Information about park roads:
Y.N.P. information office, (307) 344-7381.

Wyoming roads:
(307) 777-7777 or (800) 225-5996.

Montana roads:
(406) 444-2654 or (800) 847-4868.

From \ To	Gardiner/N.Entrance	Idaho Falls	Jackson	Livingston	Madison Junction	Mammoth Junction	Moran Junction	Norris Junction	Northeast Entrance	Old Faithful Village	Red Lodge	South Entrance	Tower Junction	West Entrance
Idaho Falls	165													
Jackson	151	90												
Livingston	54	229	206											
Madison Junction	40	126	112	94										
Mammoth Junction	5	160	146	60	34									
Moran Junction	121	121	31	175	81	115								
Norris Junction	26	139	125	81	13	21	94							
Northeast Entrance	52	198	163	107	72	47	132	59						
Old Faithful Village	57	143	98	111	17	51	67	30	89					
Red Lodge	122	268	233	123	142	117	202	129	70	159				
South Entrance	94	148	58	148	54	88	27	67	105	40	175			
Tower Junction	23	169	134	78	43	18	103	30	29	60	99	76		
West Entrance	53	112	126	108	14	48	95	27	86	31	156	68	57	
West Thumb Junction	73	159	79	127	33	69	48	46	83	19	153	21	54	47

KEY TO SYMBOLS

RECREATIONAL ACTIVITIES

[🚶] Trailhead

[🚶] Self-guiding trail with Yellowstone Assn. leaflet available

[🚶] Recommended short walk

[🚶] Recommended short walk with leaflet available

[🎣] Fishing (a few of the many good spots)

[🚲] Biking

[🎭] Amphitheater

[🐎] Horsepacking trail

[🔭] Bird-watching spot

[⛵] Boat launch site

[🐴] Horse corral

FACILITIES

[⛺] Campground

[🏪] Store

[✉] Post office

[🍴] Restaurant, cafeteria, or lunch counter

[🛏] Inn, hotel, or cabins

[⛽] Service station

[➕] Clinic or hospital

AIDS TO TRAVELERS

[🍱] Picnic area

[☎] Public telephone

[P] Parking

[👤] Visitor center or ranger station

[🚻] Rest room

[♿] Wheelchair access

[✈] Commercial airport

[?] Information station/bookstore

OTHER SYMBOLS USED

[GEO.1] through [GEO.26] points of geological interest explained in the Geological History chapter

★★ Don't miss!

★ Worth making time for

The background colors of the special topics hint at their subject matter.

Pale yellow: geology and geography

Green: natural history

Blue: human history

Beige: park information

Note: On geyser basin maps, parallel black lines indicate steps.

THE FIVE APPROACHES TO
YELLOWSTONE NATIONAL PARK

Yellowstone National Park covers an area of 3467 square miles (8980 sq km), most of which is undeveloped mountain and forest land. In spite of this huge size, almost all of the most interesting sights are available to visitors along or close to the more than 300 miles (483 km) of roads. Because there's so much to see and do and so many people who want to use the limited housing and camping facilities, advance planning is essential.

Your first decision will be which way to enter. The five approach roads are described below, along with a general idea of the scenery you'll encounter and the available activities and facilities.

Arriving by Air

If you plan to start your trip by air, consider flying to Billings, Montana, the largest city in the vicinity of the park, with the most connecting flights. You can rent a car there to drive conveniently to any entrance except the South Entrance.

Closest airport options other than Billings are: Jackson, Wyoming, the closest commercial airport to the South Entrance; Cody, Wyoming, for the East Entrance; Bozeman, Montana, for the north or west; and West Yellowstone, Montana, for the West Entrance.

If you want to begin in Idaho Falls, Idaho, several airlines can serve you. Many people begin a western trip from Salt Lake City, Utah, which is a much longer drive but is especially well served by airlines and is relatively convenient to Grand Teton National Park and the South Entrance of Yellowstone.

I. WEST ENTRANCE Page 25

There are several good reasons to approach Yellowstone along U.S. Highway 191 to its West Entrance. First, you'll find ample tourist accommodations in Bozeman, in the Big Sky area, and in West Yellowstone, Montana. Second, the scenery through

The Gallatin River Canyon opens out a few miles north of the park boundary.

Key to the Approach Roads

the Gallatin River canyon, though not the most spectacular of the approaches, can be a delightful introduction to the Rocky Mountains. The third advantage of coming this way is that the Gallatin River and Gallatin National Forest abound in opportunities for camping, hiking, fishing, kayaking, and float trips, while numerous guest ranches offer western hospitality. Horseback trips for a few hours up to a few days can be arranged.

This entrance gives geyser enthusiasts the closest access to the unique geysers and hot springs in the western half of the park. It's about 90 miles (145 km) from Bozeman to the West Entrance; then 30 miles (48 km) farther to Upper Geyser Basin in Old Faithful Village, or 27 miles (43 km) to Norris Geyser Basin.

Besides U.S. 191 from Bozeman, you can reach the West Entrance from the northwest (on U.S. 287) and from the southwest (on U.S. 20 and Interstate 15). Montana towns northwest of the park include two where vacationers might want to linger, Ennis and Virginia City. Ennis is a center for trout fishing, and Virginia City and Alder Gulch were famous for gold mining in the 19th century. In Virginia City, the capital of the Territory of Montana from 1865 to 1876, you can visit several restored historical buildings. The town boasts two small museums and performances all summer, both in an opera house and a former brewery.

Idaho towns somewhat farther from Yellowstone but with lodgings and other visitor facilities include Rexburg and St. Anthony on U.S. 20, and Idaho Falls and Pocatello on Interstate 15. While the latter two are served by major airlines and car rental companies and have many accommodations, both of these towns of 50,000 people are more than 100 miles (160 km) from Yellowstone's West Entrance.

II. SOUTH ENTRANCE Page 111

Mountain lovers and backcountry hikers would do well to choose the South Entrance. The entire southern section of the park, about one quarter of the whole, is remote mountain country of undeveloped high meadow and forest. The southeast section of the park, together with large areas outside park borders, comprise a vast wilderness, probably the largest area in the contiguous United States without roads. If your main goal is canoeing or fishing on Lewis and Shoshone lakes, the South Entrance is for you. This is also one of the two closest ways to reach Yellowstone Lake.

Within a half-day's drive outside the park's South Entrance are wonderful examples of the beautiful scenery for which Wyoming is famous. The mountains and lakes of Grand Teton National Park are visited annually by one million more people than is Yellowstone.

The Tetons are some of the most strikingly beautiful mountains in the world.

The largest town in the area is Jackson, serving visitors summer and winter and located about 58 miles (93 km) south of Yellowstone. Smaller Wyoming towns somewhat farther from Yellowstone but with less expensive tourist facilities are Dubois to the southeast of Yellowstone and Alpine on the Idaho/Wyoming state line. Dubois is 83 miles (134 km) from the South Entrance; Alpine is 37 miles (60 km) south of Jackson.

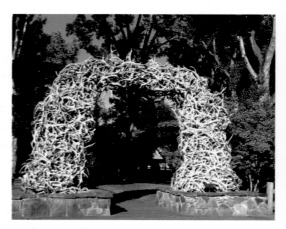

Each corner of Jackson's central square is adorned with elk antlers.

III. EAST ENTRANCE   Page 146

The East Entrance will be your first choice as a way to enter Yellowstone if you're interested in Native American lore or western museums (in Cody), or horseback riding and guest ranches. It's relatively close to Yellowstone Lake, convenient for those who want to do some boating or fishing there.

Between Cody and the park, you can indulge in every sort of outdoor activity, from golf and fishing to backpacking and windsurfing. Attractions include the Buffalo Bill Dam, with its visitor center and ten square miles (26 sq km) of reservoir, and Buffalo Bill State Park, which borders the reservoir and provides places to camp, picnic, or

Rock formations called hoodoos along the road from Cody to the East Entrance.

launch boats. The Buffalo Bill Cody Scenic Byway (U.S. Highways 14/16/20) passes through several areas of hoodoos visible from the road. It's 53 miles (85 km) from Cody to the East Entrance of Yellowstone.

IV. NORTHEAST ENTRANCE   Page 181

The Northeast Entrance is the closest one to Billings, Montana, but it's not the fastest way to get to the park from Billings—the fastest is by going through the North Entrance, described below. Two high, spectacular mountain roads approach Yellowstone from the northeast.

The most popular road, the Beartooth Scenic Byway (U.S. 212), crosses the Beartooth Range on a series of switchbacks between Red Lodge and Cooke City. The late CBS news correspondent Charles Kuralt asserted in his 1979 book, *Dateline America*, that "the most beautiful road in America is U.S. 212, which leaves Red Lodge, climbs to Beartooth Pass at eleven thousand feet, and drops down into the northeast entrance of Yellowstone Park." Most visitors agree with him when they see the tremendous panoramas and exquisitely colored wildflowers, especially above timberline.

The distance from Billings to the Northeast Entrance this way is about 130 miles (209 km). Allow about four hours to enjoy it.

An alternative if you're coming from east of the park is the Chief Joseph Scenic Byway (Wyoming 296), which crosses the Absaroka Range. Paving of this beautiful route has recently been completed. It affords breathtaking views of the surrounding countryside and access to the Sunlight Basin area with its ranches and summer homes. The Chief Joseph Highway joins U.S. 212 a few miles east of Cooke City. The distance from Billings to the Northeast Entrance this way is about 150 miles (240 km); from Cody, about 80 miles (130 km).

Visitors suffering from a fear of heights should be forewarned that there are several switchbacks on these roads with long views to the valleys far below.

Little Bear Creek runs through a field of flowers below Beartooth Butte.

The Northeast Entrance was the last to be opened, in 1936. It still has the fewest cars passing through it of any of the entrances. Cooke City and Silver Gate just outside the park have tourist accommodations, as does Red Lodge.

V. NORTH ENTRANCE   Page 236

The North Entrance was the first, and for years the most popular, way to enter Yellowstone. Lower in elevation than any of the others, this entrance has always been

The Yellowstone River is popular for rafting, kayaking, and fishing.

the most accessible by road (and formerly by rail) from Montana towns such as Helena, Butte, Billings, or Bozeman.

You reach the North Entrance via Interstate 90 to Livingston, turning south on U.S. 89. Following the north-flowing Yellowstone River, you pass through serene Paradise Valley, now famous as a resort area for movie stars and other high-profile Americans.

The distance from Livingston to Gardiner, the small town at the park's northern boundary, is 54 miles (87 km). The section of park road from Gardiner to Cooke City is the only park road kept open to motor vehicles all winter.

Approaches to the West Entrance

ROAD LOGS AND DESTINATIONS

Approaches to the West Entrance

Most people approach the West Entrance from Bozeman, Montana, north of Yellowstone Park. Taking U.S. Highway 191 through the Gallatin Canyon, you traverse pleasant mountain scenery without crossing any high mountain passes. On this route, you can find all types of accommodations, from motels to guest ranches to luxury resorts, many of which provide guided fishing and horseback riding trips. About halfway along the 90-plus miles (145 km) from Bozeman to West Yellowstone is the road to the famous ski resort of Big Sky. More than 20 miles (32 km) of U.S. 191 pass inside the western edge of Yellowstone.

If you're approaching from the west or south rather than by the Gallatin River canyon route, there are two other good roads you might take. They are U.S. 287 and the road from Pocatello, Idaho Falls, and Ashton, Idaho (Interstate 15, then U.S. 20). The Ashton to West Yellowstone drive is described in the other direction on pages 106–9.

BOZEMAN, MONTANA
Population (2000): 27,500
Bozeman is a small but bustling town and one of Montana's oldest, established in 1864. The former agricultural college, now Montana State University, is the home of the **Museum of the Rockies**, with a planetarium and excellent dinosaur and geology exhibits.

FROM BOZEMAN TO THE WEST ENTRANCE

You'll need about 2 hours driving time to cover the distance from the Bozeman area to West Yellowstone. The road follows the Gallatin River up its beautiful mountain-bound canyon. Take Interstate 90 west to Montana Highway 85, which leads to U.S. 191, or take U.S. 191 due west out of town and then follow it south.

The village of Gallatin Gateway is 15 miles (24 km) from Bozeman, just off the highway. As you pass near it, you'll see the restored **Gallatin Gateway Inn**, built as the terminus of the Chicago, Milwaukee, St. Paul, and Pacific Railroad (nicknamed the Milwaukee Road), which operated a branch line to this inn from 1927 to 1961. In those years, park visitors arriving by train were met at the inn by the classic yellow park concessionaire's buses.

Soon you'll be following the canyon of the **Gallatin River**, which flows north out of the park. The river has long been famous for its trout. Fishing scenes in the movie *A River Runs Through It* were filmed here in the 1990s. Guest ranches and private vacation cabins are numerous in the canyon.

Much of this highway is in the Gallatin National Forest, and there are several Forest Service campgrounds and trailheads along it. Approximately halfway between Bozeman and West Yellowstone (43 miles/69 km from Bozeman) is the turnoff to **Big Sky**. Motels and eating establishments are plentiful, and you'll find a small chapel near the turnoff. Since TV journalist Chet Huntley began it in the early 1970s, Big Sky has become a major vacation resort and skiing center. Before that, this part of the Gallatin Valley was fertile farmland; it was known for its lettuce and provided oats and hay for Yellowstone Park horses in the very early years.

Lone Mountain from the Big Sky road.

Above Big Sky stands the pyramid of **Lone Mountain**, a *glacial horn* carved by the action of glaciers.

Signs of the area's historic volcanic eruptions begin to appear about 12 miles (20 km) south of the Big Sky Junction. Eroded gray and yellow rock formations above the road are made of the same welded volcanic ash that you'll see topping Crown and Lava buttes just inside the park.

ALONG U.S. 191 IN THE PARK

Approximately 60 miles (96 km) from Bozeman, Highway 191 enters the northwestern corner of Yellowstone and continues inside the park for about 20 miles (32 km), crossing in and out of Wyoming and Montana. There are no campgrounds, picnic areas, or rest rooms along this stretch of road, but there is access to several trails into the backcountry, both in the park and in Gallatin National Forest. This road was first built in 1910–11 and now passes through land that was added to the park in 1929.

Road Log

0.0/20.5 Yellowstone National Park boundary. Just a large sign marks the edge of the park here; there's no entrance fee to pay until you reach the West Entrance station.

This short stretch of U.S. 191 is the only road within the park where the speed limit is 55 miles per hour rather than 45. The only park road used by large trucks, it's open year round.

The mountains northeast of the road (to your left as you enter the park) are **Crown Butte** (elevation 8051 ft/2454 m) and **Lava Butte** (7904 ft/2409 m). Crown Butte resembles a crown when

Entering park territory, you are greeted by the volcanic cone of Black Butte.

seen from the south. Geologists tell us that both Crown Butte and Lava Butte (a mile or two farther along) are topped with *Huckleberry Ridge tuff*, the 2-million-year-old welded volcanic ash that can be seen in several localities in the park. Here the tuff overlies *shale*, a sedimentary rock rich in clays. Shale weathers and erodes easily, producing landslides that sometimes encroach upon the road.

0.9/19.6 🚶 🐎 🚻 Dailey Creek Trailhead. Small parking area and Dailey Creek crossing. Dailey Creek was named for one of the first families to winter in the valley on the other side of the Gallatin Range. The family arrived in 1866 and still had a ranch there in the 1930s.

Lodgepole Creek joins the Gallatin from the (west) side opposite Dailey Creek. Note that locals pronounce the word creek like CRICK, to rhyme with trick.

All trails in this part of the park are long, steep ones that lead into the

Gallatin Range. Dailey, Black Butte, and Specimen Creek trails all join with the Sky Rim Trail 5 miles or more away and 3000 feet up (about 8 km away and 900 m up). The Sky Rim Trail affords spectacular mountain views to the very hardy climber or horseback rider. Also, some stumps of petrified wood are preserved there, but they are harder to reach and less interesting than those on Specimen Ridge in the Lamar River valley. Both grizzlies and black bears live in this northwest corner of Yellowstone.

Along the far side of the river, you'll see red-tipped white stakes marking the park boundary.

2.6/17.9 🚶 Black Butte Creek Trailhead; parking area on the west, trail on the east. This is the shortest but steepest of the trails that connect to the Sky Rim Trail.

3.0/17.5 The almost perfect cone shape of **Black Butte** looms over the road to the east. Geologists call Black Butte an *igneous intrusion*. This means that it's made of rock that rose as a molten mass from deep within the earth, but stopped and crystallized before reaching the earth's surface. Since the overlying rocks eroded away, we can now see the intrusion. Black Butte's rock is about 50 million years old.

3.9/16.6 There's a tiny stream called **Wickiup Creek** here. A *wickiup* was a temporary shelter used by nomadic tribes of Native Americans. Long poles placed in a circle with their tips joined together were covered with skins or brush. There was a group of these hunting lodges near the stream here in the early days of the park.

4.6/15.9 🚶 ⛟ Specimen Creek Trailhead. This trail connects to the Sky Rim, High Lake, and Sportsman Lake trails. In spite of its name, this is not the best route to take to see petrified wood specimens. A ranger or local resident can best advise you on how to reach them. Remember that no samples may be removed from the park. Two easier ways to see petrified trees are by hiking from Yellowstone's northern approach road north of Gardiner, Montana, and at Petrified Tree near Tower-Roosevelt Junction.

To the east is **Lightning Hill**, so named when rangers from the now-razed ranger station near Wickiup Creek used to climb it to check for lightning-caused fires.

6.1/14.4 To the west, **Snowslide Creek** cascades into the Gallatin River in an area that's marshy except when the creek dries up in late summer. On the far side of the river along here, you can see remnants of the original road through Gallatin Canyon.

7.1/13.4 Terminal Monument Creek crossing. The strange name of this creek stems from a wooden post placed up the hill to the northeast that marks the northwest corner of the state of Wyoming.

7.5/13.0 Gallatin River Bridge.

7.6/11.9 🚶 ⛟ Bacon Rind Creek Trail begins 0.3 mile (0.5 km) up the side road to the west. After the first 2.5 miles (4 km), the trail continues out of the park into the Lee Metcalf Wilderness. The century-old name Bacon Rind Creek probably referred to breakfast around the campfire or to an old way to bait bears by hanging bacon rind in a tree.

As you travel south, you begin to see the *snags*, that is, standing burned trees left from the Fan fire, one of 1988's many Yellowstone fires.

9.3/11.2 🚶 🐎 ⛵ Fan Creek and Fawn Pass trailheads. Fan Creek flows into the Gallatin from the northeast through a valley that 19th century geologists thought looked like a large fan, because of its radiating minor valleys. Both trails take hikers and riders into the southern expanses of the Gallatin Range.

🚶 To see an undisturbed, beautiful mountain valley, you might follow the start of the Fan Creek Trail for about 2 miles (3 km), turning northeast at the trail junction.

10.5/10.0 From this point south, we no longer follow the Gallatin River. The river flows west from its source in the high Gallatin Mountains, then turns north here and meanders through the flat floodplain that you've just traversed if traveling southward. This is also the Montana/Wyoming state line.

10.9/9.6 🚶 Bighorn Pass Trailhead. The sign indicates a short side road primarily for unloading horse trailers. The Bighorn Pass Trail follows the Gallatin River almost to its source at Gallatin Lake some 12 miles (19 km) away and 2000 feet (610 m) up. Both the Bighorn Pass and Fawn Pass trails continue across the high mountains and all the way to the Grand Loop Road between Mammoth and Norris. Looking east up the Gallatin River here, you see Bannock Peak (10,332 ft/3149 m), with Quadrant Mountain (10,213 ft/3113 m) behind it.

In the 1920s, citizens and Milwaukee Road officials were eyeing the Bighorn Pass Trail route as an attractive place to build a road or a railroad. We must thank National Park Service's first director, Stephen Mather, and Yellowstone Park Superintendent Horace Albright for their foresight in objecting to these plans. Long before designated wilderness areas were thought of, Mather wrote to Albright: "We must keep a large area of Yellowstone in a state of untouched wildness if we are to be faithful to our trust as protectors of the wild life with which the park abounds." The road was not built, nor was the railroad company even allowed to conduct a survey.

12.0/8.5 Divide Lake, at an elevation of about 7250 feet (2210 m), takes its name from the fact that water flows from this vicinity into two different watersheds. To the north all streams flow to the Gallatin River, while to the south they flow to the Madison River. These rivers (along with the Jefferson River) join to form the Missouri River, and their waters eventually flow to the Atlantic Ocean.

14.0/6.5 Pass Creek and ⛵ **Grayling Creek** join here. U.S. 191 parallels Grayling Creek until that creek's southern exit from the park, crossing it three or four times. The old road crossed the creek a dozen or more times, so that the builders could avoid excavating the sidehills.

The road skirts a severely burned area at the northwestern reach of the 1988 North Fork fire.

20.3/0.2 Tepee Creek crossing.

20.5/0.0 Yellowstone National Park boundary. Here U.S. 191 leaves the park.

From Outside the Park Boundary to West Yellowstone

From here U.S. 191 descends into the valley of the Madison River and reaches the town of West Yellowstone and the West Entrance in about 11 miles (18 km). Off to the west and southwest, you may see parts of the Snowcrest, Centennial, and Henrys Lake ranges beyond Hebgen Lake. To the east is the high but relatively flat and tree-covered Yellowstone Plateau.

[🚶] At 1.4 miles (2.3 km) outside the park boundary and about 9.5 miles (15 km) north of West Yellowstone is the parking area for the **Gneiss Creek Trailhead**, next to the private Fir Ridge Cemetery road. This long trail soon enters park territory and crosses the meadows of the Madison River valley. It is described from the other end at mile 7.6/6.3 on the West Entrance Road.

At the nearby junction with U.S. 287, you may want to take a side trip of less than 20 miles (32 km) to visit Hebgen Lake and Quake Lake, where you can see a remarkable landslide and learn about the devastating earthquake of 1959.

Quake Lake

If you're entering or leaving the park via the West Entrance, it's worthwhile to allow time for a visit to Earthquake Lake (often shortened to Quake Lake), northwest of West Yellowstone on U.S. 287. This is the site of the devastating August 17, 1959, earthquake and huge landslide that killed 28 people, most of them campers in a now-buried campground.

The landslide, caused by an earthquake that registered 7.1 on the Richter scale, dammed the Madison River, forming the lake. This earthquake affected the geysers in Yellowstone's Upper Geyser Basin—some 35 miles away.

Start your visit at the Forest Service visitor center where you'll find exhibits and information about

Quake Lake was created by a huge landslide.

the earthquake and how a potential Madison River flood was avoided. Hebgen Dam, completed in 1915, cracked but did not give way in the quake.

The next 8 miles (13 km) of U.S. 191 take you through an old stand of lodgepole pines, past a Forest Service campground and the Yellowstone Airport, and into West Yellowstone.

WEST YELLOWSTONE, MONTANA
Population: 1200
Motel and hotel accommodations and other tourist facilities are available throughout the year in the town of West Yellowstone. It's possible to travel by public bus between West Yellowstone and Bozeman, the only regularly scheduled public bus connection between one of the gateway communities and a larger city.

In winter, you can arrange snowcoach transportation from West Yellowstone to Old Faithful Village through the park concessionaire and several other companies. A snowcoach, with its front skis and back tracks, can carry 10 to 12 people in relative comfort over unplowed roads. In addition to serving as a starting point for snowcoaches, West Yellowstone is a major center for snowmobile rental.

West Yellowstone's first post office was established as Riverside in 1908, but the town soon changed its name to Yellowstone, Montana. This proved confusing, so in 1920 the name became West Yellowstone; the locals now simply call it West.

Snowcoach

Before 1908 the Union Pacific Railroad reached only to Idaho Falls, and visitors to the park traveled a day or more by stagecoach to reach the West Entrance. Then, until 1961, the U.P.'s Oregon Short Line served the town and this entrance to Yellowstone.

The former railroad station is now The Museum of the Yellowstone, featuring the history of the railroad era in this area and exhibits about wildlife, the Hebgen Lake earthquake, and the 1988 fires. Another West Yellowstone attraction is the nonprofit Grizzly Discovery Center, home to seven grizzlies, a Kodiak bear, and ten gray wolves.

Both the museum and the animal habitat are located on the town's main street leading into the park. Taking the main east-west street of West Yellowstone a few blocks east brings you to the West Entrance.

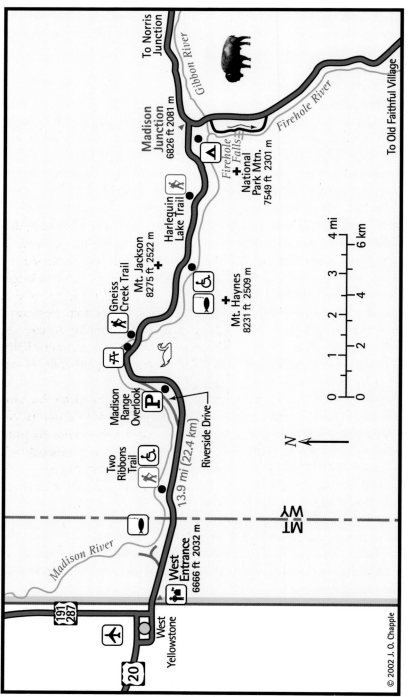

West Entrance to Madison Junction

© 2002 J. O. Chapple

From the West Entrance to Madison Junction

The West Entrance is the most popular way to enter Yellowstone, welcoming over 3000 visitors each day in the summer months. In fact, it's second only to Grand Canyon National Park's South Rim as a busy national park entrance.

From West Yellowstone, this entrance road passes through stands of lodgepole pine, much of it burned in the 1988 North Fork fire, the largest of that year's devastating fires. The Madison River is tepid all winter from geothermal runoff, which prevents ice from forming and provides habitat for the rare and beautiful trumpeter swan, making this entrance road one of the most likely places to see swans, especially in winter. There's also a strong possibility of seeing elk or bison.

The route you follow by taking this entrance road approximates that used by early-day trappers, Native Americans, and some would-be gold miners. No gold in minable quantities was ever discovered within what is now the park. Stagecoach lines used this route to bring visitors into the new national park from 1880 until 1917, when buses and cars replaced them completely.

It's about 14 miles (22 km) from the West Entrance to Madison Junction and the Grand Loop Road.

Road Log

NOTE: There are several very short side roads along this entrance road. The mileage for such roads is given at approximately the midpoint between the two ways to enter the loop.

0.0/13.9 Yellowstone National Park boundary.

0.1/13.8 Side road to the offices and warehouses of Hamilton Stores. Yellowstone's West Section Ranger Station is also on this road, but it is not a visitor center.

Hamilton Stores is the longest running concession in the entire national park system. Charles A. Hamilton purchased his first store in 1915 at Upper

Geyser Basin. Since acquiring the Haynes Picture Shops in 1968, the concession has grown to 14 stores around the park. Summer employees are predominantly college students and retirees.

0.3/13.6 👤 West Entrance station. Stop here to pay the entrance fee (see the "Travel Tips" for fee information). For backcountry permits, you'll find the backcountry office a short walk to the southeast of the entrance station.

0.8/13.1 🚲 🚶 Unmarked gravel road to the north leads to Madison River fishing access about 1.3 miles (2 km) away; fly fishing only. Over the years, this large meadow has been called Riverside and the Barns (for extensive horse barns here in the early years, later used by park buses). Stagecoach drivers 100 years ago dubbed this area Christmas Tree Park, because a very old forest fire burn had been overgrown by a new forest of uniform lodgepoles.

The Madison River

A world famous trout fishing stream, the Madison is extremely rich in the calcium bicarbonate needed for abundant plant growth, which furnishes hiding places for insects and trout. The river flows westward out of the park through Hebgen and Quake lakes, then turns north, and eventually joins the Gallatin and Jefferson to form the Missouri River near Three Forks, Montana. Members of the Lewis and Clark Expedition of 1803–6 named the three rivers but did not follow any of them into what is now park territory, since their mission was to reach the Pacific Ocean by the most direct route possible.

The three rivers were named for Thomas Jefferson, the visionary third U.S. president, who conceived and authorized the Lewis and Clark Expedition; James Madison, Jefferson's secretary of state, who became the fourth U.S. president in 1809; and Albert Gallatin, secretary of the treasury under Jefferson.

Along the river was the site of one of the Wylie Camping Company's lunch stations, beginning in 1909. William W. Wylie and his successors provided stagecoach passengers and then motorists with low-cost tent camps and lunch stops into the 1940s.

1.7/12.2 Paved road for river access.

2.2/11.7 Montana/Wyoming state line. A small portion of the park is in Montana and even less in Idaho. This is because the original Yellowstone boundaries were set in relation to their distance from natural landmarks, before the states' boundaries had been established. As one example, in 1872 Congress set the western boundary of the park to run "fifteen miles west of the most western point of Madison Lake" (present-day Shoshone Lake).

3.0/10.9 🚶 ♿ Unmarked side road to the north leads to the western end of an accessible boardwalk, the **Two Ribbons Trail**, with an interpretive display about the fire phenomena encountered along the trail. This is a three-quarter mile (1.2 km) loop walk that splits in two, with one branch near the river, the other slightly away from it.

Between here and the east end of the Two Ribbons Trail is a stand of lodgepole pines that burned in the 1988 North Fork fire. Walking among such dead standing trees, or snags, can be unsafe. They don't have deep roots and can easily topple over. Park policy states that the trees should be left where they fall, except when they're obstructing roads or trails.

There were definitely some positive aftereffects of the fires. Fifty-five kinds of birds and 24 kinds of mammals use these snags for nesting, perching, and food.

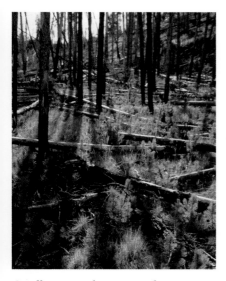

Small green saplings are replacing burned lodgepole pines all over the park.

Such trees also help prevent soil erosion and provide nutrients to fungi, young trees, and other plants. Wildflowers were especially abundant in the first few years after the fire. And far from spoiling the vista, the fire has opened up views of the Madison River and the distant Gallatin and Madison mountain ranges.

3.5/10.4 East end of Two Ribbons Trail.

4.1/9.8 Near here was the Riverside mail station and later a soldier station in the earliest years of the park, when small groups of U.S. Cavalry troops were sent on patrol to outlying areas. Later, a steep mail route called the Norris Slide climbed the plateau to descend at Fountain Flats.

4.9/9.0 🚗 Riverside Drive (west end) parallels the river for a little more than a mile.

5.6/8.3 Mountain overlook. This turnout has particularly good views of the Madison Range to the northwest (outside of the park) and the Gallatin Range (partly inside, partly outside of the park) to the north.

6.1/7.8 Riverside Drive (east end).

7.5/6.4 🏕(4) 🚻♿ 🚗 Madison River picnic area in a pleasant shady spot.

7.6/6.3 Madison River Bridge, often called the Seven-Mile Bridge, is about that far from the West Entrance station. 🚶 Parking for **Gneiss Creek Trailhead** is on the east side of the bridge. This nearly level 14-mile (23 km) trail traverses the Madison Valley, where moose, grouse, grizzly bears, and biting flies abound. The trail meets U.S. High- way 191 a short distance outside the western park boundary. Gneiss (pronounced NICE) Creek gets its name

A Tale of Two Photographers

William H. Jackson (1843–1942), for whom Mount Jackson was named, was the photographer who took some of the first photographs of Yellowstone. He accompanied the 1871 Hayden Survey around what was soon to become the world's first national park, and his photographs contributed to its formation. Also a painter, Jackson created four murals for the Department of Interior building in Washington, D.C. at the age of 92 and continued to visit Yellowstone until the age of 97.

Mammoth Terraces and Hotel in the late 19th century. W. H. Jackson climbed to unusual vantage points for his photographs.

The skiing party of F. J. Haynes passes Obsidian cliff in winter 1886–87.

It's fitting that Mount Haynes and Mount Jackson should be located near each other (about half a mile apart). Mount Haynes was named for Yellowstone photographer and concessionaire, **Frank Jay Haynes** (1853–1921), official Park Photographer starting in 1883. Haynes published early road guides to the park, operated stagecoach lines, and ran the Haynes Picture Shops. His shops were popular small stores that sold photographs and postcards in the days when few people had cameras of their own.

from the outcrops of *Precambrian gneiss,* a very old granite-like rock found in the mountains near the creek's headwaters.

7.8/6.1 [H] Interpretive displays about trumpeter swans and the historical use of this entrance road.

This part of the Madison River is a favorite nesting area and is now closed as sensitive habitat. Although their status in the park is rather precarious, these swans have never been listed as an endangered species because they are more numerous elsewhere.

8.6/5.3 West end of Madison Canyon.

9.7/4.2 [P] [↩] River access road and informational sign about *talus* (pronounced TAY-luhs), the geological name for the steeply sloping mass of rock debris across the river. To fishermen this is the Madison Notch.

Immediately north of the road is a good example of columnar jointing in volcanic rock on **Mount Jackson**. Look for the regular columns of rock several yards (or meters) high near the top of the mountain. (See the explanation of columnar jointing—"Basalt Columns"—in the road log "From Tower Junction to Canyon Junction.")

10.3/3.6 [↩] [♿] The only wheelchair accessible fishing ramp presently available in the park. About a half mile (0.8 km) to the south across the river is the cliff face of **Mount Haynes**.

12.1/1.8 [P] Informational sign about the Madison Plateau.

[🚶] The side road here is a convenient place to park for the **Harlequin Lake**

Trailhead, which is on the opposite side of the main road and slightly to the east. This is an easy half-mile (0.8 km) trail through burned lodgepoles to a delightful lily pad pond. The name Harlequin is for a type of duck found during the summer in the park, primarily along the Yellowstone River.

Beaver lodge in Harlequin Lake.

Near here the entrance road skirts the edge of the Yellowstone caldera (see "What is the Yellowstone Caldera?"). Although numerous calderas have been discovered in the Rockies in the past few decades, Yellowstone's is the largest. In fact, it's one of the largest in the world.

12.5/1.4 [P] "Beetle-Killed and Fire-Scarred" interpretive sign.

12.8/1.1 [P] An interpretive sign shows the Madison elk herd's summer and winter ranges.

13.7/0.2 [▲] [🏕][♿] [≋]Entrance to **Madison Campground**; wheelchair accessible rest room on Loop A. This campground, opened in 1961, is one of the largest in the park. Some of its 280 sites overlook the Madison River. Nearby is an amphitheater for the park rangers' evening lectures.

13.9/0.0 Madison Junction. To the northeast about 13 miles (21 km) away are Norris Junction and Norris Geyser Basin. Upper Geyser Basin and Old Faithful Village are 17 miles (27 km) to the south.

What Is the Yellowstone Caldera?

The road approaching Madison Junction from the west enters one of the major geological features of Yellowstone Park, the *caldera*, or huge crater, that formed 630,000 years ago. At that time, a vast volcanic explosion occurred, which blew out at least 1000 times as much rock as the Mount St. Helens eruption in Washington State did in 1980. The molten rock from a huge underground chamber was blown high into the air and then settled as volcanic ash (now called the *Lava Creek tuff*). The chamber extended from here east beyond the present-day Canyon Village and Fishing Bridge Junction areas and south almost to the edge of the park. Its boundary is shown by the dashed line on the map given to park visitors and on the map at the beginning of the "Geological History" chapter.

The ash settled out partly over the land north of here but was also carried to much of the northern Rockies and eastward to the Great Plains, as far as Iowa. So much rock was expelled, along with superheated water and other gases at high pressure, that the roof of this partly emptied chamber collapsed, leaving a large hole, the caldera.

The volcanic activity did not cease after the ground collapsed inward. More molten rock rose into the chamber, forcing large volumes of thick, tacky lava out onto the caldera floor. The lava flows continued intermittently over the course of a few hundred thousand years, partly filling the caldera and building up a large, high flat area. This explains why today the caldera no longer appears like a hole or crater.

The cliffs you can see across the river from the entrance road west of Madison Junction are the northern edge of the high flat area now called the Madison Plateau. The Madison Plateau reaches southwest approximately to the Idaho line, occupying 250 square miles (650 sq km) of territory. You can see good examples of its lava close up along the drive through Firehole River Canyon just south of Madison Junction. The caldera is roughly oval, about 30 by 45 miles (48 by 72 km), and partly surrounded by cliffs, like a volcano's crater but far larger. Cliffs extend along the road for about 8 miles (13 km) eastward past Madison Junction to Gibbon Falls, forming the northern wall of the caldera.

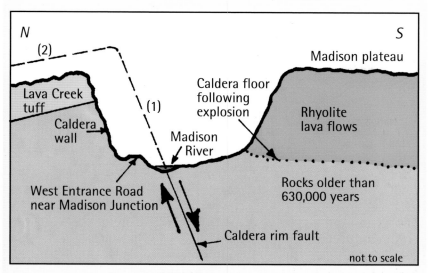

Figure 1. Cross section of the Yellowstone caldera rim.
This north-to-south cross section shows the northern rim of the Yellowstone caldera. When the Lava Creek tuff erupted and covered the older rocks 630,000 years ago, the ground surface then collapsed into the space left by the erupted tuff and so created the caldera. The arrows show the relative motion of the fault at the edge of the collapsed part. Rhyolite lavas later flowed out and covered the caldera floor. The dashed lines show approximately: (1) where the original caldera edge at the fault surface was before erosion and (2) where the surface of the tuff was outside the caldera before erosion.

Madison Junction to Old Faithful Village

From Madison Junction to Old Faithful Village

This section of the Grand Loop Road leads south to Upper Geyser Basin at Old Faithful Village, 17 miles (27 km) away. There are three side roads of interest. Firehole Canyon Drive closely parallels the canyon of the Firehole River and runs one way north to south. A few miles farther south, the Fountain Flats Road takes you to a walking or bicycle trail. The third side road is the Firehole Lake Drive—a one-way road (south to north) where you might catch an eruption of Great Fountain or White Dome geyser or stroll around steaming Firehole Lake.

On the main road you'll find numerous turnouts for access to the Firehole River. Before you reach Old Faithful, you'll pass four thermal areas. These are the Fountain Paint Pot area and the geyser basins called Midway, Biscuit, and Black Sand.

Road Log

NOTE: The name Old Faithful is used in the park to refer to both the village and the geyser. Mileage in this road log goes to and from the Old Faithful Visitor Center.

0.0/17.0 Madison Junction, intersecting with the Grand Loop Road, the figure eight road that has taken visitors to the major features of the park for over 100 years. Norris Junction and Norris Geyser Basin are to the northeast; Old Faithful Village is to the south.

0.1/16.9 ⊼(12) 🚻(2) ? Madison picnic area and information station/bookstore. The only wheelchair accessible rest rooms in this part of the park are located in Loop A of the Madison Campground (described on page 37), just to the west. However, drinking water and flush toilets are available here, unlike most picnic areas.

The information station has a park ranger on duty, and the bookstore is staffed by volunteers and employees of the Yellowstone Association. This building was opened in 1929 as a museum of history and is one of the remaining neo-rustic style interpretative buildings designed by architect Herbert Maier. The building is also one of the six National

Historic Landmarks in Yellowstone. Just behind it are the amphitheater for evening lectures and a path to the Madison Campground. There's also a plaque relating the long-accepted story (now considered an oversimplification) of how Yellowstone became the first national park (see "The National Park Idea").

The Gibbon and Firehole rivers join here to form the Madison River, which flows west out of the park. The name Madison Junction, originally applied to the river junction, also applies to the road junction.

The prominent rise to the southwest beyond the rivers is **National Park Mountain**. Its cliffs form the edge of the Madison Plateau.

The National Park Idea

At the junction of the Gibbon and Firehole rivers, members of the Washburn Expedition camped in September, 1870, after exploring much of what is now Yellowstone Park. In his reminiscences many years later, one of the expedition's leaders, Nathaniel P. Langford, credited fellow expedition member Cornelius Hedges with originating the national park idea at that time and upon this spot. For a few years in the middle of the 20th century, an annual pageant was held at Madison to reenact the story of the National Park idea.

Historians now point out that Hedges was only one of several forward-thinking men (including Langford himself) who believed in preserving this area for the enjoyment of all future generations and preventing it from being divided up and commercially exploited. These men worked to persuade Congress and the American people to set aside this unique area as the first national park in the entire world. There is no proof that this campfire conversation did *not* take place, but neither is there any proof that it did. Perhaps we should preserve this creation story as part of Yellowstone's heritage.

0.4/16.6 Gibbon River Bridge. Look for bison (also called buffalo) in the wide meadow along the river, where a large herd often spends the summer.

0.6/16.4 Firehole Canyon Drive begins. This narrow road is now one way north to south, but until it was damaged during the 1959 Hebgen Lake earthquake, it was part of the Grand Loop Road. It's about the same length as the newer main road and well worth taking.

Bison may seem placid but can be dangerous if approached too closely.

Firehole Canyon Drive*

NOTE: The mileage from the beginning of this side loop is given in parentheses. Grand Loop Road mileage continues at 2.4 miles from Madison Junction, where Firehole Canyon Drive rejoins it.

(0.4) The small spring at the left was a favorite spot for refreshing oneself, but now Yellowstone's water cannot be guaranteed safe for drinking.

Near here occurred the last of five stagecoach robberies in the park. In July of 1915, one highwayman stopped five coaches and robbed passengers of some 200 dollars. One of the victims happened to be Bernard Baruch, statesman and advisor to U.S. presidents for nearly half a century. According to Jack Haynes's booklet, *Yellowstone Stage Hold-ups*, Baruch later commented, "It was the best 50 dollars I ever spent!" The robber was never brought to justice.

(0.7) As the road climbs away from the river, look for a rhyolite flow to the left. *Rhyolite lava*, a rock rich in silica, is commonly found in Yellowstone in the form of tuff or obsidian, and occasionally as pumice.

(1.0) Firehole Falls and an interpretive display about the rhyolite flow around you. Before 1889, there were no fish occurring naturally in the Firehole River above the falls, but in that year the river was stocked with brook trout, and soon the upstream reach became a favorite with many park fishermen.

There are cascades in the river both above and below the falls. All are caused by the varying resistance that different rocks offer to river erosion.

Rhyolite and the Plateau of Fire

Lava is molten rock that reaches the earth's surface, and rhyolite is one type of lava. Rhyolite lava, which formed the rocks exposed along Firehole Canyon Drive, is very stiff and does not flow readily (that is, it's highly *viscous*), behaving much like asphalt or molasses. It's so stiff that a lot of force is required to push it out from within the earth. As it's being pushed out, it rips fragments from the rocks through which it's flowing and carries them to the surface.

If you stop at Firehole Falls, look closely at the rock face around the parking area. Portions of the rock consist of thin layers—a pencil thickness or less—that extend in the same direction as the original flow motion. This rock cooled very quickly. It didn't have time to form crystals throughout, but ended up consisting mostly of what geologists term *glass*. The very dark layers you can see are glass, and the light layers are mostly very tiny crystals of the minerals quartz and feldspar. Embedded in the rhyolite are rock fragments that have sharp, jagged edges. These were the bits of rock that the lava ripped out and carried along as it came toward the surface.

When it was flowing slowly, the lava's temperature would have been about

1200°F (650°C). Where the moving surface cracked apart, it would have glowed a bright orange until cooled by the air.

The northern edge of the Madison Plateau is where Firehole Canyon Drive begins, but the plateau extends southwestward about 30 miles (50 km) to the Idaho boundary. Imagine the number of flows and the total amount of lava that must have flowed to create this massive plateau.

The slow movement of rhyolite to form the Madison Plateau contrasts sharply with the previous events: massive explosive eruptions that resulted in the Yellowstone caldera. It was the caldera floor onto which the rhyolites later flowed.

(2.0) 🛁(2) Swimming area—one of two places near park roads where the water is really warm enough for swimming. (Read about the other in the road log "From the North Entrance to Mammoth Hot Springs.") The water of the Firehole here is a pleasant temperature—about 75°F (24°C), neither warm nor cold. A stairway and a couple of rocky paths lead down to the water. There's no lifeguard on duty, but park rangers check the area periodically. If you choose to swim here, you will not be lonely: about 50 cars were parked along the road one recent warm July afternoon. The rest rooms on the side of the road away from the river are large enough for changing clothes.

(2.2) 🚣 Just before Firehole Canyon Drive rejoins the Grand Loop Road, a sign announces "Firehole Cascade." A blocked-off stretch of former highway provides a short walkway to the best of the cascades and to fishing access, for fly fishing only. Parking is along the side loop road.

~

Continuing on the Grand Loop Road
2.4/14.6 Note the "small, almond-shaped" island just above the Firehole Cascades, as mentioned in Harry J.

Norton's 1873 guide, *Wonderland Illustrated*. Here, according to Norton, two members of his party camped for the night and returned in the morning "with glowing descriptions of the sighing and singing of the merry water-sprites who lulled them to sleep in their island couch. . . . "

🚣 This stretch of river abounds in rainbow trout, while further upriver, brook and brown trout are more common.

From the point where the one-way Firehole Canyon Drive rejoins the Grand Loop Road, lodgepole pines grow directly out of some of the rocks in the Firehole River. Somehow, they find enough soil for their roots.

4.5/12.5 🪑(12) 🛁 ♿ Firehole River picnic area.

5.6/11.4 Fountain Flats Drive leads off to the south. This was the 1882 road to Upper Geyser Basin, later called the Fountain Freight Road. The present more scenic road section of the Grand Loop Road replaced it a few years later. Beyond the first mile (1.6 km), this flat loop road is closed to cars, with generous parking provided. It's recommended for bicycles, which may travel it in either direction for about 5 miles (8 km).

Fountain Flats Drive is the best approach to the Sentinel Meadows Trailhead, but there's a shorter way (at mile 11.3/5.7) to get to the Fairy Falls Trailhead or to reach Imperial Geyser.

Fountain Flats was named for a major geyser in the Fountain Paint Pot area—Fountain Geyser, a spectacular performer from the 1870s into the 1930s and again in recent years.

NOTE: The area from Fountain Flats Drive to Biscuit Basin (mile 13.8/3.2) is closed for bear management from mid March to Memorial Day. (See page 126 about Bear Management Areas.)

The Firehole River

Contrary to what you might think, the Firehole River did not get its name from the fact that hot springs and geysers adorn its banks for many miles and pour their hot waters into the stream. In the early 19th century, hole was a word for a mountain-bound valley, and the Burnt Hole or Fire Hole was a burnt-over section of the Madison River Valley. Trappers (perhaps even the famous Jim Bridger) transferred the latter name to the river. Bridger is credited with having concocted the notion (not supported by scientists!) that the water flowed downhill here so fast that the rocks were heated by the friction.

Although the Firehole's name had another origin, in some places hot springs in the bed of the river *do* keep the rocks hot. Perhaps early trappers forded this river in their bare feet, since they needed to keep their boots or moccasins dry, as well as their powder. What is known for sure is that in 1870 Nathaniel Langford discovered a hot spring vent in the river while crossing it near Castle Geyser in Upper Geyser Basin. These facts certainly contribute to the aptness of the name.

The temperature of the Firehole is definitely influenced by the gallons of runoff water contributed by all the geothermal sources from Lone Star Geyser (the geyser that's farthest upstream) to the springs along Fountain Flats Drive. The river's temperature rises a total of almost 25°F (14°C) in this meandering stretch of about 13 miles (21 km).

Fountain Flats Drive and trail access

🏕(12) 🏨 ♿ 🚲 After the bridge crosses the creek, a short dirt road leads to **Nez Perce Creek picnic area**. Nez Perce Creek and the Firehole River come together just to the north, creating one of the prettiest picnic spots in the park.

Marshall House, a primitive park hostel later called Firehole Hotel, was built at this site in 1884. It was abandoned after Fountain Hotel was built (in 1891), but stood until the 1930s. For a short time there was also a jail here, built to incarcerate those who violated park laws, but almost never used.

Beyond the picnic area you'll see steam rising to the left from **Hygeia Spring** (Hygeia was the Greek goddess of health). Though occupants of the Marshall House used the water of this spring for bathing and cooking, now it's lukewarm.

Near the river is **Maidens Grave Spring**, named in memory of the wife of the winter hotel keeper at Marshall House. Her gravestone is between the present-day picnic area and the Firehole River's confluence with Nez Perce Creek.

As you continue on Fountain Flats Drive, you'll be in an area heavily burned by the North Fork fire of 1988.

Until the mid 1990s, this road continued to a thermal area, two trailheads, and a pair of fishing lakes. The road was closed off in an effort to mitigate impact on the wetland area and to create an additional biking opportunity. You have the option of turning back at the turning circle or leaving your car to walk about a quarter mile (0.4 km) to Ojo Caliente Spring.

[bike] Bicyclists and hikers can continue on to rejoin the Grand Loop Road less than 4 miles (6.4 km) from here.

[▲] [♿] One of the two wheelchair accessible campsites in Yellowstone is at Goose Lake, a little more than a mile (less than 2 km) from the turning circle and parking area.

~

Continuing south on foot (extension of Fountain Flats Drive)

Ojo Caliente Spring is a beautiful greenish blue to deep blue spring (its color depends on the time of day). Stay a safe distance away: the thin silica crust

Ojo Caliente is the most accessible of the River Group of hot springs and small geysers.

that overlies the superheated water can be dangerous. Ojo Caliente means "hot spring" in Spanish.

Northeast of the trail bridge across the Firehole and east of Ojo Caliente Spring is Pocket Basin, an interesting area of hot springs, small geysers, and mud pots.

It's best to ask the advice of a ranger before walking anywhere off the main trails of the park. This area is especially full of hazards, and there are no warning signs. In fact, visitors have been severely burned in this area. One person died and two were seriously injured from falling into one of these hot springs in the summer of 2000. Never walk alone in hazardous geyser basins such as this one.

An Explosion Crater: Pocket Basin

Geologists have found evidence that Pocket Basin is the crater left from a *hydrothermal explosion* (or *steam explosion*) some 10,000 years ago. As the region warmed, glaciers started to melt, and a glacial ice dam broke, suddenly lowering the lake level behind it and releasing pressure below the former lake. The pressure drop caused the hot water in the underlying rocks to flash into steam, blasting large rock fragments to the surface and leaving a hole. This is called an *explosion crater*.

The blasting happened because steam occupies about one thousand times the volume of the same amount of liquid water. Since the steam could not escape to the atmosphere fast enough, it created a huge explosion. The result of this violent event was an oval depression about a mile (1.6 km) across and a large assortment of interesting and very active mud pots over the ridge to the east of the former road.

🚶 **Sentinel Meadow Trail** goes west just across the bridge near Ojo Caliente Spring. It's about a 2.2-mile (3.5 km) walk to the Queens Laundry hot spring. On the way are several other springs and at least eight small geysers in the Sentinel Meadow Group of hot springs. Be aware that the whole area may be too wet for hiking before late July and that the trail provides no shade.

Sentinel Meadow was named in 1872 for the high geyserite mounds or cones that seem to guard it like sentinels. In the southwest corner of a large marshy area is the very hot spring called **Queens Laundry**. Here a two-room bathhouse was begun in 1881 by Superintendent Norris. The bathhouse was never completed, but the ruins are still there.

🚶 Another trail to Sentinel Meadow leaves the former road (now only for walking and bicycling) about a mile (1.6 km) south of the bridge near Ojo Caliente. This trail forks to access the Fairy Meadows Group of hot springs to the northwest; on the southwest fork are the Fairy Creek Group, Imperial and Spray geysers, and Fairy Falls.

Goose and Feather lakes are slightly farther along the main trail on the left. Goose has some rainbow and brook trout.

In another mile or so, the main trail to Fairy Falls takes off to the west, described from the other end at mile 11.3/5.7.

Continuing on the Grand Loop Road

6.0/11.0 P "Chief Joseph Story" interpretive sign. The Nez Perce tribe passed through this part of the park in the summer of 1877. Their name means "pierced nose" in French, but tribal members had stopped piercing their noses by the 1830s. In English the name is pronounced nez-PURS.

6.1/10.9 Nez Perce Creek bridge. The road enters a broad meadow, Fountain Flats, where elk can often be seen.

◄ **Nez Perce Creek** was first called the East Fork of the Firehole, but the name was changed to commemorate the tribe's passage eastward up this creek.

6.4/10.6 🚶 Mary Mountain Trailhead (also called Nez Perce Creek Trail). This was the stagecoach road from Fountain Flats to the Canyon area in the first years of the park. Near Mary Lake there's a stretch as steep as a stairway where stagecoach passengers were asked to walk so the horses could make the grade. Mary Mountain and Mary Lake were named for Mary Clark of Chicago, an 1873 visitor who crossed the park here and was said to have had a lovely singing voice.

At the start of the Mary Mountain trail, the low hills of thermally cemented glacial gravel, called the Porcupine Hills, have some hot springs at their base. The trail passes through an extensively burned area and prime grizzly bear country. It is 11 miles (18 km) to Mary Lake (no fish there) and another 9 miles (14.5 km) or more to a point on the Grand Loop Road between Canyon and Fishing Bridge junctions. No overnight camping is allowed anywhere on this trail.

7.4/9.6 Entering the Lower Geyser Basin area. These meadows may be carpeted with purple fringed gentians in August.

The Lower Geyser Basin is somewhat lower in altitude and downriver from the Upper Geyser Basin. The explorers who placed names on the land while passing through on horseback or on foot were much more aware of the topography than we are in our powerful cars and buses.

To the west about 4 miles (6.5 km) away are the small round mountains called the **Twin Buttes**. These buttes are mounds of debris left behind while the glaciers covered Lower Geyser Basin. The hot steam in this thermal area caused some of the ice to melt and release its load of rocks and gravel. As more ice moved over this area it melted, leaving more rocks and gravel. When the glacier retreated, hot vapors continued to rise from below, permeated the hills of debris, cooled, and precipitated out silica, which cemented the hills to form the Twin Buttes.

8.0/9.0 P 🏋🦽 (2) Entrance to Fountain Paint Pot parking for those traveling south. If you take this half-mile (0.8 km) walk, you can see all four principal types of hydrothermal discharge: geysers, hot springs, steam vents, and mud pots. At the start of the trail, an informative Yellowstone Association leaflet is available.

Lower Geyser Basin

Seventeen hot spring groups covering about 5 square miles (13 sq km) nestle in the valley of Lower Geyser Basin. Not all are accessible by trail or boardwalk. The basin's most exciting feature is Great Fountain Geyser, which is easy to reach on Firehole Lake Drive (at mile 9.0/8.0). At Great Fountain expect to see some of the world's most exciting geyser eruptions.

Near the Fountain Hotel site (see below) is the Thud Group of thermal features—in an area closed to the public. Looking east from the road, you might see frequently erupting Kidney Spring and Thud Spring, notable for the 1948 cleaning-out it was given by ranger George Marler. He found an amazing hodgepodge of things in it, including a pitchfork, a 40-gallon metal drum, a tree, and a section of a 1913 guidebook!

Historical Fountain Hotel

The Fountain Hotel, located less than one-half mile (0.8 km) from the Fountain Paint Pot area of the basin, opened in 1891. It was an unusually elegant place for its remote location, having electric lights, steam heat, and hot spring

water in the baths. It was the place where bears were first fed hotel garbage to entertain the tourists. In 1917, when motorization of park transportation made a hotel here unnecessary, Fountain Hotel was permanently closed.

Leather Pool provided hot water to the Fountain Hotel (Ely Cook photo).

Fountain Paint Pot Loop Walk★

NOTE: [♿] Visitors in wheelchairs should be aware that there are stairs at the point farthest from the parking lot.

[🎨] **Celestine Pool** (probably from Latin *celestinus*, meaning heavenly or sky blue) is the large, quiet pool nearest the parking lot. A tragic event occurred here in 1981, when a young man tried to rescue his dog after it jumped into the pool.

Both man and dog died as a result of contact with the scalding water.

Walking straight up the boardwalk, you come to **Silex Spring**, a large, pale blue pool that sometimes erupts as a geyser. Silex means "silica" in Latin. Although called a spring, Silex was known to erupt until 1979, then reactivated briefly in 2000.

Fountain Paint Pot is the largest easily accessible paint pot in the park. A *paint pot* is an area of hot mud delicately tinted by iron oxides. Bubbles of carbon dioxide and rotten-egg-smelling hydrogen sulfide gases escape through fine clay and silica. The paint pot's fascinating bubbling activity is dependent upon the amount of ground water available, which usually decreases as summer progresses. Overall, Fountain Paint Pot's area is gradually increasing, and the boardwalk has to be moved periodically to accommodate it. **[GEO.20]**

A 19th century visitor, Gen. John Gibbon, remarked that the paint pots are like "a group of politicians, each one trying to outdo the other"—and he said something about mudslinging in the same connection.

At the top of the hill, you can often hear a loud, high-pitched, and persistent hissing sound coming from a jumble of rocks next to bubbling mud. This is a *fumarole*, a vent where steam and other gases escape from deep underground. When water from rain and snow seeps down from the surface, it flashes into gas as it meets the extremely hot rock below.

Red Spouter formed in a grassy area soon after the 1959 Hebgen Lake earthquake. When the water table is high, its two large vents or pools are perpetual spouters. A *perpetual spouter* erupts continuously. When there's less water, Red Spouter's pools become noisy fumaroles. The gray crater sometimes sports bright red patches.

Fountain Paint Pot

Leather Pool was named for the brown bacteria that used to line it. But after the 1959 Hebgen Lake earthquake, it became a clear blue pool. The brown color has returned to the rocks lining the pool, but the water remains fairly clear. A trace of the former pipeline to Fountain Hotel can still be seen.

At a slightly lower level, you'll pass **Fountain Geyser** (not the same as Great Fountain Geyser) to the north of the boardwalk. It and sometimes its neighbor **Morning Geyser** were major attractions for the hotel guests—rather like Old Faithful still is today for guests at Old Faithful Inn.

A Fountain Hotel guest of 1899 wrote a vivid description of an eruption of Morning Geyser. Guests were aroused about midnight one August night by gongs and bells and porters shouting, "The new geyser is playing!" Tourists rushed to the geyser basin in all states of dress and undress. "Upward into the black night shot a stupendous column of water three hundred feet high. The porters were the first to arrive and playing their red calcium lights on the wonderful body of falling water gave us a display of fire and water that must be seen to be appreciated. . . . "

When active, Fountain may erupt as high as 100 feet (30 m). Since both Fountain and Morning geysers have years-long dormant periods, catching one or both erupting is a treat you can't count on. However, Fountain was recently erupting quite regularly every 7 to 8 hours.

The geysers of the Fountain Group are interdependent, exhibiting what scientists call *exchange of function*. This means that the underground plumbing of each influences the others a great deal. These geysers are consequently irregular and mostly unpredictable.

Geysers of two other groups, the Kaleidoscope and Sprinkler groups, can sometimes be seen erupting as you stand on the boardwalks above or near Fountain. There has been more activity in this area in the past ten years than ever before, according to those who've been watching closely.

Twig Geyser, at the base of the steps, can be seen erupting a few feet high (a meter or two) about half the time.

Jet Geyser built its formation from six vents along a long break in the sinter. It erupts every few minutes up to 20 feet (6 m) high when either Fountain or Morning geyser is active.

Spasm Geyser (near the bend in the boardwalk) plays about 3 feet high (1 m), often beginning to erupt 2 or 3 hours before Fountain. Spasm has a yellow-stained cone and pale green water. Its rocky edge is the result of a hydrothermal explosion this geyser experienced over 30 years ago.

Clepsydra Geyser (pronounced CLEP-si-drah), farther from the boardwalk than Spasm Geyser, clearly exhibits the geysers' exchange of function. If Fountain Geyser is not active, Clepsydra rarely stops playing, but when Fountain is active, Clepsydra sometimes pauses. Before Fountain reactivated in the late 1990s, Clepsydra's spurts were as high as 45 feet (14 m); lately they have been lower.

Clepsydra is the ancient Greek word for water clock (literally, "to steal water"). The name was applied to this geyser in the 1870s, because at that time its eruptions could be expected regularly every 3 minutes. As you tour the park you'll find that early park explorers, officials, and guides drew on their classical education, choosing Greek and Latin names for many features.

Jelly Spring (its official name, although it has sometimes erupted as a geyser) becomes lined with thick, jelly-like masses of cyanobacteria during its long dormant periods. Some scientists think that the microorganisms in Jelly Spring have helped it deposit its gelatinous geyserite. (See "What Makes the Colors?" later in this road log, for more about these microorganisms.)

Several more geysers, as well as many hot springs, cover the flats between here and the river. You may catch sight of them erupting from the boardwalk, but there's no public access to the area.

Clepsydra Geyser erupts from two major jets and several minor ones. Spasm Geyser's two vents are in the foreground.

Geyserite

As you tour the geyser basins of Yellowstone, you'll notice that a white or pale gray brittle rock surrounds the geysers and hot springs and forms gravelly areas. The chemical name for this rock is *hydrous silicon dioxide*. Other names for it are *siliceous sinter*, *geyserite*, or sometimes simply *sinter* or *silica*.

The volcanic rhyolite that underlies most of the park's thermal areas contains a lot of silica. When hot water percolates through the rhyolite, silica dissolves and is brought to the surface. There, the water cools and precipitates the silica as geyserite. In some places this process creates vast, nearly flat rocky areas, such as here at Fountain Flats.

Bacteria that thrive in these hot waters sometimes act as templates, controlling the shapes that the geyserite takes. In some places and over many centuries, the silica deposits may build fantastic formations, such as those of Castle and Grotto geysers at Upper Geyser Basin.

Continuing on the Grand Loop Road

8.2/8.8 **P** 🚻 ♿ **(2)** Fountain Paint Pot. Closest parking area entrance for those traveling north.

9.0/8.0 White Creek crossing; Firehole Lake Drive begins. This side road runs one way south to north, providing access to Great Fountain Geyser and other thermal features.

Firehole Lake Drive★

NOTE: The mileage from the beginning of this side road is given in parentheses. Grand Loop Road mileage continues where Firehole Lake Drive rejoins it.

⟨♿⟩ ⟨♿⟩ All thermal features are accessible along this drive.

(0.0) The dead pines standing in this marshy area have white "socks," a result of absorbing silica from the hot spring runoff water surrounding their roots. You can tell that many mature trees were killed when thermal runoff switched direction to flow toward them. Unlike the lodgepoles killed by fire, most of these dead trees continue to stand for decades.

(0.65) **Broken Egg Spring** resembles an upturned egg with the shell broken off.

DNA Fingerprinting Started Here!

A team of biologists led by Dr. Thomas Brock found an extremely important *thermophilic*, or heat-loving, bacterium in a hot spring near here in 1965. The bacterium is *Thermus aquaticus*. An enzyme called *Taq polymerase* derived from this bacterium has contributed to medical diagnosis and to DNA fingerprinting. This enzyme is useful specifically because of its unusually high heat stability.

Now many researchers are bioprospecting throughout Yellowstone's geothermal areas for other thermophiles that may prove useful or even help to solve the mystery of the origin of life on earth.

White Creek Hot Springs

You can reach the White Creek hot springs group by a narrow trail leading up from the Great Fountain Geyser parking area. Octopus Spring, near the tree line, is a particularly beautiful pool. Its runoff channel has delicate pink filamentous bacteria (*Thermocrinis ruber)* growing at about 176°F (80°C).

White Creek was named for the white deposits it flows through. To impress your friends, you might like to learn the name of one of these springs, Botryoidal Spring (pronounced bah-tree-OY-dul) from the Greek word for a cluster of grapes. It's recently become an active geyser, erupting frequently with unusual masses of bubbles.

(0.8) **Firehole Spring** is actually a perpetual spouter rather than a spring. In 1888, George L. Henderson, a tour guide and the namer of many Yellowstone features, wrote: "Every few seconds there arise great globes that seem to revolve like chariot wheels as they rise toward the surface. Then they come faster and faster until they seem to glide into each other and rise into one magnificent dome of liquid splendor. . . . " The runoff channels are lined with some of the park's most beautiful, many-colored bacteria.

When you look northward, the beautiful mountain you see in the distance is 10,336-foot (3150 m) **Mount Holmes**. William H. Holmes (1846-

1933) was an artist and geologist who climbed this mountain as a member of the 1878 Hayden Geological Survey, a government-sponsored expedition. In his later years, Holmes was most noted for his work in American archaeology.

(0.9) **Surprise Pool** is a deep black— not blue—pool (for the reason, see "Black Water & Travertine," later in this section). An 1895 observer wrote, "If a handful of gravel is thrown into it, it will bubble and sparkle, exactly like bromo seltzer." The modern visitor would substitute "Alka-Seltzer." But please remember that throwing anything into a thermal feature not only destroys its beauty but is illegal. The phenomenon happens because any disturbance causes a bubbling reaction in *superheated* water, that is, water whose temperature is hotter than the boiling point.

Across the road from Surprise Pool is a group of hot springs along White Creek, which is named for the sinter deposits all along its length. Geologists have found that no cold water flows into White Creek, because any rain or groundwater must percolate through hot ground before reaching the stream.

(1.0) $\boxed{P}$ **Great Fountain Geyser**★★ ranks today as one of the three highest-spouting active geysers in Yellowstone and in the world. While eruptions of the others—Steamboat Geyser at Norris Geyser Basin and Giant Geyser at Upper Geyser Basin—are rare and unpredictable, Great Fountain is fortunately quite predictable. Eruptions usually range between 100 and 150 feet (30–45 m) high, but may go higher in an occasional superburst. The average interval between eruptions is now 10 to 12 hours. The next predicted eruption time is usually listed at Old Faithful Visitor Center as well as at the geyser.

Although there may sometimes be a shortage of park rangers to write the predicted range of times on the signboard, a knowledgeable geyser gazer is often on hand to predict the next eruption, using a formula based on the duration of the previous eruption. You may be able to gauge the nearness of an eruption yourself by watching for overflow in the previously empty basin, since the eruption usually

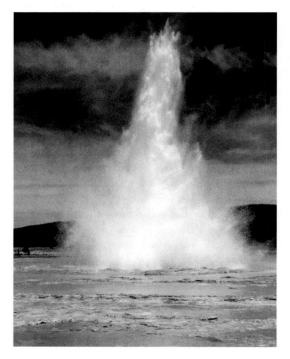

Great Fountain Geyser erupts straight into the air.

starts about 1 hour after overflow begins. Your patience will be amply rewarded!

Even the crater of Great Fountain is impressive, with a vent 16 feet (4.8 m) across surrounded by concentric rings of geyserite that extend to about 150 feet (45 m) in diameter. Its symmetry so impressed expedition leader Ferdinand V. Hayden in 1871 that he called this geyser Architectural Fountain.

This is perhaps the park's largest *fountain-type geyser*. Such geysers have a very broad pool rather than a cone or narrow vent, and they usually erupt in successively larger spurts, sometimes beginning with a dome-shaped surge.

About Yellowstone's Geysers

The number of hot springs in the park has been estimated to be around 10,000, but no one knows the exact number. There are extensive unpublished notes by early U.S. Geological Survey scientists, and inventories of the springs have been published by Allen and Day of the Carnegie Institution in 1935, by Yellowstone Park geologist George Marler in 1973 (for some thermal areas), and by several geyser enthusiasts. Only recently have researchers begun a really thorough study.

Some people are not enthralled by geyser basins. You might agree with Owen Wister, author of *The Virginian*, who visited in 1887: "I do not like them or their neighborhood. The air has drafts of stenches through it sometimes like sulphur, sometimes like a stale marsh. The ground is drilled with hissing puddles and sounds hollow as you walk, and all healthy plants and grass keep at a prudent distance. . . . "

Others of us are more like survey leader Hayden, who, according to Harry J. Norton's 1873 guidebook, "cannot compose himself in presence of a geyser in eruption; but, losing recollection of the material world for the time, rubs his hands, shouts, and dances around the object of his admiration in a paroxysm of gleeful excitement."

To learn more about geysers, you might consult the geyser books listed in the "Books about Yellowstone" chapter or contact the Geyser Observation and Study Association (see "Travel Tips" for contact information). The main source for this guide's material about geysers is *The Geysers of Yellowstone* (1995) by geologist and former ranger, T. Scott Bryan.

(1.25) **White Dome Geyser** has a 20-foot-high cone atop a 12-foot-high mound (6 m atop 3.6 m), both built up from the deposit of sinter or geyserite. To build such a mound, a hot spring or splashing geyser must have deposited sinter here steadily for centuries before the present feature. White Dome is a *cone-type geyser;* that is, a geyser whose eruption emits a steady column of water from a narrow vent within a cone. Much of the actual cone is not white, but is stained pink from a manganese compound. White Dome's unpredictable (but in most years, frequent) eruptions go as high as 30 feet (9 m).

(1.3) The jumble of interlaced channels of hot water coming from the right is aptly named **Tangled Creek**.

(1.65) **Pink Cone Geyser** is very close to the road. Its twice-daily eruptions last up to 3 hours, as high as 30 feet (9 m). It was never known to erupt until 1937.

In this area are a few other small geysers and Old Bath Lake, also called The Tank in earlier years. Researchers believe prehistoric peoples used and perhaps altered it, since artifacts have been found nearby. Tree sections dam up the spring, creating surprisingly regular sides.

Next, the road crosses over Tangled Creek several times.

(2.1) [P] Parking area for Firehole Lake and its associated hot springs (sometimes called Black Warrior Springs).

Take the boardwalk to the left of the road—and the left branch of the boardwalk—to see **Steady Geyser**, also called Black Warrior Geyser. Steady has never quit spouting in over 100 years. This perpetual spouter (technically not a geyser) may even be the world's largest, since it sometimes goes 15 feet (4.6 m) high. Notice the small oval or scallop formations built up from the mineral-laden water. These are *geyser eggs* made of travertine.

Crossing by footbridge over the steaming runoff channels, you see thousands of colonies of orange cyanobacteria and algae. The **Hot Cascades** here drain steaming water into **Hot Lake**, which is primarily a collecting basin rather than a lake, but may have hot springs within it. The outlet

Pink Cone Geyser's cone is tinted by manganese compound deposits.

(western end) of Hot Lake is cool enough for Canada geese to swim on it. They sometimes nest on grassy hummocks next to the lake. The lake created by Steady Geyser's runoff is **Black Warrior Lake**, named for its unusual dark olive green or almost black lining.

Cross the road to take the other boardwalk around **Firehole Lake** and its several spouting springs. Unlike the Firehole River, Firehole Lake and Spring got their names from the blue flame-like appearance of the large steam bubbles you can often see rising from within them.

Three small geysers on the edge of Firehole Lake may be erupting when you're here. Farthest from the road and to the east is **Artesia Geyser**, and next to it is **Gray Bulger Geyser**. Stop here to listen to the numerous small noisy holes that constantly spray water or emit steam. Nearest the road are the many vents of **Young Hopeful Geyser**, erupting almost perpetually from two craters, which formed when it underwent a steam explosion in the 1970s.

(3.3) Junction with Grand Loop Road. Opposite is the parking area for the Fountain Paint Pot area. Turn left for Old Faithful, right for Madison Junction.

Black Water and Travertine

The black color in Firehole Lake and some of the springs nearby is due to the large amount of manganese oxide being deposited. The deposits of this mineral are more extensive here than anywhere else in the park. In fact, George Henderson, tour guide in the 1880s and 90s, liked to call this part of the Firehole River valley Ebony Basin.

Around Firehole Lake is one of only four thermal areas in the park where *travertine*, which is calcium carbonate in the form deposited by hot springs, is deposited along with geyserite (silicon dioxide). Elsewhere in the park, geysers deposit only geyserite. The only other easily accessible area where both minerals are deposited is the Terrace Spring area near Madison Junction. Egg-like travertine formations exist in both Black Warrior and Firehole lakes.

Continuing on the Grand Loop Road
9.5/7.5 🌲(12) 🚻♿ Just south of a quiet meadow (unofficially called Whiskey Flats) is **Whiskey Flats picnic area**. Yellowstone Park sign maker Virgil Hall gave up making "WHISKEY FLATS" signs, when 18 of them were stolen in less than two years' time!

9.9/7.1 🅿 🚻♿(2) Midway Geyser Basin.

Midway Geyser Basin Loop Walk★★

NOTE: ♿ This route is wheelchair accessible but has a steep ramp.

🚶 The first feature you encounter on the walkway is **Excelsior Geyser**. The tremendous crater and prodigious overflow give you some idea what a stupendous geyser this must have been when active. The crater (sometimes called The Caldron in the park's early days) measures over 250 by 300 feet (75 by 90 m). The constant steaming overflow has been measured at about 4000 gallons (15,000 L) per minute. For comparison, Old Faithful Geyser takes nearly two months to throw out as much water as Excelsior's crater discharges in one day. The mustard yellow, orange, and brown runoff over the side of Excelsior's crater into the Firehole is a perennial favorite of photographers.

Early visitors called this geyser Hell's Half Acre. Park Superintendent Norris applied that name to the whole geyser basin in 1881, changing the geyser's name to Excelsior, meaning "ever higher" in Latin. When Excelsior erupted, enormous volumes of rock were thrown everywhere, and after an eruption, the Firehole River would have three times its normal volume. But these 300-foot (90 m) eruptions themselves may have destroyed the geyser. Whatever the reason, there's been only rare, minor activity during the last century.

Notice the layers and layers of laminated sinter on the crater's walls. Nearby Grand Prismatic Spring may

Excelsior Geyser (F. J. Haynes photo)

have been overflowing and depositing sinter downslope for many centuries before Excelsior blew out its crater.

If you're walking beside the crater on a cool day, engulfed in steam next to the walls' great drop-off, you may have a feeling of being at the edge of the earth. No photograph can capture that sensation.

If you take the boardwalk to the right when it forks, you'll first encounter **Turquoise Pool**, which greatly resembles the semiprecious stone. The color is caused by light reflecting from minute particles suspended in its water. Grand Prismatic Spring drains into Turquoise, and Excelsior may have an underground connection with it as well. Sometimes the water drains nearly out of sight, but it slowly returns in subsequent months.

Next along the path is **Opal Pool**, which got its name from the opalescence both of its water and its surrounding sinter. Opal is actually a geyser with rare but

sometimes high eruptions. The water in Opal Pool rises and falls with a period of about 2 hours.

Midway Geyser Basin's stellar attraction is **Grand Prismatic Spring**. The largest hot spring in the park, it measures about 250 by 350 feet (75 by 100 m). Prismatic means brilliantly colored. The central water in the spring is a brilliant blue, with blue green near the edges. Radiating out from this are rays of yellow, orange, and brown—the runoff channels. **[GEO.22]**

It's difficult to get a good photo of a spring as huge as Grand Prismatic. Some of the best are taken from the air, but if you are determined to reach a good viewpoint, there's a choice of two hills you might climb. East of the main road there's Midway Bluff, and to the southwest of Grand Prismatic is a burned-over hill skirted by the Fairy Falls Trail (described at mile 11.3/5.7).

Grand Prismatic Spring

What Makes the Colors?

Wandering through Yellowstone's thermal areas, you'll see an amazing range of colors. The centers of the hot springs may be deep blue or blue green or palest turquoise blue. The edges of the pools and their runoff channels will range from yellow through orange and red to brown, with light and dark greens here and there. What causes these different colors?

Let's start with the blue of the water. Sunlight penetrating the pool is scattered by the minute particles and molecules in the water. However, blue light is scattered more efficiently than red or yellow, so the light coming toward you appears blue. This same phenomenon occurs in the atmosphere to give us blue skies. Thus, in all but very shallow hot springs, we see blue centers. If there are some yellow or orange microorganisms growing on the sides of the pool (as at Emerald Pool in Black Sand Basin, for example), the water will appear blue green or green, since yellow and blue make green.

Scientists have found many different tiny living organisms in the hot springs, all generally called thermophilic microorganisms, meaning that they love to live in hot places. Different species of bacteria and algae thrive at different temperatures. The colors are due to the various pigments of the different organisms. *Photosynthetic* organisms (that is, those that use light as their source of energy) have a *chlorophyll* pigment, which is green. Most microorganisms have additional pigments called *carotenoids*, which are yellow, orange, and red. (Carotenoids help to color fruits and vegetables, too.)

Typically, faster moving water at the center of a runoff channel is hotter than water nearer the edges. Also, of course, the water is hotter close to the hot spring and cooler farther from the source. Non-photosynthetic bacteria live in the hottest water (up to 196°F/91°C), while at the edges of the channel, photosynthetic bacteria and algae thrive. You can usually tell where the water is hottest by the color of the mats of bacteria living in it: the lighter the color (bright yellow, for example), the hotter the water.

In general, algae have chlorophyll while bacteria lack it. Although older books about the park used the term "blue-green algae," microbiologists have recognized in the last quarter century that these blue-green organisms are actually a type of bacteria that has chlorophyll and can carry out photosynthesis. These are the microbes now called *cyanobacteria*. *Cyano-* means blue green, and chlorophyll is grass green, but cyanobacteria also contain other pigments. The microbial mats here in Yellowstone don't look blue green, because their yellow, orange, or red carotenoid pigments predominate in bright summer sunlight and mask the green chlorophyll.

As you travel in Yellowstone, you may notice colors around the hot springs other than the ones mentioned here. Not all the colors are organic; some are due to minerals. For example, iron-containing minerals are responsible for various shades of yellow and red around the acidic springs of Norris Geyser Basin. The pinks that stain some geyser cones are due to manganese-containing minerals. A great deal of

Runoff water from Firehole Spring on Firehole Lake Drive.

manganese oxide in water will turn it black. Compounds of sulfur, arsenic, and mercury create colors in some hot springs. Overall, though, most of Yellowstone's colors are due to living organisms.

—With contributions by Thomas D. Brock

~

Continuing on the Grand Loop Road 10.6/6.4 **P** ⦿ Across the Firehole River from the road is **Flood Geyser**; other geysers of lesser interest line both riverbanks. Flood was recently erupting up to 10 feet (3 m) high every 30 to 40 minutes, but it has been known to have major eruptions up to 25 feet (7.6 m). The big meander in the river is called Muleshoe Bend by fishermen, who have caught many big trout here.

11.2/5.8 Rabbit Creek crossing. Near the headwaters and elsewhere along this creek is a thermal area with paint pots and hot springs. Unfortunately, this is a dangerous area due both to downed trees and the risk of breaking through the fragile thermal crust into the very hot water below. Visit only in the company of a park ranger or other person knowledgeable about this thermal area.

Before 1970, bears were everywhere along the roads. A garbage dump near here was frequented by grizzly bears. Nearby Grizzly Pool is a spot where the bears sometimes bathed.

11.3/5.7 🚶 🚲 To the northwest a short road takes you to a large parking area for Fairy Falls Trailhead. The entire 5-mile stretch of the former Fountain Freight Road, beginning at the 1903-vintage steel bridge, is open to mountain bikes. To approach by car from the other end, turn off the Grand Loop Road at the "Fountain Flat Drive" sign at mile 5.6/11.4 instead.

There are several small geysers and hot springs near the river (and even in the parking lot). To the north is a spring with a 75-foot-wide (23 m) crater, named **Tire Pool** when two auto tires were removed from it. South of the parking lot and closer to the river is **Egeria Spring**, a name that comes from a water nymph in Roman mythology.

On the Grand Loop Road opposite this side road and partially concealed up the small hill is **Till Geyser**, named for the loose sand and gravel left by glaciers. It erupts as high as 20 feet (6 m) from several vents about every 9 hours.

To reach graceful 197-foot (60 m) **Fairy Falls** on Fairy Creek, it's a 2.2-mile (3.5 km) hike along the former road and then west on a level trail. The walk to Fairy Falls is one of the relatively few park experiences that were somewhat spoiled by the 1988 fires, but the falls itself is now easier to see and quite spectacular. **Imperial** and **Spray geysers** and some fascinating mud pots are about 3 miles (5 km) farther along the same trail, at the foot of the Twin Buttes.

11.9/5.1 🚶 Mallard Creek Trailhead on the east. This unmaintained trail reaches Mallard Lake in about 4 miles (6.5 km) and connects with the Mallard Lake Trail to descend to Old Faithful in about another 3.5 miles (5.5 km). Mallard Lake is known to geologists for the Mallard Lake dome, an area where the molten rock (or *magma*) under Yellowstone comes unusually close to the surface. [GEO.25]

12.5/4.5 For a short time in the spring you can see a waterfall cascading over the edge of the Madison Plateau if you look southwest while traveling south along this part of the road. Waterfalls enthusiast Mike Stevens, coauthor of *The Guide to Yellowstone Waterfalls and Their Discovery* (2000), calls it Unfaithful Falls for its temporary nature and proximity to Old Faithful.

13.8/3.2 P 🚶 Biscuit Basin is named for the biscuit-shaped geyserite knobs that were formerly more prevalent in this area. In addition to the three-quarter-mile (1.2 km) boardwalk around the basin, there are other trails starting from here. A recommended trail goes to 70-foot (21 m) Mystic Falls starting near Avoca Spring.

[🚶] The Artemisia Trailhead starts opposite the Biscuit Basin turnoff (look for the sign "Artemisia" with a trail symbol). Also recommended, this trail takes you southward past several interesting geysers and hot springs. It joins the paved walkway at Morning Glory Pool in less than a mile (1.5 km). Features along this trail are described from its other end on pages 89–90.

Biscuit Basin Walk [🚶]

NOTE: [♿] This hot spring area is accessible to wheelchairs, but has no curb cut.

Encountered first after you cross the footbridge to Biscuit Basin is **Black Opal Pool**, a deep green hydrothermal explosion crater. This one threw out debris sideways for hundreds of feet (perhaps 100 meters) when it exploded in 1934. Murky green **Wall Pool** next to Black Opal was formed a few years earlier, probably also by an explosion.

Sapphire Pool was delightful to watch in mid century. It was crystal clear and a beautiful color. Visitors stood transfixed, watching a string of bubbles from far below, followed by an overall sizzling, and then a surging boil that engulfed the whole spring. Then, due to the 1959 Hebgen Lake earthquake, Sapphire began erupting 125 feet (38 m). These violent eruptions increased the size of Sapphire's crater, destroyed its unique "biscuits," and changed its shape from circular to oval. By 1964, the eruptions were much smaller, and a few years later it ceased any significant activity.

Take the boardwalk loop to the right beyond Sapphire to see several other features, including the deep cavernous vent of **Black Pearl Geyser**. Black Pearl was thickly studded with quarter-inch black knobs when it was named in the first part of the 20th century. At the boardwalk curve is **Mustard Spring**, really two small geysers connected underground.

Avoca Spring is the grotto-like cone located near Mystic Falls Trailhead. Avoca was a boiling spring until 1959, when it developed into an erratic geyser.

Geyserite formations like biscuits once surrounded Sapphire Pool (W. H. Jackson historic photo).

Silver Globe Geyser, next to Avoca and connected to it, can mesmerize you when it has silvery white bubbles rising from deep within its clear pool. Here's proof of the erudition of early Yellowstone namers, especially of tour guide George Henderson: he called the geyserite arch in and over Silver Globe Geyser the Zygomatic Arch, because it reminded him of a human cheekbone.

A number of very hot features (including Avoca Spring and others to its south) are grouped into the **Silver Globe Complex**. Geyser expert T. Scott Bryan has suggested that a marked increase in activity here beginning in 1983 was linked to an Idaho earthquake of that year centered 150 miles (240 km) away at Borah Peak (Idaho's highest point).

Starting across from Avoca Spring, the **Mystic Falls Trail** is about 3.5 miles (5.6 km) round trip, with steep sections near the falls. A left turn at the first junction would lead you through backcountry to Summit Lake in 7 miles (11 km) on Yellowstone's western section of the new Continental Divide National Scenic Trail.

To reach Mystic Falls on the Little Firehole River, go left at the next trail junction instead. (The right-hand trail takes you in 0.7 mile (1 km) to an overlook of Biscuit and Upper Geyser basins.) Trail junctions are not well marked except at the falls itself. If you stay left, you'll follow the Little Firehole River to the 70-foot (21 m) drop of Mystic Falls. This delightful hike may reward you with a profusion of unusual wildflowers.

Back on the boardwalk

Shell Spring (actually a small geyser) has an irregular crater that may remind you of a clamshell. The crater has a mustard-colored lining from sulfurous deposits splashed on during its very frequent small eruptions.

Chances are good that **Jewel Geyser** (at the boardwalk junction) will erupt for you. The eruption interval averages 8 minutes, sometimes to 20 feet (6 m) high. In the 1930s, rangers found that Jewel would draw down a handkerchief placed in one vent and expel it from another during an eruption, but this practice was stopped when injuries occurred. (See "Black Sand Basin Walking Tour" for the original Handkerchief Pool.)

Two more very active geysers are located near the Biscuit Basin parking area. Out on an island in the Firehole River to the south is **Island Geyser**, which erupts most of the time. Near the

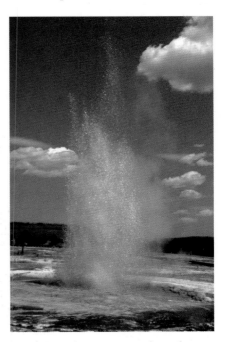

Jewel Geyser's name comes from the shiny sinter beads around its vent.

road is **Rusty Geyser**, with an iron-oxide-stained crater.

~

Continuing on the Grand Loop Road
13.9/3.1 Firehole River Bridge.

14.0/3.0 🚶 🚲 There's limited parking along the road for access to trails. A bicycle and hiking trail southeast leads to Old Faithful and passes near Daisy Geyser. A trail to the west joins the Mystic Falls Trail described earlier.

14.4/2.6 Through the burned trees or snags you may notice a red-orange stained area partway up the hill to the west. This is **Hillside Springs**, a nearly inaccessible thermal feature. Old-time stagecoach drivers called it Tomato Soup Springs.

15.4/1.6 Black Sand Basin side road southwest (right) to a large parking area. You can see all the features in this geyser basin by walking less than a mile (1.6 km). The basin is now best known for Emerald Pool at its south end. The lovely **Iron Spring Creek** meanders through the basin on its way north to join the Firehole River. There's not a lot of iron in the creek, but there *is* a large amount of reddish brown bacteria, due to the creek's thermal warming.

Black Sand Basin Walking Tour★
NOTE: This hot spring area is accessible to wheelchairs, but has no curb cut.

📷 If you take the sidewalk a short distance back along the entrance road, you'll see a couple of spouters, appropriately named **The Grumbler** (splashing angrily below the sidewalk) and **Spouter Geyser**. Spouter's runoff has fed the double oblong of **Opalescent Pool**, long a popular subject for color photographers, but with Spouter not very active, Opalescent Pool has become smaller and less colorful.

The geyserite mound southeast of the parking area indicates that there has been a geyser here for a very long time. It's been seen (and heard!) to erupt enough times to earn the name **Whistle Geyser**. Its rare eruptions are characterized by a powerful steam phase, described in a 1931 newspaper article as sounding like "about four locomotives at a distance, with a shrill, ringing tone to it."

As you start along the main boardwalk, unbeautiful **Ragged Spring** and **Ragged Spring's Annex** are the first features you meet. These two pools may erupt together to 6 or 8 feet (about 2 m).

Cliff Geyser across the creek is likely to be erupting, and its major eruptions may go to 40 feet (12 m) high from a full pool, then drain the pool suddenly and completely.

Large and gloriously colored **Green Spring** is to the left of the main walkway in a pleasant location near the creek.

Turning right when the boardwalk forks, you'll have difficulty locating **Handkerchief Pool** among the group of small- to medium-sized bubbling and spouting holes, all unmarked. Tourists used to place a handkerchief in the water near the edge, watch it be drawn out of sight by convection currents in the water, and then reappear, sometimes in another vent.

During the 1920s, someone jammed logs into Handkerchief Pool, effectively

Handkerchief Pool was once famous for drawing down and regurgitating tourists' handkerchiefs.

killing it. Some years later sufficient trash was removed from the pool to partially restore its activity, but it's now filled with sinter. Thick beds of cyanobacteria usually surround it. Occasionally in recent years, it's come back to life as a small geyser.

Rainbow Pool and **Sunset Lake** are brightly colored big pools at the boardwalk's end. You may already have seen Sunset Lake erupting from a distance. Up close, if conditions are right you can appreciate its size, the impressive concentric waves caused by its eruptions, and the reflections of its colors in the steam. Because it's now much hotter than Rainbow Pool, there's likely to be a prodigious amount of steam around Sunset, except in a strong wind. Rainbow has particularly beautiful bacterial mats around its edges.

A separate stretch of boardwalk to the south takes you to **Emerald Pool**. This is one of the most famous pools in Yellowstone and is a truly unusual deep emerald green at its center with orange around the edges. The bacteria can grow inside this pool due to its relatively cool

Emerald Pool's color is created by the combination of blue water and yellow bacteria.

temperature (around 150°F/66°C). But watch out! It's *not* cool enough to touch!

A trail you might want to take from here joins the main walkways around Upper Geyser Basin in just under a mile (1.5 km). Park in the Black Sand Basin parking lot and cross the Grand Loop Road (carefully!) opposite the parking lot entrance. The first thermal feature on this former main road segment is Black Sand Pool in about 0.3 mile (0.5 km). Features on this trail are described from its Daisy Geyser end on pages 95–96.

Continuing on the Grand Loop Road
15.8/1.2 Old Faithful interchange. Built in 1969, this urban-type interchange has been called a "disorienting concrete merry-go-round, the park's most intrusive feature" by Eric J. Sandeen of the University of Wyoming.

Take the ramp to the right for Old Faithful Village and Upper Geyser Basin. Continue straight for West Thumb Junction.

16.3/0.7 (2) After taking the off-ramp to the Old Faithful area, you then take the first left turn for a service station, general store, and the Old Faithful Inn.

NOTE: Parking in front of the inn is for guests only. Continue past this turn and follow the signs to much more parking.

16.9/0.1 The second available left (after "Do Not Enter" signs) goes to the Old Faithful Visitor Center, a logical first stop, and the West Parking Area. Old Faithful Geyser is just to the other side of the visitor center.

17.0/0.0 Old Faithful Village and large parking lot for the visitor center and many other facilities.

Old Faithful Village

⬛ ⊟(2) ⬗(3) 🛏(2) ✉ ⛱ **P**(2) After you turn toward Old Faithful Village at the second interchange, the second turn to the left takes you to a fully equipped service station, where car repairs and towing are available; a cafeteria; shops; and the new **Snow Lodge** with its restaurants and associated cabins (open in winter as well as summer). The last curve on the access road leads to the **Old Faithful Lodge** (including a cafeteria and cabins) and the East Parking Area. A picnic area is located at this parking area's southern edge, which is also the place to park recreational vehicles.

🛈 The **Old Faithful Visitor Center** provides books, videotapes, maps, geyser predictions, and ranger-interpreters ready to answer your questions.

🚻♿ Wheelchair accessible rest rooms are available at the visitor center, inn, lodge, and Snow Lodge.

✚ 🛈 ✉ Across the west parking area from the visitor center is a post office, as well as a clinic, ranger station, and backcountry office.

If you've arranged lodging at Old Faithful, you'll find that there are two faces to this village. From about nine in the morning to six in the evening there are cars and people everywhere. But later in the evening, at night, and in the early morning you may find, if not exactly solitude, at least a delightful opportunity to enjoy this long-famous area in relative quiet.

Lodgings

NOTE: There is no overnight camping in the Old Faithful area, and all lodging must be reserved in advance.

There are four types of lodgings at Old Faithful, all filled by reservations (see the "Travel Tips" chapter for details):

- **Old Faithful Inn**, which is the most interesting (and one of the most expensive)
- The new **Snow Lodge**, completed in the summer of 1999, which has the most modern accommodations

- The **Snow Lodge cabins**, which are comfortable and modern
- The **cabins** behind the **Old Faithful Lodge**, most of which lack private bathrooms.

Confusingly, but in keeping with early park concessionaires' idea of a lodge, **Old Faithful Lodge** itself has no sleeping rooms at all. Instead, it was built in the 1920s as a spacious recreation hall with a great view of the geyser. Modern needs have dictated that the space be divided for use as a cafeteria, gift shop, desks for cabin rental and activities, and several small snack shops. Showers are available at the lodge even for people not staying in the cabins.

You can find six cafeterias and restaurants at Old Faithful. In addition to those in the inn and lodge, the Snow Lodge has one grill and one family-style restaurant, and the general stores have lunch counters.

Old Faithful Inn★★

🛏 🍴 Reservations to stay in Old Faithful Inn must usually be made several months in advance, but occasionally a room becomes available close to the time you need it. Whether or not you stay in the inn, you'll enjoy seeing it, both

Old Faithful Village

Center section and porte cochere of Old Faithful Inn.

inside and out. This National Historic Landmark is a delightful example of early 20th century western American architecture.

The inn was built in the fall and winter of 1903–4, at a time when visitors were increasingly complaining about the lack of a good place to stay at Upper Geyser Basin. Before that time, most stagecoach tours of the park could allow only half a day here. Coaches stopped at the popular Fountain Hotel and at Lake or Canyon the following night.

The inn architect, Robert C. Reamer, was only 30 years old at the time the inn was built. He situated the building so that visitors driving up to the front door could see Old Faithful Geyser as they arrived. Reamer chose native materials for the inn: rhyolite for the foundations and porch pylons, lodgepole pine for the interior and exterior details, and wrought iron, which was worked on the site, for various items in the lobby.

A few years after the inn opened, guidebook writer Reau Campbell put it this way:

> Who shall describe this most charming, most unique, queer, quaint, fascinating place? . . . The stairways have the steps of logs split in half with the flat side up; the banisters and newel posts are of knotted, gnarled and twisted branches of the native trees. The galleries are supported by columns and braces cut from trees bent under the weight of snows and grown to fantastic shapes . . . the

foundation stones, innocent of the stone-cutters' chisels, were rolled in from the woods with the lichen still on their rugged sides. . . . Here is where you will wish to stay all summer. . . .

Old Faithful Inn's magnificent lobby by morning light.

Lights were electric from the outset, powered by a steam generator, and there was hot water and central heating, true luxuries for a wilderness hotel at the time. Ten rooms had private baths; even today, there are no more than that in the Old House, as the central portion of the inn is called.

The original log building had 140 rooms. Wings, also designed by Reamer, were completed in 1913 (the east wing) and 1928 (the west wing), bringing the present-day total to about 325 rooms open to guests.

If you have time to take one of the twice-daily tours of the inn, led by a knowledgeable inn employee, you'll learn much more about it. At least step inside to see Reamer's majestic lobby, with its 85-foot (26 m) roof ridge exposed above two floors of balconies and its tremendous stone fireplace and wrought iron clock (now electrified). Most of the original inn furniture has had to be replaced, but desks on the balconies are among the pieces that remain.

The dining room requires reservations but is otherwise informal. Guests of the early days were required to dress for dinner and to be precisely on time. They were entertained by chamber music easily audible from the first balcony's open window. In fact, the author's mother played piano in the Ladies' Ensemble for tea in the afternoons and dancing in the evenings in 1939. A pianist now plays from about 6:00 to

Writing desk designed by architect Robert Reamer and detail of glass lampshade.

10:00 every evening. Where else in the world can you enjoy a pleasant dinner or a refreshing drink and at the same time look out the window to watch a free-roaming bison calmly rubbing his head on a nearby tree? It has happened at Old Faithful Inn!

Twice in its history the inn has been damaged or threatened by the forces of nature. In August of 1959, as a result of the Hebgen Lake earthquake, rocks from the top of the dining room chimney fell through the roof; the chimney was rebuilt in 1987. Then in 1988, the North Fork fire came so close to the inn that people all over the country were holding their breaths in the hope it would be saved. Fierce winds blew embers across the area from the western to eastern hills, and some cabins and employee lodgings were burned. Fortunately, the presence of the huge parking lots and a last minute wind shift saved this delightful landmark. We must also thank the sprinkler system wisely installed the year before.

Hikes from Old Faithful Village

In addition to the walking tours of the Upper Geyser Basin (described in the next section), two other short walks begin from Old Faithful Village.

🚶 Take the **Mallard Lake Trail** for a short and easy walk to the **Pipeline Creek Group** of pools and mud pots. The hot springs have had this name at least since the 1920s, when a pipeline ran nearby. The lake is almost 3.5 miles (5.6 km) away and a 700-foot (210 m) climb.

You'll find the trailhead behind the Old Faithful Lodge cabins. Cross the footbridge over the Firehole River. In about 0.5 mile (0.8 km), there's a short side trail at the left toward four or more mud-filled springs, one a growler that churns like a washing machine. Watch your step and keep small children firmly under control. After about another mile (1.6 km), you cross Pipeline Creek, where, unusually for a geyser basin, pink monkeyflowers (*Mimulus lewisii*) grow.

🚶 **Fern Cascades Trail.** You may encounter some downed lodgepoles on

Pink monkeyflowers along the Mallard Lake Trail.

this moderately steep 2.5-mile (4 km) loop, which takes you to some rather small white water rapids on Iron Spring Creek. Access to the trail is through the employee housing area across the Grand Loop Road from the clinic and ranger station parking lot. The trail intersects with a part of the Howard Eaton Trail that passes Lone Star Geyser (see page 99 for a shorter trail to Lone Star).

Old Faithful Geyser★★

Old Faithful, the most famous geyser in the world, was named when members of the Washburn Expedition noticed its regularity. This group of men explored the area in 1870 and helped to encourage Congress to set it aside as a park.

Not only is Old Faithful Geyser the top priority for most visitors to see here, it's extremely accessible. Parking is close by, and generous boardwalks and benches border two sides of the geyser's mound. If you happen to be in Old Faithful Inn when the geyser erupts, you can watch it from the porch roof just off the first balcony. In fact, Old Faithful, true to its name, will probably erupt for you even if your time here is very limited. [GEO.19]

The *Haynes Guides* offered some advice about photographing Old Faithful, suggesting that the photographer not stand too close to it and try to catch the best part of the eruption, which may not be at the beginning of the geyser's activity. "Most people photograph this first display," wrote Mr. Haynes, "and are changing film about the time the geyser attains its maximum height."

Old Faithful Geyser

How Faithful Is Old Faithful?

Old Faithful has *never* in recorded time erupted "every hour on the hour," as you may have heard. Here are some figures given for average expected intervals between eruptions: 60 to 65 minutes, 1870 (Langford's journal); 65.5 minutes, 1964 (*Haynes Guide*); 78 minutes, 1990 (Bryan's *Geysers of Yellowstone*); and 88 minutes, 2001 (visitor center records). These figures do not show the range of intervals, which has always been on the order of 0.5 to 1.75 hours.

Seismic activity *can* affect Old Faithful. Following the strong earthquake at Borah Peak, Idaho, in 1983, the average interval between eruptions became greater, at least for a while. Geologists suspect that the geyser may someday seal itself off: a probe sent down its conduit a few years ago revealed a very narrow throat about 22 feet (6.5 m) down, and there's another constriction about 70 (21 m) feet down. Silica may continue building up there, but how fast is anybody's guess. On the other hand, the geyser's water may actually be eroding away the narrow section. No one knows for sure.

In recent years, there's been a rumor that the geyser is losing its power or becoming less regular or much less frequent. The truth is that the average interval between eruptions has lengthened by a few minutes, but the average height has remained about the same for at least 130 years, varying from 106 to 184 feet (32–56 m), averaging about 145 feet (44 m). Eruptions range in length from 1.5 to about 5 minutes.

Rangers and geyser enthusiasts can predict the next eruption time quite accurately, using a simple formula derived from observing the duration of the previous eruption. A relatively short duration means a shorter interval is predicted, while a longer duration leads to a longer interval.

Upper Geyser Basin

Upper Geyser Basin stretches in a right triangle from Old Faithful geyser north and west, mostly along the Firehole River. The hot springs and geysers draw upon the local groundwater for their source of water but also upon deep underground reservoirs. This hydrothermal area contains more than 20 percent of all the geysers in the world, as well as thousands of non-erupting hot springs. T. Scott Bryan, in his book, *The Geysers of Yellowstone*, writes: "To properly see the Upper Basin one *must* spend two or three days in order to wait for the large and famous geysers to erupt as well as to experience the smaller features. There are minor details to be observed in the basin, too—the colorations, forest life, thermophilic communities, and so on—many of which are found nowhere else in the world. To spend less time is to cheat oneself."

What exactly is a geyser? A *geyser* is a hot spring that throws forth jets of water and steam intermittently. As you wander through the area, you may want to guess which seemingly placid hot pools or deep holes may be active geysers, even if they don't erupt while you're watching. Here are some telltale signs of active geysers:

- A deep or wide white crater that does not look cracked and dry
- Areas downhill from the crater that are devoid of life due to hot water
- Puddles of water around a crater when it hasn't been raining
- Dead but standing trees nearby, indicating a relatively new geyser
- Concentric rims or formations of the pale brittle rock called geyserite.

The Old Faithful interchange bypasses most of the thermal features. Before it was built, the Grand Loop Road ran past many of them, including Morning Glory Pool and Grotto and Castle geysers. The only current access to these fascinating but sensitive features is by foot or bicycle.

Vandalism to the geysers and pools has decreased noticeably since the re-routing of traffic, but the road relocation has made it difficult for older or disabled visitors or for those with very little time to view such less-accessible marvels as Grand Geyser and Black Sand Pool. It's some consolation that a wheelchair may be borrowed from the visitor center.

Even the hardy should not be surprised if hills that don't look steep set you to puffing and your heart to beating fast—it's the altitude! A few conveniently located benches are especially welcome on the hilly parts of Geyser Hill.

Precautions for Your Geyser Walks

- There is **no drinking water** available at any point on these trails.
- The only **rest room** is a chemical toilet near Morning Glory Pool.
- **Stay on the walkways** and **watch children vigilantly**; the water is hot and the crust near the hot springs and geysers is thin and brittle.
- **Do not touch the water**, since you can be scalded at 120°F (49°C) and the temperature in these pools and geysers ranges from 142° to 205°F (61–96°C).

Planning your geyser walk

Here are some ways to visit the geysers:

1. Join one of the ranger-inter-preter led tours (1.5 or 2 hours long) listed in the *Yellowstone Today* newspaper you receive as you enter the park.

2. If you have only an hour or two and prefer to be on your own, walk around the Geyser Hill loop. This walk is the beginning of Geyser Route One, described below, and is about 1.3 miles (2 km) round trip.

An early morning stroll around Geyser Hill yields this view of Upper Geyser Basin and Old Faithful Inn.

3. If you have half a day or so, check the visitor center for predicted geyser eruption times, then follow one of the geyser routes described here to try to catch one or more eruptions and see other features on the way. Castle, Grand, Riverside, and Daisy geysers put on rewarding shows. Unfortunately, Grand Geyser may require a long wait, because its eruptions can only be predicted to within about a 4-hour span. Take books and games to entertain yourself while you wait!

4. A tour for true geyser lovers can be taken by those who have one or several days to spend. Wait for one or more of the predicted geyser eruptions, linger over your favorite parts of the basin, or extend your walk to Observation Point, Solitary Geyser, Black Sand Pool, or the extension of the trail beyond Morning Glory Pool.

5. To stay away from crowds, tour the basin at 7 or 8 AM or during the last daylight hours in the evening. These can be wonderful times for picture taking.

TWO WALKING TOURS THROUGH UPPER GEYSER BASIN

Described here are two routes you might take through Upper Geyser Basin. Any combination of walkways is possible, and there's much to see. You might follow one of these Geyser Routes exactly, or plan your own route with the aid of the map below or the large map in the leaflet that's available both at the visitor center and from the boxes near Old Faithful Geyser.

Geyser Route One: Geyser Hill and beyond

NOTE: This trail is mostly boardwalk and is not fully wheelchair accessible.

Geyser Route One is about 3.5 miles (5.6 km) round trip and takes you to three of the two-star features listed in the "Best Sights" chart in the Introduction. (Castle and Daisy Geysers are on Geyser Route Two, which begins on page 00.) Extending your walk beyond Morning Glory Pool to Biscuit Basin adds another 1.5 miles (2.4 km) or so. For just the shorter Geyser Hill loop, start near Old Faithful Geyser as below, but return from near North Goggles Geyser (the area labeled (C) on the map and described on pages 90–92).

Starting from the visitor center, circle partway around Old Faithful Geyser, keeping the geyser on your left. There may be bison around the area; allow them plenty of space. Sometimes fat yellow-bellied marmots make their homes under boardwalks around the basin, and elk may be grazing in the meadow. Incidentally, the old wooden boardwalks were replaced in 1997–98 with boards made from 100 percent recycled plastic, a gift from the Lever Brothers Company (now Unilever). Some people call them jugwalks.

As you walk toward the Firehole River, notice that Old Faithful and two or three other small features are on a huge mound some 200 feet (60 m) across and 12 to 15 feet (3.6–4.6 m) high. One or more hot springs must have been overflowing and depositing geyserite here for centuries to build such a mound. Tree stumps in the area are encrusted with this geyserite. One study hints that Old Faithful was probably born as a geyser not more than 700 years ago.

The trail to Geyser Hill starts down the hill to the right across the Firehole River footbridge.

BLUE STAR AND CHINESE SPRING SIDE TRAIL

If you take the left fork before going down to cross the river and walk around Geyser Hill, you can take a short side trip to three hot springs. This might be a good way to spend half an hour or so while waiting for Old Faithful to erupt, keeping the geyser in view as you walk.

The name of **Blue Star Spring** comes from its geyserite border, shaped like an irregular four-pointed star. After a

Upper Geyser Basin

bison fell in during spring of 1997, the hot spring began a hitherto unseen boiling and doming-up activity. Organisms in the runoff from this spring create a fan of color you can see from across the Firehole.

Blue Star Spring's thin crust sets off the unusual deep blue of its water.

Down the hill are two bubbling springs, first **East Chinaman Spring** and then the famous **Chinese Spring**, where an Asian laundryman (actually Japanese) used to draw his supply of water and one day accidentally caused an eruption.

Beyond Chinese Spring the walkway goes to benches that are ideally located for watching Beehive Geyser erupt across the river. Continuing past the benches returns you to Old Faithful Inn and Geyser. Retrace your steps from Chinese Spring to follow the main path.

Back on the main walkway

Stop on the footbridge across the **Firehole River**. Nowhere is the river more beautiful than in this area on the way to Geyser Hill. Wildflowers abound at least until midsummer, the river itself is crystal clear, and the brightly stained banks add to the magical effect.

OBSERVATION POINT/ SOLITARY GEYSER SIDE LOOP

Just over the bridge and partway up the hill begins the trail to **Observation Point**, a climb of about 150 feet (45 m) in elevation in less than half a mile (0.8 km). Observation Point gives you an excellent view overlooking much of Upper Geyser Basin, and it's a fine place to watch Old Faithful. You can continue to Solitary Geyser on this trail, which rejoins the Geyser Hill walkway, or you can retrace your steps down from Observation Point.

Like Chinese Spring near Old Faithful Geyser, **Solitary Geyser** was misused in earlier days, but in this case, the misuse was officially sanctioned. Its water was piped down to the Old Faithful Geyser Baths, across the Firehole River from Beehive Geyser, beginning in 1915. Its replacement, the Old

The author learned to swim at the Old Faithful Swimming Pool, housed in this building.

Faithful Swimming Pool, was used until 1948. Solitary Geyser now commonly erupts less than 6 feet (2 m) high every few minutes, and its water is definitely too hot for bathing! Solitary's pool is surrounded by interesting geyserite egg formations.

Back on the main walkway

If you don't go to Observation Point, climb the paved trail along the river and take the left fork (closer to the river) to walk around Geyser Hill and follow the route described here. (The walkway to the right is described in the other direction on pages 90–92 and labeled (C) on the Upper Geyser Basin map.)

Sulphide Spring, the first feature on your right after the walkways split, lives up to its name by emitting a strong hydrogen sulphide odor, the smell of rotten eggs. The waters of Sulphide Spring and of nearby Infant Geyser are acidic, in contrast to the alkaline water typical of most Geyser Hill springs.

Anemone Geyser (or Geysers) was named by geologist Walter Weed in the 1880s, but whether for the sea anemone or for the flower, no one is quite sure. The larger of the two vents, the one closer to the boardwalk, may erupt as often as every 7 to 10 minutes, unless an extended eruption of the smaller one increases the length of the intervals. It's entertaining to watch the larger crater fill with water, begin splashing, erupt for a few seconds—as high as 8 feet (2.5 m)—then drain away with a sucking sound.

Plume Geyser, a short distance from Anemone and on the opposite side of the boardwalk, was created by a small steam explosion in 1922, then made itself a new vent in another explosion 50 years later. Plume plays up to 40 feet (12 m) in a plume or feathery jet that spews out at an angle about every 40 minutes.

The eruptions of **Beehive Geyser★** are a glorious sight but not really predictable. Nonetheless, the activity of an indicator geyser a few feet away sometimes gives ranger-interpreters a chance to alert visitors to an impending eruption.

Although not totally reliable, the indicator has been noted in writings about the park since 1875 or earlier. It usually starts erupting 10 to 25 minutes before Beehive, allowing people around the visitor center to get to Geyser Hill or at least to the viewing benches north of Old Faithful and next to the river in time for the eruption. Late 20th century visitors were lucky: Beehive erupted about every 10 to 16 hours for about 5 minutes.

Historian Hiram Chittenden wrote of Beehive in the late 19th century: "The symmetry of its cone is only surpassed by the regularity of its water column. From an artistic point of view it is the most perfect geyser in the Park." Beehive's needle of water is breathtaking even from a distance; the roar of the steam is an extra thrill when you're standing close.

As you leave Beehive, there are several minor geysers to your right (northeast)

Beehive Geyser jets to 150 or 200 feet (45–60 m).

above the boardwalk. All are difficult to see and not currently active, though they may bubble or steam.

Depression Geyser's blue-green pool looks quiet until it erupts 6 to 10 feet (2–3 m); this happens about every 6 hours. **Arrowhead** and **Heart springs** are quiet pools whose shapes illustrate their names, except that Arrowhead may have got its name from a Native American artifact found within it.

The Lion Geyser Group has four cones. The largest and closest to the boardwalk is **Lion Geyser**. It roars like a lion when it gushes steam from its vent before all but the first of its cyclic eruptions, and its formation looks to some like a reclining lion when seen from the south. Farther back from the boardwalk, right to left as you stand near Lion, are **Big Cub Geyser**, **Lioness Geyser**, and **Little Cub Geyser**.

Lion has 5- or 6-minute eruptions up to 70 feet (21 m) and always plays in a series of eruptions spaced 1 to 1.5 hours apart, with many hours or days between the cycles. Lioness and Big Cub have been inactive in recent years but sometimes boil vigorously, while Little Cub erupts about every 70 to 100 minutes up to 10 feet high (3 m). The washed look of Little Cub's formation tells you it's a frequent geyser. In fact, Little Cub has never been dormant in the history of the park.

In 1889 a British visitor toured the Upper Geyser Basin, noted the "pretty and fanciful" names assigned to all the geysers, and wrote about the group you see here: "The first mound that I encountered belonged to a goblin splashing in his tub. I heard him kick, pull a shower-bath on his shoulders, gasp, crack his joints, and rub himself down with a towel; then he let the water out of the bath, as a thoughtful man should, and it all sank down out of sight till another goblin arrived. Yet they called this place the Lioness and the Cubs." The visitor was the 24-year-old Rudyard Kipling.

Goggles Spring and **North Goggles Geyser**, the latter with an interesting collection of geyserite eggs around its cone, are just beyond the Lion Group. To turn back toward Old Faithful, take the right-hand fork at the walkway intersection (see pages 90–92 for the features you will see).

Heading away from Geyser Hill, the main path now takes you through the trees along the Firehole River. You pass nondescript thermal pools, one called Frog Pond, because it actually has frogs in the spring, and Liberty Pool. The last spring was named after its first eruption on July 4, 1887. Across the river, Sprinkler Geyser may be spouting, as it does at least half the time.

Tardy Geyser is the first one you encounter in a group called the Sawmill Complex. The underground plumbing of Tardy and several other geysers is connected in an exchange of function with Sawmill Geyser, so that members of the group influence each other's eruptions. Look closely when the water in Tardy's crater is low, and you can see uniform coin- or biscuit-shaped geyserite knobs around the edge, as you can also in Sawmill's crater. Tardy's eruptions are 10 to 15 feet (3–4.5 m) high.

Sawmill Geyser is the tallest—up to about 50 feet (15 m)—and the longest erupting of the group. You'll find it erupting about 30 percent of the time, with intervals between eruptions typically ranging from 1 to 3 hours. Its water spins about in a circle in the crater during eruptions, sounding like the moving wooden parts in an old water-powered sawmill. Behind Sawmill (to the west) is **Uncertain Geyser**, a small hole in Sawmill's formation. Sometimes called Sawmill's Satellite Vent, Uncertain erupts when others in the group are quiet, as high as 15 feet (45 m).

SIDE TRAIL TOWARD THE RIVER

If you turn left at Sawmill to cross the river and visit Castle Geyser, you'll pass **Churn Geyser**—not very active now but known to erupt to 10 feet (3 m). **Scalloped** and **South Scalloped springs** are on your right. The water deep down in Scalloped Spring reverberates in its cavern with a satisfying gurgle. The low water level was not Scalloped Spring's normal state—the spring was probably illegally induced to erupt at some time in the past.

The cone high above the river to the right (downstream) is called **Deleted Teakettle Geyser**. Its strange moniker is due to someone having added "deleted" to the records, resulting in that word becoming part of its name. The formation to the left (upriver) is **Chimney Cone** (though sometimes signed as Chimney Geyser).

Across and downriver you may make out some steaming and spouting springs called the **Terra Cotta Springs**. Needy tourists seem to have found one of them, **Washtub Spring**, useful as a laundry tub. An 1883 guidebook advised: "Sometimes the clothes are returned with one or two pieces missing, but generally they are all safely restored in due time."

This geyser route now returns to the main path without crossing the river. Across the Firehole and up the short hill are unique Castle Geyser and its neighbors (described in Geyser Route Two).

~

Back on the main walkway

To see a few more features in the interdependent Sawmill Complex, take the small loop to the east rather than the straight walkway. These include geysers called **Penta** (named for its five vents), which rarely erupts when Sawmill is active, but may go to 25 feet (7.5 m); **Spasmodic**, with its many vents; and **Old Tardy**. Last encountered before you rejoin the main walk is delicately colored **Belgian Spring**, where a tragedy occurred in 1929: a newspaper editor from Belgium died after falling into this pool.

Turn right to rejoin the straight part of the boardwalk. We'll pick up the missed section of the main walkway on the way back labeled (B) on the Upper Geyser Basin map and described on page 90.

You're approaching what many geyser lovers consider the most exciting geyser of all to watch: Grand Geyser. Before reaching Grand you'll come to some small geysers connected to it underground, including **Rift Geyser**, which seems like just an innocuous group of cracks, but, when active, can influence Grand's eruptions; **Triplet Geysers**, of which only **West Triplet** erupts with any frequency now; and **Percolator Geyser**, which *does* sound like coffee percolating. Percolator Geyser has upon occasion been known to play for 2 hours or so before Grand's eruption. West Triplet is located closest to the boardwalk, and Percolator is in the middle of a direct line from West Triplet to Grand.

How Does a Geyser Work?

After you've seen some geysers, you'll probably want to know how a geyser works. The basic requirements are a water source, a heat source, and some rather complicated plumbing.

The Sources and the Plumbing

Snowmelt and rainfall provide the water by soaking into the ground locally and from the surrounding mountain ranges. The water flows deep into the geyser basin as groundwater, reaching many hundreds of feet (meters) below ground level, as shown in the diagram.

The still-hot volcanic rocks found below Yellowstone's geyser basins provide the source for heating the water. The rocks continually receive more heat where there is magma (molten rock) a few miles below.

The plumbing that all geysers have consists of a vent connected to a narrow crack that goes down into the hot rocks, widening into chambers and narrowing into channels as it goes and intersecting a multitude of tiny cracks and pores that feed water into the geyser.

What Happens to the Water

Let's follow the cycle at the point just after an eruption has ended.

1. The vent and crack have been largely emptied of water. A small part of the water that shot up into the air falls back into the geyser vent and drains down the crack. Of course, this water is much cooler than when it shot out.

2. More water now starts to fill the crack by seeping in from the sides. This water is already very hot from having passed through hot rocks. Much hotter water enters the crack deeper down and pushes the overlying water up.

Time-out here to mention three properties of hot water that clarify why geysers act as they do.

- The boiling temperature of water is higher at higher pressures. The weight of a column of water raises the pressure at the bottom, which raises the boiling temperature, making it superheated water.

- The same weight of water occupies far more space as steam than it does as liquid water—on the order of a thousand times more space.

- Superheated water flashes into steam if the pressure on it is lowered to ordinary atmospheric pressure.

Now back inside the geyser:

3. As more water enters the crack (or *fissure*), the water level rises toward the surface. The added weight of water increases the pressure near the bottom. The hot water heats the somewhat cooler water already in the fissure. The water level rises past the very narrow parts of the vent.

4. As the superheated water continues to rise in the fissure, it starts to boil

gently, forming small steam bubbles that rise and heat the overlying water. Because the deeper boiling water is under higher pressure, it boils at higher temperature, and its steam heats the upper water to its boiling point. More

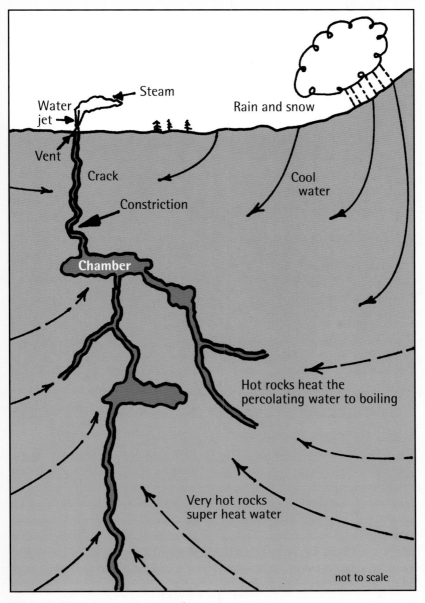

Figure 2. How Does a Geyser Work?

bubbles form, raising the column of water and bubbles in the crack until it reaches the surface at the vent. Up to this point, the water pressure at depth has been increasing.

5. When water starts to spill out of the vent, the column of water in the fissure is at its greatest height. More steam bubbles from below displace liquid water, some of which spills out at the top. With more steam in the column, now the weight of the water becomes less, more boiling occurs, even below the constricted parts, and water comes out faster.

6. Next, the steam from below rushes through the constriction like a jet engine exhaust. The water is being pushed rapidly toward the surface and spurts out. This greatly reduces the pressure inside, letting the steam blow the water column out of the vent. The geyser is erupting—an exponentially accelerating catastrophe!

7. When all the steam has managed to escape from below the constriction, there's nothing more to push on the water, and not much water there, so the eruption stops. Then the cycle begins again.

There's more about geysers in the "Geological History" chapter.

Watching powerful **Grand Geyser★★** from close by is an unparalleled experience for its raw natural energy. Maybe the obligation to wait a long time in the hot sun (or in below-zero temperatures in the winter!) adds to the thrill when it does erupt, but it's truly a stellar attraction.

Grand erupts from a rather large vent a safe distance from the boardwalk and benches. Early in the park's history, Grand erupted only at widely spaced intervals, but the interval gradually decreased between 1930 and the 1980s. In recent years, the range of time between eruptions is from about 7 to 15 hours, but most often between 10 and 13 hours. Your wait for Grand may be long, but it's very likely to be rewarding, since Grand has become the world's tallest predictable geyser.

Don't mistake **Turban Geyser** (the more impressive geyserite mound to the north of Grand) for the main attraction, although Turban will oblige you with 5 minutes of play every 17 to 35 minutes. The blobs of geyserite in its crater do resemble turban headdresses, but please don't go off the boardwalk to get a closer look! Turban erupts about 5 feet (1.5 m) above its rim, except that for an hour or two after Grand has erupted, it may go to 20 feet (6 m).

The relationship between Turban's eruptions and the overflow and ebbing away of water in Grand's pool can indicate how soon Grand will next erupt. When Turban erupts without lowering Grand's pool, waves will begin to disturb the water surface more and more vigorously, and Grand's eruption will usually begin.

When Grand finally begins, a wonderful roaring from underground will accompany a tremendous burst of water up to 150 or 200 feet (45–60 m). But that's not all—Grand may put forth as many as four of these bursts—or even more. Some people claim the first part of the second burst is always the most fun.

Observer James C. Fennel wrote a description of Grand's first burst in 1892 that's valid years later. "[W]ith earthshaking and tremendous rumbling that sounds like smothered thunder, the fountain without receiving warning of attack is shot aloft into the air two hundred feet in an immense column of steam and water. . . . From the main column numberless jets are discharged at all heights and angles draping the Colossus in an agitated fringework of ever-changing patterns. . . ."

Grand Geyser and its smaller neighbor, Vent Geyser, put on a wonderful show.

Vent Geyser next to Turban might be called Companion Geyser: its eruptions always accompany Grand and sometimes Turban. It erupts as high as 70 feet (21 m) at a slight angle and may continue after Grand's eruption for an hour or more.

In approximately the next quarter mile (0.4 km), there are only five named springs before the bridge over the Firehole. You pass springs connected to Grand called **Economic Geyser** (named for its habit of reclaiming almost all its erupted water), **East Economic Geyser**, and **Wave Spring**, and come to **Beauty Pool★★** and neighboring **Chromatic Pool**.

Beauty and Chromatic pools illustrate extremely well the exchange of function between connected thermal features. In fact, the two-star rating may belong to Chromatic Pool and not to Beauty when you're visiting. Beauty Pool was for a time in recent years decidedly the more beautiful of the two, then in 1995 Chromatic Pool became hotter and therefore more colorful for about two months. The situation then reversed itself again. The range of color in the hotter of the two pools is remarkable: the center may be blue to emerald green, with yellow, gold, orange, and brown bacteria indicating gradually cooling water at the edges.

Just across the Firehole bridge you'll find **Inkwell Spring**, whose almost constantly bubbling water leaves inky stains on its cone from manganese oxide deposits.

The trail passes **Oblong Geyser** at quite a distance, due to the fact that Oblong can erupt as high as 25 feet (7.5 m) in a large boiling dome, pouring a huge

Beauty Pool shows a full range of color in its water and bacterial mats (1997).

volume of water into the Firehole River. You can infer its long history from the wide buildup of geyserite to Oblong's west. Oblong has been active recently, erupting about every one to three days, but it goes through periodic dormancies, and, as with all of Yellowstone's features, its activity could change at any time.

On a short spur to the right beyond Oblong you can visit **Giant Geyser** and its neighbors. This group is interdependent and connected to Grotto Geyser to the north as well. Some of the smaller features here are (left to right): **Bijou Geyser** (French for "jewel"), which plays almost constantly from its bacteria-covered cone, **Catfish Geyser**, and **Mastiff Geyser**. Mastiff's name may refer to its growling sound or to its watchdog function next to Giant. It has had periods of amazing energy. Usually Mastiff and Catfish have erupted simultaneously with Giant.

Beginning in the middle of 1996, tremendous eruptions of Giant Geyser occurred frequently. Since 1955 there had been eruptions *years* apart, but for a time in the late 1990s they were occurring four or five *days* apart and providing great excitement among geyser gazers— and even the older geyser gazer geezers.

With eruptions sometimes reaching 250 feet (76 m), Giant has built a massive 12-foot-high cone (3.6 m) with an enormous central cavity. An estimated 1 million gallons of water (nearly 4 million L) pours out during an eruption. Giant Geyser ranks with the rarely erupting Excelsior and Steamboat Geyser as Yellowstone's three most powerful.

A short distance north of Giant, this route joins the paved walkway. Next, the bizarrely shaped **Grotto Geyser** is the

Giant Geyser displays its incredible power.

central attraction. Grotto's unique cone has probably been built up over fallen trees that became encrusted with geyserite. The interval between Grotto's eruptions varies from 7 hours to a day or two. Its normal eruptions are as long as 3.5 hours, but it can erupt for more than a day at a time, starting with high bursts and settling to about 15 feet (4.5 m) for the major part of its eruption. It's better to take Grotto's picture when it's not erupting, so that water and steam don't obscure the view of its remarkable formation.

Three geysers near Grotto erupt briefly just before or during Grotto's long eruptions. They are **Rocket Geyser**, which erupts from its cone in unison with Grotto, sometimes up to 50 feet (15 m); **Grotto Fountain Geyser**, which can throw a thin stream of water up to 65 feet (20 m) and precedes most of Grotto's

Grotto Geyser has the park's most grotesque cone.

eruptions; and smaller **South Grotto Fountain Geyser.** The last two are far back from the walkway.

Spa Geyser was named for the mineral spring in Belgium that gave its name to all such springs used for medicinal bathing. Don't try bathing in this spa— the water is over 190°F (88°C)! Spa's infrequent but explosive eruptions, sometimes as much as 60 feet (18 m) high, are linked to Grotto's activity.

RIVERSIDE GEYSER SPUR

Turn east toward the river at Spa Geyser to see the most gracefully situated and aesthetically satisfying geyser eruption in the park. **Riverside Geyser★★** has been for a century the park's most regular geyser. A 1909 guidebook stated that it erupted every 8 hours for about 15 minutes. It is predictable to within about half an hour, now erupting about every 6 or 7 hours. Check its predicted eruption

times at the visitor center.

During its eruption, Riverside ejects water from several vents in its chair-like formation on the far side of the Firehole. Water overflowing the edges of the formation indicates that it will erupt within an hour or so, while water beginning to spout from the highest hole at the left means the eruption will occur in about one-half hour. The first few minutes of the eruption are the most spectacular, with water arching over the river up to 75 feet (23 m) from the cone. The eruption continues for about 20 minutes. Some eruptions spread a veritable curtain of droplets out over the river.

Back on the main walkway

On the far side of the bridge are two geysers so closely related that they are always mentioned together and are effectively one geyser. In recent years they've been relatively inactive and they are never pre-

Riverside Geyser's spray creates a rainbow in the sunlight.

dictable. **Fan Geyser**'s eruptions come from 11 vents, some with water spouting as high as 125 feet (38 m) and over the trail. One vent even jets water *downward* toward the Firehole. **Mortar Geyser**, whose name may come from the cannon-like sound of its eruptions, has fewer vents and lower jets of water—up to 80 feet (24 m). The joint eruptions may occur every few days in active periods, and geyser experts can sometimes guess when these spectacular eruptions are near. Patient geyser gazers wait for hours or even overnight for the privilege of seeing these spectacular eruptions.

Spiteful Geyser is closer to the walkway than Fan and Mortar. Dormant in the early 1990s, it more recently emitted a constant spray toward the boardwalk. Witness its

angry-seeming spitting and you'll understand the name. Opposite Spiteful is an unnamed feature that is unofficially called the **Norris Pools**. In 1998, these pools underwent a major change and the southern one became a geyser that sometimes erupts when Fan and Mortar are active.

🚻♿ A rest room is off the trail to the right.

Morning Glory Pool

Morning Glory Pool, on a short spur to the left, is famous for its brilliant blue color and tube shape, which make it resemble the common morning glory blossom. But late in the season when its temperature drops, the pool turns green, yellow, and brown. Morning Glory's great fame may account for the tremendous vandalism it has suffered. In one cleaning-out in 1950, rangers found 112 different kinds of foreign objects, including logs, nearly 100 dollars in coins, and "delicate items of underclothing." Vandalism was one reason why the Grand Loop Road was relocated a considerable distance away from this pool over 30 years ago.

EXTENSION TO BISCUIT BASIN

NOTE: This extension can also be approached from the other end by parking at Biscuit Basin (see page 62). To head back to Old Faithful, skip to page 90 for the features you'll see.

[🔍] The unpaved trail from Morning Glory Pool to Biscuit Basin takes you about 0.8 mile (1.3 km) over a hill to several splendid springs and geysers. Since few people explore beyond Morning Glory, it's a great place to escape the crowds and see some Yellowstone treasures. The following description identifies the unmarked thermal features on this trail for you. Be sure to stay on the trail!

Three or four small geysers line the riverbanks just beyond Morning Glory Pool. Look for **Sentinel Geyser** on an island near the east side of the Firehole River when the water is high. **Green Star Spring** is a little farther downstream and across the river.

About 0.4 mile (0.6 km) from the Morning Glory area are two geysers below the rock wall that supported the old road.

Artemisia Geyser takes its name from the scientific name for sagebrush (*Artemisia tridentata*), which shares its gray-green color with some of the geyserite deposits under the water at the turquoise blue pool's edge. Its eruptions surge as much as 30 feet (9 m) with very little warning, at intervals ranging from 9 to 32 hours. Uphill from Artemisia are two milky bubblers, one with a beautiful mossy overhang and rust-stained edge.

Atomizer Geyser (also called Restless Geyser) consists of the two small cones between Artemisia and the slope down to the river. It's named for the device that breaks a liquid down into a fine spray. Atomizer's spraying, from the cone farthest from the river, takes place only during major eruptions. Such eruptions, which may go to 50 feet (15 m) high and last 10 minutes, occur about twice a day.

More small geysers line both sides of the river near here, but they are difficult to see through the trees. One of these was so directly a creation of the 1959 Hebgen Lake earthquake that it's called **Seismic Geyser.** It erupted as high as 75 feet (23 m) during the following 15 years. In 1999 and 2000, a new and unnamed vent close to Seismic erupted frequently as high as 20 feet (6 m) and sometimes much higher. Geyser gazers call it **Aftershock Geyser.**

Across the river from Seismic and from the trail, another very short-lived geyser, called **Fantail Geyser** for its angled eruptions, performed impressively for one spring and summer (1986), then almost not at all since.

There are three pools near the trail beyond Atomizer. **Gem Pool** is the oblong one that overflows constantly. East of Gem Pool is **Bear Den Spring**, where, in spite of bubbling water at the bottom, a crawl space under the rock ledge served at least once (in 1958) as a bear's winter home.

Pinto Spring and **Sprite Pool** are smaller round springs with little or no overflow. Then it's about 0.3 mile (0.5 km) downhill to pale sapphire blue **Mirror Pool**, with yellow to brown bacteria around the edges.

Finally, you pass **Cauliflower Geyser** south of the small footbridge before you reach the highway. The "cauliflowers" are the same type of formation as the biscuits of Biscuit Basin, but bigger. They are nodules of geyserite.

⌘ At the footbridge near Cauliflower Geyser, a trail leading north parallels the Grand Loop Road to join the Mallard Creek and Fairy Falls trails about 2 miles (3.2 km) from Biscuit Basin.

Geyser Route One features you may have missed

As you return from Morning Glory Pool, you'll have the chance to see a few hot springs and geysers you missed if you took the recommended side trails on the way out. Three stretches of the main trail are described below in sections labeled (A), (B), and (C). These letters correspond to labels on the Upper Geyser Basin map, page 77.

(A) After recrossing the bridge over the Firehole near Fan and Mortar geysers, continue straight ahead (unless Riverside Geyser is about to erupt, in which case, don't miss it!). Here you'll pass the **Chain Lakes Complex**, which consists of several hot springs and geysers related both to each other and to the Grotto Complex. The **Bottomless Pit** was described by the geologist Albert C. Peale of the 1878 Hayden Survey as "a beautiful blue cavern-like spring of great depth." **Link Geyser** has had eruptions up to 100 feet (30 m) high—but not since the late 1980s.

Culvert Geyser has an interesting story. Road engineers building the original Grand Loop Road (now the walkway) buried one spring nearby and built a culvert around this one. This gave Culvert Geyser the energy to enlarge its cra-

ter and begin spouting to 2 feet (0.6 m), which it continued to do for some years. It now has a beautiful green center and a prominent overhanging edge.

(B) Between Grand Geyser and Sawmill Geyser, the straight walkway has only three small springs. **Bulger Spring** (on the right as you walk toward Old Faithful Village) is actually a small geyser. The seemingly unremarkable springs on the left are interesting because they are not connected underground, according to geyser expert T. Scott Bryan, although their apertures are only 1 foot (0.3 m) apart. **Crystal Spring**, named for its very clear water, is connected to the Grand Geyser Complex, but **Crystal Spring's Geyser** (a round hole very near the edge of Crystal Spring's runoff channel) is a member of the Sawmill Complex.

(C) Back on Geyser Hill. When the boardwalk splits near North Goggles Geyser, turn left to take the upper part of the loop and see the features you missed at the start of Geyser Route One.

Ear Spring is obviously named for its shape and used to be called the "Devil's Ear." *Haynes Guide* in the 1920s reported that "it not only resembles an ear in shape, but the lobe is pierced and the earring is a tiny geyser. It is here that messages are transmitted, so the story goes, to regions below." Sometimes Ear Spring's water becomes superheated (hotter than boiling), and bubbling occurs around its rim.

The western end of the trail to Solitary Geyser and Observation Point joins the main boardwalk between Ear Spring and nearby Beach Spring. In rainy summers, the meadow north of here is filled with wildflowers.

Beach Spring in the boardwalk's corner may get its name from the beach-like terrace over which its water intermittently flows, from the sandy color of the sinter in its central bowl, or perhaps from the sound it makes during boiling periods: like surf at a beach. If you watch for a few minutes, you may be hypnotized by seeing the water rise, bubble, and fall repeatedly a short way down in the bowl.

Aurum Geyser, whose name means gold in Latin, gets its color from iron oxide inside its tiny geyserite mound. Aurum erupts for about 1 minute at intervals varying from 2.5 to 12 hours but averaging about 4 hours, sometimes spraying the boardwalk with spurts up to 25 feet (8 m) high.

Doublet Pool was called The Quaker by 19th century tour guide, George Henderson. Standing near it, you can sometimes hear and feel vibrations, probably caused by the collapse of steam bubbles within the pool. Its overhanging geyserite ledge is unusually wide and thin (and dangerous!), and you can see other ledges partway down, indicating previously lower water levels.

Sponge Geyser is barely a geyser at all, but it may have been one in the past or at least has been building its cone for a very long time. It resembles a sponge both in its highly perforated surface and its light beige color. When active, its water boils up to the rim, then sinks out of sight.

Pump Geyser and two small vents nearby called **The Pump** can be counted on to splash more or less vigorously almost without a break. They do sound very much like pumps.

Giantess Geyser rests in a deep pool high atop Geyser Hill. The boardwalk is placed a safe distance away, because when the geyser is active, it can erupt as high as 200 feet (60 m) with very little warning. Giantess is surely the queen of the hill, with influence over many other springs and geysers; her eruptions are known to affect Vault, Teakettle, Infant, Sponge, Doublet, Beach, Ear, Plume, and Beehive. Early writers who saw Gi-

Giantess Geyser erupts in 1899, by F. J. Haynes.

antess erupt described "globular masses of vapor" that were "domed at the top like a crystal cupola." Steam phases, which can alternate with water phases, make a deafening roar that may be heard a mile away. Eruptions can last many hours—one induced by the 1959 earthquake lasted over four days. However, their rarity (an average of three per year since 1984) means that you'll have to be very lucky to see one, as was Nathaniel Langford, who named it in 1870.

Closer to the boardwalk are deep-welled Teakettle Spring, the punchbowl-shaped crater, and Vault Geyser. **Teakettle Spring** is an excellent example of how springs change with time. Until 1947, its crater was full to the rim. Now the water level sits deep out of sight, but the bubbling from inside still sounds rather like a teakettle.

Some of **Vault Geyser**'s eruptions occur after Giantess starts and may go to 15 feet (4.5 m), but it can erupt independently of Giantess. An unusual attribute of Vault is that it erupts from far below ground level rather than first filling its crater, as most geysers do.

Active once or twice a month, **Dome Geyser** sits high and alone up the hill to the east.

Infant Geyser sometimes has tiny eruptions when Giantess Geyser is active. Note its oval cavity with an unusual deep red lining and cloudy, acidic water.

Geyser Route Two: Castle and Daisy Geysers and an extension to Black Sand Pool

NOTE: This is an approved bicycle route all the way to Biscuit Basin about 2.5 miles (4 km) to the north. To reach Biscuit Basin, turn left on the northern trail to the Daisy Group, then turn immediately right.

[符] [&] [♿] The 2.4 miles (4 km) round trip to view Castle and Daisy geysers on Geyser RouteTwo is paved and can be traversed by wheelchair or bicycle. You may shorten the distance a little by parking in the lot for the general store near Old Faithful Inn. The side trail past Daisy Geyser to Punch Bowl Spring and Black Sand Pool (not fully paved and not open to bicycling) can add another mile (1.6 km) to this excursion. Consult the Upper Geyser Basin map on page 77.

From the visitor center, follow the former main road past the east wing of Old Faithful Inn, keeping Old Faithful Geyser on your right. After passing the inn's parking area and the side trail to Chinese Spring, you'll see a large meadow on your right, where bison and elk can find grass even in winter due to warming from hot springs.

West of the store and service station, you may see steam surprisingly close to the buildings. The steam comes from the Myriad Group, where hundreds of hot springs have been counted, including at least one historically interesting feature. **Round Geyser** erupted as high as 150 feet (46 m) in a few widely spaced years, with long dormancies in between. It rivaled the height of Old Faithful itself. There's no public access to the area.

Castle Geyser★ is the first thermal feature you come to—about a half mile (0.8 km) from the visitor center. This cone-type geyser erupts from the center of a large geyserite edifice that looks very much like a turreted medieval castle. Castle's cone is about 12 feet (3.5 m) high and 6 feet (1.2 m) in diameter. Eruptions, which usually occur about every 10 to 12 hours, are predictable within a 2-hour time frame, and predicted times are posted in the visitor center.

Castle Geyser is Yellowstone's largest regularly erupting cone-type geyser.

Castle typically erupts explosively for 15 to 20 minutes in its water phase, spouting to as high as 100 feet (30 m). Then 30 to 45 minutes of steam phase follow, accompanied by a thrilling roar. Castle is changeable and has displayed other types of eruption patterns in the past. It's also thousands of years old. A hot spring predating the geyser probably built up its mound of geyserite during tens of thousands of years.

CASTLE'S NEIGHBORS TOWARD THE RIVER

Tortoise Shell Spring boils violently in its geyserite cone. It's one of the hottest springs in the park—207°F (97°C) or hotter—and seems to have no connection with neighboring Castle Geyser. According to some close observers, you can visualize not just the shell but the head, tail, and legs of a tortoise in the spring's shape. Campers in the early days used this superheated spring to boil their food.

On the boardwalk corner between Tortoise Shell Spring and Crested Pool is **Tilt Geyser**, a group of little vents that erupt from a few inches to 6 feet (10–200 cm) high. Tilt would be unremarkable if it weren't for the amazing noises it makes at the end of an eruption: a loud sucking sound and a final loud gurgle as the whirlpool of water disappears.

Crested Pool★ is 42 feet (13 m) deep and sometimes boils as high as 10 feet (3 m). According to one of the first guidebook writers, Harry J. Norton (1873): "For delicacy of coloring and beauty of ornamentation it surpasses

Crested Pool has an almost perfectly symmetrical ten-sided rim.

any we visited. It is more quiet than others, yet its surface is gently rippled by constant vibrations. . . ."

Sad to relate, in 1970 a nine-year-old boy was scalded to death in a few seconds in the superheated water of this pool. The guardrail here and additional warnings of danger throughout the geyser basins were erected in response to the tragedy. Old names for Crested Pool, such as Fire Basin and Devil's Well, may have been apt after all.

~

Back on the main walkway

Across the pavement from Castle is a fenced hot spring called **Shield Pool** for its shape.

Leaving Castle and continuing on the paved trail, you'll pass a meadow where a few springs quietly give off steam. This area had a short-lived geyser in 1986, when **South Orange Geyser** erupted quite regularly.

Look through the trees to the right, just before the walkway comes close to the Firehole River, to see a brilliantly colored mound the shape of a kiln, alive with microorganisms in the runoff from **Limekiln Springs**. This is a favorite subject for color photographers.

Before you reach the path to Daisy Geyser, the Round Spring Group of springs and occasional spouters to the west makes the idea of cutting across this open space very unwise (as well as forbidden!).

If you started from the visitor center, you will have traveled a little more than a mile (1.8 km) by the time you reach the first (southern) path to Daisy and the sign: "Daisy Geyser may erupt within x minutes of y." The time is posted both here and at the visitor center after the

first eruption or two of the day. The path to the west here and the bicycle path a short distance north both pass the Daisy Group of geysers. They rejoin west of those geysers to become one path toward Black Sand Basin.

To your east you can see the distinctive cone of Giant Geyser. It's described on page 86.

Daisy Geyser is the only regularly and predictably active geyser in the group at the top of the small hill, but there are about ten closely related springs and geysers in this group. Two of the geysers have interesting names. Park geologist George Marler named **Radiator Geyser** for sounding like a boiling car radiator. Its eruptions are mostly subterranean when Daisy is active, but above ground when Splendid is active. **Daisy's Thief Geyser**, when it first appeared in 1942, used to erupt occasionally *instead of* Daisy, lowering the water in Daisy and preventing its normal eruption. Later, it seemed to serve as a precursor to Daisy. The Thief has now been dormant for many years and is hard to see. Sometimes, nearby **Bonita Pool** would overflow and Daisy would become dormant.

Daisy Geyser★ was dormant from 1960 to 1971 but can now be counted on to erupt about every 2 hours as high as 75 feet (21 m). Its eruption lasts 3 or 4 minutes, always followed by a steam phase with a roar like that of an old steam engine.

Geologist Marler proved by experiment that Daisy's eruptions would be much longer if so much cooled water did not flow back into the crater. It's not known whether Daisy's name came from a popular old expression: "Hey, it's a

Daisy Geyser erupts dependably and at a graceful angle.

daisy!" (slang for first-rate) or from the nickname of an early assistant superintendent. Watch out for the northern side of Daisy during an eruption. Many people, including the author, have been unwilling recipients of a "geyser kiss" from Daisy!

Splendid Geyser may have the most on-again-off-again history of eruption activity of any of Yellowstone's geysers, starting with its first mention in 1834 by explorer Warren A. Ferris. It has been known to erupt over 200 feet (61 m) high in its active periods, and eruptions sometimes seem to be caused by falling barometric pressure.

Splendid and its neighbor Daisy sometimes erupt simultaneously. This unpredictable occurrence is breathtaking—they may both jet to more than 100 feet (30 m).

The relatively recent (mid 1990s) simultaneous eruptions of Daisy and Splendid provide a fine example of the reason we should never pronounce a geyser dead. An article about Yellowstone Park in a 1940 *National Geographic Magazine* stated: "Daisy sprang into existence in 1892 with the demise of Splendid Geyser, fifty feet away." But Splendid wasn't dead, just dormant for about half a century!

There may be an east-west fissure or deep underground connection between Splendid Geyser and Giant Geyser, which is about 1200 feet (360 m) to the east. In 1951 and the mid 1990s, these two magnificent geysers ceased dormancy and entered very active periods within a few months of each other.

Comet Geyser's cone is to the west of Daisy and closer to the northern walkway. Deposition of minerals from water droplets splashing almost constantly has built the cone.

Extension to Black Sand Pool

If you continue west where the two walkways around Daisy become one, you'll see the **White Pyramid** (or White Throne), the cone of an extinct geyser, across the meadow to the north. At its base is small but active **Pyramid Geyser**.

A little farther west is the almost perfectly circular **Punch Bowl Spring★**. The center of this beautiful spring boils a foot or so above its rim, which is nearly 2 feet (0.6 m) in height. It overflows constantly, creating a colorful runoff channel.

It's a short distance to **Black Sand Pool★**, the last major feature on this route. Black Sand acts infrequently as a geyser and has a large and colorful runoff stream to its west. The area at the base of the runoff was named Specimen Lake (when it had more water) for the "specimens" of still-standing silicified trees killed by Black Sand's runoff. In and around Black Sand Pool you'll see good examples of the black obsidian sand (a volcanic glass) that gives the pool and the geyser basin to its southwest their names.

The small but deep, dangerous crater just across the path and south of Black Sand Pool is called **Demon's Cave**. Avoid going near its overhanging ledge.

You can continue from here to Black Sand Basin (described on pages 64–66) or turn back to the Daisy Group.

🚲 If you return via the northern path past Daisy, you'll meet the bicycle path to Biscuit Basin. Biscuit Basin is 1.3 miles (2.1 km) from here (described on pages 62–64). This path (a former service road) goes through meadow and burned forest and passes near a large hot spring, **Cyclops Spring.**

The ridge at the south end of the bicycle path is **Wylie Hill**, the site of a tent camp from the 1890s until 1916. William W. Wylie set up several such inexpensive camps around the park for stagecoach passengers. His managers at this camp piped water from Punch Bowl Spring to the tents, in this case without apparent deleterious effect to the spring.

A short distance beyond the bicycle path, Geyser Route Two ends at the main walkway. To return to the Old Faithful Village area, turn right. To see more of the geyser basin, turn left. Grotto Geyser is just up the short hill, and Riverside Geyser is not far beyond. The walk from Grotto to Morning Glory Pool is described on pages 86–88.

From Old Faithful Village to West Thumb Junction

From Old Faithful to West Thumb is a distance of about 19 miles (31 km), as measured from the visitor center. Worth stopping for on the way are Kepler Cascades, Lone Star Geyser Trail, and Isa Lake at the western crossing of the Continental Divide, as well as the views from Shoshone Point and from above West Thumb Junction.

Road Log

0.0/19.4 Old Faithful Village and Visitor Center. Follow signs to exit the area or to find facilities in the village (described on page 67, map on page 68).

1.6/17.8 Old Faithful Interchange with the Grand Loop Road. West Thumb Junction is to the east, Madison Junction to the north.

2.3/17.1 Employee housing area on the south. Slow down for the pedestrian crossing!

2.6/16.8 🚶 Small unpaved parking area for trails to Fern Cascades (west) and Lone Star Geyser (south). The Lone Star Geyser Trail is a section of the old Howard Eaton trail. For a shorter walk to Lone Star Geyser, park at mile 4.2/15.2. (See page 71 for the Fern Cascades Trail.)

Fire damage from the 1988 North Fork fire is obvious all around.

3.2/16.2 Firehole River bridge. Prior to 1970, the area near the pond south of the bridge was the site of a bear feeding grounds, called the Bears Playground.

Through the snags, you can see the edge of the Madison Plateau. It extends southwest as far as the Bechler River in the corner of the park and as far north as the Madison River. This plateau is a huge, relatively young, lava flow—that is, about 100,000–200,000 years old.

4.1/15.3 P Kepler Cascades of the Firehole River. Kepler was the given name of the 12-year-old son of Wyoming Territory's Governor John Hoyt. The boy was with his father in a group searching for suitable routes from Wyoming into the park in 1881, and he was

97

Old Faithful Village to West Thumb Junction

© 2002 J. O. Chapple

Kepler Cascades tumbles down a gorge near Old Faithful Village.

such a good sport, that Superintendent Norris decided to name these pretty cascades for him.

The Firehole River has cut a deep gorge in the Madison Plateau lava here. Where the erosion is continuing, a series of cascades or small waterfalls drops a total of more than 100 feet (30 m). Downstream from the viewing platform, the canyon narrows radically. These steep walls below the cascades (called Devil's Gate or Devil's Gorge) claimed the life of a Yellowstone Park employee who was climbing here in 1976.

Hell and the Devil in Yellowstone

The first observers of Yellowstone Park's features were often reminded of the Prince of Darkness and his abode. As historian Aubrey L. Haines writes in *Yellowstone Place Names: Mirrors of History* (1996): "For a time, the devil had a proprietary interest in thirty-nine Park features, with the word 'hell' appearing in eight others and 'Satan' in one. But in the last half century, he has been largely dispossessed, so that his influence is now minimal. A mere three place names remain: Devils Thumb and Devils Kitchen at Mammoth Hot Springs, in addition to the Devils Den . . . " (located near Tower Fall).

Park Archivist Lee Whittlesey, in his book *Yellowstone Place Names*, adds Devil's Stairway (on the former Mary Mountain road), and for the revised edition he has found two more: Devil's Well near Icebox Canyon and Devil's Inkstand on Mount Washburn.

4.2/15.2 🚶 🚲 🐎 **Lone Star Geyser Trailhead.** A short road to the west leads to the parking area. This round trip of about 4.5 miles (7 km) is a level trail also suitable for biking, since it is a former automobile road. The route soon passes the source of the Old Faithful Village water supply.

In about 1.5 miles (2.4 km), the Spring Creek Trail intersects this one. You can follow it up to the Grand Loop Road, but coming *down* the Spring Creek Trail might be more to your liking (description at mile 8.2/11.2).

The Lone Star Trail passes some small hot springs and a beautiful meadow before reaching the geyser. **Lone Star Geyser** erupts to as high as 45 feet (14 m) from a pink-stained steep cone as wide as it is tall—about 10 feet (3 m) in each dimension.

Lone Star's eruptions occur almost exactly three hours apart, and the interval has averaged 2.5 to 3 hours with no interruption ever since the park was founded. Rangers no longer post eruption predictions at the Old Faithful Visitor Center, but you can help other visitors by recording the time of any eruption you witness in the logbook near the geyser.

The backcountry trail continues past Lone Star's thermal area to Shoshone Lake and Geyser Basin (another 6.2 mi/ 10 km). Before the lake, a (southern) branch leads to the vast and undeveloped Bechler Region in the park's southwest. A much closer trail to Shoshone Lake is at mile 10.5/8.9, the DeLacy Creek Trailhead.

6.5/12.9 Scaup Lake to the north. A scaup is a type of duck related to the canvasback and sometimes seen in the park.

Not far from here, along Spring Creek (which the road then followed), the most profitable—to the robber!—of Yellowstone's five stagecoach robberies took place. The victims of this 1908 crime called it "the greatest stage coach hold up and highway robbery in the 20th century." One man was able to stop 17 coaches and take more than $2000 in money and jewelry from the passengers. He was never caught.

Scaup Lake was the center of a more recent scandal, according to Alston Chase's controversial 1986 book, *Playing God in Yellowstone*. This was one of the places in the park where geologists were allowed to use dynamite as part of a 1980 borehole project, possibly causing the extinction of a rare species of salamander.

6.8/12.6 **P** Small pond, Congress Lake (named because it "just sits there and does nothing") to the south, and large parking area a little farther east for easy trail access down Spring Creek Trail.

As the road climbs you may see patches of snow along the road, even in July.

7.2/12.2 🌲 **(10)** 🚻 ♿ Spring Creek picnic area on the right (south).

8.2/11.2 🚶 🚻 Spring Creek and Divide Lookout trailheads.

The **Spring Creek Trail** follows the creek and the Firehole River for a total of about 6 miles (9.5 km) from this trailhead to the Lone Star Trailhead parking area (at mile 4.2/15.2). The trail uses the route of an 1890s stagecoach road through Spring Creek canyon, described in early literature as "one of the prettiest short trips on the Loop," and as having "irregular walls" and "rock needles pointing skyward."

Spring Creek was named for the several small cold springs that flow out from beneath the rhyolite along its course. The downside of having so many springs is that parts of the trail are marshy, while the upside is that wildflowers thrive here. On the east side of a 20-foot-high (6 m) rock located partway down the trail is a turtle shape engraved by natural forces. The rock has always been called Turtle Rock and was the site of the successful stagecoach robbery described above. The trail could be highly recommended were it not so difficult to get through the narrow part of the canyon at Turtle Rock—you must either climb a steep talus slope or suffer wet feet wading the stream.

The steep **Divide Lookout Trail** goes to the site of a former fire tower about 2.5 miles (4 km) south of the road and nearly 8800 feet (2680 m) above sea level.

Along the road between here and Isa Lake, as well as east of the lake, you can spot beautiful patches of altered rhyolite in some of the road cuts and hillsides. There are many colors: cream, yellow, orange, salmon pink, red, dark brown. At some time in the past, hot water and gases altered the minerals in these rocks, creating the colors.

9.3/10.1 P **Isa Lake** has parking space at both ends, 0.2 mile apart. The lake was named in 1893 for a Cincinnati tourist, Isabel Jelke, but was sometimes called Two Ocean Lake because of its location.

Water lilies cover Isa Lake in midsummer.

It's directly on the Continental Divide at an elevation of 8262 feet (2518 m).

The flow directions from the two ends of this lake are the opposite of what you'd expect. The seeming paradox will become clear to you with a look at the sketch and explanation in "Understanding the Continental Divide."

This high point on the road is called **Craig Pass**, named for the first tourist to cross the pass on the "new" road in 1891. From near Craig Pass, logs to build Old Faithful Inn were cut in the winter of 1903–4 and dragged down on sledges.

Understanding the Continental Divide

Driving between Old Faithful and West Thumb, you twice pass signs identifying the Continental Divide. This makes it difficult to understand the concept of the divide or to visualize where the water is going. Maps show the Continental Divide as a thin line crossing irregularly from the park's western boundary to leave the park near the southeast corner. What does this line represent?

A *divide* is a geographer's term for the topographic boundary between adjacent drainage basins or watersheds. Runoff from precipitation that falls on one side of the divide will find its way into one stream system; on the other side of the divide, surface runoff discharges into another stream system.

The Continental Divide, (also known as the Great Divide) is the main watershed boundary of the North American continent. As shown in Figure 3, the divide separates areas that drain to the Pacific Ocean (green) and the Atlantic Ocean (lighter green). The area around Old Faithful Village drains to the Atlantic Ocean via the Firehole River, a tributary of the Madison River. About 9 miles east of Old Faithful, the Grand Loop Road crosses the Continental Divide at Craig Pass, entering the watershed of the Lewis River, which flows to the Pacific Ocean via the Snake and Columbia rivers. A raindrop falling on one side of Craig Pass may be destined for Astoria, Oregon, while a drop falling a few feet away on the other side of the pass could meet the Gulf of Mexico near New Orleans.

Figure 3. Map of stream flow directions and the Continental Divide.

Isa Lake is situated right across this line at Craig Pass. This is a rare type of place where the top of the divide is actually flat enough to permit a small depression where a pond can form. Looking at the lake, you would think that the water from its southwestern outlet would flow to the Pacific and that from the northeastern outlet to the Atlantic, but this is not so.

In this area the Continental Divide doubles back on itself and the road crosses it again, as you can see from the sketch. Using the old name, *continental watershed*, might make it easier to visualize.

—With contributions by Linton A. Brown

The grade descending northeastward from Isa Lake was so steep in the early days of the first stagecoach road that drivers dubbed it Corkscrew Hill. According to Lee Whittlesey's book *Yellowstone Place Names*, drivers enjoyed terrifying the "dudes" by rushing down this narrow and tortuous hill. Since that time, realignment has reduced the grade so much that you hardly notice the hill.

10.5/8.9 🚶 ⛵ DeLacy Creek Trailhead opposite the parking area. **DeLacy Creek Trail** leads through forest and meadow south 3.5 miles (5.6 km) to the shore of Shoshone Lake, and connects with trails around that lake and along Lewis Lake channel to Lewis Lake and the South Entrance road. During most of the summer, it may be hard to keep your boots dry. Parallel deep tracks show heavy use by hikers and fishermen.

Walter W. DeLacy, for whom the creek was named, was an army captain and civil engineer who passed through this part of future park territory in 1863 with a party of prospectors. Shoshone Lake was called DeLacy's Lake for a time, in honor of his discovery that it is part of the Snake River drainage, not of the Madison River drainage, as previously believed.

10.8/8.6 🪑(11) 🔭 DeLacy Creek picnic area on a short side road.

11.1/8.3 P Shoshone Point turnout for a view of distant Shoshone Lake. The Teton Range about 50 miles (80 km) away may also be seen on a clear day.

In 1914, here on the Grand Loop Road, a stagecoach robber stole more than $1000 in cash and jewelry from 165 passengers. This time (unlike after other similar incidents) the robber was caught and served time in prison. He was Edward Trafton, a notorious horse thief and robber.

Shoshone Lake can be reached only by hiking, riding horseback (trailhead at 4.2/15.2), or paddling a canoe up the Lewis River from its neighbor, Lewis Lake—or on skis in winter. Shoshone is the second largest lake in Yellowstone and sports a major geyser basin near its western shore.

Before it was called Shoshone, this large lake bore the name Madison Lake and then the names of several men who named it for themselves. Finally, Prof. Frank Bradley, chief geologist of the 1872 Hayden Expedition to Yellowstone, decided it should be named for the Indians who frequented it. The Shoshoni tribe—their name probably meaning "grass house people"—lived in the area between the mountains of Wyoming and the present state of Oregon and as far south as Nevada.

The Grand Loop Road crosses the east summit (at 8521 ft/2597 m) before reaching the next crossing of the Continental Divide.

15.3/4.1 Continental Divide (8391 ft/ 2558 m). This is the east side of the Continental Divide's loop. Though it's more than 100 feet (30 m) higher than Craig Pass, this point lacks a name. Now you've left the Columbia River tributary area (see the sketch in "Understanding the Continental Divide").

About 1 mile (1.6 km) to the southwest of this point, old maps showed an unnamed lake, later a "Two Ocean Pond." Although old-timers claimed to have seen this lake (and to have fished it) as early as 1915 and as late as 1938, recent maps made from aerial photos do not show it. Was it a transient meltwater pond or a shallow lake that became a meadow? It remains a mystery.

15.6/3.8 ⋔ **(14)** 🔟 ♿ Divide picnic area (also called East Divide) on the left (north).

18.7/0.7 Ⓟ A wide area in the road just after a major curve provides parking for a panoramic view of Yellowstone Lake. This spot was called Lake View as early as the 1890s. Between then and now the lodgepoles grew tall but then burned, allowing us to see lake and mountains in a 180° arc once again.

Lake View Panorama

If the day is clear you can see, left to right (north to south):

West Thumb Bay's north edge in middle ground.

Absaroka Range in the distance—these are 50-million-year-old volcanic mountains. Absaroka was the name that the Crow called themselves, meaning "children of the large-beaked bird" and pronounced ab-SAHR-o-ka. Due east of the viewpoint are four closely grouped, pyramid-shaped peaks: Doane, Langford, and Stevenson are inside the park (and all more than 10,000 ft/3050 m high), and Plentycoups, the highest at 10,937 feet (3334 m), on the eastern border.

Duck Lake in middle ground, **West Thumb Bay**'s south edge in the background, with more Absarokas behind it.

Flat Mountain just beyond the bay (elevation 9168 ft/2794 m), noted for its red cliffs.

Mt. Sheridan at the far right and relatively close to the viewer (elevation 10,305 ft/ 3141 m).

Referring to this lake view, explorers David E. Folsom and Charles W. Cook wrote prophetically in 1869:

> We ascended the summit of a neighboring hill and took a final look at Yellowstone Lake. Nestled among the forest-crowned hills which bounded our vision lay this inland sea, its crystal waves dancing and sparkling in the sunlight as if laughing with joy for their wild freedom. It is a scene of transcendent beauty which has been viewed by few white men, and we felt glad to have looked upon it before its primeval solitude should be broken by the crowds of pleasure seekers which at no distant day will throng to its shores.

For a similar view completely off the highway, take the Yellowstone Lake Overlook Trail from West Thumb Junction (described on page 131).

19.0/0.4 Ⓟ 🚶 Short, steep, unmaintained trail to **Duck Lake**. This little lake has an unusual geologic history. About 10,000 years ago a glacial ice dam gave way and allowed water to drain out quickly. Removal of the load of water drastically lowered the pressure above a group of hot springs, allowing the superheated water to flash to steam. Duck Lake is an explosion crater filled with water. **[GEO.16]**

There's a good trail to Duck Lake from West Thumb Geyser Basin.

19.4/0.0 West Thumb Junction. For West Thumb Geyser Basin turn left (north), then turn right (east) immediately. For Fishing Bridge Junction and other points on the Grand Loop Road, also turn left (north). Grant Village and the South Entrance are to the south, Old Faithful Village to the west.

West Thumb Geyser Basin and facilities at West Thumb are described on pages 130–35 and Grant Village on pages 126–28.

The Bechler Region

Proceeding counterclockwise from the West Entrance, the next roads that go into the park are a pair of very short ones that don't connect with any other Yellowstone roads. Thus, they can't really be called entrance roads. This corner of the park is called the Bechler Region. More popularly, people call it the Cascade Corner, because it's so well supplied with water and contains so many waterfalls. It's a great place for backpackers and horsepackers (and recently llama packers) who want to escape the crowds, but a long trip for most day visitors.

Access to the Bechler Ranger Station and Cave Falls is on good highways from southeastern Idaho or via a very poor and primitive dirt road called Grassy Lake Road (or Ashton-Flagg Ranch Road), which runs outside the park's southern boundary. We'll only describe the better route here. If you want to take the Grassy Lake Road, inquire locally about its current condition before starting on it. From Ashton to the Bechler Ranger Station is 23 miles (37 km); from West Yellowstone to Bechler is about 80 miles (130 km).

FROM WEST YELLOWSTONE OR ASHTON TO THE BECHLER REGION

Not far west of West Yellowstone, Montana, on U.S. Highway 20 is Targhee Pass, used by the Bannock tribe on their annual trek to hunt buffalo. South of the pass is a wide fertile valley, a checkerboard of private and national forest lands. State parks near Henrys Lake and Island Park Reservoir offer camping and hiking possibilities and fishing for trout and whitefish. Harriman State Park on Island Park Reservoir is an important wintering spot for trumpeter swans and home to a variety of other wildlife. The park also has a visitor center and over 20 miles (32 km) of trails.

In describing a trail running along the west boundary of the park, Carl Schreier, in his book *Hiking Yellowstone Trails*, tells us: "This side of the park boundary is easy to keep track of because the forest is clear-cut up to the edge of

The Bechler Region and Environs

the park. From outer space, this is the second most visible man-made feature on earth. The most visible is the Great Wall of China." However, the Forest Service has done considerable replanting in Targhee National Forest.

Traveling along U.S. 20 between West Yellowstone and Ashton, Idaho, you might take one or both of the following side excursions in Targhee National Forest.

Side excursion to Big Springs

A side road leading east from U.S. 20 at the tiny town of Macks Inn takes you in 3 or 4 miles (5–6 km) to **Big Springs**, a source of Henrys Fork of the Snake River and a truly beautiful spot. Small rafts or boats without motors may use part of the river, and there's a trail along it.

Side excursion to Mesa Falls

For a delightful short trip very close to the western edge of Yellowstone, visit Upper and Lower Mesa falls on Idaho Highway 47. These two beautiful waterfalls on Henrys Fork cascade over the edge of lava that flowed from the Yellowstone caldera over half a million

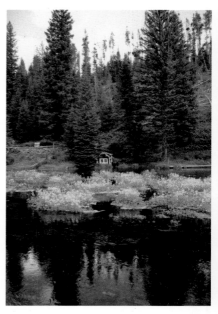

Big Springs harbors islands of flowers.

years ago. This lava flowed over the eastern section of a much older, similar crater, the Island Park caldera. (For an explanation of these calderas, see the "Geological History" chapter.) **[GEO.8]**

To reach Upper and Lower Mesa falls from the north, take Idaho 47, which intersects U.S. 20 about 36 miles south of West Yellowstone. Coming from southeastern Idaho, go east from Ashton about 5 miles (8 km) and then north on Idaho 47.

The 114-foot (35 m) **Upper Mesa Falls** is about 12 miles (19 km) from the U.S. 20 turnoff. Following the short trail leading to the falls, you stand above its

Upper Mesa Falls waters a lush green garden of moss.

exhilarating roar. The Big Falls Inn has been reconstructed as an interpretive center, with full access for wheelchairs.

A short distance south of Upper Mesa Falls is the turnoff for the less spectacular, 65-foot (20 m) **Lower Mesa Falls**, with its attractive 1930s stonework.

There are three Forest Service campgrounds along Idaho 47. Near

Warm River, the road drops steeply over the Island Park caldera rim. The contrast between forested mountain terrain and gently rolling farmland is sudden and striking. Potatoes, barley, and alfalfa are grown in these fertile plains. To the east you'll catch views of the Tetons.

~

Continuing to the Bechler Region
About 6 miles (9.5 km) east of Ashton on Idaho 47, Green Timber Road goes east. Take Green Timber Road to reach the Bechler Region of the park in about another 17 miles (27 km). Before long, the pavement changes to a good quality gravel surface, just as you enter Targhee National Forest. You cross into Wyoming just before reaching the roads leading to Bechler Ranger Station and Cave Falls.

The Bechler Region, or Cascade Corner, and Its Water
Named for Gustavus Bechler, a topographer who entered the area with the 1872 Hayden Expedition, the Bechler Region is best characterized in one word: water. Streams and marshes are everywhere. The park ranger at Bechler remarked on June 30 in a recent year: "Bechler Meadows is a lake!" The whole corner abounds in waterfalls. Within a 10-mile (16 km) radius of Bechler Ranger Station are Cave, Bechler, and spectacularly beautiful Union Falls (250 ft/76 m high), as well as Rainbow, Iris, Colonnade, Ouzel, Dunanda, Silver Scarf, and Terraced falls. Farther along the trails are others too numerous to mention.

The drawbacks to all this water are several: hikers must wait until the latter part of the summer to enjoy the area—and even then must be prepared to ford streams that may be as deep as mid thigh—and mosquitoes and other pesky insects like it here, too. Fortunately, they die off in late summer.

In the 1920s, this copious supply of water inspired repeated proposals to dam the Bechler or Fall rivers and deliver the water to Idaho farmers, allowing the use of Yellowstone Park water for irrigation or even removing the Bechler Region from park territory. But Yellowstone's supporters were successful in defeating the several bills and amendments introduced in Congress.

Around the same time, a member of the National Parks Association, writing about his exploration of the area, stated a bit cheekily: "Persons living near a national park who feel themselves harmed by their situation must bear their burden cheerfully" (quoted in *The Yellowstone Story* by Aubrey L. Haines). Idaho potato farmers get water instead from Grassy Lake Reservoir (built in the late 1930s) and from Jackson Lake.

IN YELLOWSTONE'S BECHLER REGION

The two road logs below tell you about the road to the ranger station and then the one to Cave Falls.

Road Log

0.0 Take the left turn (north) for the ranger station and (**0.1**) cross the Yellowstone Park boundary.

1.1 🏕 🚻♿ The **Bechler Ranger Station** is housed in a building dating from 1911. A ranger is available every day in summer from 8 AM to 4:30 PM to issue the required fishing and overnight camping permits and to answer questions.

🚶 🐎 🎣 Since Cascade Corner is a totally undeveloped area, horseback, llama, and backpacking trips, hiking, and fishing are the only activities here. At the ranger station, you can pick up a free guide to day trips that start from the station or from Cave Falls. Many long trails lead into the backcountry, starting from here or from the Grassy Lake Road. Backcountry trail books and good maps are essential for these trails.

To reach Cave Falls, continue eastward on Green Timber Road instead of turning toward the Bechler Ranger Station.

▲ A National Forest campground is just 0.2 mile (0.3 km) outside the boundary, but there are no camping facilities inside the park in this area.

Road Log

0.0 Yellowstone Park boundary. Here you are closer to the Fall River, and the elevation is a little lower than at the Bechler Ranger Station boundary crossing.

0.3 🚶 **South Boundary Trail** is to the east; **Bechler River Trail** is marked to the west. If you want to join the South Boundary Trail here, you must ford the wide and deep Fall River. The western part of the Bechler River Trail loop reaches the ranger station in about 2 miles (3 km). Follow the road for the northern part of the trail, which will take you to Bechler Falls.

0.9 🅿 Parking area to the right for a short trail and views of **Cave Falls** of the Fall River. This waterfall is remarkable for its breadth—it's 250 feet wide and 20 feet high (76 m by 6 m).

1.1 🪧(4) 🚶 🚻♿(2) The road to the left at the fork loops around a picnic area. It takes you to the **Bechler River Trailhead**, leading north along the river. **Bechler Falls** of the Bechler River is about a mile (1.5 km) up the trail.

Cave Falls takes its name from a large cave to the left of the picture.

Approaches to the South Entrance

You'll be entering Yellowstone through the South Entrance if you include a visit to Grand Teton National Park in your travel plans. It's also the closest entrance for those interested in water sports or in backcountry hiking in the relatively undeveloped southern one-third of the park. The spectacular Tetons loom above the valleys from east or west and afford splendid photographing opportunities.

As much as nine thousand years ago, Native Americans left evidence that they were here. Then in the last two centuries, many colorful characters have passed through Jackson Hole. Beaver trappers came as early as the 1820s, and gold prospectors followed in the 1860s, but the latter never found pay dirt in commercial quantities. Some people found this a good place to escape the law, but many came as homesteaders and established ranches. By the beginning of the 20th century, dude ranches were catering to wealthy Easterners. Today tourism and cattle are both important to the economy.

Jackson, Wyoming, has an airport and rental car agencies. Accommodations are plentiful, as are outdoor activities of every kind. The distance from Jackson to the South Entrance is 58 miles (93 km).

There's another way to approach Yellowstone's South Entrance, one that comes from the southeast rather than passing through Jackson. It follows U.S. Highways 26 and 287 from the town of Dubois near the northern end of the Wind River Range, across beautiful Togwotee Pass, and northwest to reach Yellowstone.

JACKSON, WYOMING, AND ENVIRONS
Population: 8650

Since World War II, Jackson has become a full-blown summer and winter tourist center, replete with motels, restaurants, shops, and sports outfitters. Perhaps symbolic of its cachet, Pres. Bill Clinton and family chose the area twice in the mid 1990s for their August vacation. And, not surprisingly, you pay more here for most accommodations and restaurant food than in any other gateway city

Approaches to the South Entrance

around Yellowstone. There are numerous upscale ranches, houses, and condominiums in and around Jackson.

Fur trappers named the large valley east of the Teton Range Jackson's Hole for a fellow trapper. A hole to them meant this type of valley surrounded by mountains. In 1895, a wagon road was completed from West Thumb in Yellowstone Park through the South Entrance to the new Wyoming settlements to the southeast.

This is an area with many things to do; in fact, you need a day or more just to visit the most outstanding stops in Grand Teton National Park, with perhaps a boat trip or a short hike.

A Sampling of Summer Activities in Jackson Hole
- In and near Jackson: rodeos and "shootouts," chairlift at Snow King, National Wildlife Art Museum, National Fish Hatchery
- In Teton Village: aerial tram to Rendezvous Mountain, Grand Teton Music Festival classical concerts in July and August
- In and around Grand Teton National Park: ranger-led hikes and campfire lectures, float trips and white-water rafting trips, horseback riding and pack trips, fishing, climbing, and biking

The **Snake River** has its source in the southern backcountry of Yellowstone, then traverses Jackson Hole. Its name does not come from the snake-like path it takes through the area, but rather from the French Canadian trapper name for the Shoshoni tribe: Snakes (*Serpents* in French). According to some researchers, the trappers misunderstood the sign Shoshoni people used to identify themselves: a sinuous hand motion with index finger extended, indicating that they were grass weavers. Instead, the trappers thought the sign meant the track of a snake.

Grand Teton National Park came into being in 1929 after much disagreement between advocates for adding the Teton country to Yellowstone and local ranchers interested in keeping the land private. At that time, Congress decided not to extend Yellowstone Park in this direction, but simply placed the land in the public domain. Grand Teton reached its present size only in 1950, with the addition of the part of Jackson Hole that includes the outer road (U.S. Highways 26/89/191).

For complete information about this park, write to The Superintendent, Grand Teton National Park, P.O. Drawer 170, Moose, WY 83012; call (307) 739-3300; or visit the National Park Service Web site at www.nps.gov/grte.

FROM JACKSON TO MORAN JUNCTION

As you leave town going north on U.S. Highway 89/191 from the center of Jackson, you'll pass the National Wildlife Art Museum, the National Elk Refuge, and the National Fish Hatchery. At Gros Ventre Junction, a paved road to the northeast leads to a campground and the town of Kelly.

A few miles farther north is the **Jackson Hole Airport**, its runway newly lengthened by 600 feet to better accommodate large jet aircraft. The runway is completely within Grand Teton National Park.

At **Moose Junction**, about 13 miles (21 km) north of Jackson, you'll have to choose your route to Jackson Lake Junction. Either turn onto Teton Park Road, which takes you closer to the lakes and mountains, or stay on U.S. Highways 26/89/191, a bit longer, yet faster and with equally spectacular views. On each road, there are lots of turnouts and several interpretive displays.

The wide Snake River flows past the Tetons.

Northwest of Moose Junction is a Grand Teton National Park entrance station. Visitor centers are at Moose and Colter Bay; a ranger station is at South Jenny Lake. We'll describe only the eastern highway route here.

U.S. Highways 26/89/191

Continuing straight north beyond Moose Junction, the highway intersects with Antelope Flats Road, which leads to several campgrounds, the town of Kelly, and the Gros Ventre slide. "Gros ventre"—pronounced GROW VAUNT here—

means big belly in French. The low mountain range here and a subgroup of the Blackfeet tribe share this name.

The **Gros Ventre Slide** can be seen east of the main highway. It's interesting to compare this landslide with the Quake Lake slide near the West Entrance to Yellowstone (see page 30). The Quake Lake slide buried a campground and killed 28 people in 1959 as the result of a very strong earthquake. The Gros Ventre landslide occurred when the unusually wet spring of 1925 caused sandstone layers overlying slippery shale to give way suddenly, shaken by a relatively minor earthquake. The landslide itself killed no one, but two years later the natural dam it had created suddenly gave way, flooding the town of Kelly downriver and killing six of its citizens.

Eighteen miles (29 km) from Moose Junction you reach Moran Junction. (See "From Moran Junction to the South Entrance" below.)

FROM DUBOIS TO MORAN JUNCTION

Instead of traveling via Jackson from the south, you may choose to reach the South Entrance via the southeast, from Dubois.

Dubois, Wyoming

Population: 950

A small western town with one main street, Dubois (called DOO-boys by residents) is about 83 miles (134 km) from the South Entrance on an excellent road over high Togwotee (TOE-guh-dee) Pass. Dubois has inexpensive motels, several restaurants, and the National Bighorn Sheep Interpretive Center, where tours can be arranged to visit the sheep's fall and winter range.

U.S. Highways 26 and 287

Outside the town, once a center for the production of railway ties, are now cattle and guest ranches. Spectacular striped hills, composed of alternating red and white layers of sedimentary rock, line the road west of town.

Shoshone and Bridger-Teton national forests offer two high-altitude picnic areas and two campgrounds as you cross **Togwotee Pass**, at 9544 feet (2909 m) a higher mountain pass than any inside Yellowstone. Togwotee was a medicine man and chief of the Sheepeater tribe. He led early explorers across this pass and guided Gen. Philip H. Sheridan on his expedition in 1882.

After you cross the pass, rolling hills and meadows greet the eye, with high mountains on all sides. You descend to the Buffalo Fork of the Snake River and cross the east boundary of Grand Teton National Park. Reaching Moran Junction, you may continue toward Yellowstone or turn left for the Tetons or Jackson.

The Tetons and How They Got So High

The name Tetons (Les Trois Tetons—The Three Teats in the somewhat indecent French of the early trappers) comes from the three great summits you can see from the Idaho side, although there are many more than three peaks in the range. These mountains are truly awe inspiring: 12 peaks exceed 12,000 feet (3650 m), and the Grand Teton is 13,770 feet (4197 m) high.

The striking difference in elevation from that of Jackson Hole is what makes these mountains so special. There aren't a lot of places where you can gaze up at a sky full of mountain peaks whose tops are 5000 to 7500 feet (1500–2300 m) above you while you stand at their base—with no foothills in between! As author Owen Wister wrote over 100 years ago: "The way in which they come up without any heralding of foothills seems as though they rose from the sea."

How did these mountains get so high? The eminent author John McPhee, although not a geologist, describes the process like this in his book, *Rising from the Plains*: "The crust extends, the earth stretches, the land pulls apart—and one result is a north-south-trending normal fault, fifty miles long. On the two sides of this fault, blocks of country swing [as though] on distant hinges like a facing pair of trapdoors—one rising, one sagging. The rising side is the rock of the nascent Tetons, carrying upward on its back the stratified deposits. . . ."

Geologists have proven that the Tetons certainly *did* rise, though not from the sea, as it seemed to Wister. This range of mountains was formed as part of the east-west pulling apart of the North American plate—an activity that is still going on from Arizona to Idaho and Wyoming. In the Teton area, the pulling finally overcame the strength of the rocks, and they broke to form a *fault*, that is, a fracture in the earth where the two sides move past each other. This fault runs roughly north to south and slants down steeply to the east. The more the rocks are pulled apart, the more space needs to be filled in. The block that is sinking helps to fill the gap that would otherwise develop.

The steepness of the mountain front that looms over Jackson Hole testifies to the strength and resistance to erosion of the 2.7-billion-year-old rocks recently exposed by the fault. The fault is still active, the land continues to sink, and the mountains continue to rise, but streams have brought sediments in to fill the valley floor. This process has been going on for about 9 million years so far.

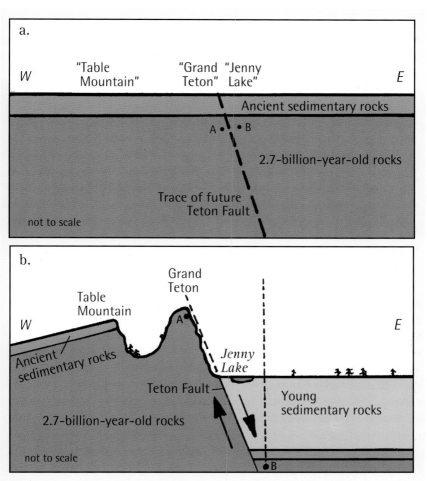

Figure 4. Cross sections showing the formation of the Teton Range.
View looking north, **4a**, shows the situation just before faulting started, where the features named in quotation marks are not yet formed. **4b** shows the situation today. The fault is indicated by a solid line, which continues as a dashed line in order to show where the fault was before the rocks were eroded. Point B started out opposite point A, but the eastern side moved down while the western side rose, separating the two points by about 19,000 feet (5800 m). Primarily we notice how the Grand Teton towers over Jenny Lake, but the tension pulling the plates apart is east-west. This tension is relieved by having point B moved eastward, along with its block of continent, as is indicated by the vertical dotted line. The Ancient sedimentary rocks, which are about 600 million years old, were deposited before the faulting, whereas the Young sedimentary rocks have been forming since the faulting, especially on the lake bottoms.

FROM MORAN JUNCTION TO THE SOUTH ENTRANCE

One of two Teton Park entrance stations is located at **Moran Junction**, just north of where U.S. 26/287 joins U.S. 89/191. Going north for about 3.5 miles

(5.5 km) takes you to Jackson Lake Junction, where the Teton Park Road joins the U.S. highway.

South of the junction is **Jackson Lake Dam**, first completed in 1911 and rebuilt in 1989. The dam has raised the water level of Jackson Lake as much as 39 feet (12 m). In August and September of dry years, drawdown for irrigation creates ugly mud flats in the northern section of Jackson Lake.

Mt. Moran rises majestically over Willow Flats and Jackson Lake.

A short distance north of Jackson Lake Junction is the turnoff for **Jackson Lake Lodge**, famous for its luxurious accommodations and its views of the mountains. It was built by John D. Rockefeller, Jr. and opened in 1955.

The next turnoff to the west is for **Colter Bay Village**. It has complete visitor facilities, including a campground, a marina, and the Indian Arts Museum, where Native American guest artists demonstrate traditional crafts. About a mile beyond the Colter Bay turnoff is one for **Leeks Marina** and the University of Wyoming/National Park Service environmental research center.

In the last 10 miles (16 km) of highway within Grand Teton National Park, there are four picnic areas and the **Lizard Creek campground**. You'll find another picnic area along the Rockefeller Parkway just to the north.

Stretching about 7 miles (11 km) between Grand Teton and Yellowstone parks is the **John D. Rockefeller, Jr., Memorial Parkway**. Congress created the parkway in 1972 in recognition of Rockefeller's work in establishing or expanding several national parks, including Teton Park. Though called a parkway, it's more than just a road; it encompasses many acres of land between the two big parks.

About 2 miles (3 km) from the Yellowstone boundary is **Flagg Ranch Resort** (with new facilities opened in 1996), where you'll find cabins and motel-style rooms, campsites with full RV hookups, a restaurant, general store, laundry, and service station. In winter, Flagg Ranch is the southern point of departure for snowmobiles and snowcoaches to travel over the unplowed roads to Old

Faithful. The entrance road to Flagg Ranch is also the eastern end of the Grassy Lake Road, along which there are eight free campsites. This area suffered a forest fire in the summer of 2000.

About 10 miles (16 km) west of Flagg Ranch, at Grassy Lake Reservoir's eastern tip, is **Beula Lake Trailhead**. This trail, at first climbing rather steeply, goes less than 3 miles (5 km) into Yellowstone to a lake prized for its cutthroat trout (catch and release only). Farther along the Grassy Lake Road are other trailheads for backcountry trails into Yellowstone. Backcountry trail books and topographic maps are essential for hiking these trails.

To the east of the Rockefeller Parkway between Flagg Ranch and Yellowstone's South Entrance rises **Huckleberry Mountain**, topped with 2-million-year-old Huckleberry Ridge tuff.

To Old Faithful

Yellowstone Lake

West Thumb Jct.
7803 ft 2378m

West Thumb Geyser
Basin map, p. 132

Grant Village

Grant Village
map, p. 127

Riddle Lake

7988 ft
2435 m

Riddle
Lake Tr.

Dogshead
& Lewis R.
Channel Tr.

DIVIDE

Lewis Lake

Heart
Lake Tr.

Aster Cr.

Hot
Springs

PITCHSTONE

Lewis Falls

RED

MOUNTAINS

Heart Lake

PLATEAU

Mt. Sheridan
10,305 ft
3141 m

Pitchstone
Plateau Tr.

N

21.5 mi (34.6 km)

Lewis River

| 0 | 1 | 2 | 3 mi |
| 0 | 1 2 3 4 | 5 km |

Moose Falls

Crawfish Cr.

Snake River

Moose
Falls Tr.

Tanager Lake

South Entrance
6886 ft 2099 m

South
Boundary Tr.

**ROCKEFELLER
PARKWAY**

To Jackson

© 2002 J. O. Chapple

South Entrance to West Thumb Junction

From the South Entrance to West Thumb Junction

Along this entrance road, you'll find two fine waterfalls and views into Lewis River Canyon. Just east of West Thumb Junction is West Thumb Geyser Basin.

Engineer Hiram Chittenden reported the South Entrance Road in 1900 as being "in a wretched condition and a disgrace to the Government." Improved very gradually, it was not heavily used until after the establishment of Grand Teton National Park. It's now the second most popular entrance.

It's about 21 miles (35 km) from the South Entrance to West Thumb Junction and the Grand Loop Road.

Road Log

0.0/21.5 Yellowstone Park boundary.

0.1/21.4 👫 South Entrance station. Stop here to pay the entrance fee (see "Travel Tips" for fee information). For backcountry, boating, or fishing permits, visit the ranger station.

👫 The **Snake River Ranger Station**, built in the 1990s, is at the right (east) just beyond the entrance station.

🚶 To take the South Boundary Trail to the east, you must ford the river either near the ranger station or south of the park boundary. Prospector Walter DeLacy wrote in 1863 of hot springs with high cones near the junction of the Snake and Lewis rivers, but access is difficult, so most of us will not see them. There used to be a hand-propelled cable ferry that park employees used in crossing the Snake River, until it was washed away in 1995.

🚶 The **South Boundary Trailhead** to the west is much more accessible. You can find it by walking through the government housing area and going in a straight line from the north edge of the horse corral, where you see a trail sign to Grassy Lake and "Bechler Ranger Station 24 mi." In less than 1 mile (1.5 km), you glimpse Tanager Lake, but the trail bypasses it. The lake was named after the official park bird, the western tanager. The most interesting feature of this trail is the perfectly straight vista created by the downing of lodgepole pines, which are still lying about. At the turn of the 20th century, they were cut down to mark the south boundary. Even today, hunters need to know exactly where the boundary is. Moose are sometimes seen around the lake, and mosquitoes and biting flies may be plentiful, even in late summer.

0.2/21.3 ⊼**(15)** 🚻⛐**(3)** Snake River picnic area, between the road and the Lewis River.

🚶 ⬅ A pleasant 1-mile (1.6 km) trail from the north end of the picnic area takes you to Moose Falls. The first 0.4 mile (0.6 km), a popular area with fishermen, follows the Lewis River after its confluence with the Snake.

1.5/20.0 P Bridge and parking for **Moose Falls** of Crawfish Creek. A trail a few hundred feet long (perhaps 100 meters) takes you down to the brink of a delightful, small waterfall in a mossy sylvan setting. Near the falls and overlook, you can find shiny jet-black swirls of *ob-*

Moose Falls rushes over hard lava toward the Lewis River.

sidian (volcanic glass) in the rock. Crawfish Creek is named for the small freshwater crustaceans that thrive in its thermally warmed water, same as crayfish or crawdads.

The long, gradual ascent of the road beginning here takes you up the southern flank of the Yellowstone caldera.

4.2/17.3 South end of Lewis River Canyon. Fire damage that begins just north of here is from the 1988 Snake River complex of fires. You can still see where the fire crossed the canyon and burned down into it.

6.7/14.8 P An interpretive sign about the 1988 fires.

6.8/14.7 P Best overlook of several possible ones (only usable when going north) at the north end of **Lewis Canyon**. Don't stop on the dangerously soft gravel shoulders along here—use the areas with widened pavement.

The rocks in the upper portions of the cliffs you see across the canyon are Lava Creek tuff, part of the vast eruption that formed the Yellowstone caldera 630,000 years ago. The Lewis River has cut down through these easily eroded rocks and is now exposing older lavas at the bottom of the canyon. Younger rhyolite lavas are west of the road. (For more about the caldera, see "Yellowstone Volcanism" in the "Geological History" chapter.) **[GEO.10]**

8.0/13.5 Approximate point where the Lewis River begins to cut its canyon.

8.3/13.2 🚶 Pitchstone Plateau Trailhead. This trail climbs steadily from the road to the plateau and then descends gradually some 1500 feet (475 m) in its 18-mile (29 km) course across the pla- teau to Grassy Lake Reservoir just south of the park.

The Eight Plateaus

Over the years of Yellowstone Park's history, explorers and geologists have discovered and named eight plateaus within the much larger Yellowstone plateau (see map for locations). Four were created by volcanic flows; the other four simply fit the definition of a *plateau*; that is, an extensive raised land area that is relatively flat.

1. **Pitchstone Plateau** is a geologically new expanse of rhyolite lava that flowed out of the caldera only 70,000 to 80,000 years ago in the most recent of the 30 or so relatively small eruptions of lava and ash since the last great caldera explosion. Since rain and snowmelt percolate rapidly through this ground, few streams are created, and trees grow only along the ridges. Today's hiker can find the pressure ridges caused by the wrinkling of lava that cooled at the surface. *Pitchstone* is another name for obsidian or volcanic glass, but such glass is not especially common on this plateau.

Approximate Locations of Yellowstone Plateaus

© 2002 J. O. Chapple

2. **Two Ocean Plateau** is a non-volcanic, high, rolling area about 10,000 feet (3050 m) high in the remote Thorofare corner. Its name comes from an area just south of the park boundary, from which creeks flow toward the two oceans. Not far from Two Ocean Pass are the sources of both the Snake and the Yellowstone rivers. Mountain man Jim Bridger knew the plateau well and may have been its discoverer in the early 19th century.

3. **Mirror Plateau** has an average elevation of about 9000 feet (2750 m).

It takes its name from little Mirror Lake, which is located on the drainage divide between the Lamar and Yellowstone rivers.

4. **Buffalo Plateau** was first seen and named by a group of prospectors in 1870, when it was a grazing ground for thousands of buffalo.

5. **Blacktail Deer Plateau** is an expanse of grass- and tree-covered glacial debris about 7000 feet (2130 m) high.

6. **Solfatara Plateau** is a small and fairly recent volcanic flow dating back 105,000 years. The first known *solfatara*, near Naples, Italy, is a volcanic crater that exhales hydrogen sulfide, sulfur dioxide, and steam. In Yellowstone, the Solfatara Plateau is an area with many fumaroles, where your nose may easily detect sulfurous gases.

7. **Central Plateau** is centered in the lower loop of the Grand Loop Road. The Nez Perce lava flow on this plateau is 160,000 years old.

8. **Madison Plateau** is the result of several lava flows of different ages. The West Entrance Road and the Grand Loop Road near Old Faithful both pass along its edges.

10.2/11.3 P **Lewis Falls** parking along the road on both sides of the Lewis River bridge. Here the flow of the Lewis River turns sharply from south to east. A rocky climb to the top of the falls on the upstream side of the bridge provides a pleasant short hike.

The river is gradually cutting down through the Pitchstone Plateau lavas that filled the Yellowstone caldera to over-

Lewis Falls drops about 30 feet (9 m).

flowing in this area. You can tell that the lavas cooled quickly from the presence of black shiny obsidian, where the lava cooled too fast to form crystals. Lewis Falls is approximately at the caldera's southern boundary.

East of the bridge, the river turns south again. The wide, calm river in its peaceful meadow gives no hint of the deep canyon it's scouring a few miles downstream. Soggy meadows like this one are good places to find moose, who love to browse standing in water.

11.4/10.1 🏞(10) 🏚🚻(2) ⛺ ⛵ 🚣 A short side road to the west leads to **Lewis Lake Campground**, picnic area, and boat launch site. The campground has about 85 sites available on a first-come, first-served basis. There are no showers here. Ironically, this campground may be closed early in the summer due to excess water.

Lewis Lake formed where the rocks of the caldera rim resisted erosion by the Lewis River, creating a natural dam. The lake is about 3 miles (4 km) long and nearly as wide, with a maximum depth of 108 feet (33 m). Anglers catch unusually large nonnative lake trout and brown trout here.

The lake was named for Captain Meriwether Lewis of the famous 1803–6 Lewis and Clark Expedition. Although the men did not enter the park's territory, the expedition added a great deal to the knowledge of the vast American west and bestirred the public's curiosity about it.

All types of boats up to 40 feet in length are permitted on Lewis Lake. A popular option is to launch a canoe here and follow the western shore of the lake to the channel that connects to Shoshone Lake about 3 miles (5 km) to the north. Both boating and overnight permits are required.

14.3/7.2 ⚐ 🦌 🏕 Heart Lake Trailhead, from a large parking area on a short side road to the east. The trail is heavily used by both hikers and horseback parties. Before reaching Heart Lake in about 7 miles (11 km), you'll notice the many hot springs and small geysers along Witch Creek. The trail's first 4 or 5 miles are relatively flat. Then it passes along the side of Factory Hill at the northern edge of the Red Mountains before descending about 500 feet (150 m) to reach the lake, which abounds in large trout. From this trail you can also climb to the summit of Mount Sheridan—a 2700-foot (820 m) climb in about 3 miles (5 km).

Heart Lake Geyser Basin saw the tragic death of Yellowstone's Research Geologist Roderick A. Hutchinson and a colleague in an avalanche in March 1997. Hutchinson contributed much to the understanding of the park's thermal areas in his 27 years as a staff member.

◄ Historians believe that Heart Lake was named for an 1840s hunter named Hart Hunney and that the spelling was changed from Hart to Heart in the 1870s because of the lake's shape. However, you can see from the map of Yellowstone that Lewis Lake is the one that's more conventionally heart-shaped! Heart Lake has both cutthroat and lake trout; in fact, it yielded the largest fish ever caught in the park—a 42 pound (19 kg) lake trout.

14.5/7.0 ⚐ 🏕 ◄ Dogshead and Lewis River Channel trailheads to the west. These are two routes to the same place, Shoshone Lake, the second largest lake in Yellowstone.

Dogshead Creek flows south into Lewis Lake. The Dog's-Heads in Greece are a range of hills where a famous Roman victory was won, but whether this was the source of the name in Yellowstone, or whether the name originally referred to a coyote or wolf, no one knows for sure. The **Dogshead Trail** is the shorter but less interesting of the two trails, reaching Shoshone Lake in about 4.5 miles (7 km).

The **Lewis River Channel Trail** reaches the channel in 3 miles (4.8 km) and Shoshone Lake in about 7 miles (11 km), skirting Lewis Lake on the way. The channel is a favorite with fishermen in the fall, when brown trout are spawning.

If you're traveling south, you'll see the **Red Mountains** looming almost ahead of you in this area, with Mount Sheridan their highest point. Mount

Sheridan sports one of the three fire towers remaining in the park.

17.4/4.1 🚶 **Riddle Lake Trailhead** to the east. An easy hike of about 4.5 miles (7 km) round trip traverses burned forest and meadows full of wildflowers to the lake, covered with lily pads and backed by Mount Sheridan. Before mid July this trail may be soggy, and it's usually closed for bear management until that time.

The name Riddle Lake is an old one. Early hunters who thought this lake was located directly on the Continental Divide and drained to both oceans may have called it "Riddle" Lake. The name Biddle Lake sometimes shows up on old maps in this location or where Jackson Lake is, presumably honoring Nicholas Biddle, the Philadelphia publisher of William Clark's map. Riddle Lake actually drains into Yellowstone Lake and thence to the Atlantic Ocean. A U.S. Geological Survey party in 1885 decided no riddle should be without a solution, so they named the lake's outlet "Solution Creek."

Bear Management Areas

In recent summers, the Riddle Lake area has been closed until mid July for bear management. This means that the park's Bear Management Office has designated this as one of the areas in which to limit bear/human interactions in an effort to keep bears from becoming habituated to people and especially to allow grizzly bears large areas of wilderness without human contact. Humans are thus less likely to be injured, and bears do not have to be relocated or killed. The program, inaugurated in 1983, appears to be paying off in the relatively few cases of bears injuring people and the apparent increase in the bear population. (There's more about bears in the "Living Things" chapter.)

17.5/4.0 Crossing the Continental Divide. The land here is so nearly flat that you wouldn't notice a divide if it weren't for the sign.

19.8/1.7 Grant Village side road to the east.

🛈 This road passes the law enforcement ranger station and in less than 1 mile (1.6 km) reaches the village, the newest facility in the park. Named for Ulysses S. Grant, the president who signed the act establishing the park in 1872, Grant Village was built between the late 1960s and the 1990s. The Snake River complex of forest fires threatened the settlement in 1988 and burned some campground buildings.

FACILITIES AT GRANT VILLAGE

🛈 🛈 🛈 As you enter the Grant Village area, you'll find a service station and mini-store on the left, with the backcountry office between them.

🛈 🛈 🛈 The large general store with lunch counter and the registration

Grant Village

building for arranging accommodations in the motel rooms are slightly farther along on the right.

✉ ❶(2) 👥 ♨ Grant also has a post office, a family restaurant and **The Lake House** (for breakfast and dinner only), a cocktail lounge, the **Grant Visitor Center**, and an amphitheater for ranger lectures. An excellent exhibit about the 1988 Yellowstone fires and the park's history of fire is on display at the visitor center.

Grant Village is situated along West Thumb Bay.

⚠️ On the way to the campground are a self-service laundry and showers.

🚻 ⛱️(10) 🏪♿(2) Near the entrance to the campground is a small ranger station and a picnic area with some fire grates.

🏪♿ Wheelchair accessible rest rooms are available at the general store, family restaurant, visitor center, laundry building, and picnic area.

🚤(2) Boats of all kinds may be launched on Yellowstone Lake from the boat ramp at the edge of the campground, but the launching area may be closed until late July due to high water. Another boat launch site can be found at the marina at the end of the first road you encounter upon entering the village. The Grant area is the best part of the lake for sailboats. Required permits and regulations for boating are available at the visitor center. (See page 140 for more about lake recreation.)

Politics and Grant Village

The construction of Grant Village had a long and complicated history, starting from preliminary surveys of the area in 1947. At that time the National Park Service decided it was desirable to relocate West Thumb's facilities farther away from the thermal features of the geyser basin. Construction at Grant began somewhat later and was halted as many as seven times for various reasons, according to Alston Chase's controversial 1986 book, *Playing God in Yellowstone*.

A major difficulty with this site is its proximity to several important trout spawning streams, where grizzly bears like to fish in late spring and early summer. The expensive large marina at the east end of the village was closed for many years due to undercutting of the shoreline by the lake's waves.

In spite of these problems, Grant Village has become a convenient and heavily used area for campers, boaters, and other tourists. It has 425 campsites and 300 motel rooms.

20.8/0.7 Thumb Creek bridge. This is one of the prime trout spawning creeks in the area.

21.5/0.0 West Thumb Junction. West Thumb Geyser Basin is described in the next section; Fishing Bridge Junction is to the northeast; Old Faithful Village and Madison Junction are to the west (straight ahead).

From West Thumb Junction to Fishing Bridge Junction

The Grand Loop Road going north from West Thumb follows the lakeshore closely most of the way to Fishing Bridge Junction, almost 21 miles (33 km) away. You'll catch glimpses of America's highest large freshwater lake and its surrounding mountains. The Absaroka Range is beyond the lake to the east, and the Red Mountains are to the south. There are many places to pull over by the lakeside to look, take pictures, picnic, or fish.

Road Log

NOTE: There are several short side roads along this stretch of the Grand Loop Road. The mileage for such roads is given at approximately the midpoint between the two ways to enter the road.

Evening at West Thumb Geyser Basin with alpenglow on the distant Absarokas.

West Thumb Junction to Fishing Bridge Junction

0.0/20.6 From West Thumb Junction the road north goes toward Bridge Bay Marina, Lake Village, and Fishing Bridge Junction. To the west is Old Faithful Village; to the south is the South Entrance and Grand Teton National Park.

0.2/20.4 Turn into the parking area for West Thumb Geyser Basin, the information and bookstore building, and a picnic area.

WEST THUMB

West Thumb Geyser Basin—just east of the junction—is the most beautifully situated thermal area in the park and is well worth visiting.

West Thumb history and facilities

NOTE: Consult the map of West Thumb Geyser Basin on the next page for West Thumb facilities.

P ? C The information and bookstore building, where the Yellowstone Association sells books and pamphlets, is housed in the former ranger station dating from 1925, now used as a warming hut in winter.

⊼(5) 🛏️ 🚻 ♿(4) 🚶 Reached from this parking lot are the West Thumb picnic area, two hiking trails, and the West Thumb Geyser Basin boardwalks. There is no running water.

The rather strange name of this spot, West Thumb, refers to the shape of this bay in Yellowstone Lake. Early explorers thought the lake resembled a hand with fingers protruding southward. Early surveyors even thought for a while that there was a fifth finger. When it turned out that the small body of water was not connected to the larger lake, it was named Delusion Lake.

You could take a steamboat from West Thumb to a dock at Lake Hotel from the 1890s until soon after automobiles were allowed into the park in 1915. At that time the steamboat line was abandoned as unprofitable.

Until 1989, there were various facilities for visitors at West Thumb, but these were moved to Grant Village to separate them from the fragile hot spring area. It was discovered that the gas station's underground storage tank was located where the ground temperature is one degree below the flash point of gasoline!

West Thumb Bay is actually a flooded explosion crater formed within the main Yellowstone caldera at some time during the last 150,000 years. Water for its hot springs and geysers comes up through fractures at the edge of this crater.

The lake's water level is now well above its level of 50 years ago, contributing to the periodic drowning of some of West Thumb's lakeside thermal features. Two factors may have caused the water level to rise: a general warming of the climate is one. The other is that this whole area is measurably tilting toward the south, attributed by geologists to uplift in the center of the Yellowstone caldera. It is as if there were a dam at Yellowstone Lake's outlet and it had recently been raised higher. For more about this tilting, see "Are We Due for Another Caldera Eruption?" in the "Geological History" chapter.

Two short hikes from West Thumb

🚶 **Yellowstone Lake Overlook Trail** is a loop of a little over 2 miles (3.2 km). Start by walking southwest from the West Thumb parking lot. After crossing the South Entrance Road (where there's limited roadside parking), turn right for the shortest way to the top of "Savage Hill," so called by concessionaire employees, who call themselves Savages. Pass a riot of wildflowers in the burned forest, and notice a couple of modest combinations of mud pots, fumaroles, and hot pools on your way up the moderately strenuous 400-foot (120 m) climb. On a clear day, you'll be rewarded with a fantastic view of much of the lake and its surrounding mountains.

You can take the **Duck Lake Trail** northwest from the same West Thumb parking area. Duck Lake

Trailhead is shown by a painted pedestrian crosswalk that crosses the Grand Loop Road north of West Thumb Junction. This hike is about one-half mile (0.8 km) through burned forest to a view of Duck Lake and another one-third mile (0.5 km) to its shore. Since Duck Lake is in an explosion crater, the last part of the trail goes steeply up and down over the crater's edge.

West Thumb Geyser Basin★

The boardwalk around West Thumb Geyser Basin is about one-half mile (0.8 km) long. It takes you to the main portion of this basin, which has few geysers but is outstanding for its scenic setting and beautiful hot springs. Since there is less sulfur in the chemical mix brought up from below, the rotten egg smell so common to other basins is less strong here.

In some seasons and some years, the colors in and around the hot springs

West Thumb Geyser Basin

are spectacular. Thermal features are changeable, however, so if the colors you see are rather ordinary at the time you're here, come back another time! Bison, deer, and waterfowl are often seen in the area.

NOTE: ⟨&⟩ The boardwalk through the basin is nearly level and accessible to wheelchairs, but on the hill farthest from the parking lot, assistance may be required.

⟨⟩ If you turn right at the boardwalk's T intersection behind the bookstore and rest rooms, then stay right at the next fork, you'll encounter **Thumb Paint Pots**. [GEO.21]

The paint pots were named Mud Puffs originally and perhaps more appropriately. The mud is formed by the action of sulfuric acid in the water on the rock it passes through. The famed pastel colors of these paint pots have hardly been visible in recent years, and there may be more water than mud here. At drier times, it's as much fun to listen to the sounds the mud pots make as it is to look at them.

Seismograph and **Bluebell pools**, on a spur to the right, differ from each other in temperature and sometimes in coloring. There may be extremely thick, colorful mats of bacteria and algae in the pools' runoff. (These mats are explained in "What Makes the Colors" on page 59.)

Above the boardwalk are **Lakeside Spring** and **Venting Pool**, unremarkable features when they're cool. However, when Lakeside Spring's water is hot, its microorganisms are beautifully colored. A sign explains the West Thumb caldera. Look in the water for a remnant of the concrete that supported

Fishing Cone in the late 1800s, by W. H. Jackson.

a boat dock here a century ago.

When Yellowstone Lake is high, the next features are entirely or almost submerged. **Lakeshore Geyser** has a sizeable cone, indicating considerable activity and a lower water level in the past—geologists tell us sinter cones like these usually aren't built under water.

A pool to the left of the boardwalk shows what happens when thoughtless visitors throw things into hot springs, filling the vents and causing the water to cool. Ugly brown microorganism mats cover the bottom or float to the top.

Fishing Cone is the most famous feature at West Thumb. It was where "unfortunate trout find catching and cooking painfully near together," as historian Chittenden wrote in 1895. In other words, early day tourists could catch a fish here and cook it without removing it from the hook. Regulations now prohibit fishing at or near West Thumb, since at least five people have perished over the years after falling into these hot springs.

Two more cones (**Big Cone** and **Little Cone**) complete features at the lakeshore before the path leaves the lake. Little Cone is above the boardwalk, well away from the water.

You'll next encounter Black Pool at the left and Abyss Pool a bit farther on at the right. Out in the runoff channel of Abyss is **King Geyser**, whose eruptions are extremely rare but discharge an impressive amount of water when they occur.

In 1991, **Black Pool** became much hotter than before and erupted for a brief period. This activity killed the bacterial mats, whose oranges and browns had combined with the usual blue of the water to give the pool an almost black color. Now Black Pool is often a lovely blue or green and is gradually cooling.

Black Pool turned blue in 1991.

West Thumb is anything but a static place! Proof of this is given by the recent history of **Abyss Pool**. A very explosive geyser in the early years of the 20th century, Abyss then became dormant for something like 80 years. Then in 1991 and 1992, it erupted numerous times up to 100 feet (30 m) high, causing some of the nearby pools to drain. Since then, Abyss has quieted, but no one can guess how long it may remain that way. At 53 feet (16 m) deep, it's one of the park's deepest pools. It's sometimes difficult to see the bottom through the lightly bubbling blue-green water.

On the boardwalk's hilly stretch, you can see how trees standing in the hot mineral-filled water have been killed fairly recently when nearby springs became more active. The trunks have wicked the minerals up from the water, preserving themselves in a hardened, upright state.

To the west of the boardwalk intersection beyond the Twin Geysers overlook, an unnamed steam vent often makes a furious racket. Just above here, road builders many years ago diverted the steam of a fumarole away from the construction site by cramming a pipe into it. The pipe ends here.

The higher section of boardwalk returns you to the parking lot, past large hot pools called the **Painted Pools**. To see several other geysers and hot springs, follow the lower boardwalk to the left. This part of the geyser basin is especially prone to *energy surges*, that is, brief periods when hot springs become geysers and known geysers increase their frequency and size.

It's hard to believe that the now relatively calm springs called **Twin Geysers**

could ever have been the largest geysers at West Thumb and a spectacular attraction, but in some decades of the 20th century, this was the case. Rising temperature and boiling activity in 1998 preceded renewed eruptions that August and occasional eruptions since. During 1999, the temperature in one of the pools sometimes measured 203°F (95°C)—above the boiling point of water at this elevation.

The next notable feature is **Blue Funnel Spring**, an almost perfectly circular pool whose shape somewhat resembles Morning Glory Pool in Upper Geyser Basin.

Ephedra Spring was named in the 1960s for the brine fly (*Ephydra bruesi*) that is common in alkaline thermal areas and feeds on microbes growing in the hot water.

Several springs lie in an almost straight line; apparently they have developed along a slightly curving fracture under the earth. These springs include Blue Funnel, Ephedra, **Perforated Pool**, an unnamed pool with a black lining, **Percolating Spring**, **Ledge Spring**, and **Surging Spring**. Some of these springs have erupted as geysers, including Ledge Spring during the summer of 1999. On the opposite side of the walkway is **Thumb Geyser**—which has been known to erupt up to 25 feet (7.5 m)—and also **Collapsing Pool**.

Continuing on the Grand Loop Road

Turn right (north) out of the West Thumb parking area to continue along the lake toward Fishing Bridge Junction. The first steam you will see comes from the Lake Shore Group of thermal features, where there is no public access.

Lone Pine Geyser in this group has been the most interesting in recent years. It was known to erupt up to 50 feet (15 m) high as frequently as every 16 or 17 hours. Lone Pine Geyser's namesake pine tree on a nearby rock fell into the lake in 1997.

1.8/18.8 Potts Hot Spring Basin is indicated only by a small widening along the road. Please heed the "Danger—Thermal Area" and "Do Not Enter" signs. This is the northernmost group of geysers and hot springs of the West Thumb area. The sinter buildup at least 18 feet (5.5 m) high indicates that it's a very old thermal area.

The Grand Loop Road used to run right through Potts Basin, which was named for trapper Daniel Potts, who wrote about his 1826 traverse of this area.

3.9/16.7 Carrington Island is the tiny, rocky bird roost just off shore, submerged at times of high water, except for one tree. It's named after the zoologist of the 1871 Hayden Expedition, E. Campbell Carrington, who sketched the shoreline of Yellowstone Lake from the first boat ever known to sail upon it, the *Anna*.

5.7/14.9 **P** Small parking area on the lake side of the road. One of the two rutted, unmaintained trails across the road is a remnant of the main stagecoach road from West Thumb to Bridge Bay, used from 1902 to 1926. In this area, the builders of the Old Faithful Inn found some of the strikingly deformed logs used in the inn's interior, according to

historian Aubrey Haines. The other unmaintained trail goes up Arnica Creek to remote Beach Lake.

Arnica Creek is named after a yellow flower with heart-shaped leaves, often found in lodgepole forests. Geologist Arnold Hague, who spent many summers in the park in the 19th century, advised the use of the arnica flower to rub on sore muscles.

Invisible due to the thick stand of trees is the western end of a wave-built sandbar in the lake. A road along the shore used the sandbar as its roadbed for a few years, but it proved too difficult to maintain—rangers later called it "Hard Road to Travel."

6.6/14.0 **P** Wide spot in the road where you can stop to walk along the east end of the natural sandbar.

6.8/13.8 ⛱(3) Unmarked side road goes near the lake to **Fisherman's Access picnic area**. One table is close to the lake. Walking in the picnic area, you'll notice vestiges of the 19th century road.

7.8/12.8 ⛱(3) 🚻(2) Unmarked road to south, leading to **Park Point picnic**

The sandbar once used as a roadbed still graces Yellowstone Lake a century later.

area. From the picnic area, there's a beautiful view of the lake and the **Red Mountains** to the south. Their highest peak is **Mount Sheridan**, (10,305 ft/3141 m), named for General Sheridan, Civil War Union general, commander during the wars with Indian tribes, and a staunch supporter of the park who paid several visits to the area.

8.5/12.1 P Pumice Point, with access to the lake. This point marks the northern boundary of West Thumb Bay. *Pumice* is a porous form of volcanic glass that can be powdered and used as an abrasive.

The closest mountain across the lake to the south is **Flat Mountain** (9168 ft/ 2794 m). It marks the southeastern edge of the Yellowstone caldera.

9.7/10.9 ⛢(2) Unmarked lake access road at **Spruce Point**.

10.8/9.8 ⛢(4) **Exhibit picnic area** with an interpretive sign about the forests. Blue-green Engelmann spruce and subalpine fir trees can be found along with lodgepole pines in the moister environment near the lake. For hints about identifying these trees, see the "Living Things" chapter.

Visible out to the east in the lake is **Dot Island**, where boat operator E. C. Waters kept bison and elk penned in the early 1900s. It was a sort of zoo for the tourists who traveled between West Thumb and Lake Hotel on his boat, the *Zillah*. The hull of this boat is probably the one seen by divers in 1994 about 200 yards (180 m) out from Lake Hotel.

Yellowstone Lake

No writer has better described Yellowstone Lake than did renowned naturalist John Muir in an *Atlantic Monthly* article of 1898:

It is about twenty miles long and fifteen wide, and lies at a height of nearly 8000 feet above the level of the sea, amid dense black forests and snowy mountains. Around its winding, wavering shores, closely forested and picturesquely varied with promontories and bays, the distance is more than 100 miles. . . .

It is full of trout, and a vast multitude of birds—swans, pelicans, geese, ducks, cranes, herons, curlews, plovers, snipe—feed in it and upon its shores; and many forest animals come out of the woods, and wade a little way in shallow, sandy places to drink and look about them, and cool themselves in the free flowing breezes.

In calm weather it is a magnificent mirror for the woods and mountains and sky, now pattered with hail and rain, now roughened with sudden storms that send waves to fringe the shores and wash its border of gravel and sand. . . .

Yellowstone Lake is North America's largest high altitude lake (7732 ft/ 2357 m) at about 14 by 20 miles (23 by 32 km) in width and length and with more than 110 miles (177 km) of shoreline. The lake has an average depth of 139 feet (42 m); its deepest spot is 387 feet (118 m).

Tributaries

Approximately 125 tributary streams feed into Yellowstone Lake, mostly from the south and east. One of the streams is the Yellowstone River's source, which enters the southeast arm of the lake from the mountains in Bridger-Teton National Forest. Thus, the lake's outlet at Fishing Bridge is not really the headwaters of the Yellowstone River.

Islands

The seven named islands in Yellowstone Lake are, from largest to smallest: Frank, Stevenson, Dot, Peale, Molly (actually two islands named Sandy and Rocky), Carrington, and Pelican Roost. Frank, Peale, and Molly were named by or for members of the 1871 and 1878 Hayden surveys of the Yellowstone area. The names of the other four are explained in the road logs when they come into view.

Winter and the Lake

In winter, ice nearly 3 feet (1 m) deep covers much of the lake, except where shallow water covers hot springs. The lake freezes over by early January, and the ice doesn't break up until late May or early June. Rangers on ski patrol used to shorten their long trek to the southeast area of the park (the Thorofare) by skiing across the ice from Lake Ranger Station to Park Point on the east shore.

Science and the Lake Bottom

In recent years, scientists have explored some of the lake's bottom using a submersible robot called a Remotely Operated Vehicle (ROV). They've learned that the hottest spot in the lake is Mary Bay at the north end, where temperatures up to 212°F (100°C) have been measured—that's above the boiling point at this altitude. They've also found deep pits that may be old hydrothermal explosion craters.

At least two other hot spots in the lake are being studied. West Thumb Bay is another active area with huge hot gas eruptions that stir up food for enterprising trout. Northeast of Stevenson Island, the ROV found a deep underwater canyon containing several hydrothermal springs. Five years later, the scientists returned, just after a major earthquake had shaken the area. The canyon had disappeared!

Spires as much as 100 feet (30 m) high grow in clusters on the lake bottom at some or all of the lake's hot spots. These pinnacles are made of the siliceous shells of *diatoms*, microscopic algae that live and die near the lake bottom. Exactly how these hydrothermal features form is as yet unknown.

14.1/6.5 🏕(18) 🚻♿(2) Sand Point picnic area. The tables have no view of the beach, but there's a shore access trail with a good view of long, narrow **Stevenson Island** and the Absaroka Mountains across the lake. The island was named for James Stevenson, the skillful manager of all three Hayden surveys of Yellowstone in the 1870s. Stevenson and a companion explored the island and reported it to be a dense jungle with abundant animal tracks.

On the far side of Stevenson Island lies the wreckage of a 125-foot (38 m) wooden steamboat, the *E. C. Waters*, named for her owner. Launched in 1905, she was never licensed to carry passengers and lay aground until 1930, when her boilers were removed and used to heat the Lake Hotel. The boat's capstan has recently been added to the park's artifact collection at Mammoth.

15.4/5.2 🏕(21) 🚻♿ Gull Point Drive (south end). This is a two-way loop road about 2 miles (3 km) long, closed in times of high lake water. Gull Point marks the south edge of Bridge Bay and extends into the lake for some distance when the water level is relatively low. California gulls come to Yellowstone in mid spring to nest on the Molly Islands in the Southeast Arm of the lake.

16.9/3.7 Gull Point Drive (north end) on the lake side.

🚶 🚲 **Natural Bridge Trailhead** on the west side of the Grand Loop Road. This is the best place to begin a bike ride to the Natural Bridge, a round trip of about 2 miles (3.2 km), but there's very little space for parking here.

To hike to the Natural Bridge, it's best to turn in toward Bridge Bay Marina 0.3 mile (0.5 km) north, park in the large lot next to the marina, and follow the trail that starts from the west side of the campground and then joins the old road. Natural Bridge from there is about a 3-mile (4.5 km) round trip. Be aware that bears feed on the spawning trout in Bridge Creek early in the season, so inquire about trail closures at a visitor center before hiking here.

Natural Bridge was cut by Bridge Creek through a cliff of rhyolite lava. Its graceful arch is about 40 feet high and 30 feet across (12 m by 9 m). The Grand Loop Road passed this way for 24 years early in the 20th century. It climbed and descended a 16 percent grade before reaching this point. (This is the north end of the former road from Arnica Creek mentioned at mile 5.7/14.9.)

17.0/3.6 Bridge across the entrance to Bridge Bay. The bay did *not* get its name from this bridge, as you might think, but, like Bridge Creek, was named by Superintendent Norris after the Natural Bridge.

17.2/3.4 🏕(23) 🚻♿ ⛺ Bridge Bay Marina entrance road. Bridge Bay is one of the newer park villages, completed in the early 1960s. **Bridge Bay Campground** is the largest in the park, with 429 campsites. A picnic area with an ice machine is close to the bay.

🔊 An amphitheater for nighttime ranger-interpreter talks and slide shows is in the campground. If you attend a ranger talk, be sure to return the same way you came in—it's a vast campground with no exit signs for the unwary!

🚤 **Bridge Bay Marina**, although

located on a natural bay, was deepened in the 1970s to better accommodate large boats. It is one of only two places to launch motorized vessels on Yellowstone Lake. At the marina you can find rowboat and outboard rentals, as well as rental slips for private boats.

🎣 There's a tackle shop and mini-store, too. Lake cruises run by the park concessionaire go out for 1-hour trips several times a day, in vessels holding 47 passengers each.

The nearest food service and general store are at Lake Village (about 2 mi/3 km north). For more groceries, gasoline, and self-service laundry, continue to Fishing Bridge, another 2 miles beyond the Lake Village turnoff.

17.3/3.3 **P** Unmarked side road for fishing access or strolling along the lake. No picnic tables.

19.0/1.6 Entrance to Lake Village.

Yellowstone Lake Recreation

Swimming in Yellowstone Lake is strongly discouraged, even forbidden at West Thumb. This is due to the extremely cold water—after all, the lake's elevation is nearly 8000 feet (3400 m). On a recent hot July day the surface water temperature behind Fishing Bridge Visitor Center was 55°F (13°C), but this was rare, and lakes like this one have colder layers beneath the surface. Signs at Bridge Bay are explicit: "Warning—water extremely cold. Survival time limited to twenty minutes."

Boating is allowed from several launch sites, but motorboats are restricted to Grant Village and Bridge Bay Marina. Permits and flotation devices are required; see the "Travel Tips" for more information. Be careful when boating! The lake is famous for sudden squalls, especially in the afternoon, when waves can be as high as 6 feet. At least 40 drowning deaths have occurred on the lake in the park's history; most have involved small boats.

Fishing opens on June 15th in Yellowstone Lake, but permits and regulations must be acquired first from a ranger station, visitor center, or general store. See the "Living Things" and "Travel Tips" chapters for more about fish and fishing in the park.

FACILITIES AT LAKE VILLAGE

Lake Village has the oldest and most beautifully situated hotel in the park and serves visitors with its many other practical facilities, including the park hospital (with its own emergency heliport), a general store, ranger station, lodge, and cabins.

➕ 🌲 After the turn onto the Lake Village side road, the first right turn leads toward the shore. If you turn right again off this side road, you'll find the hospital, equipped with ten beds, a laboratory, and a pharmacy. West of the hospital there are a couple of lakefront picnic tables.

© 2002 J. O. Chapple

Lake Village

The large building at the far end of this side road is the now-closed Lake Fish Hatchery, for many years the largest game fish hatchery in the United States. From 1913 until the 1950s, fish were raised to fingerling size from harvested eggs, then planted in lakes and streams throughout the park and sent to many localities outside the park.

Wheelchair accessible rest rooms are available at Lake Hotel and Lake Lodge and outside the general store.

There are two segments of trail along the lakeshore stretching from about 1 mile (1.6 km) west of the hatchery building past Lake Hotel and Lake Lodge northeast to Fishing Bridge Junction. This was a stretch of the Grand Loop Road until the Lake bypass was constructed in the early 1970s. Biking is allowed on the segment of the old roadbed west of the hospital. The **Lakeshore Trail** eastern section begins in the meadow below Lake Lodge and continues about 1 mile (1.6 km) northeast to Fishing Bridge. Although somewhat marshy, this is a beautiful way to enjoy views of the lake and mountains.

In front of Lake Hotel, where a boat dock used to be, is a beautiful mountain panorama over the lake. Here you can see a large part of the southeastern quadrant of Yellowstone Park, from Pyramid Peak south to Mount Sheridan.

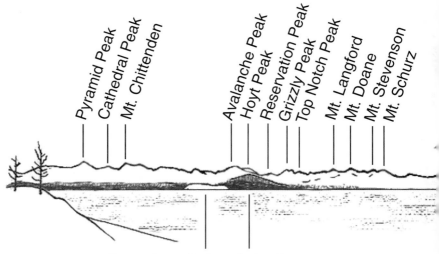

Steamboat Point   Lake Butte

Lake Hotel Panorama★

Left to right (east to southwest):

Pyramid Peak (10,508 ft/3281 m) and jagged **Cathedral Peak** (10,765 ft/3281 m).

Mt. Chittenden (10,177 ft/3102 m) and its neighboring peak to the south form a saddle on the eastern boundary of the park.

Mountains outside the park boundary.

Steamboat Point on the lakeshore.

Flat-topped **Avalanche Peak** (10,568 ft/3221 m) and **Hoyt Peak** (10,506 ft/3202m) slightly behind and to its right. In front of Avalanche and Hoyt is **Lake Butte**, covered with trees.

Reservation Peak (10,629 ft/3240 m), with its diagonal border capping of dark rock, is much farther back and to the south of the East Entrance Road.

Grizzly Peak (9948 ft/3032 m) and **Top Notch Peak** (10,238 ft/3121 m) are next (the notch is not visible from here).

The next three pyramid-shaped peaks are named for early explorers of the park:

Mt. Langford (10,750 ft/3277 m) farthest back and **Mts. Doane** (10,656 ft/3248 m) and **Stevenson** (10,352 ft/3155 m). Nathaniel P. Langford and Lt. Gustavus C. Doane were leaders of the 1870 expedition through the park. James Stevenson was geologist Ferdinand V. Hayden's manager and chief assistant on all his western ventures.

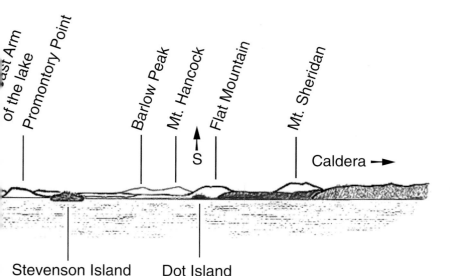

Just to the right of Mt. Stevenson is **Mt. Schurz** (11,163 ft/3402 m), named for Carl Schurz, secretary of the interior (1877–81) and strong supporter of the park.

The highest peaks in the park show their tops to the right of Mt. Schurz, and the relatively level area in front of them (to the southeast) reaches to the Thorofare Corner 30 miles away.

You can see where the **Southeast Arm** of the Lake occupies a gap in the high ground.

Promontory Point between the two arms, and the north end of **Stevenson Island** obscuring the **South Arm**.

Almost due south is the long top of **Flat Mountain** (9168 ft/2794 m), with **Dot Island** in front of it. At the left flank of Flat Mountain is the much higher **Mt. Hancock** (10,214 ft/3113 m) near the park's south boundary, and to the left of it another high mountain, **Barlow Peak** (9622 ft/2933 m). Gen. W. S. Hancock, a Union general wounded at Gettysburg, was Commander of the army's Department of Dakota in 1871, when the peak was named for him. In 1871, Capt. John Barlow led an expedition in tandem with Hayden's expedition and explored in this area.

The most westerly high mountain in sight is **Mt. Sheridan** (10,305 ft/3141 m).

To the southwest you see the low profile of the Yellowstone caldera.

Lake Hotel*

▬ ◐ Lake Hotel (called Lake Yellowstone Hotel by the concessionaire in recent years) suggests 1920s casual elegance. A string quartet or a pianist plays in the sunroom during cocktail and dinner hours, the dining room has the best food in the park, and the entire hotel is the most carefully planned and comfortable of any in Yellowstone.

From the *Haynes Guide* for 1912: "**Hotel at the Outlet.**—This spacious and elegantly appointed hotel tends greatly toward making Yellowstone Lake the resort par excellence of the Park. Here everything is so arranged that guests can spend the entire season, if they so desire, making short, easy trips of sightseeing or exploration to all points of the great reserve."

Few people have the time or inclination to spend "the entire season" these days, but the hotel has not changed much. Even in a short stay, we can appreciate its resort-like ambience and its outstanding setting. U.S. presidents Warren G. Harding and Calvin Coolidge stayed here on their trips through the park.

Lake Hotel, Yellowstone's most elegant accommodations.

The central portion of the hotel was completed in 1891, and additions were built in 1902, 1904, and 1923. You might notice that the east wing is slightly out of alignment with the hotel's central portion—this is due to a very large rock discovered underground just where the architect had planned to extend the wing.

Architect Robert Reamer added some of the colonial touches at the time of the additions, including the imposing Ionic columns, dormer windows, and small third floor balconies. He also extended the lounge toward Yellowstone Lake; guests now enjoy views in three directions from the lounge windows. The porte cochere over the hotel driveway was added in 1920. After extensive renovations took place in the early 1980s, there are now nearly 300 rooms, including those in the annex and simple cabins at the rear.

🏧 ◐ 👥 East of Lake Hotel along the shore you'll find a general store with lunch counter and the 1922 **Lake Ranger Station**, with its octagonal community room and central four-sided stone fireplace.

Lake Ranger Station

□ ◑ Beyond the store and ranger station is **Lake Lodge** and its many cabins, with 186 spaces (for two to four visitors). The lodge, built and added to between 1919 and 1929, contains the cabin registration office, cafeteria, gift shop, and self-service laundry.

Continuing on the Grand Loop Road 19.6/1.0 🚶 Elephant Back Trailhead. A 4-mile (6.4 km) trail with a loop at the top climbs **Elephant Back Mountain** about 800 feet (250 m) to a spectacular view of Yellowstone Lake. The mountain's name, one of the park's oldest, stems from the shape of its steep sides and rounded summit.

Early in the season, Elephant Back Trail may be closed due to grizzly bear activity in the area. Before you set out on a trail, it's always best to inquire about safety at a ranger station or visitor center.

Across the road from the trailhead, a short trail leads to Lake Lodge.

20.6/0.0 Fishing Bridge Junction (sometimes called Lake Junction). Fishing Bridge and the East Entrance are to the east; Mud Volcano, Hayden Valley, and Canyon Junction to the north; Lake Village, Bridge Bay Marina, and West Thumb to the southwest.

From Cody to the East Entrance

Starting your trip at Cody, you may enjoy visiting one or more of the town's four western museums or attending a rodeo. Accommodations are available in Cody and at numerous guest ranches along the road leading to Yellowstone's East Entrance, 53 miles (85 km) from the town.

Heading directly west, at Buffalo Bill Dam, you'll find a visitor center with interesting exhibits. Campgrounds and numerous places for water sports are available in the state park around the reservoir. For several miles before you reach Yellowstone, wonderfully bizarre rock formations line the road.

A longer but very scenic road over the mountains from Cody to Yellowstone is the Chief Joseph Highway. To take the longer route, go north from the center of town and turn northwest (left) on Wyoming Highway 120 in less than one-half mile. After about 17 miles (27 km), turn left (or west) on Wyoming 296 to cross Dead Indian Pass and descend to Cooke City, Montana,

Approach to the East Entrance

and the Northeast Entrance. It's a total of 81 miles (130 km) by this route from Cody to the park. (See "Approaches to the Northeast Entrance" for a description.)

CODY, WYOMING

Population: 8850

Among the Wyoming gateway communities, the growing town of Cody is rivaled only by Jackson for its complete range of tourist attractions and facilities. Cody has the advantage of having considerably lower-priced accommodations than does Jackson.

William Frederick Cody, who, with George Beck, founded the town in 1896, was world famous as Buffalo Bill, a name he won as a young man by killing more than 4000 buffaloes in a few months' time. His prowess as a hunter and Indian scout was exceeded only by his fame as a showman. From 1883 well into the 20th century, he toured the United States and Europe extensively with his Wild West spectacle. He made a fortune but lost almost all of it in well meant, but mostly unsuccessful, speculative ventures.

The town of Cody was the terminus of the Burlington Route, a railroad that operated into Cody from 1901 to 1956. Cody still has some historic buildings, including the 1902 Irma Hotel, named for Buffalo Bill's daughter.

The Buffalo Bill Historical Center houses four fine museums. For one admission price, you can visit the **Whitney Gallery of Western Art**, the **Buffalo Bill Museum**, the **Plains Indians Museum**, and the **Cody Firearms Museum**. A natural history museum is planned for early in the 21st century. Worth a stop is the **Old Trail Town** just west of town on the highway to Yellowstone. It's a collection of historic western buildings, including one used by Butch Cassidy and the Wild Bunch.

Other attractions include a nightly rodeo during summer months and, on two weekends in June, the **Plains Indian Powwow**, a social gathering that includes competitive dancing. There are two annual events in July: the **Cody Stampede** and the **Yellowstone Jazz Festival**. The Stampede is two days of "whooping it up," with parades, rodeos, barbecues, and Western entertainment.

U.S. Highways 14/16/20

This road (called the Buffalo Bill Scenic Byway by the U.S. Forest Service) goes west from Cody to Yellowstone. Just beyond the rodeo grounds, if you park near the last building on the right (north) side of the road, you can walk to the rim of the canyon of the Shoshone River (properly called the North Fork of the Shoshone) to see what's left of a geothermally heated pool at DeMaris Springs. A sulfur mine was located a bit farther along the road before World War I.

"Colter's Hell" and John Colter

The area along the Shoshone River here was called Colter's Hell by 19th century trappers. Native Americans and trappers used the Shoshone River Canyon and Sylvan Pass as an east-west passage through the high Absaroka Range. Probably the first white person to use this pass and the first to see Yellowstone's marvels was mountain man John Colter. Colter reported information about his 1806–8 traverse of the area to Capt. William Clark of the Lewis and Clark Expedition, who recorded it on a map. John Colter may have seen at least some of the hot spring basins, but if he spoke about them, people did not believe what he had to say.

A large tar spring that gave off sulfurous odors near the junction of the North and South forks of the Shoshone River came to be called Colter's Hell, and the river was called the Stinkingwater River throughout the 19th century. In 1835, "Colter's Hell" showed up in Washington Irving's version of an early explorer's journal, *The Adventures of Captain Bonneville*. Somehow the name had become transposed to the whole of the Yellowstone thermal area as a derisive term, with the implication that Colter had not seen the wonders he had described.

The dual confusion over Colter's veracity and exactly where Colter's Hell was located persisted until about 50 years ago, when historian Merrill J. Mattes determined that the name referred to hot springs in the Shoshone River Canyon and not to Yellowstone Park.

The Wyoming Legislature changed the name Stinkingwater River to Shoshone River in 1901, when Cody was first being settled and the road into Yellowstone was being improved.

You enter the Shoshone Canyon and cross the river almost simultaneously, with Rattlesnake Mountain on the north and Spirit Mountain (also called Cedar Mountain) on the south. This whole area was important to the Crow tribe. Young Crow *vision questers*, seeking to become tribal leaders and medicine men, visited the land that is now under Buffalo Bill Reservoir.

Automobile use of the Shoshone Canyon road began in 1915. Here's what it looked like to the author's grandfather, Montana mountaineer Fred Inabnit, as he drove up the old road in 1918:

> The Shoshone canyon is so narrow and winding that you can hardly see from the bench [rim of the canyon] where the valley cut through. You follow the river closely here as there is no other way possible, at times several hundred feet above it and then dipping down almost into the water. The roads are rocky,

some places on and through solid rock and up and down steep hills. . . . . The canyon is a beautiful sight, both its sides reaching up to near timber line, either perpendicular or steep. We could see the dam something over a mile away and before reaching it the road climbs way up above the river only to take another dip so as to make a good long steep climb to reach the level of the dam again. . . .

The road was reconstructed after World War II, so that traveling through it has become much less of an adventure. In fact, on the modern road you'll hardly notice the more than 3500-foot (1080 m) climb from Cody to Sylvan Pass inside the park, a distance of 60 miles (96 km).

Seven miles (11 km) from Cody and immediately beyond the long third tunnel is 353-foot (108 m) **Buffalo Bill Dam**, which was the highest in the world when completed in 1910. Looking down from the dam is rather like peering from the top of a 35-story building, with the added thrill of roaring water below creating a tremendous spray.

You may want to pick up a leaflet about the facilities available in **Buffalo Bill State Park** either at the visitor center or at the park's headquarters about 3 miles (5 km) up the road to the west.

Shoshone Canyon road in 1917, by Jack Haynes.

The road passes along the northern edge of Buffalo Bill Reservoir, crosses the Shoshone River, and then passes the little town of Wapiti. Soon after the sign about the local geology, you'll enter an area covered by what geologists call the *Absaroka Volcanics*. Around 50 million years ago, about a dozen major volcanic centers spread lava and volcanic debris over a huge area from beyond the northwest corner to well southeast of Yellowstone Park (see the map of the Absaroka Range Volcanics, below).

Look at relatively low **Jim Mountain** to the north, where you can see the edges of the old volcanic lava flow layers. In the distance beyond Jim Mountain, you may catch a glimpse of high **Dead Indian Peak**, another of many mountains made of lava.

West of Wapiti, you'll be entering America's first national forest, the **Shoshone National Forest**, created in 1891 and called at that time the Yellowstone Timber Land Reserve. It was set aside to be a cushion of protection east and south of Yellowstone.

As you drive west, you'll begin to see the fantastic rock formations or hoodoos this road is famous for. About a mile (1.6 km) into the national forest, on the left (south), is the first of many named hoodoos, **Laughing Pig Rock**.

On the north side and almost perpendicular to the road is the **Chinese Wall**, actually a *dike*, that is, a thin sheet of rock formed when magma squeezed into a vertical crack in the already existing sediments. In 4 to 5 miles (6–8 km), you'll see **Hanging Rock**, which does indeed hang almost over the road. Less than 1 mile (1.5 km) from this is **Goose Rock** at right center on the cliff top. In the same turnout area is the **Holy City**. Many equally fantastic shapes may inspire you to name them yourself.

One of the most easily recognized hoodoos is Goose Rock.

What's a Hoodoo?

To geologists, a *hoodoo* is a standing column or odd shape left when sedimentary rock has eroded unevenly. The process of making hoodoos began when the lava flows and ash falls in the extensive Absaroka Range volcanic mountains were eroded. Rain sometimes turned the slopes to mud, mud slides came surging down the mountains, filled the valleys, and hardened into *conglomerate* rock, a sedimentary rock that consists of fragments from previously formed rock. The fragments range in size from tiny up to greater than fist size.

Over the millennia, other lava flows covered some of these sediments. After relatively minor earth stresses fractured the rocks, rain and the freezing and thawing of water in the vertical cracks eroded the rock to form cliffs or columns. The tops of the columns occur where a layer of rock more resistant

Extent of Absaroka Volcanics

Map by Robert A. Chadwick. Adapted with permission from Geological Society of America Bulletin, Vol. 81, Jan., 1970.

to erosion sheltered the underlying soft layers. Some of these columns developed into the bizarre shapes called hoodoos.

Observers have used their imaginations and given names to about 60 of these hoodoos. At one of them, Chimney Rock, about 16 miles (26 km) west of Wapiti, the road goes close enough so that you can see how the flat-lying layers of pebbly rock alternate with finer-grained sandy layers.

About 20 miles (32 km) northwest of these roadside formations is another extensive area of hoodoos called Hoodoo Basin. It's in a remote spot near Yellowstone's eastern border. An easily accessible place to see hoodoos inside the park is at Devil's Den just north of Tower Fall.

In about 2 miles (3 km), you'll find the **Wapiti Ranger Station**, which dates from 1903–4 and is the oldest in the U.S. built with government funds. Midday tours of the old ranger station are sometimes offered. There's also an information center close to the road. The nearby wayside exhibit commemorates 100 years of the U.S. Department of Agriculture Forest Service, 1891 to 1991.

The rangers at Wapiti Ranger Station will give you information about the nine forest service campgrounds along this road, backcountry trails in the area, and recent bear sightings.

For a few miles after the ranger station, the valley widens, making room for many guest ranches. There are no more hoodoos for a stretch. Near Rex Hale Campground is a site called Mummy Cave (not open to the public), where archaeologists have discovered evidence that Native Americans lived here sporadically for about 9000 years. In the same area are a few petrified trees, turned to stone by the same geologic events that created similar petrified trees in the park itself.

The last two easy-to-find hoodoos near the road are **Elephant Head** and **Chimney Rock**.

Chimney Rock has eroded away from its neighboring cliff.

About 2 miles (3 km) east of Yellowstone's boundary, the road crosses the North Fork of the Shoshone, which it's been following since Cody. From here into the park, we ascend **Middle Creek**, centered between the two forks of the Shoshone.

You pass Sleeping Giant Campground and ski area (for cross-country and downhill skiing) and historic **Pahaska Tepee**, Buffalo Bill's hunting lodge, which is now open for free tours. The road from Cody is kept open this far all winter. The lodge's associated cabins and restaurant are the last facilities before entering Yellowstone.

From the East Entrance to Fishing Bridge Junction

The East Entrance Road is most noted for passing among high mountains and over Sylvan Pass as well as for spectacular views of Yellowstone Lake and of nearby mountain ranges. Sparkling Eleanor and Sylvan lakes catch your eye at the top of the pass, and farther along are viewpoints from which you can often see all the way to the Tetons. Before reaching Fishing Bridge, the road closely follows the lakeshore. It's 26 miles (42 km) from the East Entrance to Fishing Bridge Junction.

Special Caution: Much of the area accessible from the East Entrance Road, especially around the Pelican Creek drainage, is prime grizzly bear territory in the first half of the summer, when the bears are feeding on spawning trout. It is prudent to check with rangers before hiking and never to hike alone.

Road Log

0.0/26.0 Yellowstone National Park boundary.

0.1/25.9 🚻 🏪♿(2) East Entrance station. Stop here to pay the entrance fee (see the "Travel Tips" for fee information). A side road leads north to service buildings and the ranger station.

Yellowstone Park's Eastern Edge

A glance at any current map of Yellowstone Park shows that its boundaries are mostly straight, except for the eastern edge. In fact, if you look closely at that ragged edge, you can imagine the outline of a cute snub-nosed bear cub. Its ear sticks up at the Northeast Entrance, its brow and nose squiggle through the northern Absaroka Range—and you might even make a case for a right paw east of Yellowstone Lake! The original Yellowstone National Park was a perfect rectangle, its borders

East Entrance to Fishing Bridge Junction

© 2002 J. O. Chapple

specified by the 1872 act of Congress that set aside the land. The eastern border ran along the 110th meridian "passing ten miles to the eastward of the most eastern point of Yellowstone lake." Then why is this side of the park so irregular today?

In 1929, the original eastern border was revised, turning over to the Forest Service any land east of the Absaroka summits and, at the same time, annexing some of the headwaters of streams already in the park. Thus, Crow Creek and Jones Creek, which flow east out of the mountains north of Sylvan Pass to the North Fork of the Shoshone River, are entirely outside the park. Almost all the tributaries of the Lamar River (farther north) are within the park. Most of the eastern border now follows drainage divides, meandering along ridge crests and over mountain peaks.

3.0/23.0 **P** For the next mile or so, there are several parking areas and a road toward Middle Creek. Some of the turnouts provide good views of the mountains.

The original East Entrance Road followed Middle Creek more closely than it does now. A pleasant feature of the present road in early summer is that numerous small waterfalls rush down from the hillsides above. But don't drink the water—it may not be safe.

6.4/19.6 Look below the road to see a trace of the very unusual **Corkscrew Bridge** (also called Spiral Bridge). You can now see only a gently curving smooth path, but 100 years ago it was an engineering marvel. At the bottom of the Sylvan Pass grade was a large and excellent cold spring, Mammoth Crystal Spring, the source of Middle Creek. The spring is now very hard to locate.

6.9/19.1 Sylvan Pass (8541 ft/2603 m). In 1901, Army Engineer Captain Chittenden, who designed this road, wrote that Sylvan Pass is "unique among mountain passes in that it is almost entirely loosened from the cliffs on either side by the action of frost. This broken

Corkscrew Bridge afforded a manageable grade up Sylvan Pass on the original East Entrance Road.

rock varies in size from fine pebbles to pieces a cubic yard in volume." You may wonder why it was named Sylvan, meaning forested, when it's so rocky. The pass is named after the larger of the two tree-ringed lakes near it.

North of the road is **Hoyt Peak** (10,506 ft/3202 m), named for John W. Hoyt, first governor of the Territory of Wyoming and later University of Wyoming president. Hoyt Peak is part of the volcanic Absaroka Range. **[GEO.6]**

In Praise of High Mountain Passes

A Yellowstone experience that's always a delight in good weather is the opportunity to sample a high pass in the Rocky Mountains. At three places in the park, the main road climbs above 8000 feet (2440 m). Besides Sylvan Pass, the other high passes are Craig Pass between Old Faithful Village and West Thumb Junction (8262 ft/2518 m), and Dunraven Pass, the highest (8873 ft/2704 m), between Tower Fall and Canyon Junction.

What's Different about Mountain Passes?

You can tell you're in a special environment even without getting out of your car. In June and early July, there are still mounds of snow along the road. Waterfalls spill onto the road and fall down to the river.

You'll see a profusion of wildflowers in July and August. They have only a few weeks to show their splendors and produce their seeds.

Trees that grow this high on the mountainsides belong to species that have adapted to the climate, predominantly subalpine fir and whitebark pine. In very high windy places, they may show crooked growth called *krummholz*, German for crooked wood, with branches only on the side away from the wind.

Sometimes there are gorgeous vistas at or near the mountain passes. In the case of Sylvan Pass, the best views are a few miles to the west of the pass itself.

Some park animals spend the summer months this high or higher. Bears gorge themselves at the end of summer on berries and whitebark pine nuts. Especially around Dunraven Pass, you may see bighorn sheep if you look up to the crags above the road.

How Do You Feel?

At altitudes of over 8000 feet (2400 m), almost everyone feels some effects from the thinner air. You may feel dizzy, faint, or seem to have trouble getting your breath. The atmospheric pressure is 27 percent less than at sea level, thus the air around you is less dense, and you're only getting about three-quarters as much oxygen per breath. However, if you stay at high altitude for a few days, your body will usually accommodate at least partially to the reduced oxygen supply.

7.6/18.4 [⚲](2) **Eleanor Lake**, probably named in 1901 by road engineer Chittenden for his infant daughter. Look above the east end of the lake for a delightful small waterfall, named **Crecelius Cascade** for Chittenden's subordinate, who was responsible for building this stretch of road.

[🚶] You can park in the picnic area at the west side of the lake for Avalanche Peak Trail. This trail takes you in a very steep 2 miles (3.2 km) to the top of **Avalanche Peak**. Rangers sometimes lead hikes up this trail; inquire at Fishing Bridge Visitor Center.

Snow avalanches are common in this area of steep mountainsides. In the spring, park rangers fire a cannon to try to create small snowslides and prevent the snow buildup that causes greater avalanches.

An unmaintained fisherman's trail, not shown on current maps, starts south of Eleanor Lake and follows Clear Creek down to the Thorofare Trail.

8.5/17.5 Southeast end of **Sylvan Lake**.

8.7/17.3 [⚲](8) [🚻][♿] [🛶] Sylvan Lake picnic area, with tables near the lake and across the road. Fishing in Sylvan Lake is catch and release only.

The mountain visible beyond the southeast end of Sylvan Lake is the aptly named **Top Notch Peak**. Above the trees to the south and closer to the lake is **Grizzly Peak**. Look on Grizzly Peak's northwest side for an obvious *cirque*, that is, a steep-sided natural amphitheater gouged out by glacial ice.

9.1/16.9 [P] Northwest end of Sylvan Lake.

Top Notch Peak stands guard over Sylvan Lake.

11.0/15.0 [P] Teton Point turnout for the first good view of part of Yellowstone Lake, Mount Sheridan across the lake, and (on clear days) the Tetons.

12.3/13.7 The road makes a horseshoe curve to cross Cub Creek.

14.2/11.8 Unnamed ponds can be seen briefly along the road. The gas bubbles and turbid water in the ponds and colorful hillsides beyond them indicate a hydrothermally active area.

14.8/11.2 [P] Recent road improvements provide parking for an excellent panorama.

Yellowstone Lake and Mountains Panorama

Far left to right:

Three sharp peaks of the **Absarokas** poke above the trees: Grizzly, Doane, and Stevenson.

To the south are the **Tetons**, 60 miles away.

Flat Mountain at the south edge of Yellowstone Lake.

Mt. Sheridan to the right and behind Flat Mountain.

Frank Island, Yellowstone Lake's largest island, and **Dot Island**, with **West Thumb Bay** to its right. Behind and between the islands is high, flat **Thorofare** country.

To the far right is **Stevenson Island**, the long, narrow one that can become two islands when water is very high in the lake.

16.3/9.7 🏕️♿ **Lake Butte** side road to the north, about 0.8 mile (1 km) to a pretty view. The butte is the most westerly peak of Absaroka Volcanics in this part of the park.

The panoramic view from the top of this road takes in more of Yellowstone Lake and distant mountains than you can see from any other road in the park. The view stretches (right to left) from the white **Sulphur Hills** above rounded **Mary Bay** and the hydrothermally altered rocks of **Steamboat Point** to the northwest, through the distant Gallatin Range in the northwestern corner of the park, across the Yellowstone caldera to the west, to the mountains near the southern arms of the lake and to the faintly visible Tetons.

17.0/9.0 🚶🐎 Nine Mile Trailhead for the **Thorofare Trail** on a short side road to the south. This is a long pack trail that parallels the lakeshore to the park's Thorofare corner.

The southeast area of the park is called the Thorofare. The name dates from the fur-trading days of the 1820s and 1830s, when the only known southern route into the Yellowstone Plateau was by way of Two Ocean Pass and down the Yellowstone River. Today the Thorofare patrol cabin has the distinction of being the place farthest from a maintained road in the contiguous United States.

Between here and Butte Springs, we cross into the Yellowstone caldera; here the caldera rim runs approximately northeast-southwest.

18.1/7.9 Butte Springs, a small thermal area north of the road.

18.3/7.7 🏕️ ⛺(3) 🛶 Sedge Creek crossing and **Sedge Bay**, a canoe launching spot. Look out in the lake along this stretch of road to see **Pelican Roost**, a tiny rocky point that may be all but submerged in early summer.

19.6/6.4 🅿️ Three turnouts in this area afford excellent views of the lake at **Steamboat Point**. Geologist Albert C. Peale wrote in 1878 that at this spot there was located "a powerful steam vent from which a vast column of steam escapes with a continuous roar that exactly resembles the escape from a huge steam-boat," but you can no longer hear that sound. The red stain on Steamboat's formation is *cinnabar*, mercuric sulfide, which is poisonous.

Steamboat Point has two hydrothermal features, Steamboat Spring and Locomotive Vent.

20.0/6.0 [d][&] [⊼](3) Turnout at **Holmes Point**, named for W. H. Holmes after the initials W. H. H. were found on a rock here. Holmes was the artist and geologist with the 1872 and 1878 Hayden Surveys.

From this point the road follows **Mary Bay** of Yellowstone Lake for a while. Mary Bay was named for Mary Force, the girlfriend of Henry Elliot, artist with the 1871 Hayden Survey. Mary's name remains on the bay, though when Elliot returned home, he married someone else.

The rounded forms and steep sides of Mary Bay (and of Indian Pond farther west) attest to the fact that they are both steam explosion craters, formed near the end of the last glacial period. The bay has lots of underwater hot springs and the hottest spot in the lake, measured at 212°F (100°C).

21.6/4.4 Beach Springs north of the road is a small thermal area that gives off a strong sulfur odor when the lake water level is low. Here the road is actually on a sandbar. The Beach Springs area was turned into a lagoon by the buildup of sand and gravel washed in by wave action during storms on the lake.

22.7/3.3 [⚏] Short road to the northeast leads to parking for the backcountry **Pelican Valley Trail**. Until early July, this area is closed by the park administration for bear management (see page 126 for more information). Make sure you consult a ranger at Fishing Bridge Visitor Center about current grizzly bear activity in this neighborhood before using any of these trails.

22.9/3.1 [P] Parking for Indian Pond and for Storm Point Nature Trail to the south. **Indian Pond** (called Squaw Lake for some years) was named in 1880 by Superintendent Norris, who had found Indian wickiups, corrals, and lodgepoles in the area. A few years later, geologist Arnold Hague wrote that this was a favorite place for the Indians to manufacture implements, being near to stone quarries and to good hunting and fishing grounds. Notice the very steep sides of Indian Pond, which were created by a steam explosion. **[GEO.17]**

[⚏] During summer, daily ranger-led hikes cover the **Storm Point Nature Trail**'s round-trip route, a walk of a little more than 2 miles (3.2 km). You can also go down to the lake without a ranger. You might see yellow-bellied marmots or some of the local waterbirds. The circular depressions in the sandy soil are likely to be bison wallows where the animals roll, seeking warmth in winter and protection from biting insects in summer.

Storm Point, named for the storms out of the southwest that it intercepts.

The beach between Mary Bay and the outlet of the Yellowstone River is called Diamond Beach because of its sparkling sand. The lake is usually too cold for swimming, but wading can be pleasant. Just north of Storm Point is **Concretion Cove,** where early day visitors found strangely shaped rocks and thoughtlessly carried them all away long ago.

24.2/1.8 P (Unmarked) Storm Point Trailhead.

24.3/1.7 H The mouth of **Pelican Creek** is a great place to see many types of ducks, Canada geese, California gulls, and pelicans.

24.4/1.6 Pelican Creek crossing and a 1500-feet-long (460 m) causeway for the road. Pelican Creek drains the Mirror Plateau to the north.

If you could look down on Pelican Creek from above, you'd see several *oxbow lakes.* Geologists use this term for the U-shaped ponds left behind when loops in a meandering stream are cut off as the river shortens its path by connecting the two ends of the loop.

Near here in 1839, fur trapper Osborne Russell and a companion were attacked and wounded by Piegan (Blackfeet) Indians, and five other trappers were killed. The creek was named for a later incident in which a prospector shot a large bird for dinner; it was not a goose as he'd thought, but an unsavory pelican—hence the name.

24.6/1.4 🚶 **Pelican Creek Nature Trail.** This short loop (less than 1 mile/ 1.5 km) to Yellowstone Lake consists of a boardwalk across a marsh and a path through the woods.

FACILITIES AT FISHING BRIDGE VILLAGE

NOTE: See the map on page 154.

25.2/0.8 ▲ **Fishing Bridge RV Campground** road. This campground is the only place in the park where recreational vehicle owners can find a sewer hookup at each site. The nearly 350 sites must be reserved in advance. A small concession building and a self-service laundry and showers are nearby.

25.3 to 25.6/0.7 to 0.4 A short frontage road to the north parallels the main road for Fishing Bridge facilities.

(🚮 ⓪ 🏧 ♿ 🚰 From east to west along the frontage road are: an ice machine, public telephones, general store with soda fountain, and gas station. Housing for employees is also located here.

🚶 To hike on a segment of the **Howard Eaton Trail**, park along the service road a short distance behind the service station. This segment of the trail follows the east side of the Yellowstone River all the way from here to the South Rim of the Yellowstone River's canyon. It's a 6.5-mile (10.5 km) round-trip hike to view LeHardys Rapids across the river. As with all trails in this area, check first with the rangers about recent bear activity.

A Case of Bears Winning out over People

When park policy ended the feeding of bears by removing all park garbage dumps in 1970, encounters between humans and grizzly bears increased. Something had to be done, especially at Fishing Bridge, a popular spot for camping.

The bears come every year to fish in Yellowstone Lake's outlet and in its many tributaries. Now bears have been given first priority at this site. Visitors may not stay overnight, except in RVs. The campground across the main road was closed in 1990, and many cabins near the river were razed.

25.5/0.5 🚻 🏕(11) 🅿♿(2) 🛥 Road to **Fishing Bridge Visitor Center** and amphitheater. The picnic tables are to the west along the road, while rest rooms are a short distance up a trail on the op- posite side of the parking area. A pleasant sandy beach is just outside the back door of the visitor center.

Do you know what a phalarope looks like? You can find out in the museum at

Fishing from Fishing Bridge in 1925 (Frantz & Sharpe photo)

Fishing Bridge Visitor Center, one of the first buildings in the park built as a museum. Opened in 1931, it is now a National Historic Landmark. You'll find displays about lake birds, some in dioramas, as well as a grizzly bear diorama. There's also a room with exhibits about the various habitats in and around the lake and a small bookshop. (A phalarope is a small shorebird, as you can see in the museum display.)

25.7/0.3 [P] Alternate parking on the north for Howard Eaton Trail (described above) or for Fishing Bridge.

25.8/0.2 Fishing Bridge. Closed to fishing since 1973, Fishing Bridge should now be called Fish-Watching Bridge. While the crowds of anglers catching their hooks in each other's hair are gone, many people do enjoy watching the cutthroat trout and long-nosed suckers, especially during spawning season. Both trout resident in the lake and those from the outlet are believed to spawn in this part of the Yellowstone River. The park's no-fishing policy at the bridge helps the trout and allows the traffic to pass without tie-ups.

The first Fishing Bridge, built in 1903 when the East Entrance Road was completed, crossed the outlet diagonally and was a little closer to the lake. It was steeply arched to allow the passage of rowboats. The present bridge dates from 1937 and has no arch but includes much-needed walkways.

25.9/0.1 [P] [🚶] Parking for Fishing Bridge and for the **Lakeshore Trail**. Head up the steps south of the road for this pleasant, easy trail. It goes for about 2 miles (3 km) round trip along the lake to the Lake Lodge area. Parts of this trail may be marshy.

Canada geese at Yellowstone Lake.

26.0/0.0 Fishing Bridge Junction (sometimes called Lake Junction). To the southwest along the lake is West Thumb Junction, to the north are Canyon Junction and Canyon Village, and to the east is the East Entrance to the park.

From Fishing Bridge Junction to Canyon Junction

Leaving Fishing Bridge Junction and heading north, the Grand Loop Road closely follows the Yellowstone River all the way to the Grand Canyon of the Yellowstone. Highlights include the unusual thermal features of the Mud Volcano area, long views of the river as it descends gradually through the Hayden Valley, many convenient stops for fishing access and picnicking, and the summer home of bison, moose, pelicans, sandhill cranes, and Canada geese. Hayden Valley is also a favorite habitat of grizzly bears, but you seldom see them from the highway. The distance from Fishing Bridge to Canyon is 15 miles (24 km).

Road Log

0.0/15.4 Fishing Bridge Junction (sometimes called Lake Junction). Canyon Junction and Canyon Village are to the north; Lake Village, Bridge Bay Marina, and West Thumb to the south; Fishing Bridge facilities and the East Entrance to the east.

2.8/12.6 P Here and just to the north are two **LeHardys Rapids** parking areas. A boardwalk and footpaths lead to the river, where in June and early July you can spot trout leaping up the rapids on their way to spawn in Yellowstone Lake or its tributaries.

 ⚭ The walkway from the north parking lot is wheelchair accessible and marked.

Paul LeHardy met trouble at these rapids. He was a topographer accompanying a military reconnaissance of the park in 1873. At the rapids his makeshift raft was sucked to the bottom, forcing him and his partner to salvage what they could and tramp downriver to join their expedition near the falls of the Yellowstone.

4.0/11.4 ⛱(5) 🏠⚭ Loop road to a picnic area with no name.

4.7/10.7 ⛱(8) 🏠⚭ C Cascade picnic area.

4.9/10.5 Interpretive signs about trout and other wildlife.

To Tower-Roosevelt Jct.

Canyon Junction

7903 ft
2409 m

one way

Inspiration Point

Artist Point

Lower Falls

Canyon Area map, p. 171

Upper Falls

Cascade Cr.

Yellowstone River

Otter Cr.

15.4 mi

Mary Mtn. Tr.

Alum Cr.

(24.8 km)

Wrangler Lake

Sour Cr.

Yellowstone River

HAYDEN

VALLEY

Trout Cr.

Sulphur Caldron

MUD VOLCANO AREA

LeHardys Rapids

N

0   1   2   3   4 mi

0   2   4   6 km

Fishing Bridge Jct.
7817 ft   2383 m

Fishing Bridge

To East Entrance

Lake Village map, p. 141

Yellowstone Lake

© 2002 J. O. Chapple

To Bridge Bay & West Thumb Junction

Fishing Bridge Junction to Canyon Junction

5.0/10.4 禾(17) ⬚⬚⬚ Nez Perce Ford picnic area side road. No fishing is allowed in the west channel of the river here. Above and below this stretch of the river are areas extremely popular with fishermen, even though it's for catch and release only. According to data collected by the U.S. Fish and Wildlife Service, the same trout may be caught and released nine times in one season.

The Name of This Ford

The name used for many years for this spot, Buffalo Ford, stems from a winter about 50 years ago when two rangers discovered several bison frozen in the ice here. However, Nez Perce Ford has been the official name since 1981. Here the Nez Perce crossed the river as they were fleeing the U.S. Army in 1877, attempting to reach Canada. Their route began in Idaho and ended in northern Montana, where they were finally forced to surrender.

5.4/10.0 P Parking for river access and informal trails to two springs. The closer spring is surrounded by grasses, but the one nearer the river, **Cold Water Geyser**, has a considerable rock crater and a crevice filled with water and bubbles of carbon dioxide. It erupted more or less regularly for about 50 years of the 20th century. The carbon dioxide that powered this geyser is probably derived from the limestones below the caldera's volcanic rocks. There's a similar geyser near Green River, Utah.

5.8/9.6 P ⬚⬚⬚(4) Turnoff for Mud Volcano.

MUD VOLCANO AREA

If you have only a short time to spend in this thermal area, be sure to see Dragon's Mouth Spring and Mud Volcano at the north end of the walkway. For a longer visit, you might want to pick up a pamphlet from the box near the parking lot and follow the walk described below.

Unlike the water-driven basins of geysers and hot pools you find on the western Grand Loop Road, Mud Volcano is a vapor-driven system. Here steam rather than water rises from deep underground, and rain and snowmelt provide most of the water to the features. Before railings and boardwalks, early tourists considered the place "most repulsive and terrifying."

Near the center of the parking area's edge is **Mud Caldron**, a large, bubbling, gray lake that seems to have worn away or blown out the cliff behind it. In 1999, a hole created by hydrothermal action suddenly appeared in the parking lot itself.

Mud Volcano Walk

[🚶] This trail loops clockwise (left) around all the features in less than one mile (1.5 km). The climb is a little more gradual in the clockwise direction.

[♿]NOTE: Only the north length of boardwalk, which includes Dragon's Mouth Spring, is wheelchair accessible, since there are steps above Mud Volcano.

The first feature encountered, **Mud Geyser**, viewed from above, was a spectacular geyser when the park was first explored. It erupted to 40 or 50 feet (12–15 m) from its large pool and then drained dramatically. It's now usually a bubbling muddy lake with rare eruptions.

You can see evidence here that the soil is now too hot for any trees to grow. About 20 years ago a surge of local earthquake activity caused changes, including an increase in soil temperature that killed lodgepole pines, which were then blown down all around. The increased heat also created the **Cooking Hillside**, where the trail goes uphill. **Sizzling Basin** and **Churning Caldron** (up the hill) were affected, too. Sizzling Basin used to sizzle more than it does now, while Churning Caldron is now too hot for bacteria to form.

The newest large feature, south of the main walkway, is a seething mud pot, **Black Dragon's Caldron**, which formed in the winter of 1947–48. It must have begun with a terrific explosion, because trees were blown out by their roots, but no one happened to be here to see it. The pool has since grown much larger: it's about 200 feet (60 m) long. Hydrogen sulfide bubbles to the surface, causing the rotten egg smell. The black color (or sometimes a deep gray when there's lots of water) is due to iron sulfides.

Huge and very acid **Sour Lake** beyond Black Dragon's Caldron is less hot than some of its neighbors, allowing bacteria and algae to thrive and color the water green. As you can see from the steam rising beyond Sour Lake, there are more thermal features where the boardwalk doesn't go. Please don't leave the boardwalk unless you're with a ranger.

The walkway crosses quiet meadow and forest, where you may see wildlife before reaching Grizzly Fumarole. This feature changes seasonally from a large, spattering mud pot to some quiet, steaming holes, depending upon its water supply.

Mud Volcano★ is reached by boardwalk today, but in 1870, when the Washburn exploration party named it, there was only a steep hillside. Those who climbed the hill saw a cone from which mud splashed into the trees as much as 100 feet up and 200 feet away (30 and 60 m). It made a tremendous racket. However, only two years later, Superintendent Langford returned to find "the loud detonations which

Black Dragon's Caldron (1986)

resembled the discharges of a gun-boat mortar were no longer heard, and the upper part of the crater and cone had in a great measure disappeared, leaving a shapeless and unsightly hole much larger than the former crater. . . ." Today, Mud Volcano's dark gray water continues to bubble and churn inside a deep hole at the base of the hillside.

Dragon's Mouth Spring★ is still fun to visit, although its activity has diminished in recent years. The belching waters from deep within its cavern make an amazing thumping sound. You may be mesmerized by the sound and the repetition of the surging action.

Acid Hot Springs

The Mud Volcano area and Norris Geyser Basin are the two easily accessible thermal basins that have great concentrations of acid hot springs. Sulphur Caldron, across the road and just north of here, has water that is more acidic than lemon juice (with a pH of 1.3). So much acid and sulfur in the water prevent the growth of colorful bacteria and algae seen elsewhere.

Can you believe that anything can live in such an environment? Surprisingly, at least one microbe *(Sulfolobus acidocaldarius)* thrives here and actually feeds upon sulfur compounds such as hydrogen sulfide. It oxidizes the sulfur, turning it into sulfuric acid. Formerly classified as a bacterium, Sulfolobus has recently been found to belong to the domain *Archaea,* earth's oldest known organisms. It is quite content in Yellowstone, growing well even at the amazingly high temperature of 194°F (90°C). These acidic pools and soils also harbor a more complex organism, a type of alga *(Cyanidium caldarium)* that grows only in acid conditions and thrives at temperatures up to 133°F (57°C).

In the backcountry less than a mile from here, microbiologists have found a very hot pool with a diversity of life forms hitherto unimagined. Conducting studies in Yellowstone, scientists continue to learn about some of the oldest forms of life on earth.

~

Continuing on the Grand Loop Road
5.9/9.5 **P** Sulphur Caldron parking area. A hot spot burst through the pavement here in about 1980, requiring a protective fence.

Sulphur Caldron is below the level of the road. Looking down, you'll see two hot lakes and one very deep steaming and bubbling round hole. Both sulfur and the microorganisms that live on sulfur contribute to the yellow-green color. A new supporting wall had to be built at Sulphur Caldron in 1985 when the pool's acidic gases rotted the old one.

6.2/9.2 South edge of **Hayden Valley**.

The vista opens out here to take in a wide swampy valley. This is an excellent place to see wildlife, especially bison and large birds. There are several convenient turnouts along the road in the next few miles.

The valley's namesake, Dr. Ferdinand Vandiveer Hayden, directed three scientific surveys of the Yellowstone region. Educated as a medical doctor, he had a strong interest in geology and the west, leading him to persuade Congress to fund exploratory parties into this area in 1871, 1872, and 1878. The reports from his first survey helped to convince Congress to establish Yellowstone National Park in 1872.

6.3/9.1 **P** Interpretive sign about Hayden Valley.

Yellowstone Lake Was Bigger Back Then

At the south end of Hayden Valley you can see terraces across the river that mark the shoreline of the much deeper lake that was here about 10,000 years ago, at the time when the last ice age was ending. At one point, Yellowstone Lake was 270 feet higher than at present and covered the entire valley. A glacier dammed the river downstream and filled the valley with water.

The lake sediments and the *till* (clay, sand, and gravel) left by the glaciers combined to form a densely packed type of soil that water can't soak through readily. The poor drainage prevents trees from becoming established. Notice where the trees are growing now—this tree line was always higher than the water level of the lake. Now that the ice has melted, the Yellowstone River and its tributaries meander lazily across the wet valley.

6.9/8.5 **🏛** Wildlife Overlook. Hayden Valley is an excellent sanctuary for wildlife. Animals and birds you might see include bison (almost always); elk, moose, deer, coyotes, grizzly bears; Canada geese, ravens, ospreys, pelicans, gulls, sandhill cranes, marsh hawks, eagles, peregrine falcons, great blue herons, and trumpeter swans; mallard, merganser, and Barrow's goldeneye ducks.

7.4/8.0 Elk Antler Creek crossing.

7.6/7.8 **P** Turnout to the west overlooks **Trout Creek**. If you stop and look down from the cliff, you'll see a maze of waterways that are all one stream.

Meanders on Trout Creek.

Due to a landslide in the 1970s, Trout Creek's meanders now differ greatly from this 1930s sketch.

Meanders and the Northern Pacific Railway

Trout Creek is an excellent example of *meanders*, or the windings a stream forms when it flows across nearly level ground. As the water flows through this remnant of the former lake bottom, it gradually cuts through the glacial till and lake sediments. If the river encounters a small obstruction, it goes around it. As a curve develops, the water flows faster on the outside of the curve, cutting still further, while on the inside of the curve, where the water flows slower, a sandbar of deposited sediment builds up.

 Many years ago people noticed how Trout Creek's meanders resemble the Chinese yin and yang symbol, which represents the passive and active forces of the universe. In 1893, the Northern Pacific Railway, which brought tourists from the eastern U.S., chose the thousand-year-old yin-yang symbol for the logo of their Yellowstone Park Branch Line, proudly pointing out that the same symbol was found in Yellowstone.

The word meander comes from the Meander or Menderes River in western Turkey (ancient Phrygia), proverbial for its windings.

Near Trout Creek, the stagecoach road led across the Central Plateau west to Lower Geyser Basin. This road, completed in 1880, was used until the road from the Upper Geyser Basin to West Thumb over Craig Pass replaced it as the main route in 1892. Today there's only a faint trace of the 1880 road's eastern end.

7.8/7.6 Trout Creek crossing.

9.6/5.8 🚻 Turnout on the east above a large meander in the Yellowstone River. Called Grizzly Overlook, this is a good place to spot wildlife. It's also the best place to see the Sour Creek dome, a geologic feature. As you face the river with Mount Washburn to the left, the Sour Creek dome's center forms part of the eastern horizon. **[GEO.26]**

There's Molten Rock Not Far Below You

As you drive along the north end of Hayden Valley, you're about as close as the road goes to the Sour Creek dome, one of the two areas in the park that overlie molten rock—as close as 2 to 3 miles (3–5 km) below the surface.

Even a very modest rise of the Sour Creek dome affects the shorelines of Yellowstone Lake. Raising Hayden Valley raises the lake outlet (the Yellowstone River), which in turn raises the lake level. This is a different phenomenon from the rise in lake level due to sudden spring thaws that cause the Yellowstone River to flood.

For a map showing the resurgent domes and for more about the domes, see the "Geological History" chapter.

10.6/4.8 P Alum Creek bridge. Alum Creek drains some hot springs reached by the Mary Mountain Trail. Though the water may not actually contain alum (potassium aluminum sulfate), which was sometimes used to contract blood vessels, plenty of legends have risen from the belief that it does. Coach drivers were fond of telling tales about how its waters could shrink practically anything—such as the one about the guy who, upon riding his horse across the creek, found that the horse's hooves had shrunk to pinpoints. Another legend had it that water from this creek, when sprinkled on park roads, caused the distances to shrink.

Eight miles up Alum Creek, the government's first attempt to save the buffalo was made in 1895–96, a time when public sentiment was strong for trying to keep the magnificent animal from extinction. The animals were penned up for feeding in winter. Some segments of fence still stand, but no buffalo were actually saved in this effort.

Alum and other creeks join the Yellowstone River in Hayden Valley, creating an area like a small lake.

Looking south from Alum Creek, you can see the steam from Sulphur Mountain or Crater Hills hot spring and mud pot area. Early tourists who took the Central Plateau route reached this hydrothermal region by a side road. However, the area is no longer open to visitors unless accompanied by a ranger.

11.3/4.1 🚶 🏕 Mary Mountain Trailhead and interpretive sign on the east side. This is the north end of Hayden Valley and a place where waterbirds large and small love to congregate.

The Mary Mountain Trail across the road leads southwest across Hayden Valley and the Central Plateau to rejoin the Grand Loop Road near Lower Geyser Basin about 20 miles (32 km) from here. Since this is prime grizzly habitat, the entire area is closed to overnight camping.

12.4/3.0 🍴 (8) Otter Creek picnic area at the riverside.

12.6/2.8 Otter Creek crossing. Until the 1940s, Otter Creek was the site of a bear feeding ground, where tourists watched a nightly "show" of the bears eating hotel garbage. A photographer was killed by a grizzly in the same area in 1986.

13.1/2.3 Side road to Artist Point along the Grand Canyon of the Yellowstone. This 1.6-mile (2.6 km) road, **South Rim Drive**, takes you to two viewpoints for the canyon and opportunities for hiking. There are also five viewpoints on the north rim. The road first crosses the Yellowstone

Canyon Area: Village and Falls

River on **Chittenden Bridge**. Hiram Chittenden was the captain in the Corps of Engineers who built the first bridge in this locale. He planned and directed the construction of many of Yellowstone's roads between 1891 and 1906 and followed a parallel career as a historian, writing *The Yellowstone National Park: Historical and Descriptive* (1895) and three other histories of the American west.

Incidentally, this canyon was often called Grand Canyon, until Grand Canyon National Park was set aside in Arizona in 1919. Now people simply call the area Canyon or add the words "of the Yellowstone" to Grand Canyon to avoid confusion.

Here's what naturalist John Muir wrote in 1898 about Hayden Valley, the Yellowstone River, and its falls:

> For the first twenty miles its course is in a level, sunny valley lightly fringed with trees, through which it flows in silvery reaches stirred into spangles here and there by ducks and leaping trout, making no sound save a low whispering among the pebbles and the dipping willows and the sedges of its banks. Then suddenly, as if preparing for hard work, it rushes eagerly, impetuously forward rejoicing in its strength, breaks into foam-bloom, and goes thundering down into the Grand Cañon in two magnificent falls, one hundred and three hundred feet high.

South Rim Drive

Above the Yellowstone River's Upper Falls, the water "breaks into foam-bloom," in the words of John Muir.

P **⛱(4)** **🚶** Howard Eaton and Wapiti Lake trailheads are just over the bridge. There's access both for picnicking and for hiking the backcountry trails.

(0.5) **P** **🚻♿(4)** **📍** Uncle Tom's Trail parking area on your left. Here you can leave your car to see the Upper Falls, take Uncle Tom's Trail partway down the canyon, or take either the South Rim Trail or the Clear Lake Trail. You may want to pick up a Yellowstone Association pamphlet about the whole Canyon area from the dispenser near the parking area. (The symbol **📍** indicates trails on the pamphlet map.)

♿ **Uncle Tom's Overlook** at the canyon rim is a wheelchair accessible viewing area for the **Upper Falls** of the Yellowstone and **Crystal Falls** of Cascade Creek (across the canyon).

An early park tour guide and enterprising character, "Uncle Tom" Richardson, built the first crude trail into the

Uncle Tom's Overlook has a fine view of Upper Falls and Canyon Bridge.

canyon in 1898. After ferrying visitors across the Yellowstone above the Upper Falls, he would show them how to descend into the canyon with the help of wooden ladders and ropes.

Special Caution: At least ten people met their deaths falling into the canyon in the 20th century, one in 1999. Please exercise caution, stay away from the edge, and keep small children firmly under control.

Trails from Uncle Tom's Overlook

[Å] **Uncle Tom's Trail** has 328 steps in a descent of less than one-half mile (0.8 km), so it's not for the faint of heart, but it's pleasant when you reach the bottom and find yourself delightfully close to the Lower Falls. The steps are made of metallic mesh, which may seem a little scary as you descend—but there's a railing. Allow plenty of time both for rest and enjoyment. This trail was closed for some years due to damage from the 1959 Hebgen Lake earthquake and winter snows. It's no longer possible to descend to the very bottom of the canyon.

[Å] A much longer but easier and less crowded trail is **Clear Lake Trail**, which begins across the road that leads to Artist Point. It soon intersects with the Wapiti Lake Trail, where you turn left (east) to reach Clear Lake in about a mile (1.5 km). A thermal area with several steaming holes lies another few hundred yards (or meters) along the trail.

You might return the same way you came or continue on past Lilypad Lake and along the canyon rim to Artist Point. The one-way hike would be less than 3 miles (4.8 km) long if you have a drop-off and pick-up arrangement at Uncle Tom's and Artist Point parking lots. You can also hike from Uncle Tom's parking area in either direction along the South Rim Trail.

The Canyon and Falls of the Yellowstone

- Upper Falls: 109 feet (33 m)
- Lower Falls: 308 feet (93 m)
- Canyon depth: 800–1200 feet (240–360 m)
- Canyon width: 1500–4000 feet (450–1200 m) in the area of the overlooks
- Canyon length: about 20 miles (32 km) from the Upper Falls to Tower Junction.

You might wonder why you've never seen a photo showing both the Upper and Lower falls, since they're quite close together. When you look at a detailed map or wander along the canyon rim, you can understand why. The Yellowstone River makes a big bend about two-thirds of the distance downstream to the Lower Falls from the Upper Falls. There the river turns east before it cascades over the Lower Falls. **[GEO.18]**

(1.6) ♿ The side road ends at **Artist Point★★**, a must-see for the full effect of the colorful canyon and Lower Falls. Al-

though every book about Yellowstone describes or pictures this wonderful vista, there's no substitute for standing here yourself. Absorb the unbelievable coloring of the rocks, the depth of the canyon, the grace of the falls with their faint roar nearly a mile away, and the thrill of the rushing river below you. Even the attractive stonework dating from 1938 adds to the beauty of the place.

If you think you see steam in the canyon from several viewpoints, you're not mistaken. There are several hot springs, perpetual spouters, and geysers below you.

Lower Falls of the Yellowstone is by far the most often photographed of Yellowstone's many waterfalls.

Trail from Artist Point toward Point Sublime

👣 A short walk to the east along the rim of the canyon, following a part of the South Rim Trail, reveals some of the most awe-inspiring color panoramas you'll find anywhere. It's not necessary to go the entire 3 miles (4.8 km) round trip to Point Sublime to see sunset colors. Even going a few hundred yards (meters) can reveal how the sky and canyon rival each other on a beautiful evening. You can turn south (right) away from the canyon rim to pass Lilypad Lake and continue on to Ribbon Lake or else pass Clear Lake and return to Uncle Tom's parking area (see Clear Lake Trail, page 173).

There's an unparalleled view of the many pinnacles historically called **Castle Ruins**. Be very careful on the trail's steep, narrow, and slippery places, as there is no support at the canyon edge.

The trail leaves the canyon rim half a mile (0.8 km) before it reaches Point Sublime to continue on to Lilypad and Ribbon lakes and to connect with the Clear Lake Trail (trailhead at Uncle Tom's Overlook parking area).

〜

Continuing on the Grand Loop Road
Go north after the bridge (that is, turn right onto the Grand Loop Road) to reach Canyon Junction and Canyon Village, south (left) to Fishing Bridge Junction.

Canyon Colors

The colors in the Grand Canyon of the Yellowstone derive both from minerals and from living organisms. There are infinite shadings of yellow and orange, and also reds and pinks, off whites, browns, greens, and black. Most of these colors result from the weathering of the rocks and from the upward passage of hot water and steam.

Rainwater and the oxygen in the air break down the rhyolite that is the predominant rock of the canyon. At the same time, hot water and steam react with minerals in these rocks. Both processes produce iron oxides and hydrous iron oxides. These new minerals most often are the common brick red of rust, but some of the hydrated forms are bright yellow.

Some of the black shadings are probably magnetite, a jet black iron oxide, while some of the black is lichen growing on the rocks.

In moist places, such as near the hot springs at the base of the canyon, algae and moss grow and lend a lush green color to the rock surfaces. There may also be colorful microorganisms present around the few hot springs, but the living ones make a modest contribution to the riot of color in the canyon. Dead microorganisms leave no residual color.

Although you might think the Yellowstone River got its name from the yellow of this canyon, historians believe that the Native American name was for the yellow sandstone cliffs lining the river in several stretches from Billings to the river's mouth. The Hidatsa (or Minnetaree) tribe called it "Mi Tsi A-Da-Zi." French fur trappers translated that to "Roche Jaune" and English speakers to "Yellowstone." The early Native Americans who named the river probably never saw this canyon.

13.7/1.7 P 🚻♿(2) Brink of Upper Falls Road to the east. The short side road takes you to a parking area, where a very short walk takes you right to the top of Upper Falls, an exhilarating place to be.

Don't be confused by the names of the two famous falls of the Yellowstone River. Upper Falls is upstream from Lower Falls, but Lower Falls is nearly three times taller than the Upper Falls.

From the parking area, you can also reach **Crystal Falls** on Cascade Creek. Walk back along the side road, crossing the road bridge over a small creek, to the North Rim Trail sign. Then walk an easy few hundred yards (or meters) to Crystal Falls, which drops 129 feet (39 m) in three stages. When the trail forks, take the right fork for the best views of the falls. Take the left fork in order to cross on the bridge at the top of the falls or to continue on the North Rim Trail.

The cool green glen at the top of Crystal Falls was Superintendent Norris's favorite spot in the park. In 1875 he gave the name **Grotto Pool** to the "broad, deep pool of placid water, nearly hidden under the narrow shelf of rocks between the two leaps of the cataract."

14.1/1.3 A "Do Not Enter" sign marks the exit from the one-way North Rim Drive. You may enter that road by turning right at Canyon Junction (1.3 mi/2 km north of here) and continuing on past the Canyon Village facilities.

The magnificent Canyon Hotel was located just up the hill from the intersection here until it burned to the ground in 1960.

Few visitors to Canyon see Crystal Falls at close range.

Canyon Hotel

The famous Canyon Hotel, incorporating an earlier hotel, opened to guests in 1911. Arguably the all-time gem of Yellowstone Park hotels, this was the largest and most elaborate one ever built in Yellowstone.

Elegant Canyon Hotel opened for business in 1911 (Elliot W. Hunter photo).

Designed and supervised by architect Reamer, who had completed the Old Faithful Inn seven years before, Canyon Hotel was a massive and elegantly appointed hotel whose foundations were said to measure a mile around. It was five stories high and had 430 rooms, a huge lobby, and a spiral staircase reputedly copied from the Paris Opera House. The author of this guide remembers passing by as a child with her parents and being told we couldn't go there, because it was a hotel for rich people.

Canyon Hotel was built in the wintertime. Supplies were hauled the 40 miles from the Gardiner railhead on sleds pulled by six horses. Over 100 carpenters worked seven days a week to make it ready for the 1911 tourist season.

14.5/0.9 🏇 A side road leads west to the Canyon Horse Corral, from where guides will take you on one- or two-hour horseback rides along area trails during the summer months. Cascade Meadows here is a good place to see bison, elk, and birds of prey.

15.4/0.0 Canyon Junction. Canyon Village and scenic loop road ("Canyon Rim" and "Inspiration Point Road" on the signs) to the east; Dunraven Pass, Tower Fall, and Tower Junction to the north; Norris Junction and Norris Geyser Basin to the west; Fishing Bridge Junction to the south.

FACILITIES AT CANYON VILLAGE

NOTE: See the Canyon Area map on page 171.

🛢 🅰️♿ At the northeast corner of Canyon Junction is a full service gas station, including towing and maintenance.

✉️ 🔧(2) 🍴 Most of Canyon's facilities are south of the loop road, arranged in a semicircle around a very large parking lot. They include a post office, nature shop, and a general store with lunch counter.

🚻 🅰️♿ **Canyon Visitor Center** has housed a display about Yellowstone's bison since 1997. It is scheduled for renovation and will contain a major display about Yellowstone geology.

🍴(3) 🅰️♿(2) 🛏 In **Canyon Lodge** you'll find three places to eat: a dining room, a cafeteria, and a snack bar. Close by is a cocktail lounge and the registration desk for rooms in the two lodges (new in 1997 and 1999) and motel-like cabins (opened in 1957). Wheelchair accessible rest rooms are available at the cafeteria and the cocktail lounge.

🥾 A pleasant, paved trail about one-half mile (0.8 km) long leads through the woods from the "P" loop of cabins (next to P23–26) to the **Grand View** area, which can also be reached by the one-way North Rim Drive.

🔺 ♨️ North of the other facilities is the 271-site **Canyon Campground** and a building containing self-service laundry and showers. The amphitheater for ranger talks is between the campground and the service station.

North Rim Drive

After the turnoff for the campground, the remainder of this 2-mile (3 km) loop road, also called Canyon Rim Road, is designated one way in this direction (north to south).

Special Caution: At least ten people met their deaths falling into the canyon in the 20th century. Please exercise caution, stay away from the edge, and keep small children firmly under control.

(0.6) Inspiration Point side road (two way). On the way to Inspiration Point, you'll see the granite-gneiss **Glacial Boulder**, as large as a small house and surrounded by trees. Because there's no bedrock like this anywhere near, geologists have concluded that boulders like this one must have been carried from about 20 miles (32 km) north by the glacier that covered this part of the park until some 10,000 years ago. **[GEO.13]**

🚶 The strenuous Seven-Mile Hole Trail leads to the bottom of the canyon from Glacial Boulder. The "hole" refers to a good fishing spot in the Yellowstone River. The trail is not quite 7 miles (11 km) long, but it's very steep.

🚶 Less ambitious hikers might park near the boulder and use the Seven-Mile Hole Trail only to hike along the canyon rim. It's a pleasant 2.5 miles (4 km) round trip and includes a view of slim **Silver Cord Cascade** on Surface Creek, dropping 1000 feet (300 m) into the canyon from the other side.

Inspiration Point★★ was originally called Promontory Point because it protrudes into the canyon, affording fine views in both directions. You see only a slice of Lower Falls from here because of a bend in the river, but the colors of the rocks are marvelous. An earthquake in 1975 caused a large part of this promontory's rock to fall into the canyon.

Innumerable writers, artists, and photographers have tried to reproduce what they see in this canyon. One can never tire of gazing at it. Here's an early 20th century attempt to describe the colors:

> The whole gorge flames. It is as though rainbows had fallen out of the sky and hung themselves there like glorious banners. The underlying color is the clearest yellow; this flushes onward into orange. Down at the base the deepest mosses unroll their draperies of the most vivid green; browns, sweet and soft, do their blending; white rocks stand spectral; turrets of rock shoot up as crimson as though they were drenched through with blood. It is a wilderness of color. . . .
>
> —Dr. Wayland Hoyt, as quoted in the *Haynes Guides.*

Continuing on the North Rim Drive

(1.0) **P** ♿ The colors are decidedly photogenic at **Grand View**★, the first of three other stops along the road. There is no view of either falls at this point.

 Instead of driving, you can hike along the North Rim Trail, which runs from Inspiration Point at the east to Chittenden Bridge at the west.

Other turnouts for cars are at Lookout Point (for the best view of the Lower Falls from this rim) and at Brink of (Lower) Falls trailhead.

(1.2) P 🚶 At **Lookout Point** you can take the switchbacks and steps to **Red Rock Point**, a paved but very steep trail of about 1 mile (1.5 km) round trip. This is the best place to see, hear, and feel the water of the Yellowstone pounding through its narrow canyon or to take photos of Lower Falls and its mossy walls. With binoculars, you may spy osprey nests on the pillar-like formations of canyon rock.

It's hard to believe today that a little over one hundred years ago an enterprising Montanan applied to build an elevator to the bottom of the canyon at the falls. Author Owen Wister got wind of the scheme and mentioned it disparagingly to an acquaintance, who asked, "But why should your refined taste . . . interfere with the enjoyment of the plain people?" To which Wister answered, "Have the plain people told you or anybody that the one thing they lie sleepless craving for is an elevator to go up and down by those falls the way they do in hotels?" "They would like it if it was there," replied the acquaintance. Wister agreed, but asked, "Is that a reason to vulgarize a supreme place of wild natural beauty for all time?" The acting military superintendent, Capt. F. A. Boutelle, recommended against it and the elevator was never built.

Just east of here was a spot called

Grand View is a great place to see the canyon colors.

Moran Point, where artist Thomas Moran sketched in the 1870s. (Despite its name, Artist Point across the canyon was not Moran's sketching spot.) Moran subsequently painted his huge masterpiece of the Grand Canyon, which hung for many years in the nation's capitol and now belongs to the U.S. Department of the Interior. The point had become inaccessible by the mid 1900s.

(1.8) P 🚻♿ 🚶 The next parking area is for **Brink of (Lower) Falls Trail**, a strenuous but rewarding drop of some 600 feet (180 m) in about one-half mile (0.8 km). At the bottom of the trail, you stand at the very point where water tumbles over the top of thundering Lower Falls.

The canyon is not a static place. Various factors combine to insure that the steep walls will further disintegrate and that the canyon will become wider and deeper over the years. Earthquakes, storms, freezing and thawing of winter ice, the continual action of the river, and the *friable* (that is, easily crumbled) nature of the thermally altered rock all contribute to this changeable phenomenon.

(2.0) Just after Brink of (Lower) Falls parking area, the one-way loop meets the Grand Loop Road at mile 14.1/1.3. Turn right for Canyon Junction and Canyon facilities and left for South Rim Drive (page 172) or Fishing Bridge Junction.

Approaches to the Northeast Entrance

If you decide to enter Yellowstone by the Northeast Entrance, you are given the choice of two unforgettable mountain roads that lead to Cooke City and the Northeast Entrance. Most popular is the Beartooth Scenic Byway, which crosses the Beartooth Range and reaches almost 11,000 feet (3350 m) at its summit. The highway is a remarkable piece of engineering that affords spectacular views of mountains, lakes, and valleys. The summer display of wildflowers is unsurpassed, and the chance to throw snowballs in July will appeal to the kids.

A less well known but also beautiful way to reach the Northeast Entrance is by the Chief Joseph Scenic Byway, where the 8000-foot (2440 m) summit reveals other mountains and valleys in profusion.

To take the Beartooth Highway, turn south from Interstate 90 at Laurel, Montana, onto U.S. Highway 212. You'll reach Red Lodge in 43 miles (69 km)—or a total of about 60 miles (97 km) from Billings. At Red Lodge you continue on U.S. 212, which becomes the Beartooth Highway. The distance from Billings to the Northeast Entrance over this route totals about 130 miles (210 km).

The Chief Joseph Highway (Wyoming Highway 296), is easily accessible either from Billings or from Cody, Wyoming. By the Billings-Belfry-Wyoming 120-Chief Joseph Highway route, you reach the park in about 150 miles (240 km). It's less than 80 miles (130 km) from Cody by this route.

RED LODGE, MONTANA
Population: 2200

The small ranching, tourist, and summer home community of Red Lodge was built in 1884 on the site of a summer camp used by the Crow tribe, who painted their tepees with red clay.

From about 1892 to 1952, miners dug coal near Red Lodge and from several mines to the south for the Northern Pacific Railway's locomotives. Immigrants came from Austria, Croatia, Serbia, Italy, and Finland; in the 1920s, Red Lodge had some 5000 people. After the completion of the Beartooth Highway,

Approaches to the Northeast Entrance

Red Lodge began catering to increasing numbers of visitors. Now the town has festivals, fishing, and hiking in summer, and skiing from December to April. There's a historical museum and several buildings listed on the National Register of Historic Places.

THE BEARTOOTH SCENIC BYWAY

The Beartooth Highway covers the 70 miles (113 km) between Red Lodge and Yellowstone's Northeast Entrance. In *American Places* (1993), novelist and Western environmentalist Wallace Stegner wrote: "Yesterday, coming over the Beartooth Scenic Highway . . . we looked across from the 11,000-foot comb of Beartooth Pass and saw not a town, not a ranch, not a cabin, not a road or pole line, not a smoke, only miles beyond miles of forested mountains, shark-tooth peaks, the turquoise sets of lakes, bare stone, snow, wildness, serenity, the blue of distance."

You'll traverse parts of three national forests between Red Lodge and Cooke City: Custer National Forest near Red Lodge, Gallatin National Forest near Cooke City, and Shoshone National Forest in Wyoming.

This unique road first follows Rock Creek out of Red Lodge and in 8 miles (13 km) enters Custer National Forest, where there are four campgrounds on Rock Creek Road. A serious wildfire burned part of this area in August 2000.

Where Rock Creek comes down from the mountains, its valley shows the U-shape typical of a valley carved out by glaciers, with the stream at the bottom of the U.

U.S. 212 leaves the valley and climbs by way of five major switchbacks or horseshoe curves, partly following a Crow path dating from the 19th century. It was considered an engineering miracle when opened in 1936. Notice how the quick change in altitude makes your ears pop. This is caused by the rapid reduction in atmospheric pressure as you go up. (See page 156 for more about high altitude effects.) Across the valley, you can see a road built to bring chromite (chromium ore) down from a mine high in the mountains during World War II.

Rock Creek Valley nestles below the Beartooth Range.

About 20 miles (32 km) from Red Lodge, you reach the **Rock Creek Vista Point** and rest rooms. You can take the short accessible walkway to a fine view of upper Rock Creek Canyon and the mountains and plateaus to the west.

Between here and the summit of the highway, another deposit was tapped for chromite in the 1940s. Near the east summit, you'll see where winter sports enthusiasts mount their snowmobiles or take the (experts only!) ski lift. Several trails lead from both sides of the summit to the sparkling lakes of the Absaroka-Beartooth Wilderness high country.

In this rarified atmosphere, the animals you're most likely to see are the yellow-bellied marmot (related to the woodchuck) and the tiny pika, a tailless, round-eared animal. (See the "Living Things" chapter for more about the animals and plants of the mountain passes.)

In July and early August, the wildflowers are marvelous; stop at turnouts to get a closer look. It's hard to believe the flowers can

Phlox

Sugarbowl

Moss campion

Rosecrown

grow in such a hostile environment, with about a 45-day growing season, but they cling to the small amount of soil above the bedrock. Where there's a bit more soil, permafrost lurks just below their roots—this is arctic tundra. Nevertheless, you can find miniature and brilliantly colored flowers, including forget-me-nots, bluebells, moss campions, and occasionally the bitterroot, state flower of Montana.

There's snow near Beartooth Pass all year. The road is not fully plowed until late May or early June; at that time, you may be traveling through white canyons higher than your car. A little later in the summer, the snow may be pink, indicating the presence of a microscopic plant that grows on its surface and makes its meltwater unsafe to drink.

Upon crossing the Montana/Wyoming state line, you enter Shoshone National Forest, which has surprisingly few trees. Timberline at this latitude is about 10,000 feet (3000 m). On windy slopes below timberline, you'll find only the stunted trees called krummholz.

It's always windy and many degrees cooler up here than in nearby valleys. At the **West Summit** you might want to take the short side road to the top of the ridge for wonderful views of the Absaroka Range, especially to the southwest.

Twin Lakes

Descending through more switchbacks, you'll see many alpine lakes, including Frozen, Long, and Little Bear lakes near the road. These lakes are free of ice for only a few weeks of the year.

You'll pass trailheads for several backcountry hikes on the south side of Beartooth Highway's summit. The trailhead for the Beartooth High Lake Trail is at **Island Lake**, which also has a campground and a boat ramp. Be prepared for cold nights if you camp here—the elevation is about 9500 feet (2900 m).

Island Lake and dozens of others in this part of the plateau are connected by small streams and fall into patterns of straight lines. Geologists call such small, usually circular lakes in a glacial valley *paternosters*, because they resemble a rosary or string of beads.

Crystal-clear **Beartooth Lake** has a campground, picnic area, and boat ramp, and lies at the foot of a monumental beige and red cliff, **Beartooth Butte**. Not far below the summit of this butte, fossil fish have been discovered.

Why Are There Fish Fossils on Top of the Mountain?

The Beartooth Plateau is part of the large block of mountains, the Beartooth Range, which is about 75 miles long and 40 miles (120 by 65 km) across. The plateau was uplifted along nearly vertical faults and is mostly composed of very ancient granites and gneisses that are about 2.7 billion years old. When the uplift started about 50 million years ago, these ancient rocks were buried under about 12,000 feet (3660 m) of younger sedimentary rocks.

These younger rocks have largely been eroded away but remain in a few areas, such as Beartooth Butte.

The strata in the cliff face across Beartooth Lake include a lens-shaped reddish brown layer that is about a third of the way down from the top. The bright colored sediments were deposited in the brackish waters of a stream where it entered the ocean. Many fish fossils have been found in these sediments. These were among the earliest fish on earth about 400 million years ago. Today, those fish are about 10,000 feet (3050 m) above sea level, thanks to the ride they got during the Beartooth Range uplift.

Beartooth Butte is reflected in Beartooth Lake.

A couple of miles (3 km) beyond Beartooth Lake, a gravel road goes north to reach the Clay Butte Forest Service lookout tower in about 2.5 miles (4 km). In July and August, visitors are welcome to enjoy the view and the panorama of mountain photographs on display in the small building at the top. Clay Butte is another remnant of sedimentary rocks similar to Beartooth Butte, but the fish fossil strata have been eroded away.

Descending on the Beartooth Highway, you may notice the prominent white ledge across the wide valley from you. It extends for miles. This is a 100-foot-high (30 m) cliff of Pilgrim Limestone, a very tough sedimentary rock resistant to erosion. Other limestones and volcanic rocks lie above this layer.

A short side road takes you to an excellent overlook for **Pilot** and **Index peaks** to the southwest. Glaciers carved both peaks out of volcanic rocks. Pilot, the pointed one, is a glacial horn; four glaciers carved its pyramidal shape.

In this area, you'll begin to see burned trees from the 1988 Clover-Mist fire that devastated much of the northeastern quadrant of Yellowstone.

Waterfall enthusiasts should look for the lovely **Lake Creek Falls** on a bend of the old road that's supported by well-preserved rockwork. It's about 6 miles (10 km) west of the Clay Butte road. Look for a new bridge and a wide turnout north of the road to find it.

About 14 miles (23 km) east of Cooke City is the junction with Wyoming Highway 296, the Chief

Pilot and Index peaks have long served as landmarks to explorers and visitors.

Joseph Highway. To continue to the Northeast Entrance, see "The continuation of U.S. 212 to Cooke City" below.

CHIEF JOSEPH SCENIC BYWAY

Instead of taking the Beartooth Highway, you may choose to reach the Northeast Entrance via another beautiful mountain pass, using Wyoming Highway 296, the Chief Joseph Highway. Dead Indian Pass (the former name for this entire route) is nearly 3000 feet (900 m) lower than Beartooth Pass, so this route receives somewhat less snow and is plowed (though not daily) in winter.

Why Was This Route Named Dead Indian Pass?

The marker at the summit of the Chief Joseph Highway attributes the name Dead Indian Pass to an incident in 1877 involving the Nez Perce tribe and the U.S. Army. Chief Joseph led his people that year from their home in Idaho, across Yellowstone and the Absaroka Range, then down through Clarks Fork Canyon, a route considered impassable by the pursuing army. One Nez Perce was killed in the area, but about 700 members of the tribe successfully evaded the troops. The group attempted to flee to Canada but was eventually forced to surrender to the army not far short of the Montana-Canada border.

Where their route is known, an occasional marker now points out the Nez Perce National Historic Trail.

The Nez Perce story is commonly accepted as the source of the old name for this pass, but another conflict occurred near here the following year. Col. Nelson A. Miles surprised a camp of Bannock Indians, killing and capturing many of them. 1878 was the last year of troubles between Native Americans and the government in the national park.

The section of the Clarks Fork that passes through this same canyon has now been designated a Wild and Scenic River by the U.S. Congress, preserving it from any development. Only the most experienced kayakers should consider running the Clarks Fork as it passes through what's called The Box, and then only when the water is not too high.

The Chief Joseph Highway begins at the intersection of Wyoming 296 with Wyoming 120. It's about 17 miles (27 km) north of Cody or about 32 miles (51 km) south of Belfry, Montana. The sign at the intersection says "Sunlight Basin Road."

As you drive on Wyoming 120, you can see a distinctive mountain to the east, partly flat-topped, partly craggy, and standing by itself. This is **Heart Mountain**, famous both for the shameful internment of Japanese-Americans at a camp at its base during World War II and also for the Heart Mountain fault or detachment (see "The Case of the Wandering Mountains"). Crow people called this mountain Four Tops Father or sometimes Buffalo Heart Mountain.

The first 10 miles (16 km) of Wyoming 296 climb from the dry, wide Big Horn Basin to viewpoints dominated on the northeast by a red rock butte and on the south by **Pat O'Hara Mountain**, named for an old-timer who lived near here. In geologists' parlance, the red butte is a *hogback*, a resistant ridge within steeply tilted strata.

If you stop on the way up to enjoy the view or the wildflowers, don't be surprised if you think you hear a trumpet or a saxophone! The Northwest College of Powell, Wyoming, has a jazz camp located on this side of the pass.

At the summit, there's a generous parking area, two wheelchair accessible rest rooms, and a historic marker. Here you have one of the most wonderful panoramas a Rocky Mountain pass can offer, from the Absaroka Range crossing the horizon on the south to the Beartooth Plateau on the north.

Summit View

Some of the mountains and valleys from left (south) to right (north) are:

Numerous peaks of the **Absaroka Range**, many above 11,000 feet high (3350 m).

The broad flat valley of **Sunlight Basin** way below.

The perfect pyramid of **White Mountain**.

Windy Mountain, farther away and higher, and **Steamboat Hill** in the foreground.

A little to the right and farther away than Steamboat Hill are the two peaks of **Sugar Loaf Mountain** and a flat-topped hill called **Antelope Mesa**.

The Clarks Fork River and its canyon are too deeply incised to be seen from here but are marked by the steep rise of the **Beartooth Plateau** on the far side.

The Case of the Wandering Mountains

A number of the peaks you see from the Chief Joseph Highway, including Heart Mountain, Steamboat Hill, and Cathedral Cliffs, are part of a geological enigma, the Heart Mountain detachment. By sliding along for large distances, blocks of rock have placed older sedimentary rocks on top of younger ones. Several dozen such examples, some in excess of 10 miles (16 km) across, are spread over an area 60 miles (97 km) long. It is thought that they slid southeastward along a nearly horizontal fault, the average slope of which is only two degrees.

Geologists have advanced numerous hypotheses to explain how these enormous blocks could overcome the frictional resistance and slide distances of many miles. The debate is hot and heavy with no clear solution yet in sight. Unfortunately, large parts of the area are buried under volcanic rocks, hiding any evidence that might be helpful in solving the problem.

The switchbacks west of the summit were paved in the late 1990s. There are several Shoshone National Forest campgrounds, along with ranches and summer homes.

After descending from the summit, the road goes around the "prow" of **Steamboat Hill**. Then, about 2 miles (3 km) after passing Dead Indian Creek and Campground, a gravel road (Wyoming 7GQ) leads west to mountain-ringed Sunlight Basin. One-half mile (0.8 km) beyond the gravel road turnoff, park on the right near the highest bridge in Wyoming for a breathtaking look into deep **Sunlight Gorge**.

In another 14 miles (23 km) or so, Wyoming 296 meets U.S. 212.

The continuation of U.S. 212 to Cooke City

Going west at the junction of Wyoming 296 and U.S. 212 takes you to Cooke City and Yellowstone's Northeast Entrance; east is the Beartooth Highway to Red Lodge. Wyoming 296 leads southeast over Dead Indian Pass to Wyoming 120 and Cody, Wyoming, or Belfry, Montana.

Watch for **Crazy Creek Falls**, about 2.5 miles (4 km) west of the highway junction and nearly opposite the campground with the same name. It's an unusually broad waterfall.

There are five forest service campgrounds and several trailheads between the junction and Cooke City. Those south of the Wyoming/Montana state line are in the Shoshone National Forest and those north of it in the Gallatin National Forest.

You'll find good fishing access for the **Clarks Fork River**. Clarks Fork joins the Yellowstone River near Laurel, Montana. Don't confuse this river with the Clark Fork of the Columbia in western Montana.

Cooke City & Silver Gate, Montana
Combined Population: 150 (winter), 300 (summer)
Cooke City was settled in 1870 by miners soon after gold was found. The area was first called the New World Mining District and the town, "Shoo-Fly," but the name was soon changed to honor the banker and railway magnate, Jay Cooke, Jr., who had promised to bring a railroad to the area. The mining boom peaked in the 1880s, when hundreds of mining claims were recorded in the New World District and the population exceeded 1000. Hopes for a railroad faded, and most mining claims were abandoned, but deposits of gold, copper, lead, silver, chromium, and zinc remain in these mountains.

A huge gold mine was proposed in the 1990s by a Canadian mining company. After considerable national outcry over the damage Yellowstone could suffer from mine tailings and other impacts, development was averted—at least for a time—by a land exchange and the withdrawal of the area from mining claims.

Mineral Mountain (10,531 ft/3210 m) is seen northwest of Cooke City, and **Republic Mountain** (10,170 ft/3100 m) rises to the south. Inquire locally or see the Forest Service maps for four-wheel drive roads and trails in the area.

An all-day hike or horseback trip can be made to a famous spot about 12 miles (19 km) above Cooke City to the north: Grasshopper Glacier, where grasshoppers were frozen into the ice about 300 years ago. Though it's not the only such glacier in the Beartooth, this is the one that's been known and photographed since the 1890s. There are no glaciers at all inside Yellowstone Park today.

Silver Gate, the smaller and newer town 3 miles (5 km) from Cooke City, was founded in the 1930s. The architectural standards for the town site require log construction and rustic architecture.

On the hillsides to the north, you can see how the Storm Creek fire seriously threatened Silver Gate and Cooke City in 1988. The fierce Clover-Mist fire to the south also dropped burning embers in the area. A backfire was set, destroying four buildings when it raged out of control, but in the end, both communities were spared serious damage. A sign along the road (later removed) was altered by a local wit to read "Cooked City."

There are several motels and a few restaurants in Cooke City and Silver Gate. The nearest park accommodations are about 30 miles (48 km) west in the Tower-Roosevelt area.

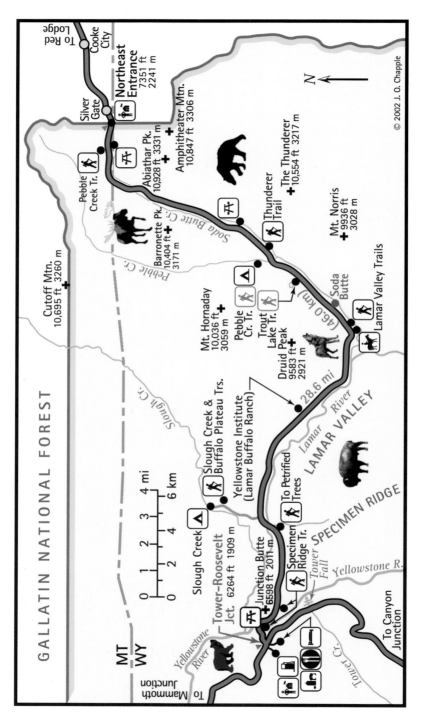

Northeast Entrance to Tower-Roosevelt Junction

© 2002 J. O. Chapple

From the Northeast Entrance to Tower-Roosevelt Junction

This area saw more human activity than any other part of park territory, both before the park was set aside and shortly thereafter. This route along Soda Butte Creek and the Lamar River was an important trail for Native Americans, trappers, and miners in the 19th century.

If miners and railroad interests had had their way in the 1880s and '90s, the Cinnabar and Clarks Fork Railway would have been built through the valley. Congress considered but rejected several bills that would have authorized a right-of-way or eliminated territory from the park's northeast corner in order to bring in a railroad.

The total distance from the Northeast Entrance to Tower-Roosevelt Junction and the Grand Loop Road is about 29 miles (46 km). At first, the road follows Soda Butte Creek. After Soda Butte, the entrance road turns toward the northwest. Here the Lamar River valley offers the chance to see part of the park's northern bison herd. Early or late in the day, you might catch a glimpse of a wolf, especially if you have binoculars or a spotting scope.

The road follows the Lamar River past Specimen Ridge, where there are petrified trees still standing upright. The Lamar joins the Yellowstone River just before Tower Junction.

Road Log

0.0/28.6 Yellowstone National Park boundary.

0.4/28.2 🚻 🔭 Northeast Entrance station. Stop here to pay the entrance fee (see

The Northeast Entrance Station, dating from 1935, is listed as a National Historic Landmark.

the "Travel Tips" for fee information). The rest room is to the east (left) of the road and outside the entrance station.

0.5/28.1 [†♠] Side road to the north for regional ranger headquarters.

1.5/27.1 [⊼](7) [🎰][♿] [⊷] Warm Creek picnic area and access for fishing in Soda Butte Creek.

1.6/27.0 [🚶] Short road to parking for the Pebble Creek Trail. The trail is a 12-mile (19 km) loop that passes between Barronette Peak and Mount Hornaday through forests, meadows, and mountain views. The trail meets this road at Pebble Creek campground.

2.2/26.4 [P] Turn out to get a good look at red-streaked **Abiathar Peak** (pronounced uh-BI-uh-ther). Paleontologist Charles Abiathar White helped the early Yellowstone expeditions, and the U.S. Geological Survey honored him with his own mountain. Behind Abiathar is **Amphitheater Peak** on the park's eastern boundary.

Abiathar Peak exhibits layers of lava and volcanic mudflows.

Timberline

What determines how far up a mountainside trees will grow? This depends on the latitude and the characteristics of the particular mountain. Factors such as rainfall, amount of wind and sun, temperature, steepness, and type of soil also affect tree growth. At Yellowstone's latitude (44–45° N), timberline is usually at 9500 to 10,000 feet (2900–3050 m). However, the upper slopes of the mountains you see in this part of the park are so steep that trees cannot grow even at 8500 or 9000 feet (2600–2750 m).

Botanists use the word *timberline* for the upper limit of fully erect trees and the expression *tree line* to mean the upper limit of all trees, including those that are stunted.

2.3/26.3 Montana/Wyoming state line. When Montana and Wyoming territories became states, surveyors intended the boundary to follow the 45th parallel, the line of latitude midway between the equator and the North Pole. However, surveying was less accurate a century ago, when the tools were a compass for observing directions and a theodolite for measuring angles. Mountainous country was especially difficult to survey. The true 45° N latitude is more than 100 yards (or meters) south of the state line in this vicinity.

3.3/25.3 First crossing of Soda Butte Creek, which the road follows for its first 15 miles (24 km) inside the park. Before

Why Do the Mountains Look Striped?

On all the nearby mountains, you can see stripes or horizontal layers, which are highlighted until midsummer by bands of snow. Abiathar Peak east of the road is layered by chocolate-colored lava flows and volcanic mud flows that were part of the Absaroka volcanic outpourings about 50 million years ago. **[GEO.5]**

Facing Abiathar from west of the highway is Barronette Peak, which is also topped by similar chocolate-colored volcanic layers. The lower slopes of Barronette, however, consist of buff to gray layers of ancient sedimentary limestones that are about 350 million years old. **[GEO.2]**

Similar sedimentary rocks underlie Abiathar Peak, but they are difficult to see from the highway. All of these rocks are practically undeformed and are still lying in nice horizontal layers, a phenomenon sometimes called layer-cake geology.

the 1930s, the road stayed on the west side of the creek; the old roadbed is now used as a cross-country ski trail.

4.2/24.4 Sign for **Barronette Peak**. The mountain to the west was named for "Yellowstone Jack" Baronett, who came to the area in 1864 to prospect for gold. (See also "Baronett's Bridge and Its Successors," page 204.) The misspelling of his name by members of the 1878 Hayden Expedition later became the officially approved form.

Early in the season, you can see dozens of small waterfalls catapulting off Barronette Peak.

7.5/21.1 🎋(2) 🚻♿ Ice Box Canyon picnic area.

7.8/20.8 North end of **Ice Box Canyon**. This steep canyon is so situated that the sun never penetrates to the bottom; in earlier years, ice remained on the east wall well into summer. There's no good

vantage point for seeing to the bottom of the canyon.

The rock exposed on the west side of the road (opposite the canyon) consists of Absaroka volcanic materials brought here roughly 50 million years ago in a mudflow of mixed rock and water called a *lahar*. Since this flow is near the Lamar Valley, geologists cannot resist calling this one the "Lamar lahar."

8.3/20.3 South end of Ice Box Canyon.

8.8/19.8 🚶 Thunderer Trailhead. This steep trail crosses a pass about 1000 feet (300 m) below the summit of **The Thunderer**, the mountain directly to the east here. The trail provides a route between The Thunderer and Abiathar Peak to reach the backcountry Cache Creek Trail.

Named for its supposed tendency to attract thunderstorms, this mountain saw the death of a lone hiker who fell from the summit in 1985.

9.5/19.1 🚶 Pebble Creek Trailhead, with a small parking area. This is a way to join the Pebble Creek Trail without passing through the campground.

9.7/18.9 ⛺ Crossing of Pebble Creek and side road to **Pebble Creek Campground**, one of the seven Yellowstone campgrounds that do not require reservations. This campground has 32 sites with chemical toilets and no showers.

🚶 For a pleasant short hike to see an interesting geologic outcrop, park at the upstream end of the campground and walk a few hundred yards (meters) along the start of the **Pebble Creek Trail**. Layers and layers of limestone about 350 million years old are exposed in cliffs in a lovely canyon cut by the creek. This limestone was laid down at the bottom of a vast sea, and looking closely at the rock reveals bits of tiny marine organisms. These fossil *crinoids*, with a cup-shaped body and a slender stem, are related to today's starfish and sea urchins. The trail continues for about 12 miles (19 km) through spectacular mountain scenery to come out at the Warm Creek picnic area.

To the northwest of the main road is **Pyramid Mountain**, and out of view behind it is **Mount Hornaday**. The latter was named for Dr. William T. Hornaday, a noted naturalist and zoo director who helped preserve the bison from extinction 100 years ago.

The road passes along the edge of the broad, swampy meadow called **Round Prairie**, where Pebble Creek and Amphitheater Creek join Soda Butte Creek.

10.9/17.7 🚶 ⛵ **Trout Lake Trailhead**. The trail marker appears partway up the trail. A rather steep but rewarding hike of about 1 mile (1.6 km) round trip takes you up a hillside strewn with wildflowers to a sparkling mountain lake with meadows on two sides.

Trout Lake was called Fish Lake when it was a major source of food for Cooke City residents. Some of the early residents broke the law and killed trout with charges of dynamite.

There's an abundance of trout in this deep lake, but they're not easy to catch. Remains of an old weir or fence for catching fish are still at the lake's outlet, a remnant from the days when fish eggs were collected here.

13.0/15.6 Soda Butte. This landmark is worth a short stop, especially if you're entering the park for the first time. It's the lone thermal feature in this corner of the park. **Soda Butte** is an extinct hot spring cone made of travertine, the same rock that forms Mammoth Hot Springs' terraces. Although it has not done any cone building during recorded history, it or its neighboring hot spring often gives off an

Soda Butte imitates the shape of Abiathar Peak a few miles away.

odor of hydrogen sulfide. Prospector A. Bart Henderson named Soda Butte in 1870. He mistakenly thought the feature was made of sodium carbonate, or washing soda. Pieces of it shine like marble.

Take the path behind Soda Butte to see a colony of cliff swallows. The seepage of warm water here was called Soda Butte Medicinal Springs by Superintendent Norris.

In the Vicinity of Soda Butte

Due east of Soda Butte is Mount Norris. Philetus W. Norris was the eccentric but effective second superintendent of the park (1877–82). He was also a prolific writer; his writings include poetry about the west, a road guide to the park, and excellent superintendent's reports that are invaluable to historians. Besides Mount Norris, several other park features carry his name, including Norris Geyser Basin and Norris Pass.

Superintendent Norris

In 1886, when the U.S. Cavalry patrolled the park, a soldier station was built just across the road from Soda Butte. Later used as a ranger station, the wooden structure was moved to the Lamar Buffalo Ranch in the 1930s. In army days, the park had 19 soldier stations, sometimes called snowshoe cabins. They were lonely outposts built to shelter soldiers on patrol in the wintertime. Scattered about the park today are about 40 patrol cabins that shelter rangers, but the rangers don't usually stay in them for weeks at a time as the soldiers often did.

The mountain to the northwest here is Druid Peak. If you're traveling west, this is the last you will see of the striated lava-topped mountains so common in this part of Yellowstone.

For the next few miles, look for wolves; the Druid pack denned near here in recent years.

14.0/14.6 🚶 🐴 Lamar River Trailhead, and a large parking area for **Specimen Ridge, Lamar Valley, Cache Creek,** and **Miller Creek trails.** This is the starting point for long trails up Specimen Ridge or into the remote backcountry. One can hike or ride horseback up the Lamar River and east of the

Mirror Plateau into mountainous areas to Yellowstone's eastern boundary and beyond.

All trails cross a sturdy footbridge over Soda Butte Creek. The apparatus near the bridge measures the flow of water.

[🚶] **Historic remnants hike.** History buffs might enjoy a short walk from this trailhead to some historic points from the 19th century. Cross the Soda Butte Creek footbridge to look for remnants of the Gardiner to Cooke City miners' road. According to the late Yellowstone historian Aubrey Haines, the two deep tracks that can still be seen paralleling Soda Butte Creek were left by miners. The men dragged an *arrastre* (a heavy apparatus for grinding ores, pronounced a-RASS-treh) along the valley.

Farther along the trail, you might look for the scant remains of a cabin built for gamekeeper Harry Yount. About 1.6 miles (2.6 km) from the parking area, you can still find chimney stones and traces of a spring box at the base of the hill near the trail junction. Over 100 years later, tall, deep green rye grass still gives away the area where Yount pastured his horses. If you reach the point where you would have to ford the Lamar River, you've gone beyond the remnants.

14.4/14.2 [🚶] [🐎] [🅿️][♿] Alternate access to the Lamar Valley trails. This one is used especially by horseback riders, who take guided pack trips into the mountains.

14.9/13.7 Located just up the hill from the present road was an especially steep section of the old road, the Jackson Grade. George Jackson squatted (that is, settled without legal claim) near here in the 1880s.

15.3/13.3 Confluence of Soda Butte Creek with the Lamar River. The Lamar River valley is a summer feeding ground for bison, so your chances of seeing them along this stretch of road are excellent.

Near here was the site of an elk corral, used to trap elk and reduce the size of the herd for about 30 years in the mid 20th century.

The Lamar River and Its Valley

The glacier-carved Lamar Valley entered the historical record as far back as 1836 in *Journal of a Trapper* by Osborne Russell. He praised the "Secluded Valley" for its "wild romantic scenery." Evening light brings forth a particularly beautiful luster.

The Lamar is a long river that originates on the eastern boundary of the park. First called the East Fork of the Yellowstone, in 1885 it was officially named for President Grover Cleveland's secretary of the interior, who bore the melodious classical name Lucius Quintus Cincinnatus Lamar. As interior secretary, Lamar was a good friend to Yellowstone. He later became an associate justice of the Supreme Court.

Death Gulch

Up Cache Creek, above where it enters the Lamar River, is an interesting hot springs area. Located about 5 miles from the road and across the creek from the trail, the area has been called Death Gulch since 1888, when geologist Walter Weed discovered that numerous animals had died there from inhaling poisonous gases. About 15 years later the hot springs in Death Gulch were named Wahb Springs after a fictional grizzly bear that met his end there in *Biography of a Grizzly*, by self-taught naturalist Ernest Thompson Seton.

Creeks with Mineral Names

A veritable mineral collection of names graces the creeks flowing into the Lamar River from the Mirror Plateau and Specimen Ridge to the southwest. On a topographic map you can find Flint, Opal, Chalcedony, Amethyst, Jasper, and Crystal creeks. Two other mineral-named creeks flow into the Yellowstone River from high on the opposite side of Specimen Ridge: Agate and Quartz creeks. All of these minerals, which contain silica, have been found in Yellowstone Park, though not necessarily near these creeks.

15.8/12.8 North of the road you may notice a rectangular, fenced-off area of lush plant growth. Biologists call this an *exclosure*, meaning an area where they've excluded all the larger browsing animals (moose, bison, elk, and deer), in order to compare the protected area with its surrounding territory. Botanists study the composition and growth rates of the vegetation in several such exclosures in the park.

narrowleaf cottonwoods and quaking aspen.

18.0/10.6 Lamar Ranger Station and summer headquarters of the Yellowstone Institute. The ranger station is a rangers' residence, not a visitor facility. The site of the former Lamar Buffalo Ranch now houses the educational branch of the Yellowstone Association. (For details about the Yellowstone Association and

16.3/12.3 Near where a former picnic area was flooded repeatedly by the river, you'll see three prominent types of trees that thrive in the relatively low altitude of the Lamar Valley: black and

Shadows lengthen in the early evening at Lamar Buffalo Ranch.

Institute, see the "Travel Tips.")

🚲 Bicycles are allowed on the service road at the north end of the cabin area for a mile (1.6 km) up Rose Creek, but, since wolves have been reintroduced in the area, anyone wishing to go there should first check with a ranger.

Buffaloes, Wolves, and Coyotes

The present location of the Lamar Ranger Station and Yellowstone Institute was the site of the Lamar Buffalo Ranch from 1907 into the 1950s. (The name buffalo was used when the park was new—zoologists prefer to call them bison.) Here bison were kept in corrals and fed on hay cut in the Lamar Valley. The imported plains herd interbred with native mountain bison, and some of their descendents live in the park today.

Wolves were brought in to the park in the mid 1990s, and an acclimatization pen for them was located on Rose Creek, a mile or so above the cabins. Considerable controversy surrounded the reintroduction of wolves to Yellowstone, but the animals are thriving.

In the Lamar Valley, you're still more likely to see a coyote than a wolf.

Four cowboys rounding up a bison in the Buffalo Ranch corral in 1935, by Jack Haynes.

Wolves will kill coyotes that are competing for food, and when the wolves were reintroduced, they began to make an immediate difference in the park's coyote population. Coyotes may be almost anywhere at almost any time of day, hunting small prey and carrion. They have little fear of man and may attack people if habituated to them.

There's more about all these animals in the "Living Things" chapter.
Special Caution: Do not feed any animals in the park. It can be dangerous for you and for them.

If you're traveling toward the Northeast Entrance along the main road, you have a long, beautiful view here of nearly 20 miles up the Lamar River valley to Saddle Mountain and other peaks in the Absaroka Range near the eastern boundary of the park.

Several miles beyond Saddle Mountain is a remote area first described by Superintendent Norris, after exploring it in 1880; he named it Hoodoo Basin. *Haynes Guide* described "tall, massed eroded rock pinnacles, which reveal to those who let loose their imaginations a large variety of forms of humans and beasts." (There's more about hoodoos on page 150.)

20.8/7.8 East end of **Lamar Canyon**. In 1885, Historian Hiram Chittenden described Lamar Canyon's many boulders as "almost spherical in shape, and, in many instances . . . as smooth as if from the hand of a stone glazier. They are piled up like billiard balls, to such a depth that the stream flows entirely out of sight beneath them."

The large outcrops along the road in this canyon consist of rocks that are among the oldest in the park, about 2.7 billion years old. In fact, there are few areas in the world where older rocks are exposed. These rocks are granites and gneisses, formed deep within the earth at a time when a mountain range was being made above them. Those mountains have long since eroded away. **[GEO.1]**

21.7/6.9 West end of Lamar Canyon.

22.8/5.8 ⏣ 🚶 ➤ 🏕 Side road to **Slough Creek Campground** and Buffalo Plateau and Slough Creek trailheads, with several bird-watching spots from turnouts. At this unreserved and unimproved campground are 29 campsites located about 2 miles (3 km) up the Slough Creek road.

🅿 🏕 To take one of the two trails, stop at the parking area before the campground.

The **Buffalo Plateau Trail** goes north to join several other trails in the Absaroka-Beartooth Wilderness. A 21-mile (34 km) loop goes from the Slough Creek Campground out of the park and back in, joining the Hellroaring Creek Trail west of Tower Junction.

🚶 The **Slough Creek Trail** is popular with fishermen. A hike of about 4 miles (6.5 km) round trip (sometimes steep) takes you through thriving wildflowers to tranquil First Meadow (as fishermen call it), where a patrol cabin for rangers' use is located.

The Slough (pronounced SLOO) Creek Trail has an unusual reason for being. Just north of the park boundary is the private Silver Tip Ranch, which is now accessible by air but was previously only reached by this trail or wagon road. At a point called the Slough Creek Transfer, supplies for the ranch are still transferred from trucks to horsedrawn vehicles kept just for traversing a particularly bad section of road through the meadows. Even now, you may see stagecoaches or wagons as you hike this trail.

23.3/5.3 Lamar River bridge and mouth of Crystal Creek, which enters the Lamar River from the south.

23.6/5.0 🚶 On an unmaintained trail, you can ascend the ridge to your south, following Crystal Creek to see some petrified trees on **Specimen Ridge**. Because it's a strenuous hike and the trees are not easy to find, get a map and instructions from the Tower Ranger Station before you go. Better yet, go with a ranger or other knowledgeable person.

Petrified Trees

South of the road is a remarkable phenomenon: high up on the slopes, trees that used to grow here have been turned to solid stone. This happened long before the caldera events that left us Yellowstone's present-day thermal features. The trees became *petrified*; that is, the wood was converted to stone by dissolved minerals in water at the time when they were covered with volcanic lava, ash, and tremendous mudflows. This was during the Eocene epoch, 50 million years ago. Other areas contain petrified wood—the best known in the United States is Petrified Forest National Park in Arizona. But Yellowstone has more well-preserved upright trees than any other known locality.

Preserved by petrification were cool-climate trees (spruce and willow, such as grow here today), temperate trees (like sycamore and walnut), and subtropical trees (like breadfruit and avocado). Researchers have concluded that the climate at the lower altitudes must have been much warmer than it is today and that the trees common to cooler climates were washed down—some still upright—in mudflows from higher altitudes. There must also have been much more rainfall, perhaps 50 to 60 inches (130–150 cm) per year, compared to today's 15 to 18 inches (38–45 cm) per year. This area may have resembled present-day Guatemala.

On a lighter note, historian Hiram Chittenden contributes the following, inspired by tales told by trappers: "Sage brush, grass, prairie fowl, antelope, elk, and bears may there be seen as perfect as in actual life.

> Even flowers are blooming in colors of crystal,
> And birds soar with wings spread in motionless flight,
> While the air floats with music and perfumes siliceous,
> And the sun and the moon shine with petrified light!"

Another entertaining version of the story has birds sitting on "peetrified" branches, singing peetrified songs.

In present-day Yellowstone, only one of the standing petrified trees is easy to reach—the others require strenuous off-trail climbs. To see this specimen, take the short side road west of Tower Junction, described at mile 16.7/1.4 in the road log "From Mammoth Junction to Tower Junction."

24.4/4.2 P This wide turnout at the south side of the road is the best place to try to see petrified trees near the top of Specimen Ridge. You can see them only with good binoculars and you need to know exactly where to look.

On the opposite side of the road not far from here was Little America, a 1930s camp for men of the Civilian Conservation Corps, who found the weather in this valley early and late in the season to be a lot like Antarctica. The original Little America, on the continent of Ant- arctica, had been established by Richard Byrd late in 1928. Today this area is called Little America Flats.

Traces the Glaciers Left Here

In the 4 miles (6 km) between the Lamar River bridge and Junction Butte, you'll see a particularly rich collection of evidence that this valley was buried in ice not so very long ago. In fact, the ice was about a half mile thick (800 m), with its base at about the level of the highway, so that even Specimen Ridge was covered.   **[GEO.14]**

You'll see numerous small lakes and ponds on the north side of the road. These are *kettle ponds*, formed when the glacier scoured out holes in

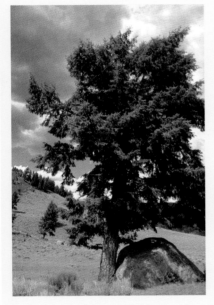

the ground and replaced the rocks or soil with ice. When the glacier retreated, boulders, gravel, and other debris left by the glacier on top of the pond ice insulated the ice from melting. Eventually, as the climate warmed, the ice melted and left round depressions that are now filled with water (kettle ponds).

[GEO.15]

What about the large boulders scattered about in this valley? These are *glacial erratics*, rock fragments that are very different from the local bedrock. They were brought from the Beartooth Range north of the park and gently dumped wherever the glacier had carried them. (For more about glaciers in Yellowstone, see the "Geological History" chapter.)

A nursery rock shielded this Douglas fir tree as a seedling.

A fascinating attribute of the glacial erratics leads some of them to be called *nursery rocks* by botanists: many of them have one Douglas fir tree growing just north or west of the boulder, where seedlings collect moisture and are protected from the wind.

🛉 Turnouts along the last 5 miles east of Tower-Roosevelt Junction provide access to many ponds, including the Trumpeter Lakes some distance from the road, where trumpeter swans have sometimes nested. Ducks and other aquatic birds, yellow-headed and red-winged blackbirds, as well as otters and muskrats sometimes make these ponds their home. However, the water may dry up by midsummer, and the birds and animals then disperse throughout the area.

26.7/1.9 🥾 Specimen Ridge Trailhead on the south. This is not a trail where you'll find petrified tree specimens, but rather a trail along the top of Specimen Ridge. You can get to the same trail at mile 27.4/1.2.

P An interpretive sign on the north side of the road explains the evidence left all around by the glaciers.

As you approach Tower Junction, keep your eyes open for black bears. The Tower area is one of the places where they like to live during the summer.

Baronett's Bridge and Its Successors

After prospector and hunter Jack Baronett built his wooden toll bridge in 1871, the trip from Gardiner to Cooke City was much easier for miners (although some of them couldn't pay the toll), as well as for park staff and visitors.

The bridge figured in the Nez Perce tribe's escape from General Howard's pursuing troops in 1877: the Nez Perce burned the bridge, delaying the troops some three hours while Chief Joseph and his people escaped up the valley of the Lamar River.

In 1880, Baronett rebuilt his bridge and continued to collect tolls until 1899, when the government finally bought the bridge. It remained here in a dilapidated state until 1905, but a steel one was built just upstream in 1903.

Look south as you cross the present concrete bridge, dedicated in 1963, and you'll see some colorful thermally altered rocks on the banks of the river. Near that spot, a worker lost his life in a tragic accident in 1939. He had

"Yellowstone Jack" Baronett's bridge over the Yellowstone River.

been lowered into a deep pit dug to explore a possible site for a new bridge foundation, but he lost consciousness and could not be hoisted out of the pit for 20 minutes. He died of exposure to hydrogen sulfide and carbon dioxide gases.

27.0/1.6 Junction Butte, just north of the road, rises above the spot where the Lamar River joins the Yellowstone.

27.4/1.2 ⛟ **(9)** 🏛️ ♿ 🚶 Yellowstone River picnic area and **Specimen Ridge Trailhead** (alternate access) on the south.

If you climb the trail above the picnic area, you'll be treated to some spectacular views into the Yellowstone River canyon and a much more extensive view of Calcite Springs than can be seen at the Calcite Springs Overlook on the other side. (The overlook is described at mile 1.7/16.6 in the road log "From Tower Junction to Canyon Junction.")

In about 2 miles (3 km) the trail leaves the canyon and continues for many miles along Specimen Ridge. A branch of this trail leads back to the highway at mile 26.7/1.9, the Specimen Ridge Trailhead.

27.7/0.9 🅿 Short side road northward to parking area. Below the point of land formed by the junction of the two rivers,

about one-half mile (0.8 km) north of this point on the road, stood the first bridge ever built over the Yellowstone River, Baronett's bridge.

27.9/0.7 Yellowstone River bridge, also called the Tower Bridge for its proximity to Tower Fall.

28.6/0.0 Tower-Roosevelt Junction. The junction here is both the joining of the Yellowstone and Lamar rivers and the intersection of the Northeast Entrance Road with the Grand Loop Road.

🏛️ ♿ 🚻 **(2)** 🚰 🏕️ Just west of the intersection is a service station and, slightly farther west, the Tower Ranger Station.

🅿 🛏️ 🍴 Follow the short road straight across the intersection (directly south) for Roosevelt Lodge, its associated cabins, and a small store.

Mammoth Hot Springs Junction is farther to the west; Tower Fall, Dunraven Pass, and Canyon Junction to the south; the Northeast Entrance to the east.

To Mammoth Jct.

Tower-Roosevelt Jct.
6264 ft   1909 m

To Northeast Entrance

Tower Fall

Lost Creek Falls, Lost Lake, & Tower Fall Trs.

Prospect Pk.
9525 ft
2903 m

Tower Fall Tr.

Tower Creek, Roosevelt Lodge, & Service Rd. Trs.

Tower Cr.

18.3 mi   (29.5 km)

Antelope Cr.

N

Chittenden Rd.

Mt. Washburn Trail

0   1   2   3 mi
0 1 2 3 4 5 km

Mt. Washburn
10,243 ft 3122 m

GRAND CANYON OF THE YELLOWSTONE

Dunraven Pk.
9904 ft 3019m

Mt. Washburn Tr.

Dunraven Pass
8873 ft 2704m

Hedges Pk.
9685 ft 2952 m

Cascade Lake Tr.

Cascade Lake

Cascade Cr.

Yellowstone   River

Canyon Junction
7903 ft 2409 m

To Norris Junction

Inspiration Point

Canyon Area map, p. 171

To Fishing Bridge Jct.

Lower Falls
Upper Falls

© 2002 J. O. Chapple

Tower-Roosevelt Junction to Canyon Junction

From Tower Junction to Canyon Junction

This stretch of road takes you first to the popular Tower Fall area, then climbs steeply to cross Dunraven Pass, opened to wagon travelers in 1905. Near the top of this highest pass in Yellowstone, you can stop for excellent mountain panoramas in three different directions. The midsummer wildflowers are outstanding.

The distance from Tower-Roosevelt Junction to Canyon Junction is about 18 miles (29 km).

Road Log

NOTE: The Tower-to-Canyon road over Dunraven Pass may be closed for rebuilding for several years in the early 2000s. Check with Yellowstone authorities before you go.

0.0/18.3 Tower-Roosevelt Junction. The main road toward the south leads to Tower Fall, Dunraven Pass, and Canyon Junction; west is Mammoth Hot Springs Junction; east is the Northeast Entrance.

Just west of the intersection is a service station and, slightly farther west, the Tower Ranger Station. On a short side road directly across from the entrance road is Roosevelt Lodge and cabins.

Roosevelt Lodge and cabins

⊟ ⓘ ⋒ ⓘ♿(2) The lodge, named for President Theodore Roosevelt, contains a dining room, wheelchair accessible rest rooms, and registration office for cabins and activities. You may arrange horseback rides, stagecoach trips, and Old West cookouts.

⛽ 🏕(3) There's a general store nearby with tables on its porch. The store sells firewood for cabin stoves and campsites.

🚶 For the unmarked, short **Lost Creek Falls Trail** (about 0.3 mi/0.5 km long), walk behind Roosevelt Lodge and go left at the signboard—don't cross the creek as you would for Lost Lake. It's a moderately steep climb with loose gravel on the trail near the top, but the 40-foot (12 m) falls and its setting are a delightful reward. In late summer, look for raspberries along the trail. Lost Creek Falls was described in Hiram Chittenden's 1903 guidebook as providing "a scene of quiet beauty rarely found in so wild and rough a country." Compared with the "wild" crowds you may find at Tower Fall, you will find this nearby but little-visited waterfall a welcome contrast!

🏃 Lost Lake is less than a mile (1.5 km) west up the Lost Lake Trail that starts behind the lodge and across the creek. It's an easier hike from the opposite end, starting near the Petrified Tree (1.4 miles west of Tower Junction). A third trail from Roosevelt goes to Tower Fall, starting behind the lodge or from the corral, reaching the waterfall in about 3.5 miles (6 km).

0.9/17.4 Rainy Lake was named because the bubbling springs in the lake make it look like it's raining on the surface.

1.1/17.2 The hill to the east of the road is **Bumpus Butte**, named for Dr. Hermon Carey Bumpus, the naturalist and educator who set up the park's first museums and roadside exhibits. In addition, Bumpus wrote and illustrated small guides to the natural features in the 1930s.

Not far from here, President Roosevelt's entourage set up camp during his two-week visit to the park in 1903.

The Springs Down by the River

At Calcite Springs Overlook, you may see steam or smell a rotten egg smell coming up from below. The Calcite Springs area is interesting to know about but only accessible to experienced and hardy hikers.

Explorers have known this thermal area since the early 1800s, sometimes calling it Burning Spring. In 1869, explorers watched as "several gallons of a black liquid ran down and hardened upon the rocks . . . it proved to be sulphur, pure enough to burn readily when ignited," quoted in Lee H. Whittlesey's *Yellowstone Place Names*.

Calcite Springs is one of the very few hot springs in the world that emits a petroleum-like material. This material apparently forms by one or both of the following processes. High water temperatures underground may cause rapid reactions in the plant or animal debris in ancient underlying sediments. Alternatively, downward seepage of the surface waters carrying dissolved plant matter and bacteria may be heated at depth, causing the organic materials to react to form oily compounds. However it forms, steam carries this material up to surface vents along the banks of the Yellowstone River.

The hot gases emitted here have the highest known concentration of hydrogen sulfide gas of any of the park's thermal areas—about five percent. Also near Calcite Spring's vents are deposits of gypsum (hydrous calcium sulfate) and pyrite (iron disulfide), and crystals of calcite (calcium carbonate) and barite (barium sulfate), in addition to the nearly pure sulfur.

1.7/16.6 P Calcite Springs Overlook. There's a short loop trail with interpretive signs here and views into the colorful canyon and across it to the Lamar Valley. This part of Yellowstone's canyon is called **The Narrows**, since it's the narrowest part of any of the four canyons of the Yellowstone River.

Bumpus Butte (at left) above Calcite Springs

Along the stretch of road between the Calcite Springs overlook and Tower Fall, there is limited parking at turnouts.

Special Caution: Several people have slipped and fallen to their deaths while climbing on the canyon side of the road between this overlook and Tower Creek bridge. Make sure you stand in a safe place to look at the views and take photos.

2.1/16.2 Overhanging Cliff, with limited parking along the road. The road excavation has undercut a fine example of columnar basalt that is 2.2 million years old. As you might suspect, landslides here have been a major problem for road builders. **[GEO.12]**

Basalt columns at Overhanging Cliff dwarf passing cars.

Basalt Columns

The area near Tower has some clear examples of basalt lavas that look like stockade fences. You can see them at the roadside at Overhanging Cliff as well as across the canyon, where two lava flows run horizontally for miles. All of these are fine examples of *columnar jointing*, that is, structures that look like closely packed, vertical logs of lava.

These basalt columns were formed when the lava flowed, stopped, cooled enough to become solid, and then continued to cool and shrink. A solidified lava flow can easily shrink in a vertical direction and still remain homogeneous and unfractured; it simply becomes a thinner lava flow. Cooling rock, however, shrinks in all directions, not just vertically. As it shrinks in the horizontal direction, cracks must form. The cracks extend and intersect with others, making columns that are polygons, with space between the columns.

The process that made the columns is very much like the formation of mud cracks. Just as the sun shining on a mud puddle causes the mud to dry, shrink, and crack, basalt shrinks into columns, but it's

Volcanic basalt columns in The Narrows of Yellowstone Canyon are separated by easily eroded sedimentary rocks.

due to cooling rather than drying. If you look at the undersides of the columns here at Overhanging Cliff, you'll see that the ends are mostly pentagons and hexagons, just like mud cracks.

2.2/16.1 **P** **Devil's Den** (with very little parking along the road) is a collection of fantastic rock formations just above Tower Fall and extending up Tower Creek's canyon. When F. V. Hayden, leader of the 1871 Hayden Expedition, named this feature, he was probably thinking of a thicket called the Devil's Den on the battlefield at Gettysburg, a battle fought only eight years before.

Devil's Hoof, with an obvious cleft, stands tall and alone in the Devil's Den jumble. The rock in these formations is not the same rock that forms the columnar jointing just to the north. The Devil's Den rocks were deposited by streams or mudflows as horizontal layers of volcanic debris. Vertical cracks formed in the beds of debris, the rain

and the river eroded material from the cracks, and pillars remained. Such formations are called hoodoos. Similar hoodoos in even more bizarre shapes occur on the approach road to the park's East Entrance.

2.4/15.9 Tower Creek bridge. Tower Creek has been found to be the coldest stream in the park, with a typical summer temperature of 45°F (7°C).

2.5/15.8 🅰(3) 🄳 🄰 🄴 **Tower Fall Campground** and picnic area one-way road to the west, and large Tower Fall parking lot to the east. The Tower Fall campground has 32 unreserved sites, pit toilets, and an amphitheater for evening ranger programs.

Tower Fall*

Tower Fall is the beautiful and popular 132-foot (40 m) waterfall on Tower Creek.

P **⌂** **⌖**(7) **⎕⎕**&(2) The Tower Fall area is extremely crowded all day, since it offers a general store with ice cream counter, as well as trails to and along the Yellowstone River. Come very early or late in the day to enjoy relative solitude.

⚘ Three trails begin in or near the Tower Fall campground. **Tower Creek Trail**, mostly used for fishing access, begins in the campground and goes almost 3 miles (5 km) up Tower Creek. The upper part of the trail's route was severely burned in the 1988 fires.

⚲ Bicyclists, as well as hikers and cross-country skiers, may use a former road (called the Old Chittenden Service Road) that goes south from the campground to rejoin the Grand Loop Road in 2 miles (3 km).

A third trail goes north from the campground's entrance road, parallels the main road (above Overhanging Cliff), and ends behind Roosevelt Lodge in a one-way distance of a little over 3 miles (5 km).

Short trails at Tower Fall

An easy, paved walkway (about 0.3 mi/0.5km round trip) takes you out to a platform at the canyon edge, where there's a fine view of Tower Fall and an interpretive sign about its hanging valley.

⚘ The trail down to the **base of Tower Fall** and into the canyon to the junction of Tower Creek and the Yellowstone River is well maintained, though rather steep—about 250 feet (76 m) down. It's a round-trip hike of a little over 1 mile (1.6 km), rewarding for the close-up view of the fall and its cool mist.

You can continue up the Yellowstone on a short, unmaintained branch of the trail to a small thermal area called Undercliff Springs. Farther upriver and on the opposite side is another, particularly malodorous, thermal area called Sulphur Beds.

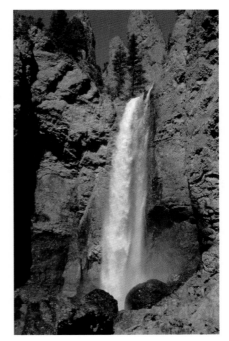

Tower Fall

Tower Fall on Tower Creek

• Tower Fall is the only waterfall in the park officially called "fall" rather than "falls." Maybe this is because of its one clean drop to the creek below. Its name derives from the many pinnacles or towers above it and was given by members of the Washburn Expedition in 1870.

• Just above Tower Creek's mouth, Antelope Creek joins the Yellowstone River. This is the location of the Bannock Ford, where large groups of Bannock Indians crossed the Yellowstone on their annual buffalo-hunting trek. It was the only good way to cross the Yellowstone until Baronett built his 1871 bridge about 2.5 miles (4 km) downstream.

• Old drawings and photographs of the waterfall show a large boulder precariously poised at the edge of the fall. Members of the 1871 Hayden expedition placed bets on when it would fall, but not until June of 1986 did it finally topple over the brink—when no one happened to be watching.

• The boulder that fell in 1986 now lies among the other large rounded hunks of granite-gneiss near the fall's base. Several of these boulders are as much as 10 feet (3 m) in diameter and may weigh up to 30 tons. According to geologists, they are 2.7-billion-year-old glacial erratics carried here from the Beartooth Range to the north and east a few tens of thousands of years ago.

• Unlike the Yellowstone River, which has cut its canyon through relatively easily eroded rocks, Tower Creek has encountered rocks that are more resistant. Also, the smaller volume of water means much less cutting power. Consequently, the Yellowstone has been able to cut down faster and leave Tower Creek perched on the side of the canyon, thus creating a *hanging valley* and a beautiful waterfall.

2.7/15.6 Tower Fall Campground one-way road ends; entrance is at mile 2.5/15.8.

The Grand Loop Road parallels Antelope Creek for about 1.5 miles (2.4 km). From 1935 until 1942 a "show herd" of about 30 bison was kept near Antelope Creek.

4.8/13.5 **P** A short road to the south leads to a parking area with access to a section of the Howard Eaton trail. The trail is now often closed for bear management (see the "Living Things" chapter, which answers the question "Where are all the bears now?").

5.6/12.7 Barred road to the northwest is the south end of the 2-mile-long (3.2 km) former service road trail that starts at Tower Fall Campground.

7.1/11.2 **P** Interpretive sign about grizzly bears and their habitat. You might spot elk or moose as well as grizzlies in the valley below or in the foothills across Antelope Creek.

7.6/10.7 ⬚P Turnout for an excellent view of Antelope Creek Valley and of several tiers of distant mountains, in a nearly 180-degree sweep.

Antelope Valley Panorama

Left to right (north to south):

Beartooth Range in the far distance outside the park; jagged **Cutoff Mountain** (10,695 ft/3260 m), with an abrupt cliff at its west end, stands out on the park's boundary. Higher and snowier mountains can be seen behind it.

Specimen Ridge (highest point, 8442 ft/2573 m) is the long, irregular, grassy mountain in the middle distance.

Amethyst Mountain (9614 ft/2930 m) is the ridge's highest point and the center of this panorama.

Grand Canyon of the Yellowstone in the middle distance. Due east of here you can see where Deep Creek's canyon joins the Yellowstone's canyon at an oblique angle.

To the southeast and across the Yellowstone River is a vast area with no maintained trails. It stretches across the **Mirror Plateau** to the headwaters of the Lamar River and the high **Absaroka Range**. Several hot spring groups emit steam in the area, including **Coffee Pot Hot Springs**.

Mt. Washburn (10,243 ft/ 3122m), with its square fire tower, is the high peak to the south.

Geological Note: There are two mountain ranges that people have trouble distinguishing between, because there's no strict line separating them. Most references use the name Beartooth for those north of the park and Absaroka for those to the east. Geologically, however, they do differ: the Beartooth are primarily built of very ancient granite-gneiss and the Absarokas of much more recent volcanic rocks.

8.2/10.1 Mae West Curve, though not an official name, is a commonly used one for this hairpin turn in the road. The famous Hollywood actress and writer of plays and films, Mae West (1892–1980), was notorious for her directness as well as for her curves.

If you look closely at the rocks in this area, you'll see that they contain innumerable angular rock pieces cemented together. This is *volcanic breccia*, evidence of the explosive volcanism of Mount Washburn some 45 million years ago. **[GEO.4]**

8.4/9.9 Chittenden Road leads 1.3 miles (2 km) up the northern slope of Mount Washburn to a view of the summit and access to the **Mount Washburn Trail**. (A part of this trail is described from the opposite end at mile 13.3/5.0). Gen. Henry Dana Washburn was the Civil War Union veteran and surveyor-general of Montana who led the 1870 expedition of the park area and was the first of his party to climb this mountain.

🚻 🚻 Rest rooms are found both at the parking area and at the fire tower. A public telephone is located at the fire tower, one of the three lookouts still in use.

🚶 🚲 You can hike or bike to the top of Mount Washburn (about 3 mi/5 km) from the parking area, but take drinking water and be prepared for sudden drastic changes of weather, including lots of wind and possible summer lightning storms. The view from the fire tower is superb. You may also access the trail from the Dunraven Pass parking area; by following this route, you avoid a narrow ridge that must be traversed just before the summit.

Expect to see bighorn sheep, which are amazingly tame here and may pose for your camera. The older rams have huge horns curved nearly in a circle, while young rams and ewes have short, slightly curved horns.

Wildflowers abound in the entire area in July and early August. It's possible to find Indian paintbrush, phlox, forget-

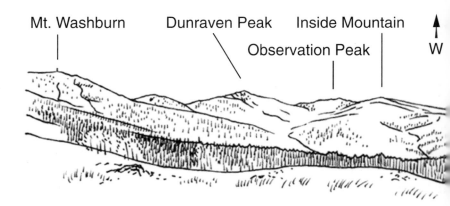

Mount Washburn North Side Panorama

Stretching from left to right (south to north):

Mt. Washburn with its fire tower, then

An unnamed round hill.

Dunraven Peak (9904 ft/3019 m) with a rocky top and **Hedges Peak** (9685 ft/2952 m) behind it (visible only from the rocky promontory). Cornelius Hedges was the Washburn expedition member who was long thought to have originated the national park idea.

The next peak is **Observation Peak** (9397 ft/2864 m), and the higher of the pair to its right is **Inside Mountain** (9681 ft/2951 m), inside the semi-circle of the Washburn Range.

A pink species of paintbrush thrives north of Dunraven Pass.

me-nots, lupine, sticky geranium, lark-spur, silky phacelia, and many others.

Even as late as mid July, you may see patches of snow. Watch for small water-falls everywhere. They're pretty to look at, but the water is not safe to drink.

10.3/8.0 **P** Mount Washburn north side view. If you stop at the wide spot in the road, a popular stop for tour buses, there's an unmarked trail out to a rocky promontory with another fine view. Even from near the road, you can see a mountain panorama totally differ-ent from the two that are 3 miles north and 4.5 miles south of this point.

Farther away in the center of the view are **Cook Peak** (9742 ft/2969 m) and **Folsom Peak** (9338 ft/2846 m), named for two of the three men who explored and wrote about this territory in 1869.

On very clear days, you can see **Electric Peak** (10,969 ft/3343 m) between Cook and Folsom, over 20 miles away.

Prospect Peak (9525 ft/2903 m), named by geologist Arnold Hague in 1885, is closer by on the right.

Peaks of the **Beartooth Range** line the far northern horizon.

13.3/5.0 Dunraven Pass★ (8873 ft/ 2704 m), the highest point reached by road in the entire park.

[🚶] [🏢] [♿] The south end of the **Mount Washburn Trail** is located here. No bicycles are allowed on this part of the trail. To hike to the top of Mount Washburn, you might prefer to start by driving up Chittenden Road (see mile 8.4/9.9), a shorter but steeper route with an elevation gain of 1500 feet in 2.25 miles (460 m in 3.6 km).

[🚶] The first half-mile (0.8 km) or so of the Mount Washburn Trail is not terribly steep and is well worth exploring for its profusion of wildflowers in July and August. Along the south-facing hillside here is one of the best flower displays in the park!

Penstemon

An interpretive sign at the trailhead explains alpine tundra and describes the rigors of the Mount Washburn trail, where elevation gain is nearly 1400 feet in about 3 miles (430 m in 5 km).

Dunraven Peak and Dunraven Pass were named for the fourth earl of Dunraven, the British sportsman who wrote *The Great Divide: Travels in the Upper Yellowstone in the Summer of 1874.* Many Europeans were first introduced to Yellowstone through reading his book. Dunraven waxes eloquent about contemplating the view from Mount Washburn.

14.8/3.5 [P] Interpretive sign about the caldera. At approximately this point, the Grand Loop Road crosses into the

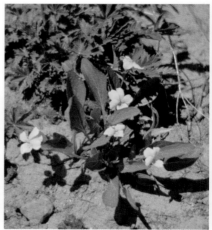

Viola

Yellowstone caldera, the major geological feature that helped to shape the Yellowstone landscape (further explained in "What is the Yellowstone Caldera?" on page 38).

The view here is worth another stop.

Washburn Hot Springs Panorama

From east to south (left to right):

Washburn Hot Springs' steam can usually be seen rising from below, as can that from two other hydrothermal areas.

Grand Canyon of the Yellowstone River's far wall is in the middle distance.

To the east are tree-covered **Mirror Plateau** and the distant **Absaroka Range**.

To the south, beyond a nearby clump of live and dead trees, is a glimpse of **Hayden Valley**.

On the clearest days you can make out the peaks of the **Tetons** 75 miles away, though Yellowstone Lake is out of sight.

Only an unmaintained trail leads from here to **Washburn Hot Springs**, which cluster on both sides of Sulphur Creek before the creek empties into the canyon of the Yellowstone. The springs can be reached from a maintained trail that descends sharply from the top of Mount Washburn down its east flank, or from the Glacial Boulder near Canyon Village.

15.9/2.4 🏕(12) 🏛♿ Dunraven Road picnic area on the west.

17.0/1.3 🏕(16) 🏛 Cascade Lake picnic area, where Cascade Lake Trail begins (south end of picnic area).

🚶 **Cascade Lake Trail** goes 4.4 miles (7 km) round trip to the lake. It's a pleasant, nearly level walk through meadows rampant with wildflowers and a mixed green and burned forest. An-

other trail branches off for a much more difficult hike to Observation Peak.

🛥 Cascade Lake is a popular catch-and-release fishing lake for cutthroat trout and grayling. It's surrounded by grass and willows, and beaver have made their lodges here. Bison, moose, and grizzly bears are sometimes seen. This lake is the source of Cascade Creek, which falls over Crystal Falls into the Yellowstone between the Upper and Lower falls.

18.3/0.0 Canyon Junction. Just to the east are Canyon Village and the one-way loop road to see the Yellowstone River canyon and waterfalls. Canyon's sights and facilities are described on page 177. South from Canyon Junction is Fishing Bridge Junction; west is Norris Junction; north are Dunraven Pass, Tower Fall, and Tower-Roosevelt Junction.

From Canyon Junction to Norris Junction

The Canyon to Norris road (historically called the Norris Cutoff) was first built in 1885–86. Although it was often in bad repair during its history, the road was substantially improved in the 1960s and provides a convenient 12-mile-long (19 km) connection between the eastern and western sides of the Grand Loop Road, providing the center part of the figure eight. There's not a lot to see on the drive, but you'll find some pleasant trails to lakes and waterfalls, as well as fly-fishing opportunities in the Gibbon River.

Road Log

0.0/11.6 Canyon Junction. To the west is Norris Junction; north are Dunraven Pass, Tower Fall, and Tower Junction. East are Canyon Village and the north rim of the Yellowstone River canyon, and south is Fishing Bridge Junction.

0.5/11.1 [🚶] [🐴] Cascade Creek Trailhead. It's about 2.5 miles (4 km) from this trailhead to the lake. This route is used by horseback groups as well as hikers. You may prefer the slightly shorter and more pleasant trail to the lake that begins north of Canyon Junction in the Cascade Lake picnic area (see mile 17.0/1.3 in the road log "From Tower Junction to Canyon Junction").

3.1/8.5 A tiny lily pond to the north may be covered with yellow blooms in midsummer. The burned forest is a result of the 1988 Wolf Lake fire.

3.5/8.1 [🚶] [⛵] Short road to generous parking for Grebe Lake Trailhead. A popular fishing spot and one of the few bodies of water in the park that may still have Montana grayling, **Grebe Lake** is about 3 miles (5 km) from the road. It was named for the western grebe (*Aechmorphus occidentalis*), a medium-large waterbird. The trail follows a former road most of the way and joins the Howard Eaton Trail east of the lake.

Grebe Lake figured prominently in the story of the second stagecoach holdup to occur in the park. In August of 1897, two masked men held up a caravan consisting of an army ambulance and 15 stagecoaches south of the lake. They got away with $630 in cash, but

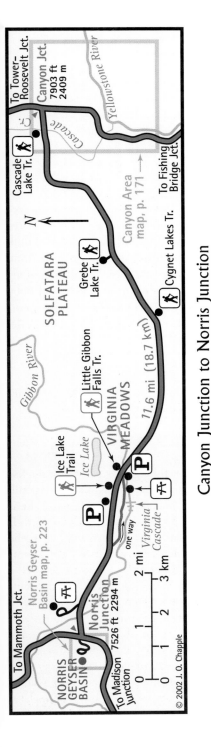

evidence found at Grebe Lake soon helped to convict the men, who served two and one-half years' imprisonment for the crime.

The whole relatively level area north of the road is called the Solfatara Plateau, where sulfur deposits, acid soil, and hot sulfurous steam abound.

4.9/6.7 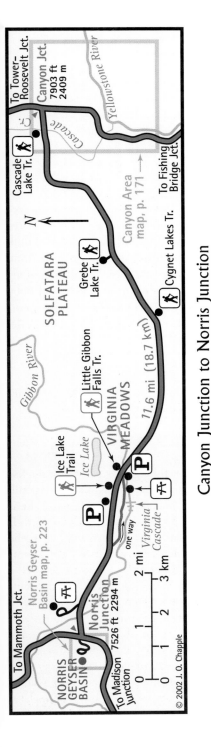 Cygnet Lakes Trailhead to the south. The lakes and their surrounding meadows are reached in about 4 miles (6.5 km); an unmaintained trail continues across the flat Central Plateau. On the trailhead sign-in box, there's a warning: "Bear Frequenting Area!"

The road turns northwest and ascends Blanding Hill, named for the foreman of the first road crew here in 1885. Until the road was realigned in 1957, this was a notoriously steep place and was the first part of the road to become impassible in early winter.

As you top the hill going west, Mount Holmes and neighboring mountains, over 13 miles (21 km) away, come into view.

7.9/3.7 Just west of the Gibbon River bridge is a parking area for the Little Gibbon Falls and Wolf Lake trailheads.

Cross the road and walk a few yards toward the river to find **Little Gibbon Falls Trail**, which is not marked at the roadside. A hike of about 1 mile (1.6 km) through Virginia Meadows and up a small hill brings you to gentle, 25-foot (7.6 m) **Little Gibbon Falls**.

Much of the remaining 2.5 miles (about 4 km) to Wolf Lake is not well maintained. North of here is one of the park's large mountainous areas with no roads or trails, which includes the

Washburn Range and its foothills.

The name Gibbon in the park comes neither from the ape nor from the famous English historian, but rather from Gen. John Gibbon. The general led a group of soldiers through Yellowstone in 1872. They ran entirely out of provisions and were subsisting on roots, squirrels, and blue jays when they encountered the Hayden Survey, who provided them with flour and sugar.

8.0/3.6 End of the one-way loop road (do not enter here) that passes the Virginia Cascade and picnic area.

8.2/3.4 🚶 ♿ ▲♿ **Ice Lake Trailhead**. This wheelchair accessible trail—relatively wide and level—is the shortest way to reach tree-bordered Ice Lake (0.3 mi/ 0.5 km from the road). The name comes from the days when ice was cut from the lake for use at the now long-gone Norris Hotel. This lake has one backcountry campsite accessible to the disabled.

Until 35 years ago, Ice Lake was repeatedly but unsuccessfully stocked with grayling. North of Ice Lake, this trail joins the long Howard Eaton Trail to the Norris campground area on the west.

To the east, the trail passes Wolf, Grebe, and Cascade lakes on its way to the Canyon area. Fishing is excellent in these three lakes, but there may be grizzlies about.

The forest was severely burned but shows patches of grass and young lodgepole pines a decade later.

8.5/3.1 P Parking on both sides of the road for the boardwalk to the **Fire and Blowdown exhibit**. A tornado-force wind tore through here in 1984, followed four years later by the big fire. In this locality there is slower regeneration of growth than in most other badly burned areas, perhaps because the soil was scorched by the burning of dry trees that were already lying down.

9.9/1.7 🏕(6) 🚌♿ **Virginia Cascade road** affords several good views of the Gibbon River's 60-foot (18 m) plunge over volcanic rock. The 2-mile (3.2 km) side road is narrow, steep, and curving—and difficult for the park to maintain. Engineer Hiram Chittenden called it "a positive menace to the lives of travelers" over 100 years ago.

Virginia Cascade and the nearby Virginia Meadows, through which the Gibbon River flows, were named for the wife of Sir Charles Gibson, head of the Yellowstone Park Association, a late 19th century hotel concessionaire.

11.0/0.6 🏕(16) 🚻♿ Norris Meadows picnic area. The Gibbon River meanders past on its way to drain Norris Geyser Basin to the west.

11.6/0.0 Norris Junction. Norris Geyser Basin is straight ahead (west), Obsidian Cliff and Mammoth Hot Springs are to the north, Madison Junction to the south (then southwest), and Canyon Junction to the east.

Norris Geyser Basin*

Give yourself a few hours at Norris Geyser Basin for a walk through a thermal area very different from all the others in the park. A ranger-interpreter is often roving in Norris Geyser Basin during daylight hours, and it's always worthwhile for a visitor to go along with him or her to learn what's currently interesting in the basin. The features at Norris change so rapidly that only someone on the spot almost daily can keep up.

🏁♿(4) 【C】 The short Norris Geyser Basin side road goes directly west from Norris Junction. At road's end, you'll find rest rooms and cold drink machines—very welcome on a hot summer day. There are no restaurants, hotels, or stores near this area.

Down a short walkway from the parking lots are a small bookstore and the **Norris Museum**, built in 1930 and now a National Historic Landmark. Inside the museum, you'll find displays about Yellowstone's and other regions' hydrothermal areas and history. Pamphlets about Norris's trails and features are available from a dispensing box near the museum. Precautions for a safe and pleasant geyser basin walk are in the "Travel Tips."

What's at Norris Geyser Basin?

About 50 of the most easily seen and interesting hot springs, geysers, and mud pots are mentioned in this guidebook. Some have such irresistible names they beg to be listed. There are actually over 180 features here, according to geyser enthusiast Rocco Paperiello's *Report on the Norris Geyser Basin for 1984*.

Two steaming springs greet you before you even start on the basin walkways. To the east of the museum is rarely erupting **Harding Geyser**, named when it first erupted in 1923 for Pres. Warren G. Harding, who visited the park that year only a month before he died.

Behind the bookstore is **Steamvalve Spring** (its official name, although the sign says Steam Valve Geyser). Have you wondered while visiting the park how engineers have managed to avoid placing roads and buildings in the path of hydrothermal activity? Steamvalve Spring is an example of a place they misjudged. Here a seemingly dead mud hole has been filled with asphalt twice, only

Porcelain Terrace → To Norris Campground
To Mammoth Jct.
PINWHEEL GEYSER
Splutter Pot Geyser
PORCELAIN BASIN
Whirligig & Little Whirligig Geysers
Blue Geyser
Constant Geyser
Porcelain Springs
Basin Geyser Ledge Geyser
Fireball Geyser
Basin Vista
Hurricane Vent
Crackling Lake
Dark Cavern Geyser
Carnegie II Drill Hole
Congress Pool
Milky Complex
Locomotive Spring
Black Growler Steam Vent
Vermilion Springs
Rediscovered Geyser
Museum
Norris Jct.
7526 ft
2294 m
RAGGED HILLS
Bathtub Spring
Book Store
Emerald Spring
Steamvalve Spring
Minute Geyser
Monarch Geyser
N
Palpitator Spring
Corporal Geyser & Dog Leg Spring
BACK BASIN
Steamboat Geyser
Vixen Geyser
Veteran Geyser
Cistern Spring
0   0.1   0.2 mi
Pearl Geyser
Tantalus Geyser
0   0.1   0.2   0.3 km
Porkchop Geyser
Bastille Geyser
Crater Spring
Black Pit Spring
Arch Steam Vent
Echinus Geyser
Muddy Sneaker Complex
Yellow Funnel Spring
Phillips Caldron
Green Dragon Spring
Gray Lakes
Puff 'n Stuff Geyser
Black Hermit's Caldron
To Madison Junction
© 2002 J. O. Chapple

Norris Geyser Basin

to come bursting through with renewed activity, erupting frequently with extraordinary rumbling noises. No more asphalt has been applied!

Loop trails divide the area open to visitors into two parts, Back Basin and Porcelain Basin. Relatively remote areas called the One Hundred Spring Plain and the Gap are hot, active, wet, and dangerous; therefore, they are not furnished with boardwalks.

Back Basin is where you'll find the sometimes predictable Echinus Geyser and Yellowstone's tallest (but notoriously erratic) geyser, Steamboat. The entire Back Basin loop is about 1.5 miles (2.4 km) around, with part of it wheelchair accessible.

Porcelain Basin is a vast, delicately tinted plain with many small geysers, hot springs, lakes, and fumaroles. The western loop around this area and the walkway to Porcelain Terrace on the east side are each about 0.5 miles (0.8 km) long. Part of the eastern walkway is wheelchair accessible.

Norris Geyser Basin in the History of Yellowstone

None of the famous early expeditions visited this geyser basin. It was not until 1872 that a man named Eugene S. Topping and his companion happened to notice steam rising far to the south from the top of Observation Peak (their name for present-day Bunsen Peak near Mammoth). Topping and party were the first known visitors to the area, but Superintendent Norris, for whom the basin is named, was the first to explore and describe it fully a few years later.

Now there's no hotel at Norris, but a succession of facilities followed each other in this area in the early years, ranging from tent camps and lunch stations to a rather fine hotel opened in 1887 and destroyed by fire the same year.

Until 1966, the Grand Loop Road cut right through the center of Norris Geyser Basin. To reduce traffic congestion and human impact on the area, as well as to eliminate the hazard of steam blowing across windshields from the geyser basin, park officials moved the road.

WALKING TOUR OF BACK BASIN

Just what Back Basin is "back" of is not obvious to present-day visitors, but the basin was in back of the museum before the Grand Loop Road was re-routed.

As you walk through Back Basin, you may wonder what has caused so many trees to fall and lie about helter-skelter, since they were not burned in the

The Grand Loop Road cut between the Norris Museum and Porcelain Basin, as shown in this H.C. Bumpus sketch from 1935.

1988 fires. Lodgepole pines have a very shallow root system, and when they grow very tall, as these have done, a strong wind can topple them easily. These trees are mostly about the same age and height; thus, winds have created a sort of domino effect among them. Park policy is to leave them lying unless they actually obstruct a path or road.

Turning south (left from the entrance walkway) near the museum, you first encounter **Emerald Spring**. Emerald may bubble due to rising gases, even when its water is below the boiling point. At times it gets hot enough to actually boil, and then it becomes a muddy brown color and may erupt as high as 26 feet (8 m).   **[GEO.23]**

Most of the time, Emerald Spring is a beautiful shade of green, combining deep blue water with a yellow sulfurous lining.

The next feature of interest is **Steamboat Geyser**, usually steaming or spouting innocently from behind a pile of yellow and orange stained rocks. But on occasion, Steamboat becomes the world's largest geyser. It has had an extremely erratic record of major eruptions, the first one noted in 1878. Since then its interval has ranged from a few days to 50 years! Eruptions were rare until the 1960s, when there were over 100 of them. Three occurred in the 1970s and at least 40 in the 1980s. Another eruption occurred in October 1991, then one in May of 2000. Steamboat's major eruptions come

with a tremendous roar and sometimes reach 380 feet (116 m), an almost unbelievable height three times that of Old Faithful. The water phase of these eruptions may last 3 to 20 minutes, followed by as much as 12 hours of the steam phase. Minor eruptions from its two vents may go to 40 or 60 feet (12–18 m).

Down the stairs and to the left (but also accessible by a longer, relatively easy path from the museum) is **Echinus Geyser★**, still Norris's star attraction, but less predictable than formerly. The name Echinus comes from the Greek word for spine. Ferdinand Hayden named it in

A thrilling Steamboat Geyser eruption in the 1960s (E. E. Mackin photo)

1878 for surrounding sinter-coated rhyolite rocks that resembled spiny sea urchins (not so evident now). Its water is very acidic, unlike the alkaline water of Yellowstone's other large geysers.

Echinus became an interesting geyser in the 1970s; into 1998 its eruptions were both large and predictable. It's still fascinating to watch the gradual filling of the crater, followed by bubbling that becomes boiling, then by exciting bursts in all directions up to about 80 feet (24 m), with huge waves of runoff water.

Photographers are inclined to be frustrated by Echinus; its prodigious amount of steam covers the sparkling water during most of the eruption. Remember to dry off your camera or eyeglass lenses immediately should they get wet in any geyser spray, because the silica in the water can leave permanent spots.

Near the upper viewing area for Echinus is **Black Pit Spring**, a very hot spring that fizzes and bubbles like oil in a frying pan.

Sparkling drops from Echinus Geyser's eruption may reach the excited spectators (1998 photo).

What Makes Norris Unique?

Extreme heat

Norris Geyser Basin is hot! The water in the springs is generally both hotter and more acidic than in the other geyser basins of Yellowstone. Here are some temperatures found in three different research drill holes:

401°F (205°C) in a hole drilled down 247 ft (75 m),

385°F (196°C) at 813 ft (248 m) deep,

460°F (238°C) at 1088 ft (332 m) deep.

Long history

Geologists infer from various evidence that geothermal activity at Norris may have been continuous since 150,000 years ago.

No big formations and few predictable geysers

Although geyserite is deposited at Norris as at other geyser basins, Norris lacks tall or grotesque formations such as you see in Upper Geyser Basin at

Old Faithful. Much of what looks like sinter at Norris is actually acid-leached volcanic rock, especially Lava Creek tuff. There are at least 70 geysers at Norris, but very few are predictable.

Change is the only constant

The whole area is so dynamic that changes in the hot springs occur constantly and rapidly. Some changes can be attributed to earthquake activity, but many are still puzzling to geologists and geochemists. Some of the variables they study here are temperature, chemical composition, amount of water and discharge, amount of sinter deposition, and acidity/alkalinity (pH).

Unique locale

Norris is uniquely situated at or near the intersection of three geologic features:
- the northwest rim of the Yellowstone caldera
- the long Norris-Mammoth corridor, a zone of faults running north-south, where the earth's surface has subsided
- a seismically active fault zone that stretches east-west between Norris and Hebgen Lake.

Special springs

Some springs far out in the One Hundred Spring Plain exhibit truly unusual phenomena. Realgar Springs deposit red and orange material that may be a previously unknown form of arsenic sulfide. Large, circular Cinder Pool suspends on its surface tiny black hollow spheres, probably made of elemental sulfur colored by iron sulfide. And then Sulphur Dust Spring's bottom is covered with powdery, pale yellow, elemental sulfur.

Seasonal disturbance

One phenomenon scientists have researched is a seasonal disturbance that often occurs in the late summer or early autumn, particularly in Back Basin. For a week or two, many features at Norris go berserk: Emerald Spring becomes cloudy, Echinus Geyser turns unpredictable (even when routinely predictable), and Green Dragon Spring and Gray Lakes turn chocolate brown and boil furiously.

During the disturbances, geologists have noted an increase in the amount of water and gas discharged, increase in the turbidity of the water, large fluctuations in water temperatures, and decreased chloride and increased acidity in some springs. Occasionally, a small hydrothermal explosion creates a new thermal feature. Some geochemists now consider it likely that the Norris seasonal disturbance stems from the mixing of groundwater from two or more different underground zones having different chemical compositions.

Leaving Echinus, the boardwalk crosses the South Fork of Tantalus Creek for the first time and passes near several features that have erupted as geysers for short periods in the recent past. **Crater Spring** and **Arch Steam Vent** are to the right (north) and left (south) of the path, respectively. **Tantalus Geyser** (formerly Decker Geyser) is out in the sinter to the north.

In the case of Tantalus Geyser, the human history is more interesting than the thermal history. In the 1960s, Mrs. Hazel Decker was so determined to see Steamboat Geyser erupt that she spent 52 consecutive days in the area, sleeping in her car in the parking lot. Whether Steamboat ever erupted for her is unknown, and a nearby geyser that had been named for her was renamed Tantalus Geyser, but a small grove of trees out in the sinter is informally called Decker Island.

Tantalus Creek, the small creek that drains both Back Basin and Porcelain Basin, is named for a king in Greek mythology. He was doubly condemned: to stand up to his chin in water that retreated whenever he stooped to drink and to reach above him for bunches of grapes that always evaded his grasp. (This myth is the source of our word "tantalize.") The creek's water level and temperature rise and fall with basin-wide geyser eruptions.

A long stretch of the Back Basin walkway passes springs of different colors, shapes, sizes, and levels of activity. Just before you reach **Black Hermit's Caldron** (away from the trail's corner), you pass another example of a geyser whose name is better than its action, **Puff 'n Stuff Geyser**. The late Park

Geologist Rick Hutchinson named it after a TV show of the early 1970s called *H. R. Pufnstuf.* The geyser gurgles below ground and sprays out some water but has never done much else.

Next is cavernous **Green Dragon Spring**, named for its usual color and its characteristic action, boiling vigorously and belching steam from three funnel-shaped vents. When the steam clears away, you can see greenish yellow crusts of sulfur and red deposits of iron on the cavern roof. Stretching away from this point are two very large hot springs called the **Gray Lakes**, whose waters are said to be in constant motion, caused by boiling springs on the bottom.

Phillips Caldron mud pot honors Charles Phillips, a park ranger who was fascinated by geysers. While stationed for the winter at Old Faithful in 1927, he mistook poisonous water hemlock growing in warm thermal runoff for edible wild parsnip and died within a few hours of eating it.

West of the path, the **Muddy Sneaker Complex** (including one small geyser) got its name from geologist Hutchinson in 1971. It was originally a violent mud pot that sprang up suddenly in the trail. "Anybody who would walk in it or below it would get their shoes or sneakers muddy," according to Hutchinson. The path has since been moved uphill.

Yellow Funnel Spring east of the path deserves its name only part of the time. Sometimes you can't see the yellow-stained funnel for the opaque green, blue, or muddy water; sometimes it's merely a steam vent. **Son of Green Dragon**, next on the west and very close to the path, sometimes acts as a small geyser.

Bastille Geyser was born in 1992 on France's Bastille Day, July 14. Just west of the boardwalk, it grew from a 2-inch (5 cm) hole to a 3-foot (1 m) crater in 8 hours during a seasonal disturbance. It erupted up to 3 feet (1 m) high every 4 or 5 minutes when active, but it has stopped erupting and has filled in its vents with sinter.

Take the short boardwalk spur to **Porkchop Geyser**. In the 1980s, it was a porkchop-shaped perpetual spouter that formed a tall ice cone from its spray in the winter. Suddenly, on September 5, 1989, Porkchop exploded. A few lucky people were watching as chunks of geyserite were upended and debris thrown about in a true hydrothermal explosion. What remains is a steaming pool surrounded by jagged boulders.

Continuing on the main boardwalk, you'll see **Pearl Geyser** and its almost translucent pearl-like deposits, now sometimes covered with mud. Pearl Geyser erupts up to 8 feet (2.4 m) high but is unpredictable.

The next feature is **Vixen Geyser**, which may erupt from its red-stained crater for a few seconds every few minutes, except for its rare major eruptions up to 35 feet (11 m). Almost all Vixen's water drains back into its rectangular vent.

Two items about Vixen should be noted. In 1876, a geyser cone was displayed at the U.S. Centennial Exhibition in Philadelphia; it may have belonged to Vixen. Vixen Geyser received its name at a time before feminism was a household word; Superintendent Norris used the then-current word for a shrewish, ill-tempered woman and got away with it! Fortunately, ideas about how to preserve our national treasures (both geysers and women) have come a long way since that time.

After crossing Tantalus Creek, you must choose between going right (east toward Echinus via Cistern Spring) or straight ahead (north toward the museum via the shortest path and past a few more features).

East toward Echinus

Near the trail junction on the left are small **Corporal Geyser** and tiny **Dog Leg Spring** with two small vents. When one of these geysers erupts the other drains.

On the right is **Veteran Geyser**, which probably derived its name from the very old sinter deposits all around. Veteran's short eruptions may go out 40 feet (12 m) at an angle, but they occur in a long-term cyclic pattern of minutes to hours that is not yet fully deciphered.

The last feature before you reach the stairs up to Steamboat Geyser is **Cistern Spring**. The remarkable colors in the runoff are unusual for Norris Basin—unless you are here during a seasonal disturbance when you may see only murky water. Cistern built its impressive terrace in the past 30 years. Bacteria color the terraces canary yellow, orange, and brown when the pool is full. True to its name as a water reservoir, Cistern's water drains drastically when neighboring Steamboat Geyser has a major eruption; without the water, the bacteria die.

North toward the museum

If you turn back from Cistern and take up the loop trail again, or if you have continued straight on at the trail junction after crossing Tantalus Creek, you'll first encounter **Palpitator Spring**. Palpitator is actually a geyser and has small but extremely long eruptions of around 3 hours. Over a hundred years ago, it was named when steam pulsing below the ground produced uncannily rhythmic beats.

You will see perpetual spouting at the center of **Fearless Geyser** at your left (west) as the trail approaches **Monarch Geyser** on the right. Behind Monarch's crater is a devastated-looking hillside, showing that Monarch was a truly regal feature at one time, though it has not had a large eruption since 1913. Before that year it could rocket to a height of 200 feet (60 m), spewing out rocks and mud "with rumblings that shake the valley" (as an 1884 guidebook states). It then became so quiet that it's sometimes called Monarch Geyser Crater. However, proving that geysers can never be pronounced dead, it began having superheated boiling periods in 1993, with an occasional burst 20 feet (6 m) high. Some researchers believe there may be an underground connection between Monarch and Steamboat geysers.

Partway up the small hill north of Monarch Geyser are **Mushroom Geyser** (named for its mushroom-shaped pedestal deposits, now gone) and Minute Geyser. **Minute Geyser** erupted at 1-minute intervals as much as 40 feet (12 m) high until about 1902. Unfortunately located near the stagecoach loading dock, Minute Geyser's vent was blocked by a large boulder thrown in by vandals. This changed the action to another vent that spouts frequently. Minute Geyser has had occasional major eruptions in recent years.

As you continue through the woods, you might notice steam rising to the left (west). One spring there (informally called **Rediscovered Geyser**) has a short path of its own.

Bathtub Spring is on its own stretch of path between the main walkway and the museum. The spring usually looks just like an old-fashioned tub filled with yellow to light brown muddy water, sometimes spouting continuously. The massive buildup of geyserite is unusual for Norris features and was probably formed during alkaline water cycles within the hot spring, since not much sinter accumulates during acidic cycles.

WALKING TOURS OF PORCELAIN BASIN

NOTE: Consult the Norris Geyser Basin map, page 223, for Porcelain Basin's walkways.

Porcelain Basin Overview

Approaching from the parking lot, turn right and pass through the museum breezeway to visit Porcelain Basin, or stop to visit the museum's geological exhibits. The far side of the breezeway affords a panoramic view of the basin and of Mount Holmes about 10 miles (16 km) beyond.

Porcelain Basin below the Norris Museum.

The acres of geyserite and acid-leached lava here give the ground the texture and colors of fine pastel tableware. Porcelain Basin is aptly named, since geyserite is made of silica, and silica and alumina are major constituents of porcelain. In the varying light between dawn and dusk, pools of opalescent water reflect different shades of blue. The basin shows delicate tints of canary yellow, sulfurous yellow green, aqua, orange, rose, coral, white, tan, and gray. Minerals like iron oxides and arsenic sulfides are responsible for much of the staining. Bright lime-green algae love the acidity in some runoff channels, while yellow, orange, and brown microorganisms thrive where the water is neutral or alkaline.

The amount of water in Porcelain Basin's aquifer seems to vary greatly. The water supply was especially low in 1996, a summer when the two Norris museums and the campground were closed as a government economy measure.

Porcelain Basin's eastern loop is partly wheelchair accessible but steep in places. An extension of the eastern loop leads toward Nuphar Lake, Porcelain Terrace Springs, and Norris Campground. Because there are few signs pointing out the named features, this is the most difficult basin in the park in which to orient yourself. The western loop is about 0.5 mile long (0.8 km) and the eastern loop a little less.

Porcelain Basin West Loop

You might begin your tour of Porcelain Basin by taking the stairs down to follow the western loop in a counterclockwise direction. This will bring you close to the greatest number of hydrothermal features.

First encountered as you bear right when the trail forks is **Black Growler Steam Vent**. One of the highest temperatures recorded at the surface of any feature in Yellowstone was in Black Growler's steam, once measured at 284°F (140°C).

North of Black Growler and a little farther from the walkway is Valentine Geyser, and even farther away (and harder to see when not erupting) is Dark Cavern Geyser. **Valentine Geyser** was called Alcove until one February 14th early in the 1900s, when the Norris hotel winter keeper watched as large amounts of rock, mud, water, and steam were blown out, forming a huge pit. It erupted quite regularly for some years to 75 or 100 feet (23–30 m), but is now irregular. This geyser has built a cone inside its alcove, the largest of any Norris geyser.

Dark Cavern Geyser usually erupts quite regularly once or twice an hour up to 20 feet (6 m) and sometimes higher and very forcefully. It seems to be connected both to Valentine and Ledge Geysers.

Ledge Geyser erupts from five vents, from which water jets out in the shape of the fingers and thumb of a hand. For its muddy eruptions, it was often called Mud Geyser in early years. Geyser expert T. Scott Bryan writes that water from the "thumb" projects at a steep angle and to a height of 125 feet (38 m), while producing an unmatched booming and roaring. But, like Steamboat Geyser in Back Basin, Ledge is totally unpredictable and has long dormant periods.

One recent summer, **Basin Geyser**, the small, steaming pool located shortly before the trail junction, had yellow monkeyflowers growing in its alcove. Another year, the temperature of its water was posted as 202°F/94°C, a temperature that's above boiling at this altitude and much too hot for flowers.

Continuing northwest

Out across the barren flats are at least eight geysers or perpetual spouters and many hot pools. The one with the most significant activity in the 1980s and '90s was **Fireball Geyser**, located 100 feet (30 m) or more from the walkway. Fireball's main jet angles to the right, while a lesser column shoots straight up. It erupts about every 2 hours.

Three geysers are near the walkway and on the right as you walk northwest. **Little Whirligig Geyser** sometimes sends up small, rapid bursts of water but is nearly dormant. **Constant Geyser** is farther from the walkway, making a triangle with the Whirligigs. Constant is not a perpetual spouter but does erupt for a few seconds several times an hour, sometimes to 30 feet (9 m).

Whirligig Geyser (sometimes called Big Whirligig) is the third of this related threesome. The water of the bigger Whirligig swirls about in its crater during eruptions and a crack on the crater's far side emits a loud chugging sound.

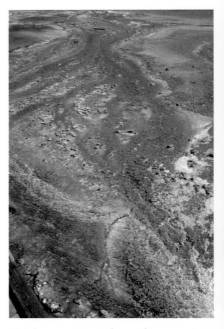

Bright green Cyanidium alga grows in a runoff channel.

Pinwheel Geyser, just east of the short spur of walkway, was a frequent performer until the ground settled some years ago, allowing runoff and sediment from above to cool and partially clog it. When this geyser is active, its runoff channel passes right across the crater of **Splutter Pot Geyser**, sometimes called the Washing Machine for its low belching water. Far out in the basin, **Blue Geyser** spouts almost perpetually.

After passing below a tree-covered hillside, the walkway brings you to **Whale's Mouth Spring**, which rather resembles an open mouth with teeth and is usually full of green water.

The jumble of high jagged rocks and

Crackling Lake takes its name from the sizzling bubbles in its water.

fallen trees bordering the basin to the west appears on park maps as the **Ragged Hills**. These hills are full of rhyolite caverns, and bears have used them for hibernation. Smart bears! The ground there can be as much as 30°F (17°C) higher than the outside temperature.

Named in the 1960s for the popping sounds from many bubbles are large, hot, opalescent, blue-green **Crackling Lake** and its neighbor **Crackling Lake Spring**, partway up the hill.

To your right as you mount the stairs from the basin is the **Milky Complex**, whose **Teal Blue Bubbler** will sometimes be spouting as you pass.

A few steps and a steep but shady path take you back to the start of this loop.

Porcelain Basin East Loop

From the stairs just below the museum, turn right (east) for the eastern loop around Porcelain Basin.

NOTE: The eastern loop is partly wheelchair accessible if you go past Bathtub Spring and around the museum to avoid the stairs (see map).

First you'll see a hillside full of steaming and bubbling fumaroles and spouters, lined in red, orange, or yellow and called **Vermilion Springs**. The variety in the colors here is due to different levels of acidity and different oxidation states of iron and sulfur. Such an area of hot sulfurous gases without pools or geysers can be called a solfatara.

Farthest from the walkway is **Locomotive Spring** (or Springs, since there are a red and a blue pool—though hard to see from the boardwalk), with occasional eruptions to 6 feet high (1.8 m).

Congress Pool next to the boardwalk became a geyser in 1891, after beginning life as a fumarole. The geyser was named for that year's Fifth International Geological Congress, and also (according to its namer, geologist Arnold Hague) "because its earliest outbursts were powerful eruptions marked by periods of rest." The congress of geologists was held in Washington, D.C., but included a Yellowstone field trip. Congress promptly settled down to become a pool, a bubbling mud pot, or sometimes a weak steam vent.

There's more action on the hillside behind Congress Pool, where in 1929 an experimental drill hole went 265 feet (81 m) down. The enormous steam pressure had threatened to blow up the drilling rig. Despite being filled with cement, the **Carnegie II Drill Hole** (near the tree line) became a perpetual spouter many years later. The ground around it pulsates, threatening a future steam explosion.

Along the trail to the north toward the Norris campground is cool **Nuphar Lake**, which carries the botanical name for the yellow pond lily, yet harbors grasses and reeds. The lake is fed by rainwater and small thermal springs and has no outlet.

This section of boardwalk ends at the foot of **Porcelain Terrace**, where thermal activity is so intense and unpredictable that boardwalks have to be rebuilt frequently. After the 1959 Hebgen Lake earthquake, fractures formed on top of the terrace and pools rich in sulfuric acid filled the fractures. This is causing the sinter to disintegrate and the hillside to crumble.

Porcelain Springs (beyond the end of the boardwalk) broke out on the west slope of Porcelain Terrace in 1971. As with most features at Norris, these springs change unpredictably from geysers to pools and back again. Sinter buildup—the most rapid in the park—has filled in some previously important springs in the basin below.

Far out in the north-central part of the basin, the large pool called **Blue Geyser** may be erupting; it's in play more often than not. Blue usually does not erupt above 15 feet (4.6 m).

Returning from Porcelain Terrace, if you bear right at the trail junction, you'll find a bench where you might rest a bit and admire the unusual and beautiful **basin vista★**. In the nearby collection of pools, each manages somehow to have a different color. The murky pools and stained sinter may be green, blue green, yellow, yellow green, reddish orange, mustard, or beige, due to different temperatures, chemical compositions, and degrees of turbidity of the water. The effect is like small jewels in the midst of desolation.

View of most of Porcelain Basin and its jewel-like pools.

Before the intersection of walkways, you'll come to **Hurricane Vent**, above the path. Now usually just a deep hole in the hillside that emits a strong odor and sometimes splashes a bit of water, a century ago it played as a geyser that whirled the water about in its crater during eruptions. At other times it was a "prodigious steam vent whose violent gusts bear a striking resemblance to the driving blasts of a tempest," according to historian Hiram Chittenden.

Colloidal Pool is a large, shallow,

funnel-shaped pool (or three or four smaller pools when the water level is low). In the past it has erupted muddy water as high as 30 feet (10 m). A *colloid* is a substance so fine grained that it is suspended indefinitely within another substance. In this case, silica and clay are suspended in water, as can be found in pools throughout Porcelain Basin.

The last interesting feature before the trail junction is the long narrow pool of **Sunday Geyser**, named in response to its large initial eruption on Sunday, July 12, 1964, but since then erupting rarely.

Turn left to return to the museum, Back Basin, or the parking lot. To the right, the path loops back along the basin's west side (see "Continuing northwest" on page 232).

From Livingston to the North Entrance

William Clark, of the 1803–6 Lewis and Clark expedition, passed the Great Bend of the Yellowstone at present-day Livingston on his return from the Pacific coast, thereby totally missing present park territory. But most visitors to the area later in the 19th and in the early 20th centuries came this way, traveling upstream along the Yellowstone River.

Approach to the North Entrance

The 54 miles (87 km) from Livingston to Gardiner traverse mountain-bound Paradise Valley, with its irrigated fields, horse and cattle ranches, and ranchettes. Area residents and guests enjoy both winter and summer sports. The area abounds in both private campgrounds and public ones managed by U.S. and Montana agencies. Fishing is immensely popular in the Yellowstone River and its tributaries. Numerous hiking or horseback trails lead into the surrounding mountains and wilderness areas.

LIVINGSTON, MONTANA
Population: 6850

The town of Livingston, probably named for railroad director Johnston Livingston, was first settled in 1882, when the tracks of the Northern Pacific Railway reached this point along the Yellowstone River. Visitors to the new national park would change trains here for Cinnabar (and later for

Gardiner, even closer to the park). Then they would connect with stagecoaches to take them through the North Entrance and on for the Grand Tour. Although passenger service has ceased, Livingston is still important as a railroad freight hub.

Livingston is a tourist, ranching, and art center with numerous 19th century buildings listed on the National Register of Historic Places, including a classic railroad depot. The Park County Museum contains a wealth of memorabilia pertaining to Yellowstone Park and to the environs of Livingston. Two 1990s movies, *A River Runs through It* and *The Horse Whisperer*, were partially filmed in and around the town.

Livingston is also well-known for its wind. The town's location east of the Rocky Mountains and north of the Yellowstone Plateau assures that it gets more wind than any other Yellowstone gateway. It's a blessing when the wind is the winter chinook from the mountains, sometimes warm and dry enough in midwinter to melt all the snow.

From Livingston to the North Entrance

To drive to Yellowstone Park from Livingston, take U.S. Highway 89 from the center of Livingston or from Interstate 90 just south of town. In about 3 miles (5 km), you pass through Rock Canyon, which has been cut by the Yellowstone River and is sometimes called Gate of the Mountains.

At the southern end of the canyon, look to the northwest to see cliffs with numerous layers of sedimentary rocks that tilt rather sharply. These roughly 400-million-year-old rocks are tilted because of deformation in this area at about the time of the major uplift that produced the Beartooth Range; the roadside exposures only hint at how complicated the deformation is. Soon after the completion of a road rebuilding project in the 1960s, blocks of this hillside slipped in a massive landslide that covered the road.

Nineteenth century explorers dubbed this the First Canyon of the Yellowstone River. Farther upstream, explorers found three other canyons cut by the Yellowstone, each more spectacular than the one before. Second Canyon, located about 15 miles (24 km) north of the North Entrance, is now called Yankee Jim Canyon. Inside the park boundaries are Third, or Black Canyon, east of Gardiner (reached only by trail) and Fourth Canyon, the Grand Canyon of the Yellowstone.

Paradise Valley, so called since at least the 1880s, spreads out before you just as you emerge from the canyon. On your left (to the east) is a part of the Beartooth Range that's sometimes called the Snowy Mountains. The highest peak visible from the valley is **Emigrant Peak** (10,921 ft/3329 m). To the west is the more rounded eastern edge of the **Gallatin Range**. Irrigation now helps overcome the low annual rainfall, making the valley hospitable to farming.

Ten or 12 miles (16–19 km) from Livingston, near Mill Creek, you begin to see effects of glaciers during the last ice age (the Pinedale), which was at its height about 25,000 years ago. Some areas are covered with large boulders dragged there by the glaciers, and a long terminal moraine appears to the east of the highway just south of Emigrant. This *terminal moraine*, the endpoint of a major Yellowstone glacier in Paradise Valley, is a mound of unsorted rocks and soil left when the glacier dropped them, much as a conveyor belt would do.

The small settlement of Emigrant is about 23 miles (37 km) south of Livingston; a road leads eastward to the tiny town of Pray and to Chico Hot Springs. Chico, settled beginning in 1864, has a resort hotel established in 1900 that was sometimes used as a clinic in its first 50 years. You might enjoy a plunge in one of Chico's two public pools supplied with natural hot spring water.

Nearby, at the mouth of Emigrant Gulch, the optimistically named Yellowstone City had 300 settlers in 1864 and could claim the title of eastern-most town in Montana Territory. Montana was not settled from east to west as you might suppose, since there was no good approach from the east before the railroad arrived. The first whites to come here were gold seekers, who prospected in Montana's western mountains. A gold strike attracted prospectors to the Emigrant area in 1863, but the prospects soon petered out, and most of the miners moved on.

Mentioned frequently in histories of Yellowstone was the ranch settled in 1868 by the Bottler brothers and located about 3 miles (5 km) south of the present site of Emigrant. Sometimes travelers wrote of its cabin, built so poorly that the wind blew through it. Yet many others found it to be a welcome way station for food and company.

England's Earl of Dunraven came through in 1874 and reported from his camping spot: "evening was drawing on apace, and the scenery was being glorified with sunset effects. The level rays of the sun lit up most brilliantly the Eastern Mountains, striking full upon the sharp angular masses of limestone, bringing out in bold relief against the sky background the cruel jaggedness of their forms, which contrasted strongly with the smooth softness of the plain beneath, penetrating and searching into the deep rifts and gorges, and defining in detail all the savage grandeur of the range."

A few miles south of Emigrant, near a wide spot in the river, you'll find a welcome **picnic and rest area**. The long mesa to the

Emigrant Peak is a prominent landmark in Paradise Valley.

east, **Hepburn Mesa**, is made up mostly of sediments, but it has a lava cap that has slowed erosion of the sediments below.

As you continue south, jagged formations to the west, called **Point of Rocks**, come into view. You can take a century-old, rough dirt road from here southwest into the **Tom Miner Basin**, named for an early prospector and poacher. This scenic basin has ranches, a forest service campground, and trails into the Gallatin Range.

For Hikers and Mineral Collectors

By following a Gallatin National Forest trail into the mountains, hikers can still find specimens of petrified wood like those preserved in Yellowstone. The petrified trees are located about a mile (1.5 km) from the end of the Tom Miner Basin Road.

The specimens inside Yellowstone Park are at the top of long and difficult trails up the western slopes of the Gallatin Range in the northwest corner. You're not allowed to collect them there. From this east side of the mountains, however, you may take home samples of petrified wood—but first ask for a free collection permit at the Forest Service Ranger Station in Gardiner. Also ask about recent bear sightings, since both black and grizzly bears live in the area.

On U.S. 89, you'll leave Paradise Valley and enter **Yankee Jim Canyon**. Here you also enter the **Gallatin National Forest**, which alternates with private land in checkerboard squares. Between here and the town of Gardiner are a forest service campground, a picnic area, and several river access points.

To create Yankee Jim Canyon, the Yellowstone River has carved through volcanic rocks to the very old Precambrian basement rocks below. James ("Yankee Jim") George took over the road-building job from a southern-born prospector named Henderson and was able to blast enough rock to make the road through the canyon passable for wagons. Then from 1874 until about 1910, he exacted a toll from all who passed by. You can see the old road clearly across the river. Sometimes the old railway roadbed is also visible.

The town of **Corwin Springs** used to have its own "plunge" or hot spring pool, using water piped from La Duke Hot Spring to the south. Near here a 5000-year-old Native American hearth was found on the Rigler Bluffs east of the river. Initially puzzled by the hearth's height and distance from the river, researchers concluded that the river must have been dammed by landslides and that Native Americans must have camped along the edge of the resulting lake.

At Corwin Springs you may cross the river and continue to the park along a parallel dirt-and-gravel road. That road passes the historic sites of the towns of Electric, which had extensive coal mines with an aerial tramway, and Cinnabar, which was the first terminus of the Northern Pacific Park Branch Line. Cinnabar claimed to be the "capital of the United States" for a few days in 1903, because President Theodore Roosevelt had left his train and communications center there while he traveled through Yellowstone. A few months later, the railroad terminus was moved to Gardiner, and not long after, Cinnabar became a ghost town.

Heat over the Hot Spring

La Duke Hot Spring and the bottom of Devil's Slide are on the property of the controversial Church Universal and Triumphant (CUT). Yellowstone Park's former Chief Ranger, Dan R. Sholly, expressed concerns about this close neighbor of the park in his 1991 book, *Guardians of Yellowstone*. Named the Royal Teton Ranch after it was purchased from multi-millionaire Malcolm Forbes in 1981, the church's 12,000-acre (49 sq km) tract of land shared 5 miles (8 km) of border with the park.

The most serious concern shared by Sholly and others involved the drilling into the La Duke Hot Spring aquifer, begun by CUT in the late 1980s. Since it's not certain to what extent Yellowstone's geothermal systems may be connected to underground systems outside the park, drawing off water to heat a spa and buildings as CUT had planned to do could have serious consequences for Mammoth Hot Springs. Sholly wrote that CUT agreed to cap its well and allow the U.S. Geological Survey to determine the relationship between its hot spring and those in Yellowstone. The drilling has been banned until further studies can be made, and all water use north of the park is being closely monitored.

In 1999, the Forest Service purchased about 7800 acres (32 sq km) of the Royal Teton Ranch, acquiring the ranch's geothermal rights and adding to the lands now available for winter grazing by Yellowstone's elk, bighorn sheep, mule deer, and pronghorn.

On the main road, less than 2 miles (3 km) south of Corwin Springs, the **La Duke Spring National Forest picnic area** is an excellent place to get a good look at **Devil's Slide** on Cinnabar Mountain. Early prospectors mistakenly thought the slide's red color was due to cinnabar, or mercuric sulfide, but it's actually sandstone and shale stained with iron oxide. The walls of the slide are made of quartz sandstone.

To the left of the slide itself, what looks like a free-standing wall is an erosion-resistant sill of diorite. A *sill* is a layer of igneous rock that, while still molten, squeezed between and parallel to layers of sedimentary rock and then cooled while below the surface. *Diorite* is an igneous rock whose composition is intermediate between granite and basalt. All of these layers formed horizontally

Devil's Slide

but were turned up to their present positions by the uplift that created the Beartooth Range to the east.

A few hundred yards (or meters) south of the picnic area, La Duke Hot Spring boils out at the roadside edge of the Yellowstone river. It's a small spring for its turbulent history.

From a short distance south of La Duke Hot Spring to Gardiner, the Yellowstone Park boundary now runs along the west bank of the Yellowstone River to the original, perfectly straight, northern boundary line.

Land was added to the park here in 1932, when a New York City game preservation company bought and presented it to the U.S. government. The goal was to provide winter range for pronghorn (often called antelope).

An airport used for helicopters and small planes squeezes between the highway and the river just outside the gateway town of Gardiner.

GARDINER, MONTANA
Population: 850
Gardiner had the reputation of a wide-open, freewheeling town when the park was new. There were 21 saloons in the 1880s. All sorts of undesirables tended to gravitate here and to nearby Mammoth Hot Springs.

Later, until train service ended in 1948, Gardiner was an outfitting station for horseback excursions into the park. The town still caters to hunters in the fall season and serves park visitors year round.

Gardiner is home to many of the people who work at Mammoth Hot Springs, headquarters for Yellowstone Park. It's also the location of warehouses and other adjuncts of the hotel and restaurant concessionaire.

A travertine quarry is located above town on a very old terrace not unlike those found at Mammoth. An old gold mine at Jardine, about 5 miles (8 km) northeast of Gardiner, reopened for a few years in the 1980s and '90s, but did not prove profitable.

[🏃] The **Yellowstone River Trail** begins outside the park but soon enters park land and follows the Yellowstone River's Black Canyon for many miles. To reach the trailhead, take the Jardine Road where U.S. 89 turns south in Gardiner, before crossing the Yellowstone River. Turn in at the private Rocky Mountain Campground and ask for parking information at the store.

North Entrance to Swan Lake Flat

From the North Entrance to Mammoth Hot Springs Junction

After you enter the park, you will follow the Gardner River through its canyon. You might spot mule deer, bison, and bighorn sheep in the canyon, particularly in winter; elk and pronghorn antelope are here year round.

This is the only entrance road that is kept plowed all winter long. It provides access to park headquarters in Mammoth Hot Springs. The road from Mammoth eastward is also kept plowed for winter access to the towns of Cooke City and Silver Gate, Montana (outside the Northeast Entrance).

It's only about 5 miles (8 km) from Gardiner to Mammoth, but the elevation gain from the North Entrance to Mammoth of nearly 1000 feet (300 m) is enough to make a noticeable difference in the climate and ecology.

Road Log

0.0/5.3 Yellowstone National Park boundary. The boundary runs along the north side of Park Street in the town of Gardiner. The road at the east end of town provides access for park personnel and passes National Park Service buildings and the concessionaire's warehouses. There the garage built for Yellowstone Park Transportation Company buses still carries the company's traditional bear symbol and the sign, "Y.P.T. Co. 1925." The visitors' route starts at the west end of Park Street. In front of the last buildings before you pass under the arch, you may notice a very old boundary marker incised with "N.B.Y.P." (Northern Boundary Yellowstone Park).

A gravel side road open to cars and mountain bikes follows the stone wall from the entrance arch toward the northwest; this is the same road that you can reach from the bridge at Corwin Springs about 8 miles (13 km) north. The road parallels the former Northern Pacific railroad bed, now within park territory. Along the road is a very old cemetery and a couple of exclosures, where biologists exclude large browsing animals in order to study the plants.

The **North Entrance Arch**, sometimes called the Roosevelt Arch, is just inside the boundary. Stagecoaches loaded passengers from the railroad station in Gardiner and passed through the arch to

The North Entrance Arch was constructed from columnar basalt quarried near Gardiner.

enter the park. Pres. Theodore Roosevelt laid the cornerstone and dedicated the arch in April 1903. It's inscribed near the top with words from the Act of Congress that set aside this land "for the benefit and enjoyment of the people."

The gateway arch was conceived by Major Chittenden of the U.S. Army Corps of Engineers and designed by architect Robert C. Reamer (designer of Old Faithful Inn and the third Canyon Hotel). Critics have pointed out the uselessness of the arch, but as the Eiffel Tower is to Paris, the arch is to Yellowstone.

0.1/5.2 **P** Sign to commemorate the 125th birthday of Yellowstone National Park in 1997.

Some Plants and A Snake Near Gardiner

Since precipitation is low (about 12–13 in/30–33 cm per year) and the elevation lower than the rest of the park, the ecology here differs from that of any other section. As the road ascends to Mammoth Hot Springs, the vegetation changes from dry

Big sagebrush lives in lower elevations and throughout the western U.S.

desert plants, such as Idaho fescue and the occasional prickly pear cactus, to higher elevation plants like Rocky Mountain juniper and rabbitbrush.

Big sagebrush (*Artemisia tridentata*) is common throughout the lower elevations. It's not related to the sage used as a kitchen herb (*Salvia officinalis*).

This is the only part of the park where rattlesnakes have sometimes been seen, but they are not common here. (See the "Living Things" chapter for more about plants and animals.)

0.5/4.8 [🚻] North Entrance station. Stop here to pay the entrance fee (see the "Travel Tips" for fee information).

The road uphill to the west near the entrance station is open to cars in one direction, from Mammoth to Gardiner—both ways for bicyclists. It was called the High Road when it and the present main route into the park were about equal in importance.

Near the entrance station, you might want to pull over and look around at the mountains.

How the Mountains Around You Got Their Names

From just inside the North Entrance gate, look toward the west to see **Electric Peak** (usually snow-capped), about 7 miles (11 km) away near the Montana/Wyoming state line. At 10,969 feet (3343 m), it's the highest peak in the Gallatin Range and was believed to be the highest in the park until 1930s surveys showed Eagle Peak in the southeast corner to be 389 feet (112 m) higher (11,358 ft/3462 m).

Electric Peak got its name from a strange experience reported by members of the 1872 Hayden expedition. While attempting to climb this peak, the men heard crackling sounds, felt electric shocks, and found their hair standing on end. This experience has not recurred as far as is known, but electric storms are indeed common during the late afternoon.

The mountain to the southwest is **Sepulcher Mountain** (9652 ft/2942 m). The name probably came from a tomblike formation in the rocks near the summit of the mountain. Both Electric and Sepulcher are made of sedimentary rocks about 100 million years old.

Slumping down toward the road from Sepulcher's northeast side is an obvious area of *hummocks*; that is, rounded humps left behind by major landslides. Geologists theorize that the underlying layer of shale on Sepulcher became water-saturated, allowing the volcanic rocks on top to slowly slide down.

To the southeast is a gradual slope to the top of 7841-foot (2390 m) **Mount Everts**. The mountain is named for Truman Everts, assessor of internal revenue of Montana Territory. But that's not why he's famous. In 1870, before there was a national park here, Everts was accidentally separated from the Washburn-Langford exploration party and lost for a total of 37 days during inclement autumn weather. Without food for much of that time, he somehow made his way from south of Yellowstone Lake to near Crescent Hill, about 12 miles (19 km) east of Mammoth. There, mountaineers Jack Baronett and George Pritchett found him, unable to walk and barely alive. When the friend who had offered a $600 reward demanded that Everts pay it, he refused, saying he would have found his way out without help! He recovered from his ordeal and survived to father a child when he was almost 75.

0.9/4.4 Ⓟ Interpretive sign about migrating animals.

1.2/4.1 🚶 Rescue Creek Trailhead. This 8-mile-long (13 km) trail was part of the primitive 19th century "Turkey Pen Road" that miners used to reach Cooke City from Gardiner. Today's trail climbs about 1200 feet (365 m) along the back of Mount Everts and then descends to rejoin the Grand Loop Road at Blacktail Deer Creek east of Mammoth.

Rescue Creek's name is the result of a misunderstanding from long ago. Ferdinand Hayden, leader of three 1870s expeditions through the park, thought that the mountain now called Mount Everts was where the lost Truman Everts had been found. Hayden named the creek that skirts the mountain accordingly, and the name has never been changed.

The field northeast of the footbridge had several uses in the early 1900s. Alfalfa and then wheat were planted on the flats near Gardiner. Part of the large field was used as a 1000-yard (914 m) target range for the U.S. Cavalry in the years when they patrolled the park (1886 to 1918); the *butts*, or trench in which the target crew operated, still remains at the north end.

To the southeast is the northern shoulder of Mount Everts, called **McMinn Bench**, where a man named Silas McMinn was allowed to mine coal from a tunnel he dug and sell it to the National Hotel at Mammoth in the late 19th century.

Gardiner or Gardner?

Why do we spell the names differently for a town and a river in the same vicinity? The river was named in the 1830s for Johnson Gardner, a rough and illiterate trapper. After 1870, the spelling on maps was Gardiner, probably the result of a mispronunciation. Since 1959, the official spelling for the river has eliminated the *i* to conform to earliest usage.

The post office at Gardiner, established in 1880, took its name from the stream. Sometimes mail consigned to the postmaster and unofficial mayor was addressed simply to "Jim on the Gardiner." The town officials have never seen fit to change that spelling.

1.6/3.7 North end of **Gardner River Canyon** and bridge over the Gardner River.

P There are wide spots for parking on both sides of the road south of the bridge. On **Eagle Nest Rock,** just east (left) of the bridge, ospreys (not eagles) nested for at least 80 years, until an earth tremor dislodged the nest. Ospreys that rebuilt the nest were harassed by ravens at one time. Check the top of this sharp rock to see if the birds are back. Eagle Nest Rock, like most of the rock in the canyon, is made of marine deposits about 100 million years old.

Across the road from Eagle Nest Rock, look out in the river to see **Split Rock**, a large boulder that fell from above and split neatly down the middle, with willows growing out of the crack. In the 1880s, the road ran on the other side of the river. You can see a remnant of an early bridge, but it's mostly covered by landslide debris.

Highway Robbery

Split Rock, a large boulder in the middle of the Gardner River, has a story. On the night of July 4, 1887, two masked highwaymen hid behind the rock, hoping to surprise the army quartermaster on his way to pay the troops. They mistakenly let the quartermaster's buggy go by and held up a stage-coach instead. The highwaymen robbed the passengers of sixteen dollars and an unusual coin with the head of Napoleon on one side.

It was this coin that eventually gave them away. One of the robbers, William James, showed the coin to some companions about two months later. This led to the arrest and subsequent imprisonment of both robbers. Ironically, the owner of the coin was Judge John F. Lacey, who later, as a member of the U.S. House of Representatives, authored the act that brought law and order to Yellowstone.

2.0/3.3 Sliding Hill is an old name for the slope to the west, where keeping the road free after landslides has been a problem since the park was new. As recently as December 1999, a slide on the east side about 6 feet (2 m) deep and 40 feet long (12 m) closed the road for several days.

The river carries away the sediment as fast as it comes down, but in doing so, continually cuts away its own banks and often undercuts the road as well, especially during the spring runoff. A small lake (appropriately called Slide Lake) perches above this point; its seepage must contribute to the landslides.

High above you is an area that bighorn sheep use for lambing. The Park Service sometimes posts "Sheep management—area closed" signs to assure that humans do not disturb the sheep.

Bighorn rams pose on the cliffs in Gardner Canyon.

2.8/2.5 As the Gardner Canyon widens out, you come to a meadow where elk like to graze. Superintendent Norris started a garden here in 1879; later gardeners were the U.S. Cavalry and a Chinese man named Sam Wo. Park employees still call this land the Chinese Garden.

2.9/2.4 At about this point you cross the halfway point between the equator and the North Pole, the 45th parallel of latitude.

3.0/2.3 Bridge over the Gardner River.

🅿️(3) Forty-Fifth Parallel picnic area to the west.

P 🚻♿(2) Parking area and trail to Boiling River on the east. **Boiling River** is one of two places near park roads where regulations allow bathing in a river warmed by hot springs. Bathing directly in any hot spring is dangerous and is not allowed in the park at all. Boiling River is not at all suitable for young children.

🚶 The trail leads about one-half mile (0.8 km) along the river to the hot spring area. The entire area is closed off until the water is low enough (usually in mid to late July) to make it safe for bathing. Hot River is an older but unofficial name used by scientists for this spot. The river does not really boil; its temperature varies in the range of 117–124°F (47–51°C), but only where the hot and cold waters mix.

3.1/2.2 Montana/Wyoming state line. The boundary was inadvertently set approximately 1200 feet (365 m) south of the 45th parallel, according to Yellowstone historian Aubrey Haines.

Local residents called the steep hill here Soap Hill when the road grade was 15 percent. Below the hill in the 1870s was a short-lived establishment called McGuirk's Medicinal Springs, where Matthew McGuirk dammed Boiling River and charged rheumatic customers to "take the waters."

Across the Gardner is a fine example of an *alluvial fan*. These are common in semi-arid regions where storms deposit huge amounts of rain in a short time span. The flooding streams race down, scouring the canyons and carrying a torrent of debris. When the stream bursts out of its canyon, it spreads out, slows down, and drops the debris, creating a fan-shaped mound.

A classic alluvial fan descends from the light-colored cliffs on Mt. Everts to the dark trees along the Gardner River.

4.1/1.2 P Lava Creek Trailhead and interpretive sign explaining Mount Everts's late spring and summer mudslides.

To take the **Lava Creek Trail**, follow the orange blazes upstream to a bridge across the Gardner River. The trail continues to the mouth of Lava Creek and then ascends Lava Creek canyon to reach Undine Falls in about 4 miles (6.5 km). It joins the Blacktail Deer Trail in another 3 miles (4.5 km).

A Quiet Geological Era Ends Violently

Sedimentation

Looking across the Gardner River at the cliff face of Mount Everts, you can see rocks whose ages span about 100 million years. The bulk of the rocks, from the level of the river to nearly the top of the cliff, were formed about 100 million years ago by the slow, gentle process of sediment deposition in fairly shallow seas, where the sandstones were probably ancient beaches. The shales were deposited when the water above them was quieter and deeper. As you drive along the base of the cliffs in the Gardner Canyon, you can look along the cliff face and distinguish the sandstones, because they form the cliffs' vertical portions. The shales (also called mudstones) erode more easily, forming the sloping parts.   **[GEO.3]**

The sedimentation occurred toward the end of a long, quiet geological episode. The Yellowstone Park area experienced this quiet period from about three billion to about 50 million years ago.

Volcanism

At the crest of the cliff on the southern end of Mount Everts—best seen from east and south of Mammoth Hot Springs—is a thin layer of volcanic tuff that resulted from violent explosions 2 million years ago.

A Sign of Violent Earth Movement

You can see another sign of re-newed activity on Mount Everts from where the road to Tower Junction descends to Yellowstone River (about 1 mi/ 1.5 km east of Mammoth Hot Springs Junction). In the left half of the photograph, you see where 100-million-year-old sediments are tilted down to-ward the north. These formerly flat-lying sediments were tilted,

Near the top of Mt. Everts is a clear example of an unconformity.

eroded to form a horizontal ground surface, and then covered with tuff. Ge-ologists call this kind of intersection an *angular unconformity*.

4.3/1.0 Side road leading east to employ-ees' housing. Located down this road is the elementary school for children of year-round park employees; junior high and high school students must go to Gardner.

4.5/0.8 ⛺ 🛶 **Mammoth Camp-ground** road to the west (right). This is the only campground in Yellowstone that's open all year. In summer it has 85 sites available on a first-come, first-served basis; fewer sites are used in winter. The amphitheater, where ranger lectures are given each evening during the summer, is located near the campground's far end.

4.6/0.7 A 180-degree curve goes up a steep hill made of ancient travertine (calcium carbonate) that is revealed by the road cut here. The travertine of this **Cedar Terrace** was deposited many centuries ago.

5.2/0.1 ▣ ✉ The clinic, post office, and **National Park Service headquarters** for Yellowstone are housed in the buildings to the left of the median land-scaped strip as you enter the Mammoth area. Facilities for visitors are slightly farther on.

Near the clinic you might notice a small log cabin dating from 1895 and built as the mail carrier's cabin. It is still used as employee housing.

5.3/0.0 Mammoth Hot Springs Junction. To the east is Tower Junction. The road south takes you past Mammoth's facilities and to the Mammoth Hot Springs terraces, then continues south to Norris Junction. To the north is the North Entrance.

FACILITIES AT MAMMOTH HOT SPRINGS

Turn left beyond the median strip, or right if you're coming from Tower Junction or the terraces, to park across the street from the visitor center.

Ⓟ 🚻 🏛(3) ♿ **Albright Visitor Center**. An elevator at the rear of the visitor center may be used to reach a wheelchair accessible rest room upstairs; other rest rooms are under the porch at the front. The building's first floor houses a ranger desk, a small bookstore, a small theater, and displays of historic paintings and photographs. On the second floor are dioramas of Yellowstone's history and of the wildlife of the northern range, especially wolves. The park's research library and archives are in the basement. A new building is being planned for the archives.

This visitor center honors the memory of Horace M. Albright, park superintendent from 1919 to 1929. Albright played an important role in the establishment of the National Park Service and became its second director.

Ⓟ 🛏 🍴(2) 🔧 🛒 Opposite the intersection with the road to Tower-Roosevelt Junction are the **Mammoth Hotel and Cabins**. Going south from the hotel toward the terraces, you'll find two restaurants and a general store, with parking across the street. There's also a service station.

Mammoth Hot Springs Hotel is open for summer and winter seasons. A succession of hotels was built on this same site, beginning with the National Hotel (1883–1936). The National Hotel's north wing, built in 1911–13, was incorporated into the present Mammoth Hotel, constructed in 1937. Cabins behind the hotel were designed by architect Robert Reamer, who also created the unique United States map in the hotel's Map Room. It's made of 15 types of

Mammoth Hot Springs Area

NOTE: Both this Mammoth area map and the terraces map on page 257 have north at the top, so they differ slightly from some official maps.

fine wood from nine countries and was carefully restored in 1997.

⊼ There are several picnic tables on the former parade ground across the road from the hotel. Others are near Opal Terrace and across the median strip from the post office.

🚻♿(4) Wheelchair accessible rest rooms are in the Mammoth Hotel lobby and the Terrace Grill, as well as in the visitor center.

The flat grassy area in the center of the Mammoth Hot Springs area was used as a parade ground when the U.S. Cavalry was in charge of the park (1886–1918). You can imagine the fine displays of horsemanship the soldiers put on for the guests at the hotel, despite fears that the hollow ground might cave in under the horses' hooves. There are still people alive who remember the years after the army left, when residents flooded the area for ice-skating each winter.

A Plant Special to Mammoth

Why are there cultivated green lawns at Mammoth, when this is supposed to be a natural and wild place? The U.S. Cavalry first created a bare parade ground at the base of the terraces but later brought in soil, seeded it with grass and clover, and installed an irrigation system. Perhaps the officers and other residents also wanted grass to help them feel at home while stationed here. This is the only place in Yellowstone where you'll see green grass lawns.

The resident elk herd at Mammoth helps keep the grass short.

The store located at the edge of the open area along the road to Tower-Roosevelt, now called a Nature Shop, was built in 1929 as the headquarters for Haynes Picture Shops. All the other buildings you see in this part of Mammoth, with one exception, are offices and workshops and housing for employees, since this is the center of administration and maintenance for the entire park.

The one public building found on the road toward Tower-Roosevelt is the **Yellowstone National Park Chapel**, the last stone building as you leave the developed area. Built in 1913 in the cruciform shape indicative of Episcopalian origin, the chapel has always been non-denominational and used for weddings as well as services. Times for Saturday mass and Sunday services are posted on the board in front of the building.

The YNP Chapel was planned by year-round residents of Mammoth, including Judge John W. Meldrum, the U.S. Commissioner for the park who served from 1894 to 1935. It was built of native sandstone by a Billings construction company and furnished in oak.

The chapel vestibule is graced with painted and stained glass windows showing Old Faithful, the Lower Falls of the Yellowstone, and common flora and fauna of the area. These windows, made and given to the park by Miss Jessie Van Brunt, were installed at the front entrance in 1939.

Animals and Holes in the Ground

Mammoth is the year-round home of a herd of **elk** (also called by its Shawnee name *wapiti*, meaning white rump). These elk are not tame, so keep a safe distance away—the park service says 25 yards (23 m) away.

In early summer, you'll see mostly cows and calves grazing and resting in

Windows in the chapel vestibule.

the shade. Sometimes they'll be on the terraces themselves, since there are fewer bugs there, and the white travertine reflects the heat away. In the autumn, the bull elk round up their harems and sound off with their peculiar bugling sound. The males with small single-pronged antlers are yearlings.

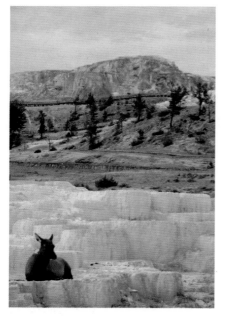

Elk at Mammoth Hot Springs like to lie on the terraces even on hot summer days.

Watch your step if you're walking on the grass! Deep burrows dug by **Uinta ground squirrels** are everywhere. This rodent, which children love to watch, appears to be a cross between a red squirrel and a yellow-bellied marmot, both of which live elsewhere in the park. These squirrels stay underground for up to seven months of the year.

Another animal you may see at the outskirts of Mammoth is the **coyote**. Coyotes are smaller and slimmer than wolves and much less shy. In fact, there have been some incidents of coyotes biting humans in recent years after they were fed human food. **Special Caution**: Do not approach or feed any animals in the park.

While walking in front of the visitor center, you'll see three holes in the ground that are much too wide and deep to be ground squirrel burrows. These are *collapse features*, where water has flowed through the travertine, weakened it, and dissolved it away until the ground above has caved in.

McCartney Cave

The hole, or collapse feature, farthest to the left as you look from the visitor center's front porch has historically been called McCartney Cave. In 1877, hotel and bathhouse proprietor James McCartney reportedly hid in this hole from Nez Perce for three days and later probably charged tourists to go down a ladder to its bottom. Here's how an 1898 guide to Yellowstone described the experience of entering the cave:

About midway between the hotel and officers' quarters, surrounded by an iron railing, is McCartney Cave. The opening is about four feet in diameter, rather oblong in shape. By means of a ladder one can descend vertically some thirty feet, thence twenty feet on an incline to the bottom of the main chamber. The venturesome may, by means of a rope and light, continue explorations 100 feet further. Far beneath, in a subterranean chamber, water can be distinctly heard by the rope-supported explorer; but the hot vapors and gases constantly arising, stimulate an earnest desire to ascend to the surface. . . .

In the winter of 1881, there was a heavy fall of snow which drifted over many of the openings in the plateau. The following spring Mr. McCartney noticed a large pair of antlers protruding, apparently, from the ground; investigating, he discovered that an unfortunate elk had broken through the crust of snow, and falling into the cave, had died, suspended by his horns, in the opening.

Hiking and biking around Mammoth

In Mammoth you can take a historic walk, the Lower Terrace walk (both described below), or other short trails for hiking or biking.

Behind and to the north of the hotel is the start of the **Old Gardiner Road** or High Road (about 4 mi/6 km long), which can only be traveled from south to north by cars (from Mammoth to Gardiner). You can bicycle either way, but you'll avoid the long uphill grade if you start at Mammoth.

You can start the **Beaver Ponds Loop Trail** at the same point as the Old Gardiner Road. A slightly steeper way to begin the loop is at Clematis Creek (it's named for a flowering vine and pronounced KLEM-a-tus or klem-A-tus). Clematis Creek is located between Liberty Cap and the U.S. Commissioner's stone house.

Although billed by the park service and several hiking books as a 5-mile (8 km) trail, to complete a loop from any point in Mammoth to Beaver Ponds requires a walk of at least 6 miles (9.5 km). The long-range views, birds, wildflowers, and the ponds themselves are delightfully worth the effort, as are the contrasts that you pass between the high desert and the moist forest microclimates. Beaver (*Castor canadensis*) are most active from dusk to dawn, so you're unlikely to see them in daytime, but you can see a dam they've built between the ponds. Incidentally, a 1996 parkwide aerial survey found about 50 active beaver lodges in the entire park.

Beaver Ponds

Another trail reached from Clematis Creek is the Howard Eaton Trail to the upper terraces and beyond (a recommended part of this trail is described on page 271).

Historic Fort Yellowstone

To get a feeling for army life a century ago here at **Fort Yellowstone**, take a ranger-guided tour or a short walk around the historic buildings described in "The Army Years" booklet available at the visitor center. This was never the kind of fort with a stockade you see in Western movies, but a permanent army post, of which there were many in 19th century Montana and Wyoming territories. Fort Yellowstone has been said to rival West Point for the quality of its architecture. Signs along the walk tell you about the buildings' use. Year-round park personnel currently occupy most buildings, so please respect their privacy.

The walk begins with **Albright Visitor Center**, the former Bachelor Officers' Quarters built in 1909. As with all the stone buildings, this one was constructed by Scottish stonemasons, who quarried the sandstone just down the hill near the Gardner River.

The cavalry decided to build new facilities in stone after a devastating 1907 fire destroyed wooden stables and killed a number of horses. The last building in the first row was the **Guard House**, also used to admit park visitors in the early years, when almost all travelers entered via the North Entrance.

The second and third rows included barracks, the post exchange, and stables, which are now used for offices and shops. Four small houses behind were non-commissioned officers' quarters and were dubbed **Soapsuds Row** when the wives took in laundry for extra money.

In 1916, when the National Park Service was formed and took over administration of Yellowstone, approximately 200 soldiers were serving in the park. Of these, 22 stayed on as park rangers. Modern national park policies, philosophies, and even ranger uniforms evolved from the base built here.

LOWER TERRACES WALKING TOUR★

The Mammoth Terraces are constantly changing! You need to approach closely to them to appreciate the variety of colors and the heat and power of the springs. Ask the rangers at the visitor center where the best current activity can be found. Walking around the lower terraces might be better called a climbing tour, since you must go up and down many stairs if you want to get close to the terraces. It's worth the effort and covers a total of about 1 mile (1.6 km).

NOTE: For a wheelchair accessible boardwalk, see the Upper Terrace Drive, beginning on page 264.

Opal Terrace

⟨♿⟩ Park at one of the several areas at the foot of the terraces. The easiest terrace to

When it's active, Opal Terrace threatens to overwhelm Executive House (1996).

get to is **Opal Spring** and **Terrace**, the only formation east of the main road.

As you approach Opal Terrace, you may wonder why a large and beautiful house would have been built so close to an active terrace. Built in 1908, the house was designed by Robert Reamer for Yellowstone Park Association president Harry W. Child. There was no spring here then, or if there was, it was tiny! Since 1926, Opal Spring deposited a foot or more (about 30 cm) of travertine each year it was active, but it has

Mammoth Hot Springs Terraces

alternated between dormant and active since 1982. Nature now usually wins out in disputes over territory, but the National Park Service must also protect the house as a cultural site.

The runoff from Opal Spring—as with many of the springs above it—flows through underground channels, not on the surface. Tracer dyes were injected down a nearby sinkhole in a recent study. It was found that the hot spring water takes about two hours to reach Boiling River about 2 miles (3 km) below Mammoth.

We'll divide the remainder of the Lower Terrace area above the road into two walks, Parts I and II.

Lower Terrace Boardwalk, Part I

🚶 Before starting up the boardwalk past Liberty Cap's cone, you might take a small side trip to see the very active lower part of Hymen Terrace, which is across Clematis Creek from the bus parking area. The spring here has been in a vigorous building phase since 1992, having eroded completely away in previous years.

Liberty Cap in about 1871, by W. H. Jackson.

Forty-five-foot-high (14 m) **Liberty Cap**, an extinct hot spring cone, is named for the conical hats given to emancipated Roman slaves, later worn during the French Revolution, and then depicted on early American coins. In 1874, the visiting British Earl of Dunraven looked at this formation and wrote: "Professor Hayden calls this the Liberty Cap; locally it goes by another name."

The spring that built Liberty Cap has been inactive at least since 1871. The formation is estimated to be about 2500 years old. Travertine may have sealed the small orifice at the top or, when the cone reached a certain height, perhaps the water pressure was insufficient to lift the hot water to the top.

Another extinct cone to the left up the walkway is named **Devil's Thumb**. Not long ago a small boy commented as he passed, "Devil's Big Toe would be a better name!"

Adjacent to Devil's Thumb is **Palette Spring**. Active in recent years, this colorful spring looks as though it could engulf Devil's Thumb in a decade or less. The texture of its sloping terrace looks rather like a giant quilt.

The walkway continues steeply uphill, past much-eroded **Hymen Terrace** (named for the Greek god of marriage) below on the north (right). Dormant since 1936, the upper section of this terrace is now almost unrecognizable as a terrace. The *Haynes Guide* for 1912 stated prophetically: "Hymen Terrace is growing fast; in fact, it is gravely feared that the openings may become choked from the abundance of depositing lime."

Hymen Terrace and Devil's Thumb in 1881, by F. J. Haynes.

If this should happen, it would be a matter of but a few days until the coloring would have disappeared, leaving the travertine rock bare and exposed to the destructive forces of the elements."

Continuing to the left when the trail forks, you will pass next to **Minerva Terrace**, named for the Roman goddess of wisdom and the arts. A short spur of boardwalk dead-ends at a part of Minerva that was very active and beautiful for most of the 1990s but sometimes inactive from late 1998 on. The boardwalk has to be changed whenever and wherever the terrace builds up too high.

At Mammoth's springs, particularly at Minerva Spring, enterprising early residents sold coated specimens to the tourists. Any item kept in this water was nicely coated in about 4 days or completely buried by calcium carbonate deposits in 11 days.

Minerva Terrace as it appeared in 1998.

Lower Terrace Boardwalk, Part II

This hike starts from the next parking area south of Liberty Cap.

Cavern Terrace had an active spring into the 1970s, but recently showed the crumbling, dark gray of eroding deposits. The boardwalk passes a large collapse feature where the travertine has caved in.

At the top of a long flight of stairs, the large fissure ridge deposit called **Mound Terrace** appears above and to the left of the boardwalk intersection. Holes and crevices in the side of Mound Terrace's white travertine may remind you of faces and other images.

Turning right at this junction eventually leads you past **Cleopatra Terrace** up many steps to **New Blue Springs**. But it's easier to reach this spot and its outstanding view from the Main Terrace overlook on Upper Terrace Drive (see page 264).

Turning left (south) above Minerva Spring instead takes you under the site of **Naiad Spring**, whose activity mainly

Part of Mound Terrace looks like a Halloween ghost mask with a screaming mouth.

formed Mound Terrace. Naiads were the water spirits of classical mythology, who were known to weep copiously.

The last terrace to the south is huge **Jupiter Terrace**. Two large hot pools at the top of Jupiter used to discharge water here. Early tour guides always pointed out Pulpit Terrace, where stalactites had grown almost together around the edges of a semicircular pool into a pulpit-shaped formation. This feature has deteriorated and can no longer be seen. The southernmost mound of this complex of terraces bears the name **Marble Terrace.**

On its own stretch of boardwalk between parking areas, little **Reservoir Springs** has been active recently and has some colorful microbial mats.

A Mountain Turning Itself Inside Out

In only 130 years of recorded history, Mammoth's terraces have grown tremendously in height and width. In fact, the average buildup of travertine in active areas is about 8 inches (20 cm) per year and can be as much as 2 feet (60 cm) in a year.

What Makes the Terraces?

The Mammoth area is underlain at depth by limestones, that is, hardened sediments consisting mostly of calcium carbonate. Hot water dissolves the limestone from deep below Mammoth and carries it through cracks to the surface. As the water rises, the pressure confining it decreases, the water cools, and hot gas, mostly carbon dioxide, escapes. The water becomes supersaturated with calcium carbonate, which precipitates out on the surface as travertine.

You might ask where all this hot water comes from, since Mammoth lies outside the Yellowstone caldera and not over the Yellowstone hot spot. The water may run along a fault in the earth from Norris Geyser Basin, or part of it may percolate here underground from the Gallatin Range. Geochemists have proven that this water has been underground for at least 60 years, probably considerably longer. Magma deep in the earth supplies the heat to maintain the water in Mammoth's hot springs at about 163°F (73°C) year-round.

Mammoth is unique in the park because of its underground limestone; Yellowstone's geyser basins, on the other hand, sit atop *igneous* rocks, that is, rocks that are or once were molten. **[GEO.24]**

Are There Geysers at Mammoth?

You will not find any geysers at Mammoth, and you may wonder why. Two factors essential to create geysers are missing here: geysers require superheated water, and they need rock harder than the limestone to provide the required plumbing and buildup of pressure.

Colors and Patterns in the Terraces

Some of the bright colors in the runoff come from mineral deposits, but most come from microorganisms that thrive in hot water. These microorganisms begin to appear just a few days after a new spring is born.

The resident bacteria and algae help extract some of the carbon dioxide from the hot spring water. Calcium carbonate is precipitated on top of the organisms, which in turn seek sunlight and begin to build up above the mineral deposits. Looking closely, you can find filamentous patterns in the formations, showing the results of this precipitation and growth.

Inactive terraces are white; long-inactive ones are various shades of gray. What causes the springs that build the terraces to vary their activity so wildly and unpredictably? The accumulating travertine tends to clog the plumbing, and varying water supply, chemistry, temperature, and frequent earthquakes may also contribute to the changes.

Some Facts and Figures about Mammoth Hot Springs

Every day at Mammoth an estimated 1.4 million gallons (5.3 million liters) of water is discharged and about two tons of new travertine are deposited. However, Mammoth is not the world's largest set of active travertine terraces; a larger one, Pamukkale (ancient Hierapolis) in southwestern Turkey, covers several square kilometers, and there may be others.

Besides the large terraces, other types of travertine features at Mammoth are cones, such as Liberty Cap; *fissure ridges,* that is, mounds of travertine fed by water rising through cracks along their center plane; and terracettes. *Terracettes* are the individual semicircles of travertine formed at the edges of a hot spring pool.

Lower Hymen Terrace is rapidly adding to its terracettes.

In over 100 years of observation, geologists have concluded that the overall thermal activity has neither declined nor increased. Over time, some hot springs seal themselves and never reopen, others cease and resume, and new ones appear with no warning.

From Mammoth Junction to Norris Junction

In the 21 miles (34 km) between Mammoth and Norris junctions there are no geysers to watch, but you'll find several other types of thermal feature as well as mountains of volcanic origin. Heading south on the Grand Loop Road, you'll pass: Upper Terrace Drive's terraces, Obsidian Cliff, Clearwater Springs, Roaring Mountain, and tiny Frying Pan Spring, with its fascinating sizzling activity.

Road Log

NOTE: See the Mammoth Hot Springs Terraces map on page 257. Mammoth's facilities are described on page 250, map on page 251.

0.0/21.0 Mammoth Hot Springs Junction. The road to the southwest (then south) takes you to the Mammoth Hot Springs terraces and then on to Norris Junction and Norris Geyser Basin. The road that begins almost opposite the Mammoth Hot Springs Hotel goes east to Tower-Roosevelt Junction. To the north is the North Entrance.

0.3/20.7 P(2) Liberty Cap and Opal Terrace. (For walking tours of the lower terraces, see pages 256–60.)

The big hill across the road from the main terraces is **Capitol Hill**, once the center of authority in the park. In 1879, Superintendent Norris built his administration building (the "Blockhouse") on top of the hill and fortified it against

possible Indian attack. It served as office and home for Norris and other civilian superintendents until it was torn down in 1909. Capitol Hill is composed of glacially transported gravel.

0.4/20.6 P Jupiter Terrace. This general area was the site of Camp Sheridan, the U.S. Army's first park headquarters, used from 1886 until 1897, by which time nearby Fort Yellowstone had supplanted it.

0.6/20.4 P Terrace Springs Trails parking area is the least convenient of the four places to park near the Lower Terraces and requires the most stair climbing.

In this area in the 1930s and '40s was

a swimming pool that used hot-spring water. It was removed by the park service about 1950.

0.8/20.2 🏠 Side road to the **Mammoth Horse Corrals** at the east. Horses may be hired through the park concessionaire for escorted 1-hour rides during the summer months. Arrangements can be made at Mammoth Hot Springs hotel or at the corrals.

There was a lodge and campground in this valley many years ago, and an enclosure where bison were confined during the summer. This show herd assured early 20th century tourists on the Grand Tour that they would see some of the then-rare beasts.

Also down this road a short way is the military cemetery, where soldiers and others who died at Mammoth were buried from 1888 to 1957. Many of the remains and gravestones were removed by the military in 1917 to Little Bighorn Battlefield National Monument (then called the Custer Battlefield). About 40 graves remain.

1.3/19.7 At the sharpest angle of the hairpin curve in the Grand Loop Road is the entrance to a side road to employee housing and a privately sponsored summer camp called the Youth Conservation Corps, for young people who do resource management and trail work.

From 1933 to 1941, this area housed the headquarters for the local Civilian Conservation Corps. The C.C.C. was a large project of Franklin Roosevelt's New Deal, during which men aged 17 to 28 were recruited throughout the U.S. They built and maintained roads, bridges, trails, and campgrounds, fought fires,

and stocked fish, learning valuable skills and often supporting destitute families in the Depression years.

🚶 A steep hike on the former Bunsen Peak Road starts in the residential area here. To locate the trailhead, turn left at the "Truck Route" sign and watch for a closed-off road with a trail sign on your left. Please respect local residents and park as well out of the way as possible. An easier approach to this trail down to the Gardner River canyon and Osprey Falls starts near Rustic Falls, described at mile 4.8/16.2 on this stretch of the Grand Loop Road.

🚶 🚫 A short trail (really a road, used as a ski trail in winter) beginning at the end of the maintenance yard leads to little Joffe Lake. The lake has some small brook trout.

The hill between the residential area and Upper Terrace Drive has traditionally been called **Formation Hill**, since it leads to the main formation or terrace.

1.8/19.2 Turnout for a good view of Canary Spring and its terrace and the whole Gardner River valley and mountains to the north.

2.0/19.0 Upper Terrace Drive (also called Mammoth Terrace Drive) begins here and leads one way to the right. No RVs, buses, or any other vehicles over 25 feet long are allowed on this road, because it's so narrow and winding.

Ⓟ 🚻 ♿ Ⓒ If your vehicle is too large for the road, leave it in the large parking area at the turnoff.

🚶 The whole loop is 1.6 miles (2.6 km) long, short enough for a pleasant walk, but many people prefer to drive and stop for the sights. Whether walking or driving, you'll find several active springs, fine views of the valley below and the surrounding mountains, and a number of interesting formations.

Upper Terrace Drive

There are two ways to access the first feature, Canary Spring, which has been quite active and beautiful in recent years.

🚹 To use the wheelchair accessible boardwalks, park on the left immediately after entering the one-way road. Follow the gradually descending boardwalk to its lower stretch.

Alternatively, drive to the first wide parking spot on the right and take the boardwalks along the top of **Main Terrace**. On this second route, a boardwalk spur passes **Cupid Spring** with its gracefully draping formations. Cupid's deposits have sealed off a feature called Cupid's Cave, named for the Roman god of love. In the early years of the park, tourists entered this cave, oblivious to the dangers of the carbon dioxide found in all such features. Where the springs have long been inactive, you might see the tall yellow-flowered *exotic* (that is, a non-native plant) called common mullein (*Verbascum thapsus*).

Walking toward **Canary Spring**, you can see pools ringed with hanging stalactites. When water pours from the spring to the scallop-edged terracettes below, microorganisms growing in the water create beautiful colored effects. One recent summer, the colors ranged from palest yellow and coral pink through yellow green, orange, and brown, contrasting with the white and gray inactive areas and the deep green of the trees. In other years, orange predominates.

On Main Terrace, **Blue Spring** is a prominent feature. You can take the many steps to the terraces and road below, passing **New Blue Springs**, which were active for part of the late 1990s after a long dormancy and an on-again-off-again career. Sometimes bubbles burst here up to 6 or 8 inches (15–20 cm) above the surface—making New Blue Springs look the most like a geyser of anything at Mammoth. This water is not boiling, however; the bubbles are carbon dioxide gas escaping from below. Across the road is the gray and deteriorating mound of **Prospect Terrace.**

The next large parking area has an informational sign about Fort Yellowstone and an outstanding view of Mammoth and the entire region. This terrace rim is called **The Esplanade**.

The road turns sharply left at The Esplanade, where **Cheops Mound** and Narrow Gauge Terrace's fissure ridge are crumbling on the right. The next small

Canary Spring has created a huge terrace, killing trees as it grows (1996).

parking area is for **Prospect Springs**, which are pools and a foot-high (30 cm) cone that were not here until about 1935. Across the road from these springs are fenced-off deep holes that emit carbon dioxide and hydrogen sulfide.

Park at New Highland Terrace for the easiest way to see the beautiful and very active lower section of **Narrow Gauge Terrace**. The old Narrow Gauge is a cracked mound of travertine (fissure ridge), named when it was thought to resemble a narrow gauge railway roadbed. To reach the active springs, walk back along the road until you see the Howard Eaton Trail uphill from the road. Take the trail a short distance to the north. The trail was recently relocated higher on the hill to accommodate the spreading runoff of Narrow Gauge. You may see a delicate layer of *calcite ice*; that is, a thin crust of travertine that can only occur on an undisturbed pool, covering some of the hot water.

New Highland Terrace is known to have been active from at least 1928 and was truly spectacular from the late 1950s into the 1970s. The many dead trees on the sides and top of this formation attest to the sequence of active growth followed by inactivity. Trees grew for many years after the hot water ceased flowing; subsequently, further hot spring activity killed the trees.

On the inside of a sharp curve is **Orange Spring Mound**, composed of several cone-type formations grown together and a fissure ridge along its long axis and colored orange by bacterial mats. A

jet at the top sometimes spouts to 3 or 4 feet (1 m). One of Orange Spring Mound's often-active hot springs is named **Tangerine Spring**.

If you stop here, notice the little travertine cone across the road, called **Little Burper** for the tiny persistent bubbles it spouts when active. From a certain angle, its shape perfectly imitates that of Bunsen Peak in the distance.

🚶 You can start a pleasant round-trip hike of about 5 miles (8 km) here at Orange Spring Mound's parking area. The trail traverses parts of the Howard Eaton and Fawn Pass trails, passing between Clagett Butte and Terrace Mountain to reach **Snow Pass** and little Summit Lake near it. To find the trail, turn your back on Orange Spring Mound and look up to the right. Pass the travertine flats of Pinyon Terrace, including some collapse features, where the gaseous carbon dioxide creates death traps for small birds.

In about 1 mile (1.5 km) you'll turn right at the intersection and begin a climb that totals about 700 feet (200 m). Stay left at the Clagett Butte Trail intersection, along a hillside that abounds in wildflowers. The top of the pass is a windy, grassy area. Summit Lake is a

Orange Spring Mound

short distance farther in the trees.

There is little evidence now, but Snow Pass was the route of the original road from Mammoth around Terrace Mountain. One early guidebook described the Snow Pass road as so steep "that it would take a loaded wagon, drawn by four mules, a half day, allowing proper time to breathe the animals on the successive terraces. . . ." Not surprisingly, they called the Snow Pass road the "Hell Gate."

Continuing on Upper Terrace Drive

Beyond Orange Spring Mound, the road descends a steep hill. Below and to the right was Bath Lake, where early tourists bathed. It has dried out and refilled sporadically over the years; the bathhouse was removed about 60 years ago. Bath Lake has been dry since 1984.

Across the road from Bath Lake, a new spring broke out in 1978. Lee Whittlesey, archivist of Yellowstone, christened it **Aphrodite Spring**, for the Greek goddess of love and beauty, but it's now called Aphrodite Terrace, since it's been inactive for many years.

Many of the small evergreen trees along Mammoth Terrace Drive are Rocky Mountain junipers. Some of these are 300 or even 500 years old, the oldest trees in the park. Limber pine trees, their needles in sets of five, also grow along the drive.

Two more features along this twisting road are worth your attention: White Elephant Back Terrace and Angel Terrace. **White Elephant Back Terrace** is another fissure ridge, built up over centuries by sporadic seepage from the springs at its

top. *Solution caves*, that is, depressions where runoff down the side has dissolved away the travertine, can be found along the north side of the "elephant." Here they're called **The Grottoes**.

Angel Terrace may have been named for its snowy whiteness or for the delicate microorganisms that sometimes live around it. Healthy trees are growing on top of the tallest gray section, while dead trees provide witness to more recent activity. Elsewhere, the hot water and bacteria are creating travertine stalactites and areas of white, yellow, orange, and salmon colors.

One of the ranger-led hikes that go off trail in the Upper Terrace area might take you to parts of the area not generally open to visitors and teach you more about the geology and the wildflowers. You may see the River Styx, a partially underground hot stream, or solution caves, such as the Stygian Caves or deep Devil's Kitchen, where tourists used to descend by ladder. They were allowed to enter the cave until someone realized that the carbon dioxide that had killed birds and small animals wasn't good for humans either! Enterprising Mammoth

Rocky Mountain juniper tree

residents even offered refreshments from a "Devil's Kitchenette" just above the cave.

A sharp curve to the right brings you back to the Grand Loop Road.

~

Continuing on the Grand Loop Road 2.1/18.9 Turnout on the east for a warming and refueling hut for skiers and snowmobilers, built in the 1990s.

3.1/17.9 P Interpretive sign about the nearby heavily burned area from 1988's North Fork fire.

The lake below the road is called **Africa Lake** for its shape, but was called "Beatty's Lake" for years, after a local truck driver named Roy Beatty lost control of his truck and drove it into the lake in 1931. In a straight line out from the turnout is the reservoir for the Mammoth Hot Springs area.

Centuries of Terrace Building

A descending series of travertine terraces passes through the Mammoth Hot Springs area from southwest to northeast, like huge stair steps. The oldest now-inactive terrace, Terrace Mountain, is the farthest to the southwest, about 2 linear miles southwest of Mammoth; while the younger and more active ones are parts of the upper and lower terraces. The most northeasterly feature in the series is Boiling River about 2 miles below Mammoth.

- **Terrace Mountain** is the oldest and highest terrace. Its travertine deposits are 400,000 years old.
- A thousand feet (300 m) below the summit of Terrace Mountain is much smaller **Pinyon Terrace**, about 10,000 years old. During its thousands of years of inactivity, its travertine has weathered into soil that supports plants and trees, but some collapse features remain.
- Next is **Highland Terrace**, crossed by Upper Terrace Drive. The named features of this upper terrace have been active only recently.
- **Main Terrace** is the flat-topped mound we look down on from Upper Terrace Drive. There the numerous springs and terraces have continued to be active on and off for the last few hundred years.
- The visitor center and many of Mammoth's other buildings are built on **Hotel Terrace** and its eastern edge, **Cedar Terrace**. The travertine of Hotel Terrace proves to be several thousand years old. Look across the terrace on a cold morning and you can see steam rising from two or more vapor vents. It is coming from hot water that flows underground toward the river from the active springs above.
- The hot spring runoff at **Boiling River** lines up neatly with this array of terraces. It has little terrace-building potential, because rain and river water dilute the dissolved calcium carbonate in the runoff.

3.7/17.3 The Hoodoos (or Silver Gate) one-way road. Go slowly to find and take the very short, unmarked loop road to the west—a remnant of the 1899 stagecoach road. Park here to look closely at these unusual rocks.

The word hoodoo can mean something that brings bad luck, but in geology, it usually refers to standing sedimentary rocks eroded into sharp spires with bizarre shapes. Actually, the other official name for this place, **Silver Gate**, is more appropriate for this slope of Terrace Mountain, since the strange shapes of the gray-white rocks are not in their original place and are not due to erosion. These rocks are lying in an immense jumble that has slid from the slopes of Terrace Mountain to the west. The rock is predominantly travertine, like that at Mammoth Hot Springs, but is much older. Notice that the trees growing among the rocks are not very large, which suggests the landslide probably occurred in a recent century.

4.4/16.6 Golden Gate at Kingman Pass (7250 ft/2210 m). When you reach Kingman Pass, you've climbed more than a thousand feet (300 m) in the short distance from Mammoth. The name Golden Gate was used as early as the 1880s and stems from the sense you get here of passing through a gateway to the park.

The Golden Gate is a canyon cut by Glen Creek through a large deposit of the Huckleberry Ridge tuff. This two-million-year-old volcanic

rock has been stained reddish yellow by iron oxide. **[GEO.7]**

At the outer edge of the road is a column of rock known as the **Pillar of Hercules**, named by 1880s tour guide George Henderson, possibly after the Pillars of Hercules that guard the Strait of Gibraltar in Europe. It has been moved three times, once in 1889 to make room for the steamboat *Zillah* to pass on a horse-drawn truck on its way to Yellowstone Lake.

4.6/16.4 [P] Rustic Falls. A sign tells about the difficulties of building the Golden Gate road, which was designed by Lt. Daniel Kingman of the Corps of Engineers in the 1880s. Incidentally, Kingman also conceived of the figure eight pattern for the Grand Loop Road.

The Pillar of Hercules at Golden Gate, by F. J. Haynes.

Rustic Falls draws water from Indian Creek and its own Glen Creek.

Rustic Falls on Glen Creek is only 47 feet high (14 m) but worth a stop.

The canyon wall across Glen Creek is part of **Bunsen Peak**, named for the 19th century German physicist, chemist, and inventor, Robert Wilhelm Eberhard von Bunsen. Bunsen studied and theo-

rized about the geysers of Iceland, as well as lending his name to the Bunsen burner used in laboratories. Bunsen Peak is a remnant of the 50-million-year-old Absaroka Volcanics and is probably a *volcanic neck*, that is, a volcano's feeder conduit that survived because it was resistant to erosion.

4.8/16.2 Swan Lake Flat opens out before you as you exit Golden Gate canyon. The area through which the Gardner River meanders was historically called Gardners Hole—"hole" was the trappers' name for a wide valley. The Gardner River flows to the southeast behind the low hills west of Swan Lake, then makes a sharp turn to the northeast, and cuts through deep Sheepeater Canyon to join the Yellowstone River near Gardiner.

[🥾] Just as you enter Swan Lake Flat is a large parking area for the Bunsen Peak, Osprey Falls, Glen Creek, and Howard Eaton trails.

[🚲] Until 1995, the road around Bunsen Peak was open to automobile traffic, but it's now available only for biking and hiking. The former road goes about 6 miles (10 km) around Bunsen Peak to end at a maintenance and residential area near Mammoth. After about 3 quite level miles (5 km) through sage flats, the old road begins the 800-foot (250 m) descent to the Mammoth area.

Hikers can climb Bunsen Peak either from the **Bunsen Peak Trail** near the

Electric Peak is the highest mountain seen from Swan Lake Flat.

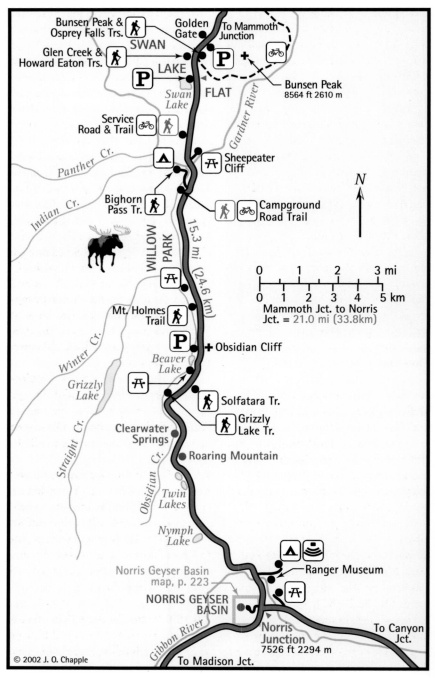

Bunsen Peak & Osprey Falls Trs.
Glen Creek & Howard Eaton Trs.
Golden Gate
To Mammoth Junction
SWAN
LAKE
FLAT
Swan Lake
Bunsen Peak
8564 ft 2610 m
Service Road & Trail
Panther Cr.
Indian Cr.
Sheepeater Cliff
Bighorn Pass Tr.
Campground Road Trail
WILLOW PARK
15.3 mi (24.6 km)
N
0   1   2   3 mi
0 1 2 3 4 5 km
Mammoth Jct. to Norris Jct. = 21.0 mi (33.8km)
Mt. Holmes Trail
Obsidian Cliff
Beaver Lake
Winter Cr.
Grizzly Lake
Solfatara Tr.
Grizzly Lake Tr.
Straight Cr.
Clearwater Springs
Roaring Mountain
Obsidian Cr.
Twin Lakes
Nymph Lake
Ranger Museum
Norris Geyser Basin map, p. 223
NORRIS GEYSER BASIN
Gibbon River
Norris Junction
7526 ft 2294 m
To Canyon Jct.
To Madison Jct.
© 2002 J. O. Chapple

Swan Lake Flat to Norris Junction

parking area or by taking the former road for about 3 miles (5 km), then climbing up from near the Osprey Falls Trailhead (see below). Either way, the elevation gain to the top is more than 1300 feet (400 m).

For another hike starting here, take the road for about 3 miles (5 km), then descend about 800 feet (250 m) in about 1 mile (1.6 km) on the **Osprey Falls Trail** to the bottom of Sheepeater Canyon. Osprey Falls is a 150-foot (46 m) waterfall in a spectacular canyon not seen by many visitors. You can get a glimpse of the falls from the road.

The **Glen Creek Trail** goes west, starting across the main road from the parking area. It follows the former Snow Pass Road to join the long Fawn Pass and Sportsman Lake trails, which cross the northwest corner of the park, or to meet the Sepulcher Loop Trail up Sepulcher Mountain.

For a delightful, easy 2-mile (3 km) hike, you can take the Glen Creek Trail for a few hundred yards (meters) until it joins the **Howard Eaton Trail**. Turn right for a gradual ascent to broad views of Swan Lake Flat and distant mountains to the south. Slightly farther on, you reach a fine panoramic view toward the Mammoth area to the north.

If you want to continue on the Howard Eaton Trail, the path goes steeply down another 2 miles (3 km) to reach Mammoth through burned Douglas fir forest. According to ranger-interpreter Orville Bach, Jr.'s, hiking book, *Exploring the Yellowstone Backcountry*, on this trail you'll find the greatest diversity of plant life of any short trail in the park. Bach also mentions the likelihood of black bears feeding on buffaloberries here in late summer.

5.7/15.3 P A short loop road (easy to spot by its lone tree) goes toward **Swan Lake** for a good place to stop and view the mountains of the southern Gallatin Range. Swan Lake is extremely shallow and has no fish. Over the years, it has sometimes been a nesting place for trumpeter and whistling swans and for ducks.

Geologists tell us that ice was almost a half mile (0.8 km) thick here during the last glaciation. At Swan Lake Flat, the ice would have piled up to over 9500 feet (2900 m) above sea level, completely covering some of the mountains in this area, including Bunsen Peak. Some rock surfaces, even near the mountaintops, have *glacial striations*, that is, small parallel grooves gouged out by small rocks trapped in the glacier ice as it moved across the solid rock.

Swan Lake is located in a unique spot, a long narrow depression that geologists call a *trough*. From here, you can see mountains for almost 360 degrees around you, as shown on pages 272–3.

7.5/13.5 🚶 🚲 **Service road** to the west is a recommended route for biking, about 2 miles (3 km) round trip, and also a pleasant, level hike. Past the electrical substation are lovely mountain views and many wildflowers. The road ends at a series of small dams where Panther Creek joins the Gardner River.

8.0/13.0 🏕(5) 🚻♿ 📷 Side road to the northeast for Sheepeater Cliff picnic area. To the left of the picnic area as you face the columnar basalt rocks is a natural amphitheater.

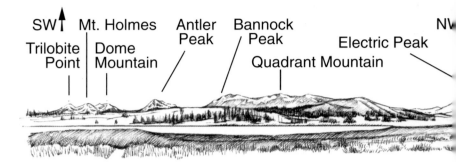

SW↑ Mt. Holmes   Antler   Bannock   NW
            Peak   Peak   Electric Peak
Trilobite   Dome
Point   Mountain   Quadrant Mountain

Swan Lake Flat Panorama

Starting to the east (left) and looking around clockwise, you'll see:

To the east and southeast are mountains of the **Washburn Range**, 9 to 12 miles (15–19 km) away.

To the south, the gently rolling terrain is part of the eroded Yellowstone caldera.

Trilobite Point (10,011 ft/3051 m), a part of Mt. Holmes, the peak farthest to the left. It was named for ancient trilobite fossils found on the mountain.

Mt. Holmes, the second highest one in this panorama (10,336 ft/3150 m), with a fire lookout on top and snow near its top most of the year.

Dome Mountain with two peaks, the higher being 9903 ft (3018 m).

Antler Peak (10,063 ft/3067 m), looking very pointed, as elk antlers are.

Bannock Peak (10,332 ft/3149 m)—barely peeking out at Quadrant's left—named for the tribe who trekked annually through this part of the park to hunt buffalo to the northeast.

Cliffs like those above the picnic tables here extend north downstream along the Gardner River through Sheepeater Canyon. You can reach a trail into the canyon from the Osprey Falls branch of the Bunsen Peak Trail, which begins at mile 4.8/16.2. Fishermen have made another trail along the Gardner.

Superintendent Norris first applied the name Sheepeater Cliffs to the expanse

Sheepeater Cliff is a popular stop for children, who love to climb here and chase the marmots.

Quadrant Mountain (10,213 ft/3113 m), the flat-topped ridge in the middle of the view, named in 1878 by members of the Hayden Survey. Their topographer, Henry Gannett, wrote that "the summit, with the northern and western slopes, forms a curved surface, roughly resembling a segment of a sphere."

Unnamed nearby hills west of Swan Lake.

Electric Peak, near the park's northern boundary, about 4 miles (6.5 km) away. At 10,969 feet (3343 m), it usually has snow—when it doesn't, a reddish area below its highest point is revealed.

Sepulcher Mountain (9652 ft/2942 m) northwest of Mammoth, with a rounded top.

Terrace Mountain to the north of Swan Lake Flat, lower than the others (8011 ft/ 2442 m) and topped by a travertine cliff.

Bunsen Peak (8564 ft/2610 m) at the far right rear as you face the lake (northeast).

of basalt cliffs farther down this canyon in 1879. The small so-called Sheepeater tribe, related to the Shoshonis, were the only Native Americans known to live in park territory. They had their own specialized mountain culture, subsisting mainly on bighorn sheep but also on small mammals, birds, fish, and native plants. In the Gardner canyon, Norris discovered remnants of shelters belonging to the Sheepeaters, who had been removed to nearby reservations before Yellowstone was established as a park.

8.1/12.9 ◄ Gardner River crossing, sometimes called the Seven-Mile Bridge (it's about that far from the Mammoth area). At this point **Obsidian Creek** flows from the south and joins the Gardner River. **Panther** and **Indian creeks** join the Gardner just west of here, creating a marshy area. Park fishing regulations allow children to fish with worms as bait on these four streams. The road follows Obsidian Creek for the next few miles south.

8.6/12.4 ⛺ **Indian Creek Campground** is at the end of a half-mile (0.8 km) side road to the west. This is one of the park's first-come, first-served campgrounds, with 75 sites. It has pit toilets only and no showers. As you cross the creek, you'll pass a warming hut used by winter visitors.

🚶 Bighorn Pass Trail starts in the campground. This trail is 19 miles (30 km) long and goes all the way to U.S. Highway 191 near the park's west boundary.

🚶 🚲 A 1.5-mile (2.4 km) round trip trail for biking and hiking, called the **Superintendent's campground road**, follows Indian Creek south just after the creek crossing. It's a good place to see birds, elk, and moose. There's an isolated walk-in campsite at the end of the road.

Indian Creek was named in 1878, when Hayden expedition members noticed the travois marks left by the annual trek of the Bannock tribe.

9.6 to 10.4/10.6 to 11.4 P Willow Park turnouts. Yellowstone has some 20 varieties of willows. Since moose love willows, this is said to be a favorite spot for them, but a frequent visitor recently quipped, "They need to take down the signs so the moose will come back there!"

Beaver are known to live in Willow Park, but your chances of seeing one are not good, except at dawn or dusk.

🐟 Obsidian Creek here meanders along its gentle, clear-watered course through the wide meadow. It's uniformly 6 to 8 feet wide and perhaps a foot deep (2 m wide by 30 cm deep). This is another good fishing spot.

10.6/10.4 P Moose Bogs. Large parking area and interpretive sign about moose. You can see both Mount Holmes and Dome Mountain from here.

11.0/10.0 🍴(6) 🚻(2) Apollinaris Spring picnic area (with plumbing!) on the west.

11.1/9.9 P **Apollinaris Spring** on the east. Limited roadside parking, more in the picnic area. The travertine masonry steps from 1925 take you to a charming spot with a cold-water spring, named in the 1880s after a German spring water that is still sold in that country.

This water contains minute amounts of several chemicals and was thought by early park visitors to be healthful, but it does not comply with current standards for drinking water. In fact, officials recommend that you don't drink from any untreated spring, lake, or river in the park due to the danger of contracting *giardiasis* (pronounced gee-ar-DI-a-sis), an intestinal disease.

11.4/9.6 🚶 Mount Holmes Trailhead. The summit of Mount Holmes is 10 miles (16 km) and 3000 vertical feet (9150 m) from this trailhead.

12.4/8.6 P Short side road to exhibit at Obsidian Cliff. **Obsidian Cliff** became a National Historic Landmark in 1996 for its importance as a prehistoric site. As long as 8800 years ago, Native Americans obtained this obsidian and made extremely sharp and valuable tools and other objects. Yellowstone obsidian points were traded extensively and have been found in archaeological digs as far away as Ohio.

A Mountain of Glass

The vertical columns of pentagonal-shaped blocks of obsidian, rising some 250 feet above the road, present a glistening, mirror-like effect when illumined by the sun's rays. The greater part of this mineral glass is jet black and quite opaque with traces of similar formation variegated with streaks of red and yellow. The construction of the roadway along its base was accomplished in a novel manner and with considerable difficulty; blasting powder being ineffectual, great fires were built around the huge blocks of glass, which, when heated, were suddenly cooled by dashing water upon them, thus shattering the blocks into small fragments. This process made possible the construction of this really wonderful roadway, probably the only piece of glass road in the world.

—from the *Haynes Guide*, 1912

Obsidian Cliff and Beaver Lake as they appeared a century ago.

Don't be disappointed when you can't see your reflection in the rock of the cliff across the road! Not only are the purest bits of obsidian far from the road, but also the Obsidian Cliff that Haynes saw has probably changed, because many early visitors chopped off bits of the cliff as souvenirs and because moss and lichens have thrived on the rock, covering up much of its shine.

Obsidian is rhyolite lava that cooled so quickly that crystals did not have time to form; thus, Obsidian Cliff is largely glass. This cliff is the western edge of a huge mass of lava that flowed and cooled here about 180,000 years ago, long after the last major Yellowstone caldera event (630,000 years ago). Though the area away from the road is now closed to the public, you can see some fine big specimens of obsidian right along the roadside south of the cliff. Several other places in the park have outcrops of obsidian, but this is by far the largest, most famous, and easiest to see.

The small gazebo that houses exhibits is itself worth looking at. It was built in 1931 from columns of quarried volcanic rock reassembled for this structure.

13.1/7.9 Beaver Lake. What lake? you may ask, since it's now largely a swampy meadow. Over many years, beavers have repeatedly dammed this lake. In fact, at one time a beaver dam said to be about 1000 feet (300 m) long and the largest in the park stretched across the lake's northern end where the outlet is.

13.4/7.6 ⛅(9) 🚻♿ Beaver Lake picnic area to the west. To the east a few yards up the small creek is a fumarole that gives off the rotten egg smell of hydrogen sulfide.

13.7/7.3 The road crosses an electric transmission line and Lemonade Creek at about this point. The creek really is the color of lemonade or maybe limeade. In *Yellowstone Place Names*, Park Archivist Lee Whittlesey quotes a story about stagecoach drivers who carried a "small bag of sugar along to treat their party to cold lemonade hardly distinguishable from the real article." Actually, the clear green water is warm, acidic, and not good to drink.

🚶 For a hike of about 2 miles round trip, you can follow the transmission line up to see a hillside full of fumaroles and to look down on or visit the hot spring area below, **Amphitheater Springs**, perhaps so named because boulders in the area look like seats carelessly arranged. Indians passing through this area found vermilion (mercuric sulfide, a red pig-

ment). This route avoids the downed timber you may encounter on the Solfatara Trail described next. The only good parking place is at Solfatara Trailhead.

13.8/7.2 🚶 Short road to the **Solfatara Trailhead** to the east. Sometimes closed due to bear activity, this unmaintained trail follows a power line and the tourist road built in 1878, passing near Amphitheater Springs and Lake of the Woods. The trail continues about 6 miles (10 km) to the Norris Campground.

14.6/6.4 🚶 Grizzly Lake Trailhead and "Fire Weather" interpretive sign. The lake is a steep 2 miles (3 km) up the trail. In another 1.5 miles (2.4 km), it joins the Mount Holmes Trail.

This is a heavily burned area where a 1976 fire left dead trees standing about. After 12 years, when the dead trees had dried out, the 1988 North Fork fire came this way, and a true firestorm resulted—a popular locale for photographers that summer.

15.5/5.5 🅿 For about 0.3 mile (0.5 km) along the road, turnouts are available on the west side where **Clearwater Springs** are located along Obsidian Creek. The only sign here says "Unstable ground—boiling water" for a good reason: visitors have been burned in the hot springs. You may no longer walk along the creek in this area, according to park regulations.

15.7/5.3 Semi-Centennial Geyser (near the "Obsidian Creek" sign) is now a sometimes steaming, sometimes scummy pool drowned by Obsidian Creek. But in 1922, the year Yellowstone Park was 50 years old, it sprang to life with a huge explosion, hurling scalding water, mud, and rocks to an estimated 300 feet (90 m) high. The expelled material destroyed nearby roadbed and trees. A few weeks later the geyser had ceased to erupt at all. Semi-Centennial is the most northerly geyser in the park.

16.0/5.0 P Roaring Mountain and **Lemonade Lake.** You'll find it hard to hear any roaring now, and only on colder days do you see steam rising from the numerous vents, but the mountain was active and sometimes very loud in the park's first 50 years. The soil is still so acidic that little grows here. Lemonade Lake is greenish when it has water, but in summer it is usually dry. An interpretive sign explains how this and other park features change over time, especially as a result of earth tremors.

16.5/4.5 North Twin Lake has a lovely green color, particularly in morning sunlight. Its water may be too acidic for pond lilies.

16.9/4.1 South Twin Lake has a darker blue-green color, and pond lilies bloom near its shores. These lakes are twins only in being next to each other and separated by a small piece of land, being similar in size, and having no fish. They differ in acidity and color. North Twin Lake is very acidic (pH 3.5), since it receives most of its water from Roaring Mountain, perhaps via underground flow. South Twin Lake is fed by creeks and is much less acidic (pH 5.9). The northern lake is about 20 feet (6 m) higher than the southern one.

The Twin Lakes Problem

Various authorities have puzzled over and disagreed about which way Twin Lakes drain. The 1986 U.S.G.S. topographical map shows no inlet or outlet for North Twin Lake and only a south-flowing outlet for South Twin Lake.

One fact about drainage here has been established, however. This general area marks the *drainage divide*, where waters flow to different basins or river drainages. North Twin Lake may have an underground outlet, which probably flows into the Gardner and Yellowstone rivers. South Twin Lake and the creeks that rise to its south and east flow to the Gibbon and Madison rivers.

17.5/3.5 P Bijah Spring is a large hot spring west of the road. Parking is restricted to a wide area slightly north of it. No one has been able to decipher the spring's name, used since the 1880s, although it might be a corruption of *bijou*, meaning jewel in French.

18.2/2.8 Nymph Lake was named in 1931 for *Nymphaea*, the botanical family of water lilies. Its water is too warm and

acidic from nearby hot spring activity to support fish. It has deep holes and contains a great variety of microorganisms and plankton.

18.4/2.6 P Frying Pan Spring, identified only by a parking space along the road and danger warnings. The unusual action of the springs on both sides of the road, reminiscent of hot grease sizzling in a pan, comes from rising gas bubbles passing through extremely porous and permeable rock and shallow water. The water is acidic enough (pH about 1.0) to eat through almost anything, but it's not extremely hot. There are other steaming springs and warm lakes nearby, and the decomposing geyserite all around indicates old thermal activity.

18.6/2.4 Hazle Lake, named for its color (and misspelled) by 1880s tour guide George Henderson.

19.4/1.6 [P] Norris Geyser Basin Overlook to the south. The overlook provides a view of the One Hundred Spring Plain, a thermal area at Norris Geyser Basin. You'll also see an extensive area that was burned in the 1988 North Fork fire.

20.2/0.8 [A] [≋] **Norris Campground** side road to the east and the **Museum of the National Park Ranger** just a mile up the same road. The campground has about 100 first-come, first-served sites and a campfire circle where campers may attend evening ranger talks.

The ranger museum building has also been a soldier station and later a ranger station. Displays here relate to park rangers throughout the United States.

20.3/0.7 [P] [C] Gibbon River bridge and a sign about the days when the U.S. Cavalry policed the park. To the southwest two different Norris Hotels have stood: one built in 1886 that burned down just after opening and another that lasted from 1901 until 1927 but was abandoned in 1917.

21.0/0.0 Norris Junction. Norris Geyser Basin is on a short side road to the west (see description on page 222), Madison Junction to the south, Canyon Junction to the east, and Mammoth Hot Springs Junction to the north.

From Norris Junction to Madison Junction

This short section (13.3 mi/21.4 km) of the Grand Loop Road follows the Gibbon River through its meadows and canyon. There's a good chance of seeing elk and buffalo on the way. Three thermal features to stop for are the Artists' Paintpots, Beryl Spring, and Terrace Spring near Madison.

Road Log

0.0/13.3 Norris Junction. Madison Junction is to the south, then southwest; Canyon Junction to the east; Norris Geyser Basin to the west; and Mammoth Hot Springs Junction to the north.

1.5/11.8 Northeast end of Elk Park. Mount Holmes dominates the northwestern horizon. Besides elk, watch for ducks, geese, and great blue herons on the meandering river.

2.5/10.8 **P** 🚶 Gibbon River Rapids at the southwest end of Elk Park. Stop in the wide parking area to walk to the rapids. There's good fishing in this part of the Gibbon River, and even better fishing between the Gibbon Falls (at mile 8.6/4.7) and Madison Junction.

2.8/10.5 **P** Wide spot in the road for parking to see the **Chocolate Pots.** There's an active cone or "pot" down below the road (very hard to see) and a large

one across the river. A large amount of ferric oxide (an iron compound) in the

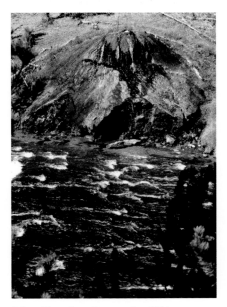

This Chocolate Pot on the Gibbon River's bank nurtures unusual microorganisms.

Norris Junction to Madison Junction

deposits causes the unusual bright orange-brown color that you see on the sides of these geyserite cones and on the river bottom. Some microorganisms apparently metabolize the iron. Bright orange and green bacteria and algae grow in the water that trickles down the sides of the cones.

3.3/10.0 **(9)** Near the north end of Gibbon Meadows is a picnic area west of the road. The terrain is very flat here, and the Gibbon River twists and turns through numerous meanders before entering its canyon just to the south.

4.2/9.1 **P** **Artists' Paintpots** parking for a pleasant trail (to the east) that takes you through partially burned woods to an interesting hydrothermal

area in about one-half mile (0.8 km). You'll see many wildflowers where the trees were burned. The paintpots' noisy mud is gray, but the area's springs and their surroundings abound in colorful clays—orange, red, and pink. Green and yellow bacteria and algae line the runoff channels.

Blood Geyser, a feature at Artists' Paintpots.

4.4/8.9 P ⌐ North end of **Gibbon Canyon** and a short side road along the river for fishing access. Tiny hot springs steam along the riverbank.

4.9/8.4 🏃 Gibbon River crossing and Monument Geyser Basin Trailhead parking area. A 700-foot (200 m) climb in about 1 mile (1.6 km) takes you to some tall and oddly shaped geyser cones, including the still slightly active Monument Geyser, also called Thermos Bottle Geyser, which is gradually sealing its own spout with sinter.

5.0/8.3 Lone Tree Rock in the Gibbon River was pointed out to tourists in the stagecoach days. At least one lodgepole still grows out of a rock here, but maybe it's not the same tree.

5.3/8.0 P Beryl Spring parking areas on both sides of the bridge, but with more room on the south. **Beryl Spring**, named for the blue-green gemstone, perpetually throws its superheated water 3 to 4 feet (1–1.2 m) into the air from the several bubbling spots in its pool.

One or more fumaroles hiss like steam engines behind Beryl, while along an old roadbed above it is a dormant paintpot and hot spring area. Both up- and downriver from Beryl are steaming hot springs, perhaps less active than in the past. According to Mary Bradshaw Richards's account, *Camping Out in the Yellowstone, 1882*, a "roarer" above the river poured forth a torrent of boiling water from a horizontal orifice, creating "frightful sounds, explosions of pent up water and steam, hissings, roarings, and earth shaking generally."

In the earliest years of the park, a very crude road paralleled the river and climbed the mesa south of here, bypassing Madison Junction.

6.0/7.3 Bridge crosses the Gibbon River. The original route to Madison Junction simply went down the middle of the river for a short distance.

High above the river to the west, the tall, pinkish gray cliffs are welded tuff, compacted volcanic ash blown out of the Yellowstone caldera 630,000 years ago. Rocks east of the river are lavas and are much younger.

Crossing the Gibbon River in 1884, by F. J. Haynes.

6.7/6.6 An unmaintained section of the Howard Eaton Trail goes uphill from here.

6.8/6.5 P C The road follows a big bend in the river at the south end of Gibbon Canyon. Rangers called this steep curve Tanker Curve for years after a tanker truck overturned here in the 1970s.

8.3/5.0 P The wide parking area on the river side of the highway lets you stop to get one of the few close views of the Lava Creek tuff available along park roads. The tuff is very thick here, because it's close to the caldera edge, and the volcanic ash was not blown far.   **[GEO. 9]**

8.6/4.7 P For a good view of **Gibbon Falls**, park at the falls itself or in the widest roadside parking area north of the falls. In the smaller areas to the south, the roadbed is too narrow for safe parking. Gibbon Falls is 84 feet (26 m) high and unusually wide. Here the river flows near the northern edge of the Yellowstone caldera.   **[GEO.11]**

You'll often see squirrels or chipmunks dashing over the rock walls. Please don't feed them—they can become dependent on handouts and then unable to forage for themselves. Least chipmunks sport black and white stripes on both cheeks and backs, while golden-mantled ground squirrels are a little larger and have reddish heads, and their stripes are only on the back.

Lacy ribbons of water fall over Gibbon Falls.

9.0/4.3 🏕(15) 🏨♿(2) Side road to Gibbon Falls picnic area near the river, an area left quite bleak by the 1988 fire.

11.0/2.3 This section of the Gibbon River shows the tendency of a river channel to meander through a nearly level valley.

11.8/1.5 🏕(3) 🏨♿ **Tuff Cliff** picnic area. An interpretive sign in the picnic area explains how tuff was created. A large section of the cliff fell as a result of the 1959 Hebgen Lake earthquake. Notice how a thick stand of lodgepole pines has grown back since the 1988 North Fork fire.

12.7/0.6 🅿(2) Terrace Spring thermal area. There's a medium-sized parking area on the north side of the road and a smaller one on the south side (closest to Madison Junction).

♿ A stroll of perhaps one-third mile (0.5 km) around this wheelchair accessible boardwalk takes you past a large hot lake, **Terrace Spring**, and two pools, the higher and cooler one called **Bath Spring**. The night of the 1959 earthquake near Hebgen Lake, a couple was bathing here in the nude—until the spring drained completely!

Orange and brown bacterial mats line the edges of the springs and their runoff channels. Wildflowers grow in the steamy places—yellow monkeyflowers in some weeks of the summer and purple fringed gentians along with tall yellow sunflowers in other weeks.

If you walk on the opposite side of the road above the Gibbon River meadow, stay on the path and watch your footing carefully. There are a few springs and hot runoff channels where interesting microorganisms grow.

13.1/0.2 🚶 Purple Mountain Trailhead. This trail can take you about 1600 feet up (490 m) in about 3 miles (5 km) to a spectacular view in all directions.

The Terrace Spring area looked like this to naturalist H. C. Bumpus in 1935.

Purple Mountain was named for the color of the rock it's made of. The welded tuff (or volcanic ash fall) contains pink crystals of a variety of the mineral feldspar that here is rich in potassium, giving an overall purplish color to the rock.

13.3/0.0 Madison Junction. To the south is Old Faithful Village, to the west are the Madison Campground and the West Entrance, and to the northeast is Norris Junction.

Geology at Terrace Spring

The water at the north end of Terrace Spring appears to be boiling but has been measured at only 141°F (61°C). The bubbling is due to carbon dioxide gas bubbles expanding as they reach the surface of the water.

Terrace Spring is an unusual place in the park, in that the waters of the springs deposit both siliceous sinter and travertine. The deposits of sinter on the surface are to be expected, since the hot water comes up through rhyolite lava rich in silica. However, it's something of a mystery where the travertine comes from, since it has to come from rocks rich in calcium. The calcium and carbon dioxide could originate from older limestones that were later covered by the rhyolite lavas.

From Mammoth Junction to Tower Junction

The road from Mammoth to Tower, a distance of about 18 miles (29 km), is kept open all year. It's the only four-season road in Yellowstone. As you pass this way, you'll encounter spectacular views of mountains near and far. You can stop to enjoy two pleasant waterfalls and the Self-Guiding Fire Trail or take a short side road to view the only petrified tree in the park reachable without a hard hike. Lava Creek has the only picnic area on this stretch of road.

Road Log

0.0/18.1 Mammoth Hot Springs Junction. To the east is Tower-Roosevelt Junction. To the south are Mammoth Terraces and Norris Junction, to the north is the North Entrance at Gardiner, Montana. For facilities at Mammoth Hot Springs, see page 251.

0.1/18.0 🐾 P 🎋(3) Short road to the west for the **Nature Shop** and some residences owned by the federal government. It's okay to park along this road to visit Opal Terrace. The picnic tables are at the edge of the former U.S. Cavalry parade ground.

0.3/17.8 P Parking across the road from the **Yellowstone National Park Chapel** (described on page 252). Beyond the chapel, another street leads to residences and government buildings.

0.5/17.6 A runoff channel called Bluff Creek goes under the road from the terraces above.

1.1/17.0 At this point you're at the lowest elevation on the entire Grand Loop Road, 6005 feet (1830 m). The mountain to the northeast is Mount Everts.

1.7/16.4 Gardner River bridge, also called Sheepeater Canyon Bridge for the canyon from which the river emerges. When completed in 1939, this was the largest bridge in Wyoming, both in length (805 ft/245 m) and height above the river (about 200 ft/60 m high). Far below and to the northeast, Lava Creek and the Gardner River flow together.

You may be able to see the basalt columns that form some of the walls of the Sheepeater Canyon, but only in late afternoon light.

Mammoth Hot Springs Junction to Tower-Roosevelt Junction

© 2002 J. O. Chapple

3.8/14.3 First view of Mammoth Hot Springs Terraces for those traveling west. Along the south edge of the road is a good example of a basalt flow with moderately developed columnar jointing. The cliffs above also look like columns. (See page 209 for an explanation of columnar jointing.)

History of the Lava Creek Trail

From mile 1.7/16.4 to mile 4.4/13.7, the road follows Lava Creek. Across the creek to the north, you can catch glimpses of the old Bannock Indian Trail that became a road soon after mining began at Cooke City in the 1870s. The Bannock made an annual trip to hunt buffalo, traveling from their winter home in Idaho across what is now the northern part of Yellowstone to Wyoming east of park territory. They followed Lava Creek and continued eastward across Blacktail Deer Plateau.

When this became a miners' road, one freighter would handle a team of six to eight horses or mules unassisted. A snub block was usually dragged behind a rear wheel to keep the wagons from backing down inadvertently on the way up. On the steep descents, when the brakes could not hold back the wagons, they were either rough-locked by chaining or tying one or both of the rear wheels to keep them from turning, or else they were slowed by dragging a tree.

This part of the former Bannock trail is now the Lava Creek Trail.

4.0/14.1 P **Undine Falls** on Lava Creek. This triple waterfall has a total drop of over 100 feet (30 m). Geologist Arnold Hague named it in 1885. In classical mythology, undines were water spirits who could earn themselves a soul by marrying a mortal and bearing his child.

Like many falls in the park, Undine has an interesting geologic origin. About 700,000 years ago, the predecessor of Lava Creek was flowing through the valley to the east of the falls and gently eroding old shales that are about 100 million years old. A basalt lava flow then erupted and flowed down the valley, filling the low areas. Lava Creek is now

At Undine Falls even the power of water cannot erode the lava very fast.

flowing over the much harder basalt and has started to cut down through it.

4.4/13.7 🏕(6) 🏞 Lava Creek picnic area, in a particularly delightful setting that used to hold a campground.

🚶 **Lava Creek Trail** can be accessed from the north side of the road by crossing the bridge over Lava Creek just east of the picnic area. Following this trail, you go mostly downhill on the 4-mile-long (6.4 km) route that ends at Mammoth Hot Springs.

5.0/13.1 🚶 **Trail to Wraith Falls** on Lupine Creek. If you're here in early to mid summer, take the time to traverse the half-mile (0.8 km) trail through the meadow to the falls, where you may see a profusion of wildflowers.

The falls itself drops over smooth rock about 90 feet (27 m), sometimes with only a trickle of water. One meaning for the word wraith is "a barely visible vaporous column," which applies well to Wraith Falls.

6.2/11.9 🚻 ⛵ Blacktail Pond (or Ponds) north of the road. In early summer, ducks and geese nest around the ponds (which at times of high water are one pond). If you walk in this vicinity, be careful of the boggy soil—locals call this area "shaky lakes"! The going may be difficult except late in the summer, when the area may be quite dry.

6.8/11.3 🚶 ⛵ **Blacktail Deer Creek Trailhead** to the north. From here, you can hike to the Black Canyon of the Yellowstone River, which is about 4 miles (6.5 km) north, with a steep descent to reach the river.

🚶 If a less strenuous hike appeals to you, you might follow the trail for the first 3.5 miles (5.6 km), as far as **Hidden Falls** on Blacktail Deer Creek. The trail climbs to extended vistas in all directions and descends to the creek in the last half mile (0.8 km) to the place where the water falls over basalt columns. On a hot summer day, there's almost no shade until you reach the creek.

Bulrushes line a pond along Blacktail Deer Creek trail.

From the same trailhead, backcountry hikers join the Rescue Creek Trail toward Gardiner or skirt the north side of Blacktail Ponds to go west on the Lava Creek Trail.

Blacktail Deer Creek was called that by prospectors even before 1870. Blacktail is another name for mule deer, which are common in this part of the park throughout the year.

Almost across the road from the Blacktail Deer Creek Trailhead, an unmaintained trail or old road goes south to a patrol cabin used by rangers.

8.0/10.1 The mountains visible to the west on clear days are part of the Gallatin Range, dominated by Electric Peak, the northernmost visible peak.

8.3/9.8 🚶 ♿ **Self-Guiding Fire Trail**. Signs call this by its original name, the "Children's Fire Trail," but the National Park Service now calls it "All-Persons' Self-Guiding Fire Trail" (perhaps to avoid the appearance of discrimination against adults). Built partly with donations from children who were concerned about the park after the 1988 fires, this easy accessible boardwalk winds in a two-thirds mile (1 km) loop through a burned area now bedecked with wildflowers. There are several benches and interpretive signs.

The service road to the south goes to a gravel pit behind the barrier. In the winter, it's used by skiers to connect with Blacktail Plateau Drive about a mile to the east. Road planners throughout the park's history have always tried to keep the necessary reserves of road maintenance materials out of sight of the Grand Loop Road.

9.5/8.6 Beginning of **Blacktail Deer Plateau Drive**, a section of the former tourist road. This 7-mile (11 km) unpaved one-way road is closed at night, after storms, and all winter. The first road built through the area, it follows a tortuous route through the hillsides, climbing 500 feet (152 m) higher than the four-season main road.

If you take Blacktail Plateau Drive, you'll pass several fine stands of aspen trees and catch views of the surrounding mountains. In about 4.5 miles, the road descends steeply into a small canyon or gorge (The Cut). The 19th century

Fireweed changes to its fall colors under lodgepole snags at Elk Creek.

Bannock trail went through here, as did the 1870 Washburn-Langford exploration party. Devil's Cut was the name used by Superintendent Norris a few years later, shortened to The Cut by geologist Arnold Hague, who thought too many park features were named for the king of the underworld.

The hill immediately northeast of The Cut is Crescent Hill, where Truman Everts was found, lost and near death, after his 37-day ordeal in the wilderness. (See page 245 for the Everts story.)

∿

Continuing on the Grand Loop Road
10.4/7.7 Phantom Lake is next to a low point on the road. The lake dries up by midsummer, which explains its name. Naturally, it has no fish.

11.7/6.4 Geode Creek crossing. A *geode* is a hollow, roughly spherical rock, with

Hellroaring Mountain

Buffalo Plateau
NE Hellroaring Creek

Black Canyon of Yellowstone River
(in middle ground)

Hellroaring Creek Panorama

Left to right (north to southeast):

Hellroaring Mountain (8359 ft/2548 m), whose conical peak is about 3.5 miles (5.6 km) to the north. The 1988 Hellroaring fire was started by an outfitter's camp stove igniting his tent. It burned thousands of acres of forest north and east of here, but of these, only spottily burned areas can be seen.

Hellroaring Creek flows south toward the observer between Hellroaring Mountain and Bull Mountain (far distance), turning west before joining the Yellowstone River. The creek got its name in 1867 when a prospector, who had gone ahead of his companions to hunt, reported: "It's a hell roarer."

Southeast of Hellroaring Mountain, notice the five or six **kettle ponds** ringed with deep green grass.

crystals lining its interior walls. There's no record of geodes being found right here.

All around you are stands of quaking aspen trees, notable for their white bark and their shivering leaves, which glisten in sunlight and turn a brilliant yellow in the autumn.

13.0/5.1 P Hellroaring Creek overlook turnout. A delightful view of mountains, valleys, and streams is visible from here.

14.5/3.6 🚶 🐎 Side road to **Hellroaring Creek Trailhead**. This is a major trailhead for horseback parties heading into the northernmost parts of the Beartooth Range in the Absaroka Primitive Area north of the park.

A short but strenuous hike goes to the Black Canyon of the Yellowstone River. The trail descends 600 or 700 feet (about 200 m) in 1 mile (1.6 km) to a suspension bridge over the river. After crossing the bridge, you can follow the Yellowstone River Trail for a mile to

The **Black Canyon of the Yellowstone River** is so deep and narrow below here that you can only see the place where it must be.

A vast expanse of treeless meadow rises gently to the north above the Yellowstone. It's part of the **Buffalo Plateau**, which stretches out of sight to the northeast.

Little Buffalo Creek flows out of the hills and into the Yellowstone River.

Garnet Hill (7060 ft/2152 m) is the nearby, partially forested low cone. The deep red silicate mineral called garnet has been found on Garnet Hill, but the examples found were not of gem quality.

The distant mountains to the right (east), nearly 30 miles (48 km) away, are part of the **Absaroka Range**.

Closer at the far right is **Specimen Ridge**, with alternating meadows and patches of trees.

Hellroaring Creek and then walk down the creek through sagebrush for about 1 more mile (1.6 km) to the confluence of Hellroaring Creek and the Yellowstone. The confluence is described by Mark C. Marschall in his *Yellowstone Trails* as "a delightful spot" with "the cold clear rushing water of the creek, the deep surging river, a sandy beach and the sheer walls of the Black Canyon of the Yellowstone. Osprey nest in these cliffs and are frequently seen flying over the river looking for trout."

15.0/3.1 🏕 **Floating Island Lake** earned its name many years ago when marshy rafts of vegetation and debris used to float on the lake. Beavers once lived in the lake but have not for many years; there are no fish. Behind the lake is Crescent Hill.

Treat yourself to a short stop here, waiting quietly by the shore for a chance to see one or more of the beautiful yellow-headed blackbirds that live around the lake. Even if you don't see them, you can often hear their unusual calls. Another bird you may hear or see on and around the lake is the American coot, which looks rather like a dark gray duck but has a white bill and red eyes.

16.2/1.9 Elk Creek crossing. This immediate area was intensely burned in the 1988 Wolf Lake fire.

16.6/1.5 Eastern end of Blacktail Plateau Drive (one way, do not enter here).

To the north, indicated by an equestrian crossing sign near the main road, is an area heavily used by riding parties from the Tower-Roosevelt corral. Down the hill is the historic site of Yancey's Hotel, where horseback and stagecoach parties from Roosevelt now come for cookouts.

16.7/1.4 Petrified Tree half-mile side road, not usable by large vehicles because it lacks turning space at the end.

It's sad to note that only one standing petrified tree remains of the many found on this hillside when the park was first explored. The surviving tree is protected by an iron cage, since souvenir hunters over the years have made off with all the others. Although the 1912 edition of the *Haynes Guide* refers to "two large stumps," editions from 1916 on include a picture of just one large standing stump. The remaining tree is (or was) a redwood, like those that grow today in California.

🚶 **Lost Lake Trail** goes south where the side road ends, following Yancey Creek for less than 1 mile (1.5 km) to quiet, lily-pad-covered Lost Lake. Near the lake, you may see moose or beaver, but reputedly no fish. Black bears are also seen frequently in this part of the park.

The trail continues another mile (1.6 km) to reach Roosevelt Lodge, passing the junction with the Lost Creek Falls Trail on the way. The last half mile (0.8 km) descends about 500 feet (150 m).

Curiously, Lost Creek does not flow

About 1914 there were still two petrified trees.

out of Lost Lake, but originates near Prospect Peak in the Washburn Range and runs past the ranger station at Tower-Roosevelt Junction. Lost Lake's outlet stream flows into Yancey Creek.

16.9/1.2 P Interpretive sign explains the difference between medium and high intensity forest fires.

17.9/0.2 👫 Side road to **Tower Ranger Station**, where you can buy a fishing license or ask questions about this part of the park.

The building nearest the road, now a private residence for park personnel, dates from 1907, when this was an outlying soldier station in a little-traveled part of the park.

18.0/0.1 🔪 🅿️🚻 🗜 Tower service station.

18.1/0.0 Tower-Roosevelt Junction. To the south on a short side road are Roosevelt Lodge and its cabins and a small general store (facilities described on page 207). East is the Northeast Entrance; south on the Grand Loop Road are Tower Fall, Dunraven Pass, and Canyon Junction; and west is Mammoth Hot Springs Junction.

NATURAL AND HUMAN HISTORY

Geological History
THE STORIES IN YELLOWSTONE'S ROCKS

Yellowstone National Park is a showcase for some of the world's best examples of spectacular geological features. In this chapter we explain the 3-billion-year development of the region and speculate about future events. These pages describe the causes and processes that created such things as the geysers, canyons, waterfalls, and mud pots of Yellowstone. We point out specific examples of these features that are visible from the road and also show their locations on the Geological Points of Interest map on the next page. The boldfaced numerals in this chapter and the road logs, such as [**GEO.1**], correspond to locations on the map.

Early geological history

The North American continent has existed for approximately 3.8 billion years, although it was not always so large. The oldest rocks in Yellowstone Park itself are about 2.7 billion years old. These are accessible at the roadside on the Northeast Entrance Road in Lamar Canyon [**GEO.1**], as well as where U.S. Highway 212 crosses over the pass in the Beartooth Range outside the Northeast Entrance, and in most of the Teton Range just south of the South Entrance.

These rocks are *granites* and *gneisses*. They are coarse-grained rocks often containing one-half inch (1 cm) mineral crystals. They formed at high temperatures—over 1100°F (600°C)—at depths in the earth of 5 to 10 miles (8–16 km). Granites form by *crystallizing*, that is, solidifying, from molten rock. Gneisses are made deep within the earth by reactions between minerals that are unstable at high temperatures and so react to transform themselves (*metamorphose*) to produce new minerals, such as mica and feldspar. These minerals are easily seen in the roadside outcrops mentioned in the paragraph above.

The granites and gneisses have since been uplifted to the surface. In fact, they were formed as the roots of a 3-billion-year-old mountain range that has long since been eroded away. Not much is known about the Yellowstone region

Geological Points of Interest in and near Yellowstone

© 2002 J. O. Chapple

Key to Map

1	Lamar Canyon	14	Lamar Valley
2	Barronette Peak	15	Kettle ponds
3	Mt. Everts	16	Duck Lake
4	Mt. Washburn	17	Indian Pond
5	Volcanic mountains	18	Falls of the Yellowstone
6	Sylvan Pass	19	Old Faithful Geyser
7	Golden Gate	20	Fountain Paint Pot
8	Mesa Falls	21	Thumb Paint Pots
9	Lava Creek Tuff	22	Grand Prismatic Spring
10	Lewis Canyon	23	Emerald Spring
11	Caldera edge	24	Mammoth Terraces
12	Basalt lava	25	Mallard Lake Dome
13	Glacial Boulder	26	Sour Creek Dome

from the time of those ancient mountains until about 80 million years ago, a time gap of 2.9 billion years.

Clues about this tremendous gap in time are sparse. The roots of a 1.6-billion-year-old mountain range are found in the Gravelly Range west of the park and the Gallatin River Canyon north of the park. Within the park, we can see sedimentary rock layers lying flat in a few cliff faces. Most *sedimentary rocks* are formed by transport of rock or mineral particles to low areas, where they are deposited. The rocks become hard when compressed by thick layers of sediment deposited on top. Transport can be by wind, streams, ocean currents, or glaciers.

The extensive flat-lying sedimentary layers in the park were deposited either in shallow seas or on land, depending upon sea level at the time. Two places to see such cliffs are at Barronette Peak (lower part of cliffs), near the Northeast Entrance [**GEO.2**] and at Mount Everts near Mammoth [**GEO.3**].

On the lower third of Barronette Peak's cliffs are alternating white and brown layers of sedimentary rocks that are approximately 350 million years old. The chocolate-colored rocks above these are part of the much younger Absaroka Range Volcanics.

The sedimentary rocks in these places were deposited between 600 and 80 million years ago. They are evidence that the much older mountains described above had already been eroded away to form a level plain at or near sea level. Today, many of these sedimentary rocks remain undeformed, except by easily identifiable recent events. One example was the general uplift that formed the Rockies and raised these sediments to their present altitude. Two factors suggest that not much was happening in the Yellowstone area during that gap of 2.9 billion years: the scarcity of rocks older than 600 million years and the fact that the 3-billion-year-old rocks appear to have been undisturbed. But this quiet was about to change dramatically!

Plate tectonics and Yellowstone

Most people today are aware that the continents move around on the earth's surface, fortunately at only a few inches (cm) per year, by a process that geologists call *plate tectonics*. Yellowstone Park is not immune to this process and, in fact, has been singled out for some special events.

The *plates* of plate tectonics are huge slabs that occupy the uppermost 60 miles (100 km) of the solid earth. They are obliged to slide around due to the uneven heating of the earth's interior. Parts of the interior rise, being hotter and less dense, while cooler portions sink, as shown in Figure 5. We don't know when the plates started to move in this manner, but it was probably some time during the first half of the earth's 4.6-billion-year existence. The diagram shows three types of upward movement from the earth's deep interior: one at mid-ocean ridges, one where plates subduct and cause some melting, and a third along rising vertical columns, called plumes.

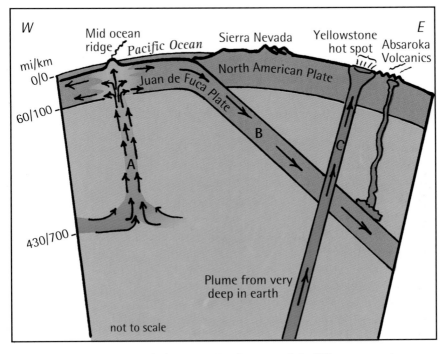

Figure 5. Plate tectonics and plume activity that created the Yellowstone region; a cross section through the earth.

This west-southwest to east-northeast cross section shows sources of magma (molten rock) that reach nearly or all the way up to the earth's surface (not drawn to scale). This sketch does not represent a single point in time. The Absaroka Volcanics and Yellowstone hot spot, for example, are both shown erupting, but the Absarokas finished erupting about 40 million years before the first Yellowstone caldera eruption. **A** is the source area at a mid-ocean ridge. Plates move apart as molten rock rises to fill the space. **B** shows how the sinking (subducting) Juan de Fuca plate arrived below the Sierra Nevada area in California, part of the plate and surroundings melted, and magma rose to create the Sierra Nevada range about 100 million years ago. As the plate continued to sink, it finally reached the area of the Absaroka Range, and more magma formed and rose to create the Absaroka volcanoes 53 to 44 million years ago. **C** shows a plume that rose under westernmost Nevada near Oregon about 17 million years ago. Then the North American plate brought the Yellowstone area over the plume about 2 million years ago. The plates are shown where they were when they were producing the Absarokas.

When plates sink deep into the earth (called subduction), they normally do so at an angle to the surface. The plates drag seafloor sediment and other near-surface rocks down to great depths, where they reach high temperatures and pressures. These rocks differ so markedly from those normally at great depth that they cause melting to occur, very much like a flux helps to melt solder. Since molten rock (called magma) is less dense than the solid rocks, it rises toward the surface. If such magma reaches the surface, it forms a chain of volcanoes, such as the Absaroka Range. Elsewhere, the magma cools and solidifies before reaching the surface, as in California's Sierra Nevada. Both the Sierra magmas and the Absaroka Range magmas were formed above the subducting plate.

Yellowstone volcanism

SUBDUCTION VOLCANISM. Volcanoes formed the Absaroka Range, which extends from the Beartooth Range north of the park for approximately 100 miles (160 km) to the southeast into Wyoming. Most of the rocks in these mountains are either lava flows or the debris that resulted when the rocks were rapidly eroded to form mudslides. The outstanding example in the park is Mount Washburn [**GEO.4**]. The Northeast Entrance Road along Soda Butte Creek [**GEO.5**] and the East Entrance Road near Sylvan Pass [**GEO.6**] both pass through fine examples of these volcanic mountains.

PLUMES. In contrast to the Absarokas, *plumes* result from hot spots very deep within the earth. The heated rocks are less dense than their neighbors and so rise as a column to the surface. Some of the rock melts on the way up. The result is an enormous concentration of heat and magma in a relatively small area near the surface. Such occurrences are rare, but two examples are the Hawaiian Islands and the Yellowstone region. This hot spot phenomenon is what gives us most of the dramatic features and thermal activity in Yellowstone.

Somewhat over 2 million years ago, the North American plate moved the Yellowstone region over a plume that was bringing large amounts of magma to not far below the surface. This molten rock shoved its way into the existing rocks, causing them to arch upward to make room. As more magma rose, a magma chamber formed and grew, which greatly increased the arching up of the overlying rocks and caused them to crack. Figure 6 shows the sequence of events that followed over the next several hundred thousand years.

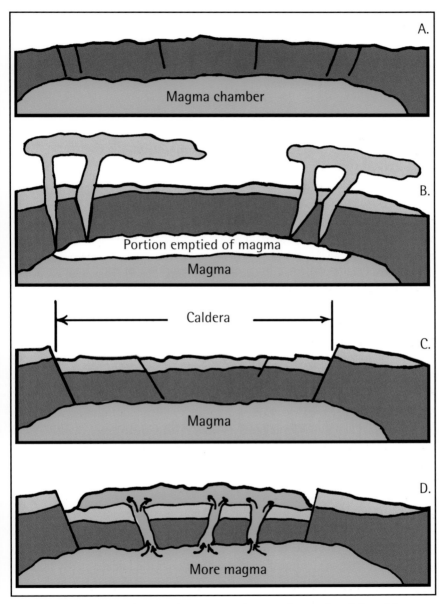

Figure 6. Cross section showing the sequence of events that produced the calderas.
  A. shows how magma (shown in red) rises into a magma chamber, forcing the overlying rocks to arch up. Cracks form in the arched rocks (in brown) and extend downward as the arching increases. In **B.** cracks reach down to the magma chamber and release some gases and molten rock, thus reducing the pressure in the chamber. Steam forms from the water dissolved in the magma, forcing the magma to blow out of the chamber and spread volcanic ash (yellow) as a thick layer as well as sending

some of it high into the air. An unsupported empty space remains in the magma chamber. In **C**. overlying rocks have collapsed into the empty space, creating a large crater or caldera many miles across. **D**. shows how the hot spot continues to deliver magma, which rises through cracks to reach the caldera floor and make Yellowstone's high plateau of rhyolite lavas (red).

(Modified from Keefer, *The Geologic Story of Yellowstone National Park,* 1971.)

HUCKLEBERRY RIDGE CALDERA EVENT. At about 2 million years ago, enough magma had flowed into the chamber so that the cracks in the overlying rocks reached down to the chamber (Figure 6B). The magma had a great deal of water dissolved in it, so as soon as the cracks released some of the pressure, this water formed steam bubbles. Water as steam occupies a much larger volume than when it is dissolved in magma—about a thousand times as much—so suddenly the magma needed a much larger space. You may have seen this kind of violent process when a car's engine overheats and steam pours out! All this steam pressure in the magma caused a huge explosive eruption of rock fragments and molten globs that rushed out of the chamber and partially emptied it.

The ejected rock and steam spread up and out as a billowing incandescent cloud, probably traveling at 50 to 100 miles (80–160 km) per hour and being pushed by the material behind it. As it traveled and expanded, the cloud cooled and deposited ash over the northern Rockies and the Great Plains. In Iowa, for example, the ash was still as much as 3 inches (8 cm) thick. The total volume of erupted ash was about 600 cubic miles (2500 cu km)! The explosion probably lasted for a period of days or weeks.

Volcanic ash, unlike wood or coal ash, is not the residue left from something that has burned, but rather fine-grained rock. An outcrop of this ash deposit can be seen in the park at Golden Gate [**GEO.7**] south of Mammoth Hot Springs, where it's called the Huckleberry Ridge *tuff*. In places, it's 550 feet (170 m) thick.

The unsupported roof of the magma chamber collapsed to create a circular depression that resembled a huge crater, called a *caldera* (Figure 6C). The plume that was the source of all the magma didn't stop, however, and continued to send up more magma. Some of this flowed out onto the caldera, partly filling it with rhyolite lava (Figure 6D). *Rhyolite* is a volcanic rock that has high silica content, which makes it very *viscous* (stiff and tacky), so that it flows very slowly. **MESA FALLS CALDERA EVENT.** The plume continued to send up more magma, now using somewhat different plumbing, and the whole caldera process was repeated, with the center of the action being just west of Yellowstone Park in the area of Island Park, Idaho. This culminated in a new major explosion 1.3 million years ago; the debris was again mostly ash. This Mesa Falls tuff can be seen at Mesa Falls [GEO.8] west of the park boundary. The eruption was smaller than the Huckleberry Ridge tuff eruption.

YELLOWSTONE CALDERA EVENT. These two major eruptions set the stage for the third and latest explosion 630,000 years ago, the one depicted in Figure 6 and the best studied. The earlier ones were similar but have been partly obscured since. This one formed the present Yellowstone caldera. Rocks and ash blown out this time are called the Lava Creek tuff. You can see this tuff on the west side of the road just north of Gibbon Falls [GEO.9], and at the top of the Lewis River Canyon cliffs on the South Entrance Road [GEO.10]. This latest eruption, with ash beds occasionally exceeding 1000 feet (300 m) in thickness, produced a volume of 240 cubic miles (1000 cu km) of ash, which makes it intermediate in scale between the two previous calderas.

In comparison with the impressive eruption at Mount St. Helens, Washington, in May 1980, the Lava Creek eruption blew out about 1000 times more rock. The Mount St. Helens output of volcanic debris was about 0.25 cubic miles (1 cu km).

The caldera resulting from the Lava Creek eruption is approximately 30 by 45 miles (48 by 72 km) across, which explains why calling it a crater is rather inadequate. A good place to see the northern edge of the caldera is along the east-west stretch of road that leads from Madison Junction to Gibbon Falls [GEO.11]. This stretch of road stays just north of the Gibbon River, which here flows almost parallel to the caldera edge. Erosion of the tuff has worn the original caldera wall back to the cliff you see on the north side of the road.

You may have noted that the intervals between the three caldera-forming events were 700,000 and 700,000 years, and the last caldera explosion was 630,000 years ago. Are we due for another soon? We'll return to that question below.

POST-CALDERA LAVAS. After the cataclysmic Yellowstone eruption, the plume kept sending up magma that erupted at intervals for several hundred thousand years. It spilled out onto the caldera floor as rhyolite flows (see "Rhyolite and the Plateau of Fire," page 43), filling much of the caldera. This explains why there is no deep hole or crater now visible in or near the Yellowstone caldera.

It is difficult to get a sense of the Yellowstone caldera when you're in the park. In fact, the existence of a caldera of this size was not proposed until the 1960s. After many years of mapping, geologists realized the following: First, all the outcrops we now call Lava Creek tuff stem from one event. Second, the tuff is seen only outside an oval area that we now know as the caldera. (Some Lava Creek tuff is also presumably buried under the later lavas that mostly fill the caldera.) Third, the tuff layers seen in other states (as far away as Iowa) are also from the Yellowstone area.

A good place to get a feel for this enormous event is along the Grand Loop Road in the vicinity of Gibbon Falls south of Norris. The 5 miles of highway between Madison Junction and Gibbon Falls parallel the caldera edge. On the north side of the road, you can see a cliff whose upper part is Lava Creek tuff. This tuff was left when the caldera, which was on the south side here, slid down along a fault during its collapse (see Figure 6C). Over the past 630,000 years, the cliff has been eroded back a bit, but it still represents that rim fault.

If you now drive past Gibbon Falls and go north toward Norris, you have moved away from the caldera and its rim. The parking area about 0.3 mile (0.5 km) from the falls allows you access to a very tall, nearly vertical wall of Lava Creek tuff, which is cream colored with hints of pink.

BASALTIC VOLCANISM. Another type of volcanic rock encountered in the park is *basalt*. Good examples can be seen near Tower Fall [**GEO.12**]. (There's a description of columnar jointing in basalt on page 209.) Since basalt contains less silica than rhyolite, basalt flows out as sheets that sometimes spread for miles. It is black due to its high iron content.

A 1.2-million-year-old basalt lava flow near Calcite Springs extends across the middle of the photo. Vertical lines in the flow are the columns of basalt formed when the lava cooled and shrank.

Glaciers reshape the landscape

At about the same time that the plume started sending up magma in the Yellowstone region, a worldwide climate change brought colder temperatures and, in some places, glaciers. Vast ice sheets covered much of Canada and spread south to the Ohio River. Elsewhere, glaciers also formed at high elevations. The broad plateaus of the park average about 8000 feet (2400 m) above sea level and so developed glaciers.

We know that worldwide there were about 20 glaciations or ice ages. Each glaciation lasted about 50,000 to 100,000 years, with shorter warm periods in between. The glaciers retreated about 10,000 years ago, resulting in the warm interglacial period we now enjoy.

Glaciers had several major effects on Yellowstone, and the last two glaciations left evidence all around. Almost the entire park was covered with ice. Often the ice was about one-half mile (800 m) thick, so that animals and plants were essentially non-existent here. Although glaciers are solid ice, they flow slowly toward lower ground at rates of a few yards (meters) per year. The glaciers were major agents that modified the landscape drastically by transporting some rocks, digging and scraping away at others, and interacting with the park's thermal areas. Some examples of this activity follow.

The glaciers' ability to transport rocks is demonstrated in the area of the Yellowstone Canyon [GEO.13] and in the Lamar River valley [GEO.14]. In both places, you see boulders as large as 10 feet (3 m) across that are clearly out of place. We know where they originated, because they match the 2.7-billion-year-old gneisses common in the Beartooth Range. These boulders are called *glacial erratics*, because they are many miles from the nearest outcrops of similar rocks.

Glacial erratics: The large boulders in this Lamar Valley photo were carried by the glacier from the Beartooth Range. Climate warming about 10,000 years ago melted the glacier, which dumped these boulders onto the land surface.

Glaciers will often gouge out holes in the ground when moving over soil or soft sediment. Look for these *kettle ponds*, or kettle holes, mostly on the north side of the Northeast Entrance Road [GEO.15].

The glaciers carried huge amounts of rock and soil along and dumped it at their downhill edges where they melted. These deposits (or *moraines*) can be seen in Paradise Valley along the Yellowstone River north of the park. Streams

This kettle pond was formed when a glacier covering this area gouged a hole in the ground. When the glacier melted, it left sand, gravel, and boulders on the ice in the hole. At a later, warmer, time the ice also melted, leaving the hole that is now filled with water.

formed from the meltwater of the glacier also carried away much of the debris and then deposited it further downstream as outwash sediments.

The hot rocks underlying parts of Yellowstone had some unusual interactions with the glaciers. The glaciers dammed many streams by simply filling the stream valley with ice. Sometimes the lake that was formed covered one of the many hot areas. Water boils at a higher temperature when under pressure. Under the increased pressure from the lake, the hot rocks heated the groundwater until it was superheated.

When the glaciers melted, the ice dam sometimes suddenly collapsed, letting the lake drain rapidly. The hot water at depth, suddenly relieved of the high pressure, boiled in a flash and created a steam explosion that blew out much of the rock around it. Examples of this type of *explosion crater*, now filled with water, are Duck Lake near West Thumb Junction **[GEO.16]** and Indian Pond near Fishing Bridge Junction **[GEO.17]**.

Carving the Canyon

The magnificent Grand Canyon of the Yellowstone, with its steeply sloping sides, colorful rocks, and spectacular waterfalls, was carved after the latest caldera-forming explosion 630,000 years ago.

Before the caldera existed, the Yellowstone River had been eroding the Absaroka volcanic rocks north of the present canyon area. Then came the Yellowstone caldera eruption, which dumped a lot of tuff; the river redug its channel through the debris. The rhyolites flowed out, nearly filling the caldera with lava, and the Yellowstone started to carve its valley into those.

Meanwhile, early glaciations must have occurred, though we can't distinguish their effects from the later ones. We do know that during the last two glaciations, the whole area was buried in ice, except for the tops of some of the highest peaks. Because the glaciers were mostly moving across rather than along the Yellowstone River valley, they were not responsible for cutting the canyon.

A glacier flowing from the Lamar River valley did block the Yellowstone valley, creating a dam and a lake that filled part of the Yellowstone Canyon. The canyon was then partly filled by lake sediments until the glacier retreated. The ice dam failed suddenly at one point during the retreat, causing a wall of water about 150 to 200 feet high (45 to 60 m) to flow north and west, rolling and carrying boulders along until they were dropped northwest of Gardiner, about 20 miles (32 km) downstream. There is evidence that this type of catastrophic flood occurred more than once.

The Yellowstone River then redug its channel in the canyon and continued eroding to its present depth. Consequently, the Grand Canyon of the Yellowstone was cut mainly by the river, and all in about 150,000 years, a very short time geologically speaking.

A number of local deep fractures permitted rainwater to seep into the earth and be warmed by the still-hot rocks. The hot water rose toward the surface, reacting with the upper rocks and breaking down their minerals, weakening the rocks. This happened near the present Upper and Lower falls of the Yellowstone and resulted in zones of weaker and stronger rocks. The river exploited this and cut down through the softer rocks very rapidly. The result is two splendid waterfalls. [GEO.18]

There are two falls because a layer of more resistant rhyolite separates the easily eroded rocks into upper and lower blocks of rock. This harder rock protected the lower soft block from being eroded. It forms the lip of the Lower Falls. The upper soft block was eroded further upstream and gives us the Upper Falls.

Geysers, fumaroles, mud pots, and hot springs

Most visitors come to Yellowstone to see geysers. There are, indeed, more geysers in Yellowstone than anywhere else in the world. What visitors also find, however, is a vast collection of places that spurt, hiss, boil, and bubble, often displaying a rainbow of colors, sometimes with a nasty smell, but always interesting.

What makes the different hydrothermal features do what they do? Basically, rain and snowmelt seep down to an area of very hot rocks. With all its young volcanics, Yellowstone has plenty of very hot rocks quite near the surface, so that water doesn't have far to go to be warmed to its boiling point, boil into steam, expand greatly, and find a way to escape upward.

Geysers such as Old Faithful [GEO.19] are one special kind of steam and hot water emitter. They need a very steady supply of hot groundwater and special plumbing that includes a narrow fissure that goes deep into the ground and that has even narrower parts along the way. (For a more specific explanation of geysers, see "How Does a Geyser Work?" on page 82.)

Changes in the shape of a geyser's plumbing, its water supply, or water temperature can change the timing, height of eruption, or volume of water. The changes are normally due to blockage of fissures by precipitation of solids onto their walls, to minor earthquakes, or to eruptions that are especially violent. Most geysers in Yellowstone erupt repetitively, but the intervals are not necessarily regular. Old Faithful Geyser is faithful in its timing, because the flow rate and temperature of the very hot water have been very constant.

The 1959 Hebgen Lake earthquake just outside the northwest corner of the park considerably altered conditions in Yellowstone. Some geysers changed their cycles, some stopped erupting, and others started up after having been quiet for years. Smaller earthquakes affect Yellowstone's hydrothermal features every year.

How do the other hydrothermal features work? Steam vents, also called *fumaroles*, are places where there's a steady flow of steam coming from a fissure in the ground. In these places, a steady downward seepage of groundwater reaches hot rocks, the water boils, and the steam is vented through the fissure.

Over time, the steam breaks down the rocks chemically where it is escaping, turning them into clays. When enough clays have been made, they tend to form a bowl-shaped soupy mass, a *mud pot*. The steam coming up through the clay will now make mud bubbles, sometimes more than 6 inches (15 cm) across. These are the delightful blurping bubbles that can be seen at several park localities, including Fountain Paint Pot [GEO.20] and Thumb Paint Pots at West Thumb Geyser Basin [GEO.21].

In this mud pot photo from near Imperial Geyser (Lower Geyser Basin), notice the three mud bubbles—two at upper left, one at lower left. You can see the trace of one that just popped at bottom left.

In other places, very hot ground water rises to the surface to make a hot pool. These deceptively inviting pools have lovely colors, but their water is at or near the boiling point. Examples are Grand Prismatic Spring [GEO.22] in Midway Geyser Basin and Emerald Spring [GEO. 23] in Norris Geyser Basin.

Most of the rocks underlying the hot water and steam features in the park are rhyolites or related igneous rocks. A major exception to this is the collection of terraced structures that have built up at Mammoth Hot Springs [GEO.24]. Before reaching the surface, hot water rising there encounters *limestone* rather than rhyolite. Limestone is sedimentary rock that was deposited in shallow seas and is mostly made up of the shells of marine organisms.

The water under the Mammoth area dissolves some of the limestone and brings it up to the surface. Here the water is under less pressure. It can no longer hold all the carbon dioxide in solution, and some of the gas bubbles escape, causing some of the dissolved limestone to deposit out, forming the terraces. This rock is a white or gray form of limestone called *travertine*.

The hot waters on Mammoth's terraces contain algae and bacteria that are orange, green, yellow, or brown and coat the travertine with color. This ever-changing palette is dependent upon the quantity and temperature of water at the particular spot.

Are we due for another caldera eruption?

We saw above that the last caldera eruption was 630,000 years ago, while the preceding two eruptions were at intervals of 700,000 and 700,000 years. Time intervals between such major eruptions are not necessarily regular, but should we worry that a new caldera explosion could occur soon? Rather than leaving the Yellowstone area or weakening, the Yellowstone hot spot appears now to be centered in the northeast portions of the park. This would be consistent with the path of the hot spot, which has been traced back in time southwestward to northwestern Nevada about 16 million years ago. Of course, it was the North American plate that moved, carrying northwestern Nevada away from the hotspot.

What evidence is there of the likelihood of a new caldera catastrophe? An increase in magma under Yellowstone would indicate an impending caldera eruption. By studying seismic waves that pass below the park, geophysicists have shown the presence of molten rock in two areas: the Mallard Lake dome [GEO.25] just east of Old Faithful and the Sour Creek dome [GEO.26] east of Hayden Valley. To indicate an impending caldera type of explosion, however, these two magma regions would need to be growing.

Neither of these domes is easy to see. Careful studies of the ground level revealed that the ground in the Sour Creek dome area rose a total of 36 inches (91 cm) between 1923 and 1984. Then it subsided somewhat for a decade but recently has been rising again. Nobody knows if the rising is due to new magma flowing into the area at depth or to steam, or a combination of the two. A similar behavior was measured at the Mallard Lake dome.

This type of uplifting area is called a *resurgent dome*. Geologists were concerned about these measurements, because they implied more magma was forcing the ground up to make room. The process looks suspiciously like what must have happened just before the Yellowstone caldera eruption 630,000 years ago. What does this heavy breathing by the earth mean about possible eruptions? Geophysicists are working to understand it. There's clearly no immediate danger—but stay tuned.

Chronology

YELLOWSTONE SINCE 1800

This chronology juxtaposes events relating to Yellowstone Park and this region with relevant events from world and United States history. "A changing America has always had an impact upon Yellowstone. . . ." wrote historian Richard A. Bartlett. World events have likewise had their impact on the park.

EXPLORATION OF YELLOWSTONE

YEAR	IN THE YELLOWSTONE REGION	IN THE U.S. OR THE WORLD
1803	Lewis and Clark set out to explore Louisiana to the Pacific, missing the Yellowstone area by about 50 miles.	Pres. Thomas Jefferson buys Louisiana from France.
1806–8	John Colter leaves Lewis and Clark and explores Yellowstone and environs.	
1808	John Jacob Astor incorporates the American Fur Company.	
1826–40	Fur trappers and adventurers visit and tell about the wonders of the area, but are usually not believed.	An estimated 60 million bison live in the Great Plains; Native Americans depend upon them.

Jim Bridger, capable guide, fur trapper, and storyteller

YEAR	IN THE YELLOWSTONE REGION	IN THE U.S. OR THE WORLD
1832		Hot Springs in Arkansas is the first area set aside for national conservation (today a national park).
1860	Capt. William F. Raynolds unsuccessfully tries to penetrate the mountains at the southeast corner of the future Yellowstone Park.	Abraham Lincoln is elected the 16th president of the U.S.
1862		Homestead Act grants free land in the west to all settlers.
1863	Nez Perce Indians are forced to sign a treaty saying they will vacate their land (then located in Idaho Territory).	President Lincoln signs a bill giving rights of way to the Central Pacific and Union Pacific railroads and guaranteeing them money for laying track. Idaho Territory is organized.
1864	Gold is found at Last Chance Gulch (later Helena, MT).	Yosemite Valley in California becomes the nation's first scenic reservation. Montana Territory is formed out of Idaho Territory.
1865	Jesuit Father Kuppens visits Yellowstone area in the company of Blackfeet.	Lewis Carroll publishes *Alice's Adventures in Wonderland*. Lincoln is assassinated.
1868	Gold is found on Clarks Fork near present Northeast Entrance to Yellowstone.	Wyoming Territory is organized.
1869	Charles W. Cook, David E. Folsom, and William Peterson successfully undertake and later write about their trip through the Yellowstone area.	Union Pacific and Central Pacific railroads join at Promontory Point, Utah. Northern Pacific Railway begins laying track west from Minnesota.
1870	Gen. Henry D. Washburn leads a quasi-official exploration of the Yellowstone area, accompanied by other prominent westerners, such as Nathaniel P. Langford, Cornelius Hedges, and Truman Everts, and a military escort under Lt. Gustavus Doane.	

Gen. Henry Dana Washburn died before he could publish his expedition diary.

Henry D Washburn
1869

YEAR	IN THE YELLOWSTONE REGION	IN THE U.S. OR THE WORLD
1871	Dr. Ferdinand V. Hayden leads the first of three congressionally funded Yellowstone expeditions. A second summer expedition, led by army captains John W. Barlow and David P. Heap, also enters the area.	Chicago Fire on October 8th destroys 3.5 sq mi of the city, most 1870 census records, and Thomas J. Hine's negatives from the Barlow-Heap Yellowstone expedition.
1872	**Yellowstone National Park** is set aside by Congress. Nathaniel P. ("National Park") Langford is the unsalaried first superintendent. Second Hayden Survey traverses the new park.	Pres. Ulysses S. Grant signs the bill authorizing the Yellowstone reservation on March 1st.

~

YELLOWSTONE NATIONAL PARK HISTORY

The Act Setting Aside the Yellowstone Reservation

The U.S. Congress preserved this land for us and for all subsequent generations in language that reserved and withdrew the land "from settlement, occupancy, or sale" and assured that it be "dedicated and set apart as a public park or pleasureing-ground for the benefit and enjoyment of the people."

	IN THE YELLOWSTONE REGION	IN THE U.S. OR THE WORLD
1873	Capt. William A. Jones leads a U.S. Army Corps of Engineers party through the new Yellowstone.	Northern Pacific Railway's financial agent, Jay Cooke & Co., fails on September 18th; stock exchange collapses on Black Friday, the next day.
1876		Gen. George A. Custer, all his men, and many of the Sioux tribe are killed in the Battle of the Little Bighorn in south central Montana Territory.
1877	Pursued by General Howard's troops, Nez Perce cross the park, kill two and frighten and wound other tourists.	

YEAR	IN THE YELLOWSTONE REGION	IN THE U.S. OR THE WORLD
1878	Supt. Philetus W. Norris hastily builds crude roads in anticipation of "Indian trouble." Members of the Bannock tribe cross the park but are killed and captured by Colonel Miles near Clarks Fork River, east of the park. Third Hayden Survey makes observations for the government.	John Wesley Powell writes *Report on the Lands of the Arid Region*, warning of the paucity of rainfall in the west.
1882	The Crow sell to the U.S. the small strip of their Montana reservation that lay in park territory. Crow, Bannock, and Shoshoni are banned by treaty from entering Yellowstone.	German engineer Gottlieb Daimler invents a gasoline-powered internal combustion engine.
1883	Northern Pacific completes its line to Cinnabar, MT, near Gardiner. The first large (but still incomplete) hotel in the park takes in guests at Mammoth Hot Springs. Lt. Dan C. Kingman of the Corps of Engineers begins planning a loop system of roads. Hunting and fishing (except with hook and line) are disallowed in the park.	Krakatoa volcano in Indonesia erupts, killing 36,000 people. Dust eruption creates brilliant sunsets around the world and lowers global temperatures for months afterward, but its caldera is only a fraction of the size of Yellowstone's.

Stagecoach tours started from Mammoth Hotel (1915 photo, Haynes Studio).

YEAR	IN THE YELLOWSTONE REGION	IN THE U.S. OR THE WORLD
1884	Wyoming territorial law becomes the law of Yellowstone to help curb vandalism, poaching, and lawlessness. Frank J. Haynes opens a photo studio at Mammoth.	George Eastman devises a way to coat photographic paper in long rolls, an invention that will soon make the use of wet glass plates obsolete.
1886	The U.S. Cavalry arrives in the park in August to bring order.	
1886–87	First winter tour of the park, during which Haynes takes the first winter photographs of Yellowstone.	The Rockies and Great Plains experience one of the most severe winters in history, one that kills some 60% of range cattle.
1888		Dry film and the inexpensive Kodak camera ("You Press the Button, We Do the Rest") make amateur photography possible and then increasingly popular.
1889	Trout are first stocked in Yellowstone's so-called barren waters.	Montana becomes the 41st U.S. state.
1890	First Haynes guidebook appears: *Practical Guide to Yellowstone National Park*, by A. B. Guptill (Haynes' accountant).	The last major confrontation between Native Americans and the U.S. Army takes place at Wounded Knee, SD. Yosemite National Park is created by act of Congress. Idaho and Wyoming become U.S. states numbers 43 and 44.
1891	Hotels are completed at Lake, Fountain, and Canyon by the Yellowstone Park Association.	The National Forest Reserves Act authorizes the president to set aside forest lands; thus begins the national forest system.
1892	Initial Fort Yellowstone construction is completed. Roads are now complete in what later becomes the southern loop of the Grand Loop Road.	First U.S. motorcar is produced by Charles and Franklin Duryea in Springfield, MA.

YEAR	IN THE YELLOWSTONE REGION	IN THE U.S. OR THE WORLD
1894	The Lacey Act protects birds and animals and punishes crimes in the park; John W. Meldrum is appointed first U. S. Commissioner of Yellowstone to enforce the act and stays nearly 40 years.	Strikes paralyze western railroads and other businesses.
1895	First attempt to save the buffalo from extinction by captive feeding and breeding at Alum Creek in Hayden Valley.	
1896		25 motorcars, the first for public sale, are produced by Duryea Motor Wagon Co.
1898	F. J. Haynes and an associate form the Monida & Yellowstone Stage Company to bring tourists through the West Entrance.	
1899	Haynes begins producing his postcards of the park.	
1900	Yellowstone has a few dozen bison (buffalo) left.	Bison are almost extinct in the U.S.
1901	Burlington Route (Chicago, Burlington & Quincy Railroad) reaches Cody, WY.	
1902	Henry G. Merry drives his Winton motorcar through the North Entrance, but cars remain illegal in the park.	
1903	Road from Cody to East Entrance and on to Fishing Bridge is completed. Pres. Theodore Roosevelt tours the park and dedicates an arch at the North Entrance. Later that year, Northern Pacific tracks reach Gardiner, MT.	Ford Motor Co. is incorporated and sells hundreds of Model As.
1904	Old Faithful Inn opens.	
1905	Dunraven Pass road is completed, linking the entire Grand Loop Road system.	National forests are placed under the jurisdiction of the Department of Agriculture, with Gifford Pinchot, a conservationist and multiple-use advocate, as chief.

YEAR	IN THE YELLOWSTONE REGION	IN THE U.S. OR THE WORLD
1907	The Union Pacific's Oregon Short Line reaches West Yellowstone.	
1911	Canyon Hotel is greatly enlarged and improved and opened to guests.	
1915	Motorcars are first admitted to Yellowstone on August 1st.	Ford produces more than 500,000 Model Ts in any color you want, as long as it's black.
1916	Yellowstone concessions are consolidated into three companies, for transportation, hotels, and permanent camps.	The National Park Service is created to manage 14 national parks and 21 national monuments; Stephen Mather becomes first director the next year.
1917	All passenger equipment used in the park is now motorized.	U.S. enters World War I.

Stephen Mather, first director of the National Park Service, poses with an elk calf.

1918	U.S. Cavalry troops leave the park, except the few who stay on as rangers.	World War I ends, having killed close to 10 million people.
1920	First chief ranger, James McBride, is appointed.	
1921	Approach road to the South Entrance from Laramie through Togwotee Pass is opened.	
1923	The Howard Eaton Trail, a 157-mile loop bridle trail, is dedicated.	Grasshoppers consume nearly everything green growing in Montana.

YEAR	IN THE YELLOWSTONE REGION	IN THE U.S. OR THE WORLD
1927	The Milwaukee Road carries rail passengers to Gallatin Gateway (near Bozeman, MT).	
1928	Several concession companies are bought out by Harry W. Childs and merged to become the long-lived Yellowstone Park Co. under William M. Nichols 8 years later.	
1929	Grand Teton National Park is created after much controversy over the possible expansion of Yellowstone Park.	U.S. stock market crashes, beginning a worldwide depression.
1930	First museums in Yellowstone are opened at Norris, Old Faithful, and Madison.	
1931	Fishing Bridge Museum opens.	
1933	The Yellowstone Library and Museum Association is formed (later the Yellowstone Association).	
1933–42	Civilian Conservation Corps serves Yellowstone.	The national C.C.C. builds bridges, fights fires, and helps pull the country out of depression.
1936	The Beartooth Highway to the Northeast Entrance from Red Lodge, MT, is opened.	

Automobiles could cross the Beartooth Plateau on the new highway—but with difficulty (1937 photo by F. W. Byerly).

1937	Mammoth Hot Springs Hotel and cottages replace older hotel at the same site.	
1941		U.S. is attacked by Japan at Pearl Harbor and enters World War II.

YEAR	IN THE YELLOWSTONE REGION	IN THE U.S. OR THE WORLD
1942	Number of park visitors drops to below 200,000 from 582,000 in 1941. Many facilities are closed.	U.S. begins gas rationing and a 35 mph speed limit.
1945		World War II ends.
1948	Annual Yellowstone Park visitation tops 1 million for the first time.	
1956	National Park Service initiates Mission '66 to improve facilities in Yellowstone and other parks.	Congress authorizes construction of the Interstate Highway system, indirectly subsidizing road users and penalizing passenger rail service.
1957	A new Canyon Lodge and some cottages in Canyon Village are opened. Hatcheries close; fish stocking in park lakes and streams ceases.	
1959–70	Frank and John Craighead conduct first intensive research on grizzly bears in and around the park.	
1959	Earthquake on August 17th near Hebgen Lake (outside West Entrance) causes 28 deaths and great damage to property. Many Yellowstone hydrothermal features register changes as a result.	
1961	End of all rail service to park entrances.	
1963	Snowmobiles travel to Old Faithful, beginning winter use of the park.	Leopold Report on wildlife management begins debate leading to major policy changes in all national parks.
1964		Congress passes Wilderness Act.
1965	Annual park visitation tops 2 million.	
1966	Goldfield Corporation purchases the Yellowstone Park Co.—soon purchased by General Host (1967).	The U.S. Department of the Interior issues the first rare and endangered species list, including 78 species.
1970	New bear management policy put in place in the park.	
1972	Yellowstone celebrates 100 years.	

YEAR	IN THE YELLOWSTONE REGION	IN THE U.S. OR THE WORLD

1973

Black bears begging near the roads were a common sight before the 1970s.

In response to the Endangered Species Act, grizzly bears are declared threatened and gray wolves endangered (a more severe classification).

Arab oil embargo raises gas prices and encourages more economical car design.

1976　Yellowstone is designated a U.S. Biosphere Reserve in the country's bicentennial year.

1978　World Heritage Site designation given to Yellowstone.

1979　Congress purchases all park concession buildings from General Host for $19.9 million. TWA Services (later TW Recreational Services) takes over hotel and food concessions.

Oil crisis occurs again due to OPEC price increases and low U.S. imports.

1980

Mount St. Helens, WA, erupts on May 18th; the volume of volcanic debris expelled is only 1/1000th of that from the Yellowstone caldera.

1983　Borah Peak earthquake in Idaho affects geysers, slowing Old Faithful's average interval.

1988　Forest fires rage through Yellowstone with a destructive severity seen only once in centuries.

The 1988 fires burned more than one-third of Yellowstone's territory.

YEAR	IN THE YELLOWSTONE REGION	IN THE U.S. OR THE WORLD
1992	Annual park visitation tops 3 million.	
1995	Wolves are introduced into Yellowstone from Canada.	World Heritage Committee adds Yellowstone to its World Heritage in Danger list.

A wolf being released in Yellowstone.

1996	U.S. government stops the Canadian Noranda Minerals company from mining near Yellowstone's northeast corner. AmFac Parks and Resorts takes over as hotel, restaurant, and activities concessionaire.	
1997	125 years as a national park celebrated throughout Yellowstone.	
2002	AmFac changes its name to Xanterra Parks and Resorts.	
2003	Delaware North Parks Services replaces Hamilton Stores as the park's general store concessionaire.	

Dates in this chronology were mostly culled from U.S. history books and from both *The People's Chronology*, edited by James Trager, and the *New York Public Library Book of Chronologies*. For Yellowstone historical information, the author is particularly indebted to *Yellowstone, A Wilderness Besieged* by Richard A. Bartlett, Aubrey L. Haines's two-volume *The Yellowstone Story*, and the 1949 *Haynes Guide*.

Living Things

A YELLOWSTONE SAMPLER

No one thought in 1872 that such a relatively small tract of land in the vast western territories would actually become a preserve for bears, wolves, bison, and thousands of other common living things. But during the next century, these animals disappeared from most of the country, and Yellowstone became an island of wilderness within a sea of human settlement.

According to modern ecologists, though, the Yellowstone island is not large enough to adequately protect the unique resources found here. Five Yellowstone birds and animals are listed as endangered or threatened under the 1973 Endangered Species Act: the whooping crane, gray wolf, bald eagle, lynx, and grizzly bear. The peregrine falcon was delisted only in 1999. We are fortunate that with time, patience, and a little luck we may still see these creatures and many others in the park.

A complete catalog of Yellowstone's living things has never been produced; it would require volumes. In this chapter, after pointing out some small living things that occur throughout the park (along with a couple of not-so-small rare snakes), we introduce you to some of the more common plants and animals living here, grouping them into three quite different *ecosystems*, or communities of organisms that function as a unit of nature.

Ecosystems are defined by the geology and soil types, the elevation, the latitude, and the amount of precipitation. The elevation in Yellowstone ranges from about 5300 feet (1615 m) to over 11,000 feet (3350 m). For every 1000-foot (300 m) increase in elevation, average daily temperatures are 3.5°F (about 2°C) lower, spring arrives about ten days later and autumn about ten days earlier. The latitude here is about that of Turin, Italy, or Bangor, Maine—between 44 and 45 degrees north. Lastly, the amount of rain and snowfall varies greatly, and the snowpack at 9000 feet (2750 m) remains almost two months longer than at 7000 feet (2130 m). More rain falls on western mountainsides than in sheltered valleys east of the mountains.

Many of the plants and animals mentioned below occur in two or more of the ecosystems. At the end of the chapter is a special section on fish and fishing.

THE SMALLEST LIFE FORMS

Microorganisms

Microorganisms are all around us, present in all parts of Yellowstone, yet individually invisible to the naked eye. Living in very hot water are ones that interest us as visitors. The thermophilic bacteria and algae form beautifully colored filaments and mats that are often seen in the runoff from hot springs and sometimes in the springs themselves. You'll see outstanding examples of these mats at Midway and Upper geyser basins and at Mammoth Hot Springs.

Lichens

As you follow trails throughout the park, you may notice a large boulder or an old tree trunk with a crusty sort of growth on it. This is probably a *lichen*, a combination of an alga and a fungus that live together *symbiotically*; that is, in a mutually beneficial relationship. An *alga* is an ancient form of life that can convert light to energy via photosynthesis, while a *fungus* obtains nourishment by breaking down organic matter (such as algae). The thousands of different species of lichen may be orange, red, yellow, green, gray, brown, or black. They can utilize water from fog and dew, and, along with the action of water and wind, they serve as one of the most important factors in breaking down rocks into soil. Lichens do not grow in the geyser basins—they cannot abide the sulfur dioxide.

Some forms of lichen commonly seen in Yellowstone are **old man's beard** (*Usnea longissima*), which hangs from tree branches in a dark green mass and can be a good source of vitamin C, and **wolf lichen** (*Letharia vulpina*), a bright yellow-green type found on sunny tree trunks and branches. In Douglas fir forests, such as grow near the Grand Canyon of the Yellowstone, you may see dark brown **horsehair lichen** (*Bryoria* sp.) hanging from branches and looking like coarse twisted hair.

Mosses and mushrooms

It takes an expert to differentiate some types of lichen from the mosses. Common sorts of **moss** form green mounds or mats and grow in moist places everywhere, and some lichens may look similar to them. Both mosses and lichens grow on other plants but derive their nutrients from air, water, and dust particles (that is, they are *epiphytic*, not parasitic).

In moist places throughout the park, you may see **mushrooms** of various shapes, colors, and sizes. Observe and admire but do not pick them unless you're an expert. It's not against regulations to pick edible plants for immediate consumption in a national park, but at least six Yellowstone mushrooms are poisonous.

Insects, amphibians, and reptiles

Let's not talk about the biting horse flies and mosquitoes that torture hikers in early summer nor about the moths that fly into the flame of your camp lantern, but only mention a few insects and larger creatures that are fun to see.

Those beautiful blue gossamer-winged insects hovering about the streams are **dragonflies** and their smaller relatives **damselflies**, both of the order *Odonata*, meaning toothed. Some dragonflies are also called darners for their resemblance to long thin darning needles. They hold their two pairs of wings horizontally, while damselflies hold their wings above the body. They can eat as many as 300 mosquitoes and other small insects a day. Look for reddish gold dragonflies in drier parts of the park.

The **water strider** (*Gerris remigis*) is also called the Jesus bug for its ability to walk on water. Its extremely long back pair of legs provides steering ability, allowing the bug to spread its body weight, while the middle pair provides oar-like power.

Living in hot spring waters is the **ephydrid fly** (*Ephydra bruesi*), whose larvae live on microorganisms. The adult flies you'll see swarming in shallow hot water may not eat at all.

Among the many types of butterflies, some conspicuous ones are the small blues like the **spring azure** (*Celastrina argiolus*), various shades of yellow ones called sulfurs (genus *Colias*), and the large yellow and black swallowtails of the family *Papilionidae*.

In August of dry years you may be surprised at the hordes of jumping short-horned **grasshoppers** (family *Acrididae* or *Locustidae*) in every field you pass. In a glacier north of Cooke City just outside the Northeast Entrance a great many grasshoppers have been preserved for some 300 years.

Not a lot of **frogs** and **toads** live in Yellowstone, and those that live here seem to be diminishing in number. Most common is the 2 to 3 inch (5–7.5 cm) **Columbia spotted frog** (*Rana luteiventris*). These tiny animals are extremely sensitive to air and water pollution, and it has recently been discovered that they're falling prey to a parasite.

Small **garter snakes** (*Thamnophis elegans* or *sirtalis*) are fairly common but harmless. Along trails in the lower altitude river valleys, you have a slight chance of seeing a **bull snake** (*Pituophis* genera), which may be up to 7 feet (2 m) long but has no poison, or a **rattlesnake** (*Crotalus viridis viridis*)—up to 4 feet (1.2 m) long and poisonous.

Three Yellowstone Ecosystems

The map shows the extent of
- the forested community of the central plateaus
- the Yellowstone, Lamar, and Gardner river valleys, and
- the Absaroka Range ecosystems.

Adapted with permission from Yellowstone Vegetation: Consequences of Environment and History in a Natural Setting *(1990), by Don G. Despain.*

I. THE FORESTED COMMUNITY OF THE CENTRAL PLATEAUS

You're likely to spend the majority of your Yellowstone visit in the central plateaus region, where most of the roads are, along with the geyser basins, the Yellowstone Canyon, and the western and northern shores of Yellowstone Lake.

The undulating terrain, much of it within the Yellowstone caldera, consists of rhyolitic lava and ash, which weathers to a coarse, sandy soil, poor in nutrients and in ability to hold water. The altitude in the central plateaus varies from about 6600 to 8000 feet (2000–2440 m). Precipitation ranges from 20 to 40 inches (50–100 cm) per year.

This area includes excellent places to see water-loving birds and large animals—the Hayden and Pelican valleys and along the shores of Yellowstone Lake. Here the soil is better but drainage is poor, creating marshy areas where trees don't do well. Grasses and sedges thrive here and create a nourishing habitat for wildlife.

Trees and shrubs of the forests and lakeshores

What you'll see most of in the central plateaus are trees, mile upon mile of **lodgepole pines** (*Pinus contorta*) with trunks close together, tall and straight, their needles growing only near the tops where they can reach sunlight. These trees got their name by serving as framework for Native American dwellings.

Lodgepole needles always grow in twos and are stiff and twisted. The reddish brown cones have short scales and a slender prickle. Some lodgepole cones can open and release seeds only in the intense heat of a fire.

Grouse whortleberry

Under stands of lodgepole you may find **grouse whortleberry** (*Vaccinium scoparium*) plants with tiny, fine leaves and white or pink hanging bells for flowers. The berries are a staple of the diet of bears, birds, and small mammals.

There are only eight species of evergreens and three of deciduous trees in the park. This is due to high altitude and poor soil, but also to the relatively short time that trees have had to become established since the end of the last ice age—about 10,000 years.

Watch for **Engelmann spruce** (*Picea engelmannii*) and **subalpine fir** (*Abies lasiocarpa*) along the drive from West Thumb Junction to Fishing Bridge Junction. These species would eventually dominate Yellowstone's forests if it weren't for the lodgepoles' superb adaptability to fire. Check the cones and needles to tell these spruce and fir trees apart. Spruce cones hang down from the branches. Their needles have sharp points but are relatively soft to the touch, occur singly on the branch, and are square in cross-section. To remember that, notice that the words spruce, sharp, soft, single, and square all start with *s*. If you crush spruce needles, they smell of camphor. Subalpine fir cones, on the other hand, sit upright on the branches, and the needles are flat and flexible.

In late summer you are welcome to eat the edible berries on shrubs along the trails. Way out in front for flavor is the **huckleberry** (*Vaccinium membranaceum*) on its short bush.

Huckleberry

Red raspberries (*Rubus idaeus*) can be found in some moist environments, as can **wild strawberries** (*Fragaria virginiana*) and **thimbleberries** (*Rubus parviflorus*), pictured on page 10.

Forest flowers

Here is a guide to some of the central plateaus' common wildflowers, arranged by color. Remember that it's against regulations to pick flowers.

PINK/RED/LAVENDER

Fireweed (*Epilobium angustifolium*) grows on its 4- or 5-foot (1.2–1.5 m) stem quickly after burns.

Fireweed

The aptly named **paintbrush** or **Indian paintbrush** (genus *Castilleja*) is Wyoming's state flower. Its color is in the *bracts*, or specialized leaves, from which the flowers arise. These bracts may be red, white, orange, yellow, or pink. The roots of the paintbrush penetrate the roots of nearby plants and steal food from them parasitically.

Indian paintbrush

Sticky geranium (*Geranium viscosissimum*) is common in damp meadows. It's a pink or rose-colored five-petaled flower with large, five- to seven-lobed leaves.

The **Everts thistle** (*Cirsium scariosum*) commemorates Truman Everts, the man who survived—in part by eating its roots—for 37 days when lost in Yellowstone in 1870. Peeled stems and roots are both edible.

Everts' thistle

Shooting star (*Dodecatheon pauciflorum*), like the houseplant cyclamen, has its petals flexed backwards and its dark *stamens* (that is, the male pollen-producing parts of a flower) projecting forward.

YELLOW
Yellow monkeyflower (*Mimulus guttatus*) thrives in the steamy atmosphere of hot spring basins, but the heat restricts it to 2 to 3 inches (5–7 cm) high there.

Shooting star

Isa Lake on the Continental Divide west of West Thumb has a splendid covering of **yellow** or **Rocky Mountain pond lilies** (*Nuphar polysepalum*), as do several ponds around Norris Junction. Native Americans roasted the large seeds and ate them like popcorn, and the rootstocks are food for muskrats. Pond lilies are pictured on page 101.

Monkeyflower

Yellow composite flowers are many and hard to distinguish. Two common ones that have distinctive leaves are **heartleaf arnica** (*Arnica cordifolia*) and **arrowleaf balsamroot** (*Balsamorhiza sagittata*). Although mentioned here to compare it to the arnica, the balsamroot is most common in the river valley ecosystem described later.

Heartleaf arnica (left) *& arrowleaf balsamroot* (above)

Blue/Purple
Lupine (genus *Lupinus*) has long spikes of pea-like flowers and many leaflets radiating out like fingers. It grows in moist soils, developing alkaloids that are poisonous to livestock late in the season.

Harebell (*Campanula rotundifolia*), called Scotch bluebell in Scotland, has hanging bells almost an inch (2 cm) long.

Harebell

The official flower of Yellowstone since 1958 is the **Western** or **Rocky Mountain fringed gentian** (*Gentiana thermalis*). It is often found near hot springs, especially in August.

Fringed gentian

Birds

Nearly 300 different bird species have been sighted in Yellowstone over the years. Here we name some birds with personality that are common to the central plateaus, first birds of the forest and then those of the lakeshore. Some of these species are also seen in the river valley and mountain pass ecosystems.

In the forests and along the rivers

You're in for a treat if you find an **American dipper** (*Cinclus mexicanus*—formerly called water ouzel) feeding on insects in cold mountain streams. Author Owen Wister observed in 1887 that "the spectacle of a little gray bird, like a fat catbird, skimming along the river like a bullet and suddenly dropping below the surface where it was shallow, and walking along the bottom with its tail sticking out in the air, filled me with such elation that I forgot the geysers and watched him." This year-round resident sometimes sings like a canary.

In the case of the **gray jay** (*Perisoreus canadensis*) and the **Clark's nutcracker** (*Nucifraga columbiana*), it's the birds that are in for a treat. Whenever you sit down for a picnic, your meal will be of interest to one of these camp robbers.

(Facing page) **Gray jay** (left) & **Clark's nutcracker** (right)

The **mountain chickadee** (*Parus gambeli*) is heard more often than seen. It's a tiny, roly-poly, light gray bird with a black head and white line over the eye. It's most common song goes *fee-bee-bee*, with the first note higher than the others; sometimes it will vary this and surprise you. The **black-capped chickadee** (*Parus atricapillus*) is also found here.

The male **mountain bluebird** (*Sialia currucoidus*) flashes by you wearing the most intense shade of sky blue imaginable, while his mate makes do with a bit of blue on her otherwise brown body. Bluebirds, a little smaller than robins, build their nests in snags.

For a few years, a colony of **cliff swallows** (*Hirundo pyrrhonota*) made their distinctive jug-shaped mud-and-stick nests under the eaves of the Old Faithful Visitor Center. More recently, fine-meshed netting has discouraged some of the nesters. This small, square-tailed, and buff-rumped swallow also nests on the back side of Soda Butte in the Lamar Valley.

Common ravens (*Corvus corax*), purplish black, large relatives of the very common crow, show up in droves to feast on carrion. They can be over 2 feet (60 cm) long and have a large beak and an annoying croak. They're very intelligent birds that can mimic human speech and learn amazingly complex behaviors.

In and around the rivers and small lakes are many types of duck, perhaps the easiest to spot being the male **mallard** (*Anas platyrhynchos*), with his iridescent green head, white neck-ring, yellow beak, and blue on the wing feathers, while the female is mottled brown with orange beak and feet and some blue feathers.

The **great blue heron** (*Ardea herodias*) likes to fish along the Madison and Firehole rivers and near Fishing Bridge. Its blue-gray feathers include some stringy ones in the breast area. As long as 4 feet (1.2 m), the heron flies and often stands with its neck in an S shape.

The **sandhill crane** (*Grus canadensis*), although similar to the heron, flies with its neck outstretched. It is a duller shade of gray and a little smaller than the heron and has a red patch over the eye. It hunts rodents, insects, and seeds in the meadows and has a bugling call.

Great blue heron & Sandhill crane

The most regal of all Yellowstone's birds is the **trumpeter swan** (*Cygnus buccinator*). Male cobs may be 5 feet (1.5 m) long with a wingspan of 7 feet (2 m), and the female pens are a little smaller. These snow white swans with coal black bills dabble (that is, go bottom up) for aquatic plants. Some trumpeter swans nest along the Madison River. Others nest in neighboring refuges, such as the

Red Rock Lakes National Wildlife Refuge in southwestern Montana, home to E. B. White's Louis, the remarkable mute swan in *The Trumpet of the Swan*. Fewer than 30 adults live in the park year-round, despite strong efforts to help them increase.

Trumpeter swan and cygnets

ALONG THE SHORES OF YELLOWSTONE LAKE

Pelican colony

The **American white pelican** (*Pelecanus erythrorynchos*) can be 5 feet (1.5 m) long and have a wingspan of 9 feet (2.7 m). Park Service regulations protect the pelican's nesting place (the lake's Molly Islands) from approach by any watercraft.

A much smaller fish-eating bird is the **osprey** (*Pandion haliaetus*). Its body is black or brown above and white below, with a black patch under the crook of its wing and powerful talons for catching fish. One can see osprey nests on high pillars or tall pines in the Grand Canyon of the Yellowstone.

The **California gull** (*Larus californicus*) nests on the islands of inland lakes, including Yellowstone Lake, and winters along the Pacific coast, turning from a brownish color when young to all white underneath and gray above as it matures.

The park has its share of **Canada geese** (*Branta canadensis*), which have become something of a pest around northern U.S. cities. This large goose is characterized by its black neck and white chin strap and its deep honking.

Small Mammals of the Forest

If something is flying over your head at dusk, it may be a **little brown bat** (*Myotis lucifugus*). Three to 4 inches (7–10 cm) long, this bat finds moths, mosquitoes, and other insects at night by echolocation (a sort of radar). It hibernates for about six months of the year.

Around the boardwalks at Old Faithful Village or at the Yellowstone Canyon, you'll see the much larger **yellow-bellied marmot** or **rockchuck** (*Marmota flaviventris*), whose low-slung body may be over 2 feet (0.7 m) long. The marmot digs burrows and spends much time underground but also loves to soak up the sun.

Nocturnal rodents are the common **deer mouse** (*Peromyscus maniculatus*)

Yellow-bellied marmots

and the much larger **bushy-tailed woodrat** (*Neotoma cinerea*). This pack rat collects and hoards miscellaneous objects, especially shiny ones. Old Faithful Inn sets up mouse motels, since the concessionaire must follow the park policy of killing no wildlife.

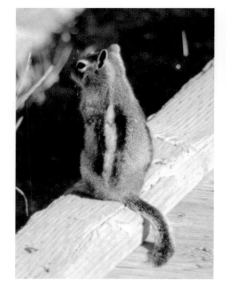

Least chipmunk (left) *& Golden-mantled ground squirrel* (right)

The smallest rodent you're likely to see in wooded areas here is the **least chipmunk** (*Tamias minimus*), 7 to 8 inches (18–21 cm) long including the bushy tail it carries straight up as it runs. It's a gray to reddish brown color with black and white stripes on both the back and face and is known for stuffing its cheeks with seeds or berries.

The way to tell a **golden-mantled ground squirrel** (*Spermophilus lateralis*) from a chipmunk is to notice that the squirrel has stripes only on the body. This squirrel is some 4 inches (10 cm) longer than its chipmunk relative and may eat insects as well as vegetable matter.

Larger mammals

Ruminants are cud-chewing, hoofed mammals with an even number of toes, and four species are common in the central plateaus: mule deer, elk, moose, and bison. Male elk, deer, and moose have antlers and shed them every year, while male and female bison have horns.

Mule deer (*Odocoileus hemionus*) are much smaller than elk and named for the size and shape of their ears; they are also called blacktail deer. Although their cousin, the **white-tailed deer** (*Odocoileus virginianus*), is the most numerous big game species in the United States, there are very few whitetails inside the park. Some live just north of Gardiner in Paradise Valley.

Rocky Mountain elk (*Cervus elaphus nelsoni*), dark brown with a light rump and tail, are of the same species as the red deer of Europe. A bull elk may be 5 feet (1.5 m) tall at the shoulder and more than 9 feet (2.7 m) long, weigh half a ton (450 kg), and carry a majestic rack of antlers several feet high. You can't tell a bull's age exactly by the number of points on his antlers, but if he has six (or even seven) points, he's a dominant male. There are as many as 35,000 elk in the park during the summers, many of which migrate north and south from the park to find winter forage. Chances of seeing elk are particularly good all along the Madison,

Mule deer & Elk

Gibbon, and Firehole rivers between Norris Junction and Old Faithful Village. Mammoth Hot Springs has its own year-round resident herd.

The largest member of the deer family, **moose** (*Alces alces shirasi*) are relatively rare in Yellowstone—probably a few hundred. They're shy of people, so seeing one is an exciting experience. Watch for an ungainly, large, dark brown animal—if it's a mature bull, it will have distinctive *palmate* antlers; that is, shaped like the palm and fingers of a hand. Both bulls and cows have a *dewlap*, a piece of hanging skin, under the throat. They eat willows and other plants that grow in shallow water all summer, but when snow is deep, they move high up to browse on fir trees.

Moose

The buffalo, more properly called the **bison** (*Bison bison*), symbolizes the wide open spaces of the American west. Ironically, the bison is also probably the most grievous case of man's wanton destruction of a natural resource in America's history. Not only did hunters nearly eradicate the bison during the last decades of the 19th century, but it was official government policy to exterminate them in order to suppress the Native American people who depended upon them.

Bison herd in winter

Yellowstone's herd is sometimes called the only surviving wild population of bison. Though not fenced in, they are not exactly the same wild bison as when the park was new. The few bison left by 1900 were crossbred here with semi-domesticated animals from Texas and northern Montana in an early successful effort to undo damage to the environment. The restoration of the bison proved so successful, in fact, that by 1940 the park was giving them away to zoos.

The calm-looking bison can be every bit as cantankerous as a farmer's bull and can sprint faster than any Olympic runner. The Park Service warns you amply about the danger of approaching bison, because many people have been injured. Bison herds graze along the Madison and Firehole rivers and in the Hayden and Lamar valleys.

The Brucellosis Problem

The late 1990s saw a difficult problem arise between the agencies responsible for protecting bison and the ranchers who graze herds of cattle on private and public property all around Yellowstone. The basic problem is that cattle in Montana have been certified free of *brucellosis*, a disease that can cause a pregnant cow to abort her calf, but does not cause abortion in bison. Ranchers fear the disease could be transmitted to cattle when the park's brucellosis-infected bison migrate to winter feeding grounds outside the park.

An interim management plan resulted in over 1000 bison being slaughtered in the winter of 1996–97, causing a huge outcry from environmental organizations, with widespread discussion in the press. From a bison herd of about 3600, this slaughter plus winterkill from the severe weather of the same winter reduced the herd to about 1600, but in a few years the count was back up to about 3000. Vaccination of park bison or other controls are being considered, despite the facts that no case of brucellosis spreading to cattle from bison has been documented and that park elk also carry brucellosis.

BEARS

Grizzly bears were probably more common here than black bears in the 19th century. Recent estimates put the number of grizzlies in the Greater Yellowstone Ecosystem at about 500 to 600 (with at least half that many in the park itself); black bears are not as closely watched, but now their number is similar or a little larger.

The so-called **black bear** (*Ursus americanus*) may be brown or cinnamon colored as well as black. To decide whether a bear you see at a distance is a black or a grizzly, try to observe its overall size. Adult black bears are usually about 3 feet (90 cm) in shoulder height and up to 5.5 feet (1.7 m) in overall length, weighing up to 250 pounds (114 kg). If you can see the face and ears clearly enough, observe their shape; black bears have a rather flat face in profile and pointed ears. Their claws are relatively short.

Black bear (left) *& Grizzly bear* (right)

In contrast, Yellowstone's **grizzly bears** (*Ursus arctos*) often have the grizzled or silver-tipped hair their name suggests but may have darker hair at certain times of the year. Grizzly boars (males) may weigh 700 pounds (318 kg) and sows 400 pounds (182 kg) and be 4.5 feet (1.4 m) in shoulder height and 6.5 feet (2 m) overall. Their most distinguishing features are a shoulder hump and extremely long claws, which help them dig roots but hinder them in climbing trees.

You can't generalize about grizzlies, according to Dick Knight, former head of the Interagency Grizzly Bear Study Team, since each year they learn new tricks and they are notoriously unpredictable.

Grizzlies eat a varied diet. When emerging from their winter dens, they find winter-killed carrion and newborn elk calves, supplemented with grasses and sedges. In early summer they fish in trout spawning streams, and throughout the summer, they eat various plants, small mammals, and insects, especially ants and army cutworm moths. In late summer and fall, they raid squirrels' middens full of whitebark pine nuts and feast on all sorts of berries. Black bears' diet is similar, except they do not dig for roots and tubers as the grizzlies do.

By mid November, the bears are hibernating in their winter dens. Although mating occurs in June and July, the fertilized egg is not implanted in the sow's uterus until after denning. This *delayed implantation* is a characteristic bears share with several of the park's smaller mammals, such as river otters and badgers. Grizzly cubs are born in the den in January or February and black bear cubs a month or two later. In the wild, bears live about 15 to 20 years.

Where Are All the Bears Now?

This is a question rangers must hear several times a day, since for at least 50 years, you were guaranteed the opportunity to see black bears along the roads and grizzly bears at the hotel garbage dumps. This situation led to lots of interaction between people and bears, and bears injured nearly 50 people each year.

In response to the problems with bears and concern about the possible extinction of the grizzly bear, the park changed its policies. The park closed dumps where bears had fed, began using bear-proof garbage cans, and strongly cautioned visitors against feeding bears or leaving unsecured food in their campsites. Also, the park management set aside Bear Management Areas, closed to humans (explained further on page 126).

As a result of these actions, a dramatic reduction of bear/human confrontations ensued. In recent years, there have been very few injuries, and very few bears have had to be relocated or killed. The park's threatened population of grizzlies is showing strong signs of recovery and could be delisted in the near future.

So the answer to: "Where are all the bears?" is that they're still here and fending for themselves very nicely. You're not likely to see grizzlies near the roads in the summertime, since they often find their favorite foods at higher altitudes away from human populations. They're most likely to be living in roadless parts of the Hayden, upper Lamar, and Pelican valleys. You'll see black bears somewhat more often, especially within a few miles of Tower-Roosevelt Junction, but also west to Mammoth Hot Springs and sometimes around Old Faithful and Madison.

Hikers should be aware that bears might be near the trails. Never approach a bear closer than 100 yards (90 m), do not hike alone, and make some noise as you go in order to let them know you're there—they don't like to be surprised! Overnight hikers must obtain a permit from a ranger station or visitor center and follow the park regulations for making camp and securing food.

In and near Yellowstone Park in over 125 years there have been ten bear-caused fatalities (two of which cannot be confirmed). Sensational media publicity when a bear has killed a human makes it seem that there have been more.

II. THE VALLEYS OF THE LOWER YELLOWSTONE, LAMAR, AND GARDNER RIVERS

The northern valleys average a little lower and drier than the central plateaus overall, and the high desert ecology along the 5 miles of road between Gardiner and Mammoth is unique in the park, for precipitation there is sometimes as low as 11 inches (28 cm) in a year. In contrast, the Lamar River valley is a little higher and has about 30 inches (76 cm) of precipitation a year.

The ecology of these river valleys is also heavily influenced by glacial scouring, which has brought down volcanic and sedimentary soils from surrounding mountains. The soil holds water well and is high in plant nutrients. These are places where bison and elk thrive.

Valley Trees

Douglas fir (*Pseudotsuga menziesii*) is the evergreen you'll often see growing singly in the lee of big boulders along the road between Mammoth Hot Springs and the Northeast Entrance (it's pictured on page 203). Its scientific name means false hemlock, and it is not really a fir (genus *Abies*) at all. The needles grow around the branch, and the hanging female cones have little tridents between their scales. An old Douglas fir will have very thick, deeply fissured bark that protects it from fires.

The **limber pine** (*Pinus flexilis*) has young branches so flexible they can be tied in knots without breaking. This pine grows at high altitudes, and its needles grow in bundles of five. Its cones are up to 8 inches (20 cm) long and green. The limber pine is common near Mammoth Hot Springs.

In the park, the shrub **Rocky Mountain juniper** (*Juniperus scopulorum*) grows only around Mammoth (it's pictured on page 266). Its scaly leaves look much like a cedar's, and its seed cones look like blue berries. Some junipers are lollipop-shaped, with bare trunks and bushy tops, a result of elk browsing on them in winter. There are examples of this tree that are several hundred years old growing around Upper Terrace Drive at Mammoth Hot Springs.

One of the three deciduous trees at home in northern Yellowstone is the **quaking aspen** (*Populus tremuloides*), which grows in sunny places on hillsides where there's abundant ground water. Aspens are distinguished by white trunks and by leaves that quake

Aspens in autumn

or shiver in the slightest breeze due to flattened leafstalks. Fire does not destroy a stand of aspen, because the trees reproduce mainly by cloning from *rhizomes*, specialized horizontal root systems full of nutrients. One unexpected positive result of the 1988 fires was aspen's spreading into burned-over meadows, where thick vegetation had previously crowded out any aspen seedlings.

Both of the area's other deciduous trees are types of cottonwood, the **narrowleaf cottonwood** (*Populus angustifolia*) and the **black cottonwood** or **balsam poplar** (*Populus balsamifera*). Look for cottonwoods along the Lamar River and at the confluence of the Lamar and Yellowstone rivers. Black cottonwood have thick, furrowed, gray bark and trunks up to 3 feet (1 m) in diameter; the narrowleaf cottonwood is much smaller.

Valley shrubs and flowers

Many plants grow only in the park's relatively lower elevations. For example, along all the rivers and some creeks are many species of **willow** (*Salix* spp.), which provide nutritious forage for elk, as do the stems, leaves, and bark of the aspen.

YELLOW

Big sagebrush (*Artemisia tridentata*) is so common in most of the west as to be a symbol of the dry western plains. It's a gray-green shrub from 2 to 10 feet (60 cm–3 m) tall, bearing three-toothed leaves on many branches (see its picture on page 244).

A similar low bush found in the northern part of the park is **common rabbitbrush** (*Chrysothamnus nauseosus*). It's a rather nondescript plant with almost needlelike leaves covered with woolly white hairs, but in late August and September it bursts out with yellow flowers.

Two yellow flowers that resemble the snapdragons are the **butter-and-eggs** (*Linaria vulgaris*) and **Dalmatian toadflax** (*Linaria dalmatica*). These are *exotics* (that is, non-native plants), introduced to Mammoth from Europe. Park managers are trying to control the spread of these and other exotics whenever possible.

Only in the high desert area between Gardiner and Mammoth will you see a cactus. It's the **plains prickly pear** (*Opuntia polycantha*), and its fleshy stems are covered with spines that are unpleasant to brush against. The

Prickly pear

rose-like flowers are usually yellow but may be pink or purple on the outside if not fully opened. Pronghorn and elk will eat prickly pear in a hard winter.

Blue/Purple

Larkspur (*Delphinium nelsoni* and other species) often grows where sagebrush is abundant. It's easy to recognize for the tubular spur that protrudes sideways from its deep purple blossom on a 1 to 2 foot (30–60 cm) stem. Larkspur is poisonous to cattle but not to sheep; elk avoid it until late summer.

Valley Birds

Yellow-headed blackbirds (*Xanthocephalus xanthocephalus*) may be seen in the reeds at Floating Island Lake west of Tower Junction or along the edges of some of that area's other ponds. The call of this blackbird is a loud "tseck."

At Floating Island Lake and many other shallow ponds in the area, you may see **American coots** (*Fulica americana*), which look rather like ducks but are actually a type of rail. Coots are slate gray with broad white bills, red eyes, and lobed feet and a habit of pumping their heads while swimming. When a flock of coots takes off, they seem to dance or skitter on the surface of the water.

You are very likely to see the distinctive **black-billed magpie** (*Pica pica*) between the North Entrance and Tower-Roosevelt Junction. Watch for a rather large black and white bird with an extremely long tail.

The **American kestrel** or **sparrow hawk** (*Falco sparverius*) is a medium-large bird with two black marks on its face, a buff-colored breast, gray wings, and a reddish brown back with black flecks across it. The kestrel swoops out of the sky to pick up its prey but lives mainly on insects. Sitting on a high perch, a kestrel will wag its tail up and down repeatedly.

The **red-tailed hawk** (*Buteo jamaicensis*) is about twice as large as the kestrel and may be gray or brown on the upper body and lighter below, with chestnut red in the top of the tail. They have been known to soar for as long as 7 hours a day while hunting. There's a breeding population near Gardiner, and red-tailed hawks may be seen throughout northern Yellowstone.

The **golden eagle** (*Aquila chrysaetos*) may be more than a yard (1 m) long and have a 7-foot (2 m) wingspread. You may sometimes see them not far from the road in the Lamar Valley. Watch for a gracefully soaring, lustrous brown bird with golden brown head and lighter colored breast. The **bald eagle** (*Haliaeetus leucocephalusi*), America's endangered national symbol, is relatively rare in the park and seldom seen outside of remote areas around southern Yellowstone Lake.

Small mammals of the river valleys

The **river otter** (*Lutra canadensis*) is a highly aquatic member of the weasel family. Three or 4 feet (1–1.2 m) long including its tail, it has lustrous, dark brown fur and a broad, rather flat head. It feeds mostly on fish, amphibians, and insects. Otters dig dens in the riverbanks or use beaver and muskrat lodges. River otters can sometimes be seen playfully sliding down a steep bank into a stream in and around the Madison, Yellowstone, and Lamar rivers, but they are *crepuscular* (that is, active at dawn or dusk) or nocturnal.

A more common aquatic mammal in Yellowstone is the **muskrat** (*Ondatra zibethicus*), a rodent that grows up to 2 feet (60 cm) long and has thick, lustrous fur that is usually dark brown. Outside of national parks, its fur is responsible for a multi-million-dollar industry. You might see them eating aquatic plants in the still ponds of the Lamar Valley or around Obsidian Creek. Their cone-shaped lodges look like beaver lodges but are less substantial.

The wide lawns at Mammoth Hot Springs or the meadows near Roosevelt Lodge are full of the holes and burrows of **Uinta ground squirrels** (*Spermophilus armatus*). Ground squirrels are half the size of marmots (only about 1 ft/30 cm long) and disappear underground for much of the year. In July or August, adults go into a sort of summer torpor called *estivation*, which may lead directly to hibernation, leaving them only about 90 days of activity.

Uinta ground squirrels

Larger mammals

The **pronghorn antelope** (*Antilocapra americana*) is the smallest but by far the

fleetest horned animal in Yellowstone. There's no point in chasing one. It can sprint up to 60 or 70 miles per hour (about 100 km/hr) and cruise at 30 to 40 mph (50–60 km/hr). In the world of animals, it's second only to the cheetah in sprinting speed and may be faster over longer distances. It's a very shy animal and will run at the slightest provocation.

Pronghorn antelope

The park herd lives between Mammoth Hot Springs and Cinnabar Mountain northwest of Gardiner. Only about 200 have been counted in recent years, and the gradually diminishing herd poses a particularly difficult dilemma for the National Park Service. Since current wildlife management policy favors letting natural processes run their course, should the pronghorn be allowed to die out, with the possibility of having to face a costly reintroduction program in the future? Or should measures be taken to prevent this?

Three members of the *Canidae* or dog family live in Yellowstone. By far the most numerous is the **coyote** (*Canis latrans*), whose population burgeoned over the many years when there were no competing wolves here. Look for a slim and crafty-looking animal with pointed nose and ears, weighing about 30 pounds (14 kg). It runs with its long, bushy, black-tipped tail between its legs. Coyotes are abundant enough in the northern valleys that you're almost sure to see one there, but they live throughout the park.

Coyote

Since the introduction of wolves, they have killed enough coyotes to reduce the population considerably. Coyotes eat mostly small rodents, stalking and pouncing on their prey, but can bring down a deer or elk when they hunt as a small pack, so the wolves must consider them competition.

Should you pronounce the coyote's name KI-yoat or ki-O-tee? Both are in the dictionaries—how you say it seems to depend upon how close you are to Spanish-speaking Mexico, where the name came from. Most residents of Wyoming and Montana say KI-yoat.

The smallest dog-like animal in Yellowstone is the **red fox** (*Vulpes vulpes*), which weighs about 15 pounds (7 kg). Some "red" foxes have white-tipped black hairs, giving them a silvery appearance.

A mature **gray wolf** (*Canis lupus*), also called a timber wolf, is likely to weigh two or three times as much as a coyote. It has a more massive body and a less pointed snout and ears. A wolf's tracks are

Gray wolf

the size of a large dog's, and its color may be anywhere from nearly white to black. You may see wolves along the Northeast Entrance Road, particularly early and late in the day. There are several turnouts in the Lamar Valley for the many eager wolf watchers.

Wolves in the West

"There has never been a documented case of a healthy wild wolf seriously injuring a human in North America," states a recent Yellowstone Foundation publication. Why then the century-long vendetta against the wolf in the U.S. west? It's true that wolves kill cattle and sheep as well as wild animals for food. Hatred of wolves was so strong when the west was being settled (particularly in the 1870s), that killing wolves was a civic duty. Trappers also profited by baiting buffalo carcasses with strychnine and then collecting and selling the wolf pelts. Officially sanctioned predator control continued here until 1926.

Things began to turn around for the wolves in the latter half of the 20th century. After extensive debate and planning, 31 wolves were trapped in western Canada in 1995 and 1996. They were kept for a few weeks in specially constructed pens and then released. Again in 1997, 10 wolves, this time from northwestern Montana, were set loose. A few years later, over 150 wolves ranged the Greater Yellowstone Ecosystem. The wolf population is well on its way to recovery.

Zoologists can now study the many interesting interactions between the wolves and other Yellowstone animals, particularly the bears. Elsewhere, wolves and bears have been reported to kill each other (although rarely). Bears are known to readily displace wolves from their kills, so there's more food for the bears than before Yellowstone's wolves came back.

III. MOUNTAIN PASSES

If you love flowers, then the mountain passes of the Absaroka Range in July and early August are places you must visit. Three passes on park roads are at least 8000 feet (2440 m) high: Dunraven, Sylvan, and Craig passes. The approach roads include three more: Togwotee, Beartooth, and Dead Indian. All of these passes are deep in snow for eight to nine months of the year; here the total precipitation amounts to about 40 or 50 inches (100–127 cm) per year.

Evergreen trees

In this ecosystem lives one species that doesn't grow well at lower altitudes: the **whitebark pine** (*Pinus albicaulis*). Its needles grow in groups of five or sometimes more. Mature trees have whitish bark and short purple cones with thick scales and sharp spines, but the trees may not produce cones until they're around 100 years old. In late summer, when the cones fall and release their tasty and nourishing seeds, birds, squirrels, and bears enjoy the feast. Subalpine fir, Engelmann spruce, and lodgepole pine also grow around some of the mountain passes.

Mountain flowers

The very best places to get out of your car and enjoy the wildflowers center on Dunraven Pass—along the Chittenden Road at the north and along the Mount Washburn Trail beginning right at the pass. There and at other high places, you'll find many of the flowers already described and those listed below, as well as dozens of others.

WHITE

White phlox (*Phlox multiflora*) is a low, mat-forming plant with small, snowy white five-petaled flowers (see its picture on page 183). It appears in sunny places soon after the snow has melted.

BLUE/PURPLE

The **forget-me-not** (*Myosotis alpestris*) is unforgettable due to its small and intense blue flowers with tiny yellow centers (or sometimes red or white centers).

Forget-me-not

Silky phacelia (*Phacelia sericea*) puts up a tall spike, dense with purple flowers with long protruding stamens, giving it a silky or feathery appearance. Insects are attracted by its strong, disagreeable odor.

Silky phacelia

Mountain mammals

Living in rock piles at high altitudes is a tiny relative of the rabbit family, the **pika** (*Ochotona princeps*), pronounced PEE-ka or PIE-ka. You may see it or hear its distinctive little "eek" in rocky places along the Yellowstone trails or at the Hoodoos (Silver Gate) near Mammoth. Pikas (also called rock rabbits or coneys) are usually less than 8 inches (20 cm) long, with round ears and no tails. They do not hibernate, but survive the winters on the large stashes of hay they've carefully dried and stored during the summers.

The **bighorn sheep** (*Ovis canadensis*) has been prized historically by hunters for the wonderful curl of horn on the mature males (see the picture on page 247), but hunting them is now strictly limited throughout the Rocky Mountains. Small herds of bighorn sheep roam around Mount Washburn and from Mount Everts north to Sheep Mountain outside the park. There were about 200 bighorns in the park in recent years, sometimes creating traffic jams along the Dunraven Pass road. In summer, you'll find bighorns only in the security of the highest places they can find.

FISH AND FISHING

You may wonder, why is it okay to catch and eat fish in Yellowstone Park when we are forbidden to kill or capture all other animals, pick wildflowers, or even take away non-living rocks? People began to question park policy toward fishing a few decades ago, and fishing practices began to change. The park now charges a fee for fishing licenses, which had always been free. As of the 2001 fishing season, all native sport fishing is catch and release only.

The number of anglers has dropped, but these anglers probably land more fish. Some people enjoy watching the fish feed, fight, and mate at Fishing Bridge or swim upstream at LeHardys Rapids to reach their spawning grounds. More important to the ecosystem, the bears and fish-eating birds, who were beginning to be deprived of a major element of their diet, now profit by the upsurge in the number of fish available.

There are about 20 species of fish in the Greater Yellowstone Ecosystem. The types of sport fish most common to Yellowstone's waters are native **cutthroat trout** (*Oncorhynchus clarki)* and four introduced species: **rainbow trout** (*Oncorhynchus mykiss)*, **brown trout** (*Salmo trutta,* brought in 1890 from Scotland and Germany), **brook trout** (*Salvelinus fontinalis)*, and **lake trout** (*Salvelinus namaycush)*. Two less common native fish are **mountain whitefish** (*Prosopium williamsoni*) and **Montana grayling** (*Thymallus arcticus montanus*).

Fisheries in Trouble

Yellowstone's fisheries currently face four problems: predation by lake trout, tapeworms, whirling disease, and the New Zealand mud snail invasion.

Lake trout

On the wall of the museum at Fishing Bridge hangs one of the largest fish ever caught in the park, a 37-pound (17-kg) lake trout pulled from Heart Lake in 1935. Although some larger lakes of southern Yellowstone were stocked with lake trout, these large predator trout were never known to live in Yellowstone Lake until a few years ago. In Yellowstone Lake, they have the capability to wipe out the lake's population of cutthroat trout, a consequence that would have a huge impact on grizzly bears, eagles, and pelicans.

The problem is being studied. Crews have gillnetted more than 20,000, and other remedies are being sought, but it's unlikely that all lake trout can ever be removed from the lake. Meanwhile, anglers must keep all lake trout they catch and bring them to a ranger for verification.

Diseases and an invasion

The tapeworm (*Diphyllobothrium* sp. in larval stage) is a parasite that has been found here since before Yellowstone was a park. It is passed back and forth between the mammals and birds on land and the fish and crustaceans in water. Fortunately, tapeworms are harmless to man after the fish is cooked, although finding worms is unaesthetic. For reasons not yet understood, fish from Yellowstone Lake were found to have fewer tapeworms in the years after the 1988 fires. The large older cutthroat are the most likely to be infected, but no one is allowed to keep these according to present regulations.

Whirling disease is a relatively recent development. It's caused by a parasite in another type of worm (the *Tubifex* worm) eaten by trout. Over 20 states have reported incidences of the disease. Although the parasite has recently been detected in older trout from two tributaries of Yellowstone Lake, whirling disease has not shown any proven population impact on Yellowstone cutthroat so far.

The New Zealand mud snail (*Potomoprygus antipodarum*) reproduces so fast that it occupies habitat at an alarming rate. It can reach a density of 30,000 per square foot and could conceivably become a problem to the fish. It has been found in the Madison River and its tributaries.

The Fires of 1988
and What They Taught Us

"Fire Rages Through Yellowstone Park!" screamed the headlines. Conflagrations throughout the greater Yellowstone area in 1988 led to a fire fighting effort that was the largest in American history. It was widely covered in all forms of media from July to September. Twenty-five thousand people confronted the fires and over $120 million was spent. When snow finally quenched the last flames, everyone had an opinion as to whether park managers had acted responsibly or had ineptly let a natural treasure be destroyed.

Fire threatens Old Faithful Village, 1988.

What happened in 1988?
Here are a few facts about the fires:
- For the park's first 100 years, fires were suppressed, but fire fighting methods became truly effective only after World War II.
- In 1988, nearly 800,000 acres (3240 sq km) were affected by the fires; that is, about 36 percent of Yellowstone's 2.2 million acres (8910 sq km). Of the total acreage burned, about 41 percent was severe *canopy burn*, meaning the

tops and branches of trees were burned, trunks partially consumed, and ground cover turned to ash. This calculates to 15 percent of Yellowstone's territory having suffered severe burn.

- Remarkably, no one was killed in the park during the fires, although there were some injuries. However, in fire-related accidents in October, a small craft pilot died in a crash near Jackson, and a firefighter in Shoshone National Forest was killed by a falling snag.

- Of the park's large animals, only elk died in any significant numbers in the fires; 257 elk, but only 9 bison, 4 deer, and 2 moose are known to have perished. Most animals remained calm and continued to graze near the fires.

- Sixty-seven buildings were lost in the greater Yellowstone area, 22 of them at Old Faithful.

- Of the more than 40 different Greater Yellowstone Ecosystem fires that year, three human-caused fires burned into the park, including the most destructive one by far, the North Fork fire. It began accidentally near a tiny creek called North Fork in Targhee National Forest, just 200 yards outside the park's western boundary.

What parts of the park burned?

The map shows the nine large fires. You can see from the map that if you enter Yellowstone at the north or west, see only the western parts of the Grand Loop Road, and exit at the south (or vice versa), you'll feel that the park was truly devastated in 1988. If you include other parts of the park in your trip, only a small part may cross burned forest. If you spend more than a day or two, you may well forget the snags and fallen timber and appreciate the lush undergrowth of small

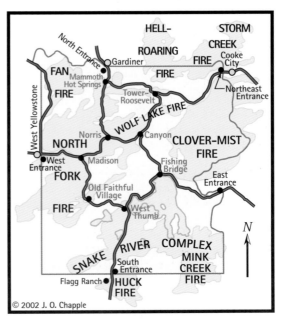

Map adapted with permission from the book Yellowstone on Fire!, *Billings Gazette, 1989.*

The Fires of 1988

lodgepoles, grasses, and wildflowers. The fires have even revealed more wildlife and opened up mountain vistas that visitors couldn't see before.

Particles in the air from natural fires in September 1996 contributed to the beauty of this sunrise scene.

What was learned from the fires?

James M. Ridenour, Director of the National Park Service from 1989 to 1993, summed up his feelings about the fires this way:

> There are two things that need clearing up. First, the Park Service, in cooperation with other government agencies, fought those fires aggressively. True, they may have started the fight a little slowly, but as soon as the fires escalated the firefighting effort grew intense.
>
> Given the intensity of the fires coupled with hot, dry weather and gusting winds, there was little the world's best firefighters could do to control this inferno. The fire was jumping normal firebreaks and leap-frogging ahead as much as half a mile. You couldn't build a firebreak big enough to stop it no matter how many bulldozers you had.
>
> The second and more important point is that the fires wouldn't have been so intense if there hadn't been so much forest litter on the forest floor. You won't get the really big fire if little fires have burned through and consumed the downed limbs and fallen trees. Periodic fires keep these fuel sources down.
>
> So after all the bitter argument, the answer still is that fires are a necessary part of our ecosystem and always have been. Yellowstone burned many times before man ever set eyes on it. There has to be coordination among agencies and strict guidelines as to when and where fires will be allowed to burn, but fighting all fires aggressively from day one would be a very expensive proposition as well as a mistake in terms of the health of the forest.
>
> —from *The National Parks Compromised: Pork Barrel Politics and America's Treasures*, 1994. Used with permission.

Strategies developed since 1988 include:

- continuing efforts to prevent human-caused fires
- detecting fires from three lookout stations (on Mounts Washburn, Holmes, and Sheridan)
- detecting fires by air after severe lightning storms
- allowing certain lightning-caused fires to burn
- igniting occasional controlled backcountry fires to reduce fuel buildup
- protecting human life, property, and designated resources, and
- suppressing all other wildfires as safely and cost-effectively as possible.

Judging from tree ring studies that show the last burn of this size was about 300 years ago, biologists conclude that the age of a forest is the most significant factor in the accumulation of fuel load that invites such a fire, regardless of human fire suppression efforts.

As Paul Schullery and John D. Varley wrote in an article evaluating the effects of the fires on Yellowstone's fish: "Where once the old rule of 'Scenery is greenery' held everywhere, now people are confronted with nature's long view: wildland, in order to remain wild, does things to itself that seem shocking to us. It has all the time in the world to regenerate and maintain itself. It scars and heals itself on a scale of centuries, and with no regard for the much briefer scale of a human lifespan."

TRAVEL TIPS

When you enter the park, you'll receive the official Yellowstone Park newspaper, *Yellowstone Today*, along with a map. The newspaper includes a half page or more of regulations and other useful information, including suggestions for your safety. Quoted below in "A to Z Information" are some of these regulations from *Yellowstone Today*, as well as other tips to help you plan your trip.

For backcountry camping, bicycling, boating, and fishing, special regulations apply and are available in full at ranger stations and visitor centers. In advance of your visit, you may obtain information from the superintendent's office at park headquarters (see the contact information in "Useful Addresses & Phone Numbers," after the A to Z listings).

The chart of all Yellowstone facilities on page 356 tells you at a glance where gasoline, food, lodging, and other services are available within the park.

A TO Z INFORMATION

Altitude sickness. Since Yellowstone's elevation averages about 8000 feet (2400 m) above sea level, visitors of any age may suffer from this condition. Minor symptoms, such as shortness of breath or loss of appetite, will usually disappear in a few days, but more serious problems, including nosebleeds, muscle pain, nausea, or rapid heartbeat, should be treated, especially if moving to a lower altitude does not seem to help. (See Medical Services below.)

Bicycling. "Bicycling is permitted on established public roads, parking areas, and designated routes. There are no bicycle paths along roadways. Bicycles are prohibited on backcountry trails and boardwalks." Listed in a brochure available at visitor centers are the designated trails for bicycling. In this guidebook, they are indicated with a bicycle symbol. Please note that most park roads are far from ideal for bicycling, since they are narrow, winding, sometimes steep, and they lack bike lanes.

Boating. Permitted on park lakes (except for Sylvan, Eleanor, and Twin lakes and Beach Springs Lagoon); motorized boating restricted to Yellowstone and Lewis lakes. Personal watercraft are not allowed on any Yellowstone waters, nor are boats exceeding 40 feet (12 m) in length or exceeding a noise level of 82 decibels (measured at 85 ft/26 m from the vessel). A Coast Guard-approved life vest is required for each person boating.

Quoting Y.N.P. Boating Regulations: "A permit is required for all vessels, including float tubes. Permits may be obtained at the following locations: South Entrance, Lewis Lake Campground, Grant Village Backcountry Office, Bridge Bay Marina and Lake Ranger Station. Non-motorized boating permits only are available at the Canyon and Mammoth backcountry offices, Bechler Ranger

Station, and West and Northeast entrances." Boating fees for motorized vessels are $20 (annual) or $10 (10-day); for non-motorized vessels it's $10 (annual) or $5 (10-day).

Boats are not allowed on rivers and streams, except that hand-propelled vessels may use the channel between Lewis and Shoshone Lakes. Detailed regulations are given with permits. Only non-motorized boats are allowed in the most remote sections of the three so-called fingers of the lake: Flat Mountain Arm, South Arm, and Southeast Arm. This is primarily to protect the nesting pelicans, terns, and seagulls.

Camping. Yellowstone has 11 campgounds and one recreational vehicle park. Sites in 4 campgrounds and the Fishing Bridge RV Park may be reserved in advance, but the other 7 campgrounds are available on a first-come, first-served basis. Campground use fees range between $10 and $15; RV park, $27. In July and August, all campgrounds in the park may be full by noon. You'll find Forest Service and privately operated campgrounds along all the roads that approach the park.

For backcountry camping, you must obtain a free permit at a ranger station or visitor center no more than 48 hours before you set out. If you wish to reserve a backcountry campsite in advance, you must pay a $20 fee. The booklet "Beyond Road's End" (obtainable from park headquarters) provides excellent backcountry information and advice.

Collecting specimens. Removing any specimens from Yellowstone is illegal. Look around you as much as you like, but take only pictures. Yellowstone and everything in it belongs to all the people.

Drinking water. It's safe in park villages and campgrounds, but water from streams and lakes cannot be guaranteed safe for drinking and must be boiled. Boiling is more effective than chemical treatment against the diarrhea-causing parasite *giardia*, which has been found in park waters.

Driving. The speed limit throughout the park is **45 mph (72 km/h)**, less where posted. Watch for animals and pedestrians. "Animal jams" are common, particularly when a bear, bison, elk, or bighorn sheep is on or near the road. Some roads are full of potholes and most are quite narrow.

Emergency telephone number. Call **911** for emergency medical, fire, or ranger response.

Entrance fees. The cost to enter the park in a private automobile is $20, good for seven days. An individual arriving on foot, on skis, or by bike pays $10 for the same period. Various types of annual passes are available. Keep your admission receipt, because you'll need it to reenter the park.

Fishing. Permitted in most Yellowstone streams and lakes, but a permit must be purchased and regulations followed. Permits cost $10 for ten days or $20 for the season. Children under 12 years of age may fish without a permit when supervised by an adult; children ages 12 through 15 must obtain a free permit.

Pick up a copy of the fishing regulations from any visitor center, ranger station, or marina in the park, or from one of the sporting goods stores in gateway communities. You are responsible for following the regulations and being able to measure your fish and identify the different species. All native sport fish species now come under catch-and-release-only rules. If you'll be fishing in Montana, Wyoming, or Idaho waters outside park boundaries, you'll need to purchase a state fishing license. (See the last section in the "Living Things" chapter for more about fish and fishing.)

Geyser basin walks. Before you set out on a walk, especially one around the geyser basins, take a few precautions to make your visit enjoyable.

The sun at this elevation can be brutal, especially between 10 AM and 4 PM, so provide yourself with a hat, a long-sleeved shirt, and sunscreen lotion. Be prepared with rain gear for the rainstorms and even hail that can come up quickly in any mountain environment, especially during the late afternoons. Take your own drinking water; there is none along the walkways.

Neither pets nor smoking are allowed in the geyser basins. The only rest rooms near most routes through the geyser basins are in the parking lots.

Photographers and anyone who wears eyeglasses should know that the spray from geysers contains silica, which can damage glass. Wipe off lenses and eyeglasses immediately if they are dampened by spray.

Park regulations state: "You must stay on the walkways and designated trails." Be sure to watch small children vigilantly. Geyserite formations are extremely brittle and can easily break through, and even pools that do not look very hot may scald you!

Hiking. Hiking in Yellowstone can mean anything from going a few hundred yards from your car to spending a week backpacking in the remotest backcountry. Although this guidebook does not include backcountry information, parts of longer backcountry trails are included here when they're not difficult and are particularly interesting.

The chart of 59 Recommended Short Walks in Yellowstone, starting on page 357, may help you plan hikes according to what part of the park you are visiting and how much time you have. It shows the approximate distance and elevation change for each walk. Marked in the road logs and on the accompanying maps with the symbols 🚶 or 🚶, these walks are recommended to anyone who wants to get away from the roads to see something fun, but especially for non-athletes, older people, and families with young children. The symbol 📖 indicates that the Yellowstone Association has printed a self-guiding pamphlet, available both at a visitor center and at the start of the walk.

Most of these recommended walks involve round trips of less than 5 miles (8 km) and are not too steep. They have no stream crossings by ford or wobbly log. The chart does not include walks that lead less than one-half mile (0.8 km) from a road.

Horseback riding. Horses are available at Canyon, Mammoth, and Tower-Roosevelt for hire from the park concessionaire.

Horsepackers. For horsepacking trips, you must obtain a backcountry permit and follow regulations available from the National Park Service.

Information sources. Ranger-interpreters answer questions, present evening amphitheater programs, and lead daytime hikes. Employees of the concessionaire provide guided bus tours and evening talks in some hotels. Books, maps, videos, and audio tours are available in visitor centers and at shops and in park villages. The Yellowstone Association prints pamphlets about several hydrothermal areas and erects interpretive signs throughout the park.

Lodging. Accommodations may fill up long before you want to visit, so it's wise to reserve several months in advance. Plan stays in more than one campground or lodging to facilitate seeing more and driving less. All hotels and cabins are reserved through AmFac Parks and Resorts. Some restaurants require reservations, too. A chart of all Yellowstone facilities is on page 356. For contact information, see "Useful Addresses & Phone Numbers" later in this chapter.

Maps. We recommend the following maps for hiking or simply learning more about Yellowstone.

Yellowstone Series Trail Maps are four maps based on U.S.G.S. 15-minute topos. (Evergreen, CO: Trails Illustrated); excellent references for all but backcountry hiking.

Yellowstone Park: Current Trails, Backcountry Campsites, North and South sections (Salt Lake City, UT: American Adventures Association); good for park details, including activity information on the reverse side.

U.S.G.S. 7-1/2-minute topographic maps of all of Yellowstone Park, available at some Yellowstone visitor centers, at bookstores and outfitting stores, or from: U.S. Geological Survey, Map Distribution, Building 41, Box 25286, Federal Center, Denver, CO 80225; strongly recommended for backcountry hiking.

Geological Map of Yellowstone National Park (Bozeman, MT: Montana State University, Dept. of Earth Sciences); explains Yellowstone geology in technical detail.

Medical services. Mammoth Hot Springs Village has a clinic open all year. Open in summer only are the clinic at Old Faithful Village and the hospital and pharmacy at Lake Village.

Pets. "Pets must be leashed. They are prohibited on any trails, in the backcountry, and in thermal basins. Pets are not allowed more than 100 feet from a road or parking area. Leaving a pet unattended and/or tied to an object is prohibited." AmFac accommodations brochures add: "Pets are not allowed in the hotel rooms; however, dogs and cats are permitted in the cabin facilities if quiet and housebroken. Pets may not be left unattended." Consider seriously whether it might be best to leave your pet at home.

Picnic areas and rest rooms. All picnic areas have tables and well-maintained rest rooms, but many do not have water. The toilets are usually of the vault (outhouse) or chemical type and are indicated in the road logs by the symbol 🚻.

Ranger stations. Go to a ranger station for backcountry camping, boating, and fishing permits, or to report a problem. There are two kinds of rangers in Yellowstone, ranger-interpreters and law enforcement rangers. The emergency phone number **911** works in the park.

Rock climbing. Rock climbing is dangerous and not recommended in Yellowstone. It is illegal in the Grand Canyon of the Yellowstone.

Swimming. There are no swimming pools in Yellowstone. "Swimming or bathing is prohibited in thermal pools or streams where water flows entirely from a thermal spring or pool." River, stream, and lake water is very cold and may contain organisms dangerous to your health.

Swimming is allowed in a few places where river and hot spring water mix naturally. Two of them are the Firehole River along Firehole Canyon Drive and a site called Boiling River in the Gardner River near Mammoth Hot Springs.

Telephones. A few are located in visitor centers, lodgings, and restaurants. Gradually, more antenna towers for cellular phones are being erected in the park.

Theft and vandalism. Both crimes have become more prevalent as the number of visitors has increased. Lock your car doors, and keep all valuables out of sight.

Yellowstone's supporting organizations

Yellowstone Association. A non-profit organization that provides funding to the park in support of educational, historical, and scientific projects. One ongoing project is the Yellowstone Institute, through which adults and families may study wildlife, wildflowers, Yellowstone history, geology, ecology, and many other topics with experts in their fields, or participate in guided hikes and horseback trips.

A special facility at the Lamar Buffalo Ranch is the headquarters, classroom, and housing for people attending Yellowstone Institute classes. To inquire about membership in the Yellowstone Association or for details about the classes, see any visitor center in the park; write The Yellowstone Association,

P.O. Box 117, Yellowstone National Park, WY 82190; call (307) 344-2294; or visit their Web site: www.YellowstoneAssociation.org.

Yellowstone Park Foundation. A non-profit organization dedicated to raising money for projects that protect, preserve, and enhance the park. The foundation funds such projects as the Wolf Restoration Project and the restoration of native cutthroat trout to Yellowstone. For further information or to send a tax-deductible gift, write: The Yellowstone Park Foundation, 37 East Main Street, Suite 4, Bozeman, MT 59715; phone: (406) 586-6303; Web site: www.ypf.org.

Greater Yellowstone Coalition. An umbrella organization of conservation groups. Members keep informed about many issues affecting the Yellowstone ecosystem. They are located at 13 South Willson, Suite 2, Bozeman; their mailing address is: P.O. Box 1874, Bozeman, MT 59771; phone: (406) 586-1593; Web site: www.greateryellowstone.org.

Geyser Observation and Study Association. GOSA is an organization of people who observe, record, and exchange information about geysers year round, including geysers elsewhere in the world. Visit their Web site at www.geyserstudy.org. For information about joining the organization and to subscribe to the bimonthly *Geyser Gazer Sput*, write: GOSA Store and Press, c/o Udo and Janet Freund, 39237 Yellowstone Street, Palmdale, CA 93551-4155; e-mail: gosastore@qnet.com.

National Parks Conservation Association. Founded more than 80 years ago, NPCA works to help the National Park Service fulfill its mission of preserving the natural and cultural resources of all national parks "for the enjoyment, education, and inspiration of this and future generations." Membership includes a subscription to their monthly magazine. Their address is: 1300 Nineteenth Street N.W., Suite 300, Washington, DC 20036; phone: (202) 223-6722; Web site: www.npca.org.

USEFUL ADDRESSES & PHONE NUMBERS

NOTE: Since Web addresses change frequently, we cannot guarantee them. The sites listed here were valid at the time of publication.

The **National Park Service Headquarters** in Yellowstone provides information about the park. You can leave your name and address at (307) 344-2111 to have a N.P.S. planning kit mailed to you; write to P.O. Box 168, Yellowstone National Park, WY 82190; phone (307) 344-7381; or see the N.P.S. Yellowstone web pages at www.nps.gov/yell.

Contact **Xanterra Parks and Resorts** to reserve park lodgings and sites at some campgrounds. Write to P.O. Box 165, Yellowstone National Park, WY 82190; phone (307) 344-7311; or visit their Web site at www.ynp-lodges.com.

State recreation and tourism offices

Idaho Parks and Recreation Dept., P.O. Box 83720, Boise, ID 83720-0065; phone: (800) 635-7820 or (208) 334-4199; Web site: www.idahoparks.org.

Montana Travel Promotion Division, P.O. Box 200533, Helena, MT 59620; phone: (800) 847-4868 or (406) 444-2654; Web site: visitmt.com.

Wyoming Division of Tourism, I-25 at College Dr., Cheyenne, WY 82002; phone: (800) 225-5996 or (307) 777-7777; Web site: wyomingtourism.org.

Chambers of Commerce

Big Sky: P.O. Box 160100, Big Sky, MT 59716; phone: (406) 995-3000 or (800) 943-4111; Web site: www.bigskychamber.com.

Billings: 815 S. 27th St. or P.O. Box 31177, Billings, MT 59107; phone: (406) 245-4111 or (800) 735-2635; Web site: www.billingscvb.visitmt.com.

Bozeman: 2000 Commerce Way, Bozeman, MT 59715; phone: (406) 586-5421 or (800) 228-4224; Web site: www.bozemanchamber.com.

Cody: 836 Sheridan Ave. or P.O. Box 2777, Cody, WY 82414; phone: (307) 587-2777; Web site: www.codychamber.org.

Cooke City & Silver Gate: P.O. Box 1071, Cooke City, MT 59020; phone: (406) 838-2495.

Dubois: 616 W. Ramshorn St. or P.O. Box 632, Dubois, WY 82513; phone: (307) 455-2556; Web site: www.dteworld.com/duboiscc.

Gardiner: P.O. Box 81, Gardiner, MT 59030; phone: (406) 848-7971; Web site: www.gardinerchamber.com.

Idaho Falls: 505 Lindsay Blvd. or P.O. Box 50498, Idaho Falls, ID 83402; phone: (208) 523-1010 or (800) 634-3246.

Island Park: P.O. Box 83, Island Park, ID 83429; phone: (208) 558-7755; Web site: www.ida.net/org/ip/ip.htm; or East Idaho Visitor Info, phone: (800) 634-3246.

Jackson: 532 N. Cache St. or P.O. Box 550, Jackson, WY 83001; phone: (307) 733-3316; Web site: www.jacksonholechamber.com.

Livingston: 303 E. Park St., Livingston, MT 59047; phone: (406) 222-0850; Web site: www.yellowstone-chamber.com.

Red Lodge: 601 N. Broadway or P.O. Box 988, Red Lodge, MT 59068; phone: (406) 446-1718; Web site: www.redlodge.com.

West Yellowstone: 100 Yellowstone Ave. or P.O. Box 458, W. Yellowstone, MT 59758; phone: (406) 646-7701; for motel reservations, (406) 646-9488; Web site: www.westyellowstonechamber.com.

U.S.D.A. Forest Service headquarters

Six national forests, administered by the Forest Service under the Department of Agriculture, either border Yellowstone Park or are very nearby. Ranger districts are listed here with phone numbers under their respective national forests if they are near the Yellowstone approach roads.

Beaverhead N.F., phone: (406) 683-3900; Madison Ranger District, phone: (406) 682-4253.

Bridger-Teton N.F., phone: (307) 739-5500.

Caribou-Targhee N.F., phone: (208) 524-7600; Ashton Ranger District (for Mesa Falls Scenic Area), phone: (208) 652-7442.

Custer N.F., phone: (406) 657-6200; Beartooth Ranger District, phone: (406) 446-2103.

Gallatin N.F., phone: (406) 587-6701; Bozeman Ranger District, phone: (406) 522-2520; Gardiner Ranger District, phone: (406) 848-7375; Hebgen Lake/Earthquake Lake areas, phone: (406) 823-6961; Livingston District, phone: (406) 222-1892.

Shoshone N.F., phone, (307) 527-6241; Clarks Fork and Wapiti Ranger Districts, phone: (307) 527-6921.

METRIC CONVERSIONS

Yellowstone National Park speed limit is 45 miles per hour (72 kilometers per hour).

1 km/hr = 0.6214 (5/8) mile/hr
1 mile/hr = 1.6093 km/hr

1 meter = 3.28 feet
1 kilometer = 0.6214 (about 5/8) mile

1 foot = 0.3048 meter
1 yard = 0.9144 meter
1 mile = 1.6093 kilometers

To convert temperatures:
From degrees Fahrenheit: subtract 32, multiply by 5, divide by 9 = degrees Celsius
From degrees Celsius: multiply by 9, divide by 5, add 32 = degrees Fahrenheit

FACILITIES IN YELLOWSTONE

Village or Junction	ATM	Auto Services[a]	Boat Ramps	Cafeteria/Restaurants	Campgrounds[b]	Gift Shops	Groceries/Fishing Supplies[c]	Laundry (Self-Service)	Lodging	Medical Clinic[d]	Nature/Photo Shops[e]	Post Office	Ranger Station[f]	Showers (Public)	Visitor Center[g]
Bridge Bay			x		x		x						x		
Canyon Village	2x	x		5x	x	x	x	x	x	x	x	x	x	x	x
Fishing Bridge	x	x		x	RVs only		x	x					x	x	x
Grant Village	x	x	x	4x	x	x	2x	x	x		x	x	x	x	x
Lake Village	x			3x		2x	x	x	x	x	x	x			
Mammoth Hot Springs	2x	x		3x	x	x	x		x	x	x	x	x		x
Old Faithful Village	3x	x		6x		2x	2x	x	x	x	x	x	x	x	x
Tower-Roosevelt		x		3x	x	x	2x	x	x		x	x	x	x	

a) Mammoth and Tower junctions have gasoline but not general auto services.
b) Additional campgrounds are at Madison and Norris junctions, as well as 4 other locations.
c) Bridge Bay has a mini-store only.
d) Lake Village has a hospital.
e) Film may be developed at Canyon, Fishing Bridge, and Old Faithful.
f) Mammoth has the backcountry and law enforcement ranger headquarters.
g) Most visitor centers are open 8 AM to 7 PM; info/book centers from 9 AM to 5 PM. Madison, Norris, and West Thumb junctions have small info/book centers only.

59 RECOMMENDED SHORT WALKS IN YELLOWSTONE

Name and Type of Walk	Round Trip or Loop Distance	Elevation Change	Road Log Mileage	Map Page
NORTHWEST CORNER (U.S. 191)				
Part of Fan Creek Trail	4 mi (6.4 km)	150 ft (45 m)	9.3/11.2	24
WEST ENTRANCE TO MADISON JCT.				
Two Ribbons Nature Trail 🦽	0.75 mi (1.2 km)	Level	3.0/10.9	32
Harlequin Lake	0.5 mi (0.8 km)	100 ft (30 m)	12.1/1.8	32
MADISON JCT. TO OLD FAITHFUL VILLAGE				
Sentinel Meadow Trail (extension of Fountain Flats Dr.)	4.4 mi (7 km)	120 ft (36 m)	5.6/11.4	40
Fountain Paint Pot Loop (partly 🦽) 🚲	0.5 mi (0.8 km)	50 ft (15 m)	8.0/9.0	40
Midway Geyser Basin Loop	0.6 mi (1 km)	50 ft (15 m)	9.9/7.1	40
Mystic Falls	3.5 mi (5.6 km)	100 ft (30 m)	13.8/3.2	77
Black Sand Basin Loop	1 mi (1.6 km)	Level	15.4/1.6	77
OLD FAITHFUL VILLAGE				
Part of Mallard Lake Trail	0.5 mi (0.8 km)	50 ft (15 m)		77
Geyser Hill and Beyond 🚲	3.5 mi (5.6 km)	50 ft (15 m)		77
Observation Point 🚲	0.5 mi (0.8 km)	150 ft (45 m)		77
Extension to Biscuit Basin 🚲	1.6 mi (2.6 km)	50 ft (15 m)		77
Castle & Daisy Geysers 🦽 🚲 🚲	2.4 mi (3.9 km)	Almost level		77
Extension to Black Sand Pool 🚲	1 mi (1.6 km)	100 ft (30 m)		77

	Distance	Elevation		Page
OLD FAITHFUL VILLAGE TO WEST THUMB JCT.				
Lone Star Geyser 🚲	4.5 mi (7.2 km)	Level	4.2/15.2	98
SOUTH ENTRANCE TO WEST THUMB JCT.				
Moose Falls	2 mi (3.2 km)	100 ft (30 m)	0.2/21.3	120
Riddle Lake	4.5 mi (7.2 km)	Level	17.4/4.1	120
WEST THUMB JCT. TO FISHING BRIDGE JCT.				
Yellowstone Lake Overlook Loop	2 mi (3.2 km)	400 ft (120 m)	0.2/20.4	132
West Thumb Geyser Basin Loop ♿ 🧒	0.5 mi (0.8 km)	Almost level	0.2/20.4	132
Natural Bridge 🚲	2 mi (3.2 km)	60 ft (18 m)	16.9/3.7	130
Lakeshore at Lake Village to Fishing Bridge	2 mi (3.2 km)	Level		141
EAST ENTRANCE TO FISHING BRIDGE JCT.				
Storm Point Nature Trail	2 mi (3.2 km)	Almost level	22.9/3.1	154
Pelican Creek Nature Trail	1 mi (1.6 km)	Level	24.6/1.4	154
FISHING BRIDGE JCT. TO CANYON JCT.				
Mud Volcano Boardwalk Loop (partly ♿) 🧒	1 mi (1.6 km)	150 ft (45 m)	5.8/9.6	164
CANYON AREA				
Uncle Tom's Trail 🧒	1 mi (1.6 km)	300 ft (90 m)		171
Clear Lake 🧒	2 mi (3.2 km)	100 ft (30 m)		171
Canyon Rim east of Artists' Point 🧒	3 mi/4.8 km	100 ft (30 m)		171
Crystal Falls 🧒	0.5 mi (0.8 km)	Almost level		171
Grand View 🧒	1 mi (1.6 km)	Level		171

Walk	Distance	Elevation	Mi	Page
Part of 7-Mile Hole Tr. (waterfall view) [icon]	2.5 mi (4 km)	Level		171
Red Rock Point (close to Lower Falls) [icon]	1 mi (1.6 km)	500 ft (150 m)	North Rim Dr.	171
Brink of (Lower) Falls [icon]	1 mi (1.6 km)	600 ft (180 m)	North Rim Dr.	171
NORTHEAST ENTRANCE TO TOWER-ROOSEVELT JCT.				
Part of Pebble Creek Trail (geologic formation)	0.5 mi (0.8 km)	Level	9.7/18.9	192
Trout Lake	1 mi (1.6 km)	200 ft (60 m)	10.9/17.7	192
Part of Lamar Valley Trail (historic remnants)	1.6 mi (2.6 km)	Almost level	14.0/14.6	192
Part of Slough Creek Trail	4 mi (6.4 km)	400 ft (120 m)	22.8/5.8	192
Part of Specimen Ridge Trail	3 mi (5 km)	150 ft (45 m)	27.4/1.2	192
TOWER-ROOSEVELT JCT. TO CANYON JCT.				
Roosevelt Lodge: Lost Creek Falls	0.6 mi (1 km)	150 ft (45 m)		206
Base of Tower Fall	1 mi (1.6 km)	250 ft (75 m)	2.5/15.8	206
Part of Mt. Washburn Trail (wildflowers)	1 mi (1.6 km)	200 ft (60 m)	13.3/5.0	206
Cascade Lake	4.4 mi (7.1 km)	Almost level	17.0/1.3	206
CANYON JCT. TO NORRIS JCT.				
Little Gibbon Falls	2 mi (3.2 km)	100 ft (30 m)	7.9/3.7	219
Ice Lake [icon]	0.6 mi (1 km)	Level	8.2/3.4	219
NORRIS GEYSER BASIN [icon]				
Back Basin Loop (partly [icon])	1.5 mi (2.4 km)	70 ft (21 m)		223
Porcelain Basin West Loop	0.5 mi (0.8 km)	100 ft (30 m)		223
Porcelain Basin East Loop (partly [icon])	0.5 mi (0.8 km)	70 ft (21 m)		223

North Entrance to Mammoth Hot Springs Jct.

Boiling River	1 mi (1.6 km)	Level	3.0/2.3	242

Mammoth Hot Springs

Beaver Ponds Loop	6 mi (9.6 km)	500 ft (150 m)		251
Lower Terrace Boardwalk, Part I 🄰	0.5 mi (0.8 km)	100 ft (30 m)		257

Mammoth Jct. to Norris Jct.

Upper Terrace Drive 🄰	1.6 mi (2.6 km)	150 ft (45 m)	2.0/19.0	257
Snow Pass	5 mi (8 km)	700 ft (210 m)	2.0/19.0	257
Part of the Howard Eaton Trail (above Mammoth) 🚲	2 mi (3.2 km)	150 ft (45 m)	4.8/16.2	270
Service Road south of Swan Lake 🚲	2 mi (3.2 km)	Level	7.5/13.5	270
Indian Creek Campground: Superintendent's Road 🚲	1.5 mi (2.4 km)	Level	8.6/12.4	270

Norris Jct. to Madison Jct.

Artists' Paintpots	1.5 mi (2.4 km)	100 ft (30 m)	4.2/9.1	280

Mammoth Jct. to Tower Jct.

Wraith Falls	1 mi (1.6 km)	Level	5.0/13.1	286
Hidden Falls on Blacktail Deer Creek	7 mi (11 km)	580 ft (175 m)	6.8/11.3	286
Self-Guiding Fire Trail ♿	0.6 mi (1 km)	Level	8.3/9.8	286
Part of Lost Lake Trail	1.8 (3 km)	Almost level	16.7/1.4	286

Walk Symbols

🚲 Biking allowed
♿ Wheelchair accessible
🄰 Self-Guiding Trail pamphlet available

BOOKS ABOUT YELLOWSTONE

SUGGESTED READING

Birds, Fish, and Mammals

Charlton, Robert E. *Yellowstone Fishing Guide: The Complete Guide to Fishing Yellowstone Waters.* Ketchum, Idaho: Lost River Press, 1995.

Herrero, Stephen. *Bear Attacks: Their Causes & Avoidance.* New York: Lyons Press, 1985.

McEneaney, Terry, and Karen McEneaney. *Birds of Yellowstone.* Boulder, CO: Roberts Rinehart Publishers, 1988.

Parks, Richard. *Fishing Yellowstone National Park.* Helena, MT: Falcon Publishing, Inc., 1998.

Schullery, Paul. *The Bears of Yellowstone.* Worland, WY: High Plains Publishing Co., 1992.

Scott, Douglas M., and A. Suvi. *Wildlife of Yellowstone and Grand Teton National Parks.* Salt Lake City: Wheelwright Press, 1988.

Varley, John D., and Paul Schullery. *Yellowstone Fishes: Ecology, History, & Angling in the Park.* Mechanicsburg, PA: Stackpole Books, 1998.

Wilkinson, Todd. Photographer: Michael H. Francis. *Yellowstone & Grand Teton National Parks: Wildlife Watcher's Guide.* Minnetonka, MN: Creative Publishing International, 1999.

Flowers and Microorganisms

Brock, Thomas D. *Life at High Temperatures.* Yellowstone National Park, WY: Yellowstone Association for Natural Science, History & Education, 1994.

Phillips, H. Wayne. *Central Rocky Mountain Wildflowers.* Helena, MT: Falcon Publishing, Inc., 1999.

Geology

Fritz, William J. *Roadside Geology of the Yellowstone Country.* Missoula, MT: Mountain Press Publishing, 1985.

Good, John M., and Kenneth L. Pierce. *Interpreting the Landscapes of Grand Teton and Yellowstone National Parks.* Moose, WY: Grand Teton Natural History Association, 1996.

Schreier, Carl. *Field Guide to Yellowstone's Geysers, Hot Springs and Fumaroles,* 2nd rev. ed. Moose, WY: Homestead Publishing, 1992.

Smith, Robert B., and Lee J. Siegel. *Windows into the Earth: The Geologic Story of Yellowstone & Grand Teton National Parks.* London: Oxford University Press, 2000.

Hiking and Backcountry Camping

Adkison, Ron. *Exploring Beyond Yellowstone.* Berkeley, CA: Wilderness Press, 1996.

Bach, Orville, Jr. *Exploring the Yellowstone Backcountry: A Guide to the Hiking Trails of Yellowstone with Additional Sections on Canoeing, Bicycling, and Cross-country Skiing.* San Francisco: Sierra Club Books, 1998.

Evans, Lisa Gollin. *An Outdoor Family Guide to Yellowstone & Grand Teton National Parks.* Seattle: Mountaineers Books, 1996.

Marschall, Mark C. *Yellowstone Trails: A Hiking Guide.* Yellowstone National Park, WY: The Yellowstone Association, 1995.

Schneider, Bill. *Hiking Yellowstone National Park.* Helena, MT: Falcon Publishing, Inc., 1997.

Schreier, Carl. *Hiking Yellowstone Trails.* Moose, WY: Homestead Publishing, 1997.

History

Bartlett, Richard A. *Yellowstone: A Wilderness Besieged.* Tucson, AZ: University of Arizona Press, 1985.

Bonney, Orrin H. and Lorraine Bonney. *Battle Drums & Geysers.* Vol. 2, *Discovery & Exploration of Yellowstone: Doane's Journal.* Houston: Bonney, 1970.

Haines, Aubrey L. *The Yellowstone Story*, 2nd rev. ed. 2 vols. Boulder, CO: University Press of Colorado, 1996.

———. *Yellowstone Place Names: Mirrors of History.* Niwot, CO: University Press of Colorado, 1996.

Whittlesey, Lee H. *Death in Yellowstone.* Boulder, CO: Roberts Rinehart Publishers, 1995.

———. *Yellowstone Place Names.* Helena, MT: Montana Historical Society Press, 1988 (new edition in press).

Photography

Meagher, Mary and Douglas B. Houston. *Yellowstone and the Biology of Time: Photographs Across a Century.* Norman, OK: University of Oklahoma Press, 1998.

Schreier, Carl. *Yellowstone: Selected Photographs.* Moose, WY: Homestead Publishing, 1989.

Whittlesey, Lee H., comp. *A Yellowstone Album: A Photographic Celebration of the First National Park.* Boulder, CO: Roberts Rinehart Publishers, 1997.

Specialized Guides

Bryan, T. Scott. *The Geysers of Yellowstone*, 3rd ed. Boulder, CO: University Press of Colorado, 2001.

Eversman, Sharon and Mary Carr. *Yellowstone Ecology: A Road Guide*. Missoula, MT: Mountain Press Publishing, 1992.

Rubinstein, Paul, Lee H. Whittlesey, and Mike Stevens. *The Guide to Yellowstone Waterfalls and Their Discovery*. Englewood, CO: Westcliffe Publishers, Inc., 2000.

Tawney, Robin. *Family Fun in Yellowstone*. Helena, MT: Falcon Publishing, Inc., 1998.

Wuerthner, George. *Yellowstone: A Visitor's Companion*. Mechanicsburg, PA: Stackpole Books, 1992.

ADDITIONAL REFERENCES

Bargar, Keith E. *Geology and Thermal History of Mammoth Hot Springs, Yellowstone National Park, Wyoming*. Washington, DC: U.S. Geological Society Bulletin 1444, 1978.

Blevins, Winfred. *Roadside History of Yellowstone Park*. Missoula, MT: Mountain Press Publishing, 1989.

Chittenden, Hiram M. *The Yellowstone National Park: Historical and Descriptive*. Cincinnati, Ohio: Robert Clarke Company, 1895.

Despain, Don G. *Yellowstone Vegetation: Consequences of Environment and History in a Natural Setting*. Boulder, CO: Roberts Rinehart Publishers, 1990.

Dunraven, Earl of. *The Great Divide: Travels in the Upper Yellowstone in the Summer of 1874*. London: Chatto and Windus, 1876.

The Geyser Gazer Sput. Palmdale, CA: The Geyser Observation and Study Association. Issued bimonthly.

Haynes, F. Jay and Jack E. Haynes. *Haynes Guides* (1912, 1923, 1937, 1949, 1961, 1964). St. Paul, MN: F. Jay Haynes; St. Paul, MN: Haynes Picture Shops, Inc.; and Bozeman, MT: Haynes Studios, Inc.

Keefer, William R. *The Geologic Story of Yellowstone National Park*. Washington, DC: U.S. Geological Survey Bulletin 1347, 1971.

Kershaw, Linda et al. *Plants of the Rocky Mountains*. Edmonton, Canada: Lone Pine Publishing, 1998.

Marler, George D. *Inventory of Thermal Features of the Firehole River Geyser Basins and Other Selected Areas of Yellowstone National Park*, 1973. USGS GD 73-018. Microfiche. Photocopy by The Geyser Observation and Study Association, ed. Lynn Stephens.

Paperiello, Rocco. *Report on the Norris Geyser Basin for 1984*. Available from The Geyser Observation and Study Association.

Parsons, Willard H. *Field Guide: Middle Rockies and Yellowstone.* Dubuque, Iowa: Kendall/Hunt Publishing Co., 1978.

White, Donald E. et al. "The Geology and Remarkable Thermal Activity of Norris Geyser Basin, YNP, WY." U.S. Geological Survey Professional Paper 1456, 1988.

Whittlesey, Lee H. *Wonderland Nomenclature: A History of the Place Names of Yellowstone National Park.* Helena, MT: Montana Historical Society Press, 1988. Microfiche.

Yellowstone Science. Yellowstone National Park, WY: Yellowstone Center for Resources. Issued quarterly.

Yellowstone Today. Yellowstone National Park, WY: Division of Interpretation, National Park Service. Issued quarterly.

INDEX

Note: Page numbers in *italics* indicate locations of definitions of terms; the letter "m" after a page number indicates a map, the letter "p," a picture.

PICTURE CREDITS

The publisher wishes to thank the following photographers and institutions for the use of illustrations:
Colorado Historical Society, pp. 36a (WHJ-39952), 62 (WHJ-503) & 133 (WHJ-4351); **Leslie Kilduff**, pp. 5, 27, 35, 46, 52, 54, 65b, 69, 70b, 70c, 85b, 87, 88b, 93a, 93b, 134, 144, 145, 172b, 209b, 220, 231, 244a, 244b, 252, 253, 254, 256, 264, 272, 279, 282, 289, 335, 346 & 384; **Haynes Foundation Collection, Montana Historical Society**, pp. 36b, 49, 65a, 91, 149, 176b, 200, 258b, 268, 281 & 315; **Record Group 79, National Archives and Records Administration, Susan Kraft, Curator, Yellowstone National Park,** pp. 78b, 197, 258a, 292, 308, 309, 311, 314; **U. S. Department of the Interior, National Park Service, Yellowstone National Park**, pp. 31, 58, 79, 86, 155, 161, 204, 225b, 275, 317a, 317b, 318, 327a, 328a, 328b, 328c, 329a, 330a, 331b, 331c, 333a, 333b, 338a, 338b, 339a, 339b & 344.

All remaining photos were taken by **Bruno Giletti**, with the exception of the one on p. 75, which was taken by the author.

The wildflower paintings by **Mary Vaux Walcott** on pp. 323, 324, 325, 326, 336 & 341 are published here with the permission of the Smithsonian Institution from Walcott's 1925 book, *North American Wildflowers*.

Sketches on pp. 168, 224 & 283 were created by **Hermon Carey Bumpus** for his 1930s Yellowstone booklets, "Trailside Notes."

Cutoff
Mtn.

Silver Gate
Cooke City

212 To Red
Lodge

Northeast
Entrance

Pebble Cr.
Soda Butte Cr.

Abiathar
Peak

Cache Cr.

YELLOWSTONE
NATIONAL
PARK

Lamar
River

Miller Cr.

Saddle
Mtn.

Pyramid
Peak

0		5		10		15		20 mi

0	5	10	15	20	25	30 km

N

Cathedral
Peak

East
Entrance

**14
16** **20** To Cody

Ivan Pass

Mt.
Langford

Eagle Peak
(Highest point
in Yellowstone)
11,358 ft 3462 m

Yellowstone R.

THOROFARE
CORNER

© 2002 J. O. Chapple

MONTANA

YNP

IDAHO

WYOMING

ABOUT THE AUTHOR

Montana native Janet Chapple has been savoring the atmosphere of Yellowstone Park since she was a child, when her father worked at Old Faithful Inn. On her many visits since then, she has combined intensive personal observation with research into the work of park experts, as well as reading widely and attending Yellowstone Institute courses. Her enthusiasm has inspired many others to accompany her on her trips. In connection with her career as a professional cellist, Janet has edited and helped write a book on music practice. She lives in Rhode Island with her husband, Bruno Giletti, professor emeritus of geological sciences at Brown University, who contributed to most of the geological explanations and drew the geological diagrams in this guidebook.

Author with a Gallatin Canyon gas pump of about the same vintage.

You can order *Yellowstone Treasures* directly from our Web site: www.yellowstonetreasures.com.